Philosophy as a Way of Life

METAPHILOSOPHY

METAPHILOSOPHY SERIES IN PHILOSOPHY

Series Editors Armen T. Marsoobian and Eric Cavallero

The Philosophy of Interpretation, edited by Joseph Margolis and Tom Rockmore (2000)
Global Justice, edited by Thomas W. Pogge (2001)
Cyberphilosophy: The Intersection of Computing and Philosophy, edited by James H. Moor and Terrell Ward Bynum (2002)
Moral and Epistemic Virtues, edited by Michael Brady and Duncan Pritchard (2003)
The Range of Pragmatism and the Limits of Philosophy, edited by Richard Shusterman (2004)
The Philosophical Challenge of September 11, edited by Tom Rockmore, Joseph Margolis, and Armen T. Marsoobian (2005)
Global Institutions and Responsibilities: Achieving Global Justice, edited by Christian Barry and Thomas W. Pogge (2005)
Genocide's Aftermath: Responsibility and Repair, edited by Claudia Card and Armen T. Marsoobian (2007)
Stem Cell Research: The Ethical Issues, edited by Lori Gruen, Laura Gravel, and Peter Singer (2008)
Cognitive Disability and Its Challenge to Moral Philosophy, edited by Eva Feder Kittay and Licia Carlson (2010)
Virtue and Vice, Moral and Epistemic, edited by Heather Battaly (2010)
Global Democracy and Exclusion, edited by Ronald Tinnevelt and Helder De Schutter (2010)
Putting Information First: Luciano Floridi and the Philosophy of Information, edited by Patrick Allo (2011)
The Pursuit of Philosophy: Some Cambridge Perspectives, edited by Alexis Papazoglou (2012)
Philosophical Engineering: Toward a Philosophy of the Web, edited by Harry Halpin and Alexandre Monnin (2014)
The Philosophy of Luck, edited by Duncan Pritchard and Lee John Whittington (2015)
Criticism and Compassion: The Ethics and Politics of Claudia Card, edited by Robin S. Dillon and Armen T. Marsoobian (2018)
Connecting Virtues: Advances in Ethics, Epistemology, and Political Philosophy, edited by Michel Croce and Maria Silvia Vaccarezza (2018)
Philosophy as a Way of Life: Historical, Contemporary, and Pedagogical Perspectives, edited by James M. Ambury, Tushar Irani, and Kathleen Wallace (2021)

Philosophy as a Way of Life

Historical, Contemporary, and Pedagogical Perspectives

Edited by

James M. Ambury, Tushar Irani, and
Kathleen Wallace

WILEY

This edition first published 2021

First published as *Metaphilosophy* volume 51, nos. 2–3 (April 2020).

Registered Office
John Wiley & Sons, Inc., 111 River Street, Hoboken, NJ 07030, USA
John Wiley & Sons Ltd, The Atrium, Southern Gate, Chichester, West Sussex, PO19 8SQ, UK

Editorial Offices
350 Main Street, Malden, MA 02148-5020, USA
9600 Garsington Road, Oxford, OX4 2DQ, UK
The Atrium, Southern Gate, Chichester, West Sussex, PO19 8SQ, UK

For details of our global editorial offices, for customer services, and for information about how to apply for permission to reuse the copyright material in this book please see our website at www.wiley.com.

Wiley also publishes its books in a variety of electronic formats and by print-on-demand. Some content that appears in standard print versions of this book may not be available in other formats.

Library of Congress Cataloging-in-Publication Data applied for
9781119746867 (paperback)

Cover Design: Wiley
Cover Image: © FabricioMacedoPhotos/ 97 Bilder/ Pixabay

Set in 10/11pt Times New Roman MT Std by SPi Global, Chennai, India

SKYC690663C-437E-4FDC-BFF6-EDE1C6CDEDCE_091520

I think that Homer said it all in the line, "Going in tandem, one perceives before the other." Human beings are simply more resourceful this way in action, speech, and thought.

—Socrates in Plato's *Protagoras*, 348c–d

CONTENTS

NOTES ON CONTRIBUTORS

James M. Ambury is an associate professor of philosophy at King's College in Wilkes-Barre, Pennsylvania, and a member of the Mellon Philosophy as a Way of Life Network. He is the coeditor (with Andy German) of *Knowledge and Ignorance of Self in Platonic Philosophy* (Cambridge, 2019) and has published articles in *Ancient Philosophy, International Philosophical Quarterly, Proceedings of the Boston Area Colloquium in Ancient Philosophy, Dionysius*, and *Plato*.

Joseph I. Breidenstein is a Ph.D. candidate at Queen's University at Kingston, Ontario, and is currently writing his dissertation on how Nietzsche was influenced by his classical education when formulating his understanding of reincarnation. His other research interests include early Greek philosophy, Bergson, Peirce, Whitehead, and Deleuze.

Caleb M. Cohoe is an associate professor of philosophy at Metropolitan State University of Denver. He has published articles on ancient Greek and Roman philosophy in a number of journals, including *Phronesis*, the *British Journal for the History of Philosophy*, *Apeiron*, and the *Philosophical Quarterly*. He has ongoing projects on Aristotle's theory of understanding and Augustine's views on happiness. He serves as one of the lead faculty advisers for the Philosophy as a Way of Life Project.

Marta Faustino is a research fellow at the Nova Institute of Philosophy (IFILNOVA) in Lisbon, where she currently coordinates the Art of Living Research Group. The main focus of her research is the relationship between philosophy and therapeutic and self-cultivating practices. She is the author of several articles on Nietzsche, Hadot, Foucault, and the Hellenistic philosophers and is the coeditor of *Nietzsche e Pessoa: Ensaios* (Tinta-da-China, 2016), *Rostos do Si* (Vendaval, 2018), and *The Late Foucault: Ethical and Political Questions* (Bloomsbury, 2020).

Stephen R. Grimm is a professor of philosophy at Fordham University. He specializes in epistemology, the philosophy of science, and the philosophy of religion, and his work has appeared in such journals as *Mind, Philosophy and Phenomenological Research*, the *British Journal for the Philosophy of Science*, and *Philosophical Studies*. He is the series editor for Oxford University Press Guides to the Good Life and is a life member of Clare Hall, Cambridge.

Javier Hidalgo is an associate professor of leadership studies at the University of Richmond. His past research has focused on the ethics and political philosophy of immigration, and his publications have appeared in such venues as the *Journal of Political Philosophy*, the *Journal of Ethics and Social Philosophy*, and the *Journal of Moral Philosophy*. His recent research explores Buddhist ethics and topics related to philosophy as a way of life.

Steven Horst is professor and chair of philosophy at Wesleyan University in Middletown, Connecticut, where he has taught since 1990. A specialist in philosophy of mind, he has published four books, most recently *Cognitive Pluralism* (MIT, 2016). He has been a visiting scholar at Boston University, Princeton, and Stanford and has received research grants from the NEH and the John Templeton Foundation.

Tushar Irani is an associate professor of philosophy and letters at Wesleyan University in Middletown, Connecticut. Apart from his interests in philosophy as a way of life, he works on issues of philosophical method, the history and practice of rhetoric, virtue ethics, and moral psychology in ancient Greek and Roman philosophy. He is the author most recently of *Plato on the Value of Philosophy: The Art of Argument in the* Gorgias *and* Phaedrus (Cambridge, 2017).

I-Kai Jeng is an assistant professor of philosophy at National Taiwan University. He is the author of "On the Final Definition of the Sophist: *Sophist* 265a10-268d5" and "Observations on Listening in Aristotle's Practical Philosophy." He specializes in Plato, especially Plato's conception of philosophy, and also works on ancient rhetoric and Aristotle's practical philosophy.

Pengbo Liu is an adjunct lecturer at Bentley University in Waltham, Massachusetts. His research interests include philosophy of mind, bioethics, and cross-cultural philosophy. His work has appeared in such journals as *Comparative Philosophy* and the *Journal of Medical Ethics*.

Paul Lodge is a professor of philosophy at the University of Oxford and a tutorial fellow in philosophy at Mansfield College, Oxford. In addition to authoring numerous articles on the philosophy of Leibniz, he is the editor and translator of *The Leibniz–De Volder Correspondence* (Yale, 2013) and the editor of *Leibniz and His Correspondents* (Cambridge, 2004), *Locke and Leibniz on Substance* (Routledge, 2015, with Tom Stoneham), and *Leibniz's Key Philosophical Writings: A Guide* (Oxford, 2020, with Lloyd Strickland).

Christopher Moore is an associate professor of philosophy and classics at Pennsylvania State University. He is the author of *Calling Philosophers Names: On the Origin of a Discipline* (Princeton, 2020) and *Socrates and Self-Knowledge* (Cambridge, 2015), coauthor of *Plato: Charmides* (Hackett, 2019), editor of two volumes on the reception of Socrates, and author of two dozen articles and chapters on early Greek philosophy.

Alberto Oya is a research fellow at the University of Girona in Spain, where he obtained his Ph.D. in philosophy. His main research interests are in philosophy of religion, with a particular focus on non-doxastic conceptions of religious faith. He is the author of *Unamuno's Religious Fictionalism* (Palgrave Macmillan, 2020).

John Sellars is a Reader in philosophy at Royal Holloway, University of London. He is also a visiting research fellow at King's College London and a member of Wolfson College, Oxford. He has written multiple books on Stoicism, including most recently a study of Marcus Aurelius (Routledge, 2020).

William Sin is an assistant professor at the Education University of Hong Kong. His main areas of research are ethics and comparative philosophy. Applying analytic philosophy to Chinese thought, his current project develops consequentialist and contractualist analyses of the demands of filial obligation. His previous publications include "Adult Children's Obligations Towards Their Parents: A Contractualist Explanation" (*Journal of Value Inquiry*, 2019) and "Confucianism, Rule-Consequentialism, and the Demands of Filial Obligations" (*Journal of Religious Ethics*, 2019).

Vitor Sommavilla is a *professor adjunto A* (equivalent to a tenure-track assistant professor) in the Department of Philosophy at Universidade Federal da Paraíba (UFPB) in Brazil. His research is dedicated primarily to moral and political philosophy and to the philosophy of action. His areas of interest include constructivism and constitutivism in ethics, theories of practical reason and value, the nature of agency, moral and political disagreement, and personal identity.

Kathleen Wallace is a professor of philosophy at Hofstra University. In addition to philosophy as a way of life, her interests include personal identity and anonymity, ethics, metaphysics, and American philosophy. She is the author of *The Network Self: Relation, Process, and Personal Identity* (Routledge, 2019). She is currently on the Board of the Society for the Advancement of American Philosophy and is also the book review editor for *Metaphilosophy*.

Simone Webb recently completed a Ph.D. in gender studies at University College London. Her thesis reads Mary Astell's writing through the lens of Michel Foucault's later work, bringing Astell and Foucault into dialogue with modern feminism. She is keenly engaged in community and public philosophy, volunteering with the Stuart Low Trust Philosophy Forum and facilitating philosophy with children through the Philosophy Foundation.

Robin Weiss teaches at the American University in Cairo. She specializes in Stoicism and is the author of several articles and book chapters on the Stoics' ethical and political philosophy, including "Cicero's Stoic Friend as Resolution to the Paradoxes of Platonic Love," in *Ancient and Medieval Conceptions of Friendship*, edited by Suzanne Stern-Gillet and Gary M. Gurtler (SUNY Press, 2014), and "Stoic Utopia" (*Apeiron*, 2015). She has also written at length on Michel Foucault's interpretation of Stoicism.

Jake Wright is a senior lecturer at the University of Minnesota Rochester's Center for Learning Innovation, an interdisciplinary center focused on the scholarship of teaching and learning. His published research focuses on the pedagogical and ethical justifications for in-class teaching practices, especially at the introductory level, including work on technology bans, inclusion of marginalized students in discussion, and overcoming students' predisposition toward naive skepticism. He holds a Ph.D. in philosophy from the University of Missouri.

INTRODUCTION

JAMES M. AMBURY, TUSHAR IRANI, AND
KATHLEEN WALLACE

> "When will you finally begin to *live* virtuously?" said Plato to an old man who told him he was attending classes on virtue. The point is not always to speculate, but also ultimately to think about applying our knowledge. Today, however, he who lives in conformity with what he teaches is taken for a dreamer.
>
> —Immanuel Kant, *Lectures on the Philosophical Encyclopedia* (qtd. Hadot 2002, xiii)

The passage above, featured in the opening pages of Pierre Hadot's classic *What Is Ancient Philosophy?* articulates a tension as real for us in the modern academy today as it was for Kant several hundred years ago, namely, how to convey the love of wisdom as not only a body of dogmatic principles and axiomatic truths but also a lived exercise that can be practiced. In fact, one might argue that the difficulty is even more acute for us than it was for the famed sage of Königsberg. In today's classroom, for instance, teachers are faced with the scientification of the humanities and the push toward assessment-based models of learning that have come to predominate in much of higher education. In such an atmosphere, the attempt to deviate from traditional classroom assignments—reinforced by rubrics and empirically verifiable models of evaluation—in favor of way-of-life experiments in pedagogy hazards the suspicious administrative eye as much as it risks the bored undergraduate eye-roll. What might such assignments look like? How does one evaluate them? And are they rigorous enough to qualify as "real" collegiate work in a discipline that is pushed more and more to justify itself as rigorous and relevant?

In terms of scholarship, we face similar challenges. The struggle for philosophy to maintain significance in our culture has increasingly driven

Philosophy as a Way of Life: Historical, Contemporary, and Pedagogical Perspectives.
Edited by James M. Ambury, Tushar Irani, and Kathleen Wallace.

Published 2021 by John Wiley & Sons Ltd.

both traditional publishing houses and specialized journals toward a vision of our discipline as one that addresses specific problems or puzzles in need of a solution. If one can solve a problem, after all, one's discipline is progressive, and therefore useful and worthwhile. Here we can think, for instance, of the mind–body problem, the problem of free will, and the problem of evil, all of which have given rise to rich and interesting philosophical scholarship that has advanced far beyond the original horizon within which such problems were first conceived. Given the prevalence of this approach, one might hesitate or even be confused about the idea of scholarship concerned with philosophy as a way of life. Under which of the standard subfields of philosophy should this scholarship be classified? Would such articles or monographs advance the literature? Would their arguments be innovative? And how would the discipline benefit in a new way from these sorts of publications?

Concerns about pedagogical rigor and the advancement of philosophy as a discipline are not without their merits. Indeed, these concerns are crucial to debates about the place of philosophy in today's academy. They should not, however, be raised at the expense of an element that has been integral to the discipline since it was first conceived. In the ancient world, philosophy, concerned as it was with problem and paradox, was also understood to be a practical guide for living, or even itself a way of life. To ignore this dimension of philosophy is not to ignore an accidental subset of the subject that can be divorced from its essential nature—it is to ignore philosophy itself. The articulation of philosophy as a way of life and its pedagogical implementation advances the love of wisdom; it is not merely an addendum to it. It is the purpose of this collection to bring historical views about philosophy as a way of life, coupled with their modern equivalents, more prevalently into the domain of the contemporary scholarly world.

The impetus for this collection of essays arose from conversations at a Summer Institute sponsored by the National Endowment for the Humanities that took place at Wesleyan University in the summer of 2018, entitled *Reviving Philosophy as a Way of Life*. Under the directors of the Institute—Meghan Sullivan (University of Notre Dame), Stephen Grimm (Fordham University), and Stephen Angle (Wesleyan University)—the participants were guided each day through a seminar about a major figure or movement in the history of philosophy by an invited expert in the field being discussed. The discussions—about Confucianism, Buddhism, Stoicism, Skepticism, existentialism, and Kantianism—all revolved around the theme of philosophy as a way of life as it appears in the texts, ideas, and methods of some of the tradition's most famous thinkers. Seminar leaders emphasized core arguments that focused on way-of-life issues and also presented techniques designed to implement these ideas into teaching, simultaneously attentive to scholarly topics suitable for the world of publication and pedagogical possibilities for the classroom. The hope of the editors of the present volume—each of whom participated in that Institute—is to continue and advance this dialogue.

Composition of This Collection

The essays in this collection fall under three general categories: history of philosophy, moral philosophy, and pedagogy. Our selection of essays was guided in large part by the recommendations of external referees, but as we made decisions during the final rounds of the reviewing process, it became clear to us that we wanted the volume to push the study of philosophy as a way of life into new directions in each category. Studies of this topic in ancient Greek and Roman philosophy have become well established over the past three decades, thanks to the careful scholarship of Pierre Hadot and more recently John Cooper. For this reason, most of the history essays selected for inclusion in this collection focus on relatively neglected approaches to the idea of philosophy as a way of life in other historical periods and traditions: one essay (by Christopher Moore) argues that already in the ancient world there were Greek writers who were happy to regard thinkers from the East as *philosophoi*, precisely because they understood philosophy to be a way of life; two essays (by Pengbo Liu and William Sin) address the topic as it appears more singularly in different schools of Chinese philosophy; one essay (by John Sellars) argues that the notion of philosophy as a way of life provides a useful framework for interpreting the views of figures in the Renaissance humanist tradition; three essays (by Joseph Breidenstein, Paul Lodge, and Simone Webb) discuss the prevalence of the topic in the thought of philosophers from the early modern period (Descartes, Leibniz, and Astell, respectively); and one essay (by Alberto Oya) assesses a key criticism of Christian philosophy as a way of life in existentialist thought of the nineteenth and twentieth centuries. To round out this group, we have also included two essays (by I-Kai Jeng and Robin Weiss) that discuss overlooked features of the idea of philosophy as a way of life in Plato and Stoicism.

We have construed the category of moral philosophy broadly in this volume to show how the study of philosophy as a way of life can contribute to present-day debates on the nature of the good life. The four essays included in this category form a coherent set. Three of them (by Caleb Cohoe and Stephen Grimm, Marta Faustino, and Javier Hidalgo) each provide a different case for the role of philosophy in a well-lived life. In making these cases, they draw on and contemporize a debate between Hadot and Cooper on the use of reason and reflection versus practical exercises in ancient ethical thought. By contrast, one essay in this set (by Vitor Sommavilla) provides a dialectical foil to the others by arguing against the ideal of a philosophical way of life, construed as it has been since Socrates as an examined life. Particularly in connection with contemporary research on the good life, we hope that these essays offer scholars some well-argued supporting and opposing views for the pursuit of philosophy as a way of life.

Our section on pedagogy includes two essays by scholars who have applied their reflections on philosophy as a way of life to the classroom. One essay (by Jake Wright) argues for the benefits of a way-of-life approach to teaching an introductory-level philosophy course through the assignment of immersive exercises that make the value of philosophical theory and investigation apparent to students in their lives. The other essay (by Steven Horst) offers an example of such exercises, identifying and discussing in the process various challenges that a professor may encounter in teaching such a course. Together, both essays enlarge the sense of possibilities open to professors who are interested in exploring what a course designed around the idea of philosophy as a way of life might look like.

The essays in this collection demonstrate that philosophy as a way of life has been a recurrent theme and strand in the history of philosophy, and that it continues to be a topic of interest for scholars working in ethics today. We suspect that these essays have only scratched the surface and hope that they are not only interesting in their own right but will also stimulate further research in this area. We also hope that philosophers will consider whether and how their current commitments, practices, and methods may constitute or contribute to a philosophical way of life. The contemporary philosophical world is quite diverse and rich in method, subject area, and scope, with many different visions of what philosophy should be and do. How might some of these visions be understood as philosophical ways of life (or practices) or suggest a particular role for philosophy in the modern world? If philosophy as a way of life is not only a historically interesting aspect of our discipline but also an ongoing dimension of the way in which philosophy is currently practiced, how might this be articulated?

Reference

Hadot, Pierre. 2002. *What Is Ancient Philosophy?* Translated by Michael Chase. Cambridge, Mass.: Harvard University Press.

PART 1

HISTORY OF PHILOSOPHY

CHAPTER 1

ANCIENT GREEK *PHILOSOPHIA* IN INDIA AS A WAY OF LIFE

CHRISTOPHER MOORE

1. Introduction: Studying Philosophical Ways of Life

The question animating this essay is whether the Greeks themselves thought of philosophy as a way of life. The answer might be thought an uncontroversial affirmative, and so it may be. But the details are not so clear, and one can imagine a broad range of counter-cases, where ancient practice seems little different from a modern practice not admitted to be a genuine or robust "way of life." This we see by rearticulating the question in a twofold way: as one concerning the way the Greeks thought of *philosophoi* ("philosophers"); and as one concerning how they thought of the *bioi* ("ways of life") that such philosophoi could be thought to have lived. Aristotelian investigation into first principles need not come caparisoned in the garb of a way of life; Cynic unconventionalism need not depend on rational argument.

Here I provide new evidence, based on material from Greek historiography that may be largely unfamiliar to philosophers, that the Greeks did think of *philosophia* as a distinctive *bios*, and that, equivalently, they acknowledged a way of life identifiable as that lived by philosophoi. The evidence is that the Greeks recognized philosophia and philosophoi, and explicitly in these terms, in India in the late fourth century BCE among those traditionally called gymnosophists. These were the decades of Alexander and his generals' conquests in Asia, at just the time of Aristotle's death, and thus at the very beginning of the Hellenistic period. This recognition illuminates the Greek conception of philosophia by the end of the first century and a half of its use, a period decisive in the discipline's

Philosophy as a Way of Life: Historical, Contemporary, and Pedagogical Perspectives.
Edited by James M. Ambury, Tushar Irani, and Kathleen Wallace.

Published 2021 by John Wiley & Sons Ltd.

increasingly settled self-understanding. We must allow for much dynamism before that point, since the concept and the practices that it incorporated underwent significant specification, reevaluation, and occasionally technicalization and colloquialization; but while it never grew wholly stable, it came to have canonical connotations by then.[1] I show that the Greeks in India identified philosophoi by their practical life, social position, and cultural-intellectual contributions. That the Greeks did not—in order to admit the Indian intellectuals into the practice of philosophia—have to observe their participation in a shared canon of literature (on the assumption that philosophia means membership in an institutional-disciplinary network) or have to appraise the relevant cognitive or investigatory attitudes as theoretical or disinterested in the right way (on the assumption that philosophia means "love of wisdom" in some noninstrumental sense) shows that philosophia was for them in fact an identifiable "bios," a livelihood or lifestyle, separable from an individual group ("Greek philosophoi") or attitude. This does not require that every use of philosophia implies an equally full-bodied way of life. Recent contributions on the conception of philosphia advanced by Aristotle, whose work provides the largest and most contemporaneous corpus of relevant usages, show that he, and thus other Greeks, treated philosophia in a range of ways, from a specific topic of research, namely, of first principles, to the name for the kind of leisure directed more at self-study than mere dissipation (Moore 2019a and forthcoming a). And at a Hellenistic outpost in Afghanistan, Ai Khanoum, one could find—as one could also find at Delphi by the end of the fourth century—public inscriptions of the maxim *Philosophos ginou*, "Be philosophical"; this appears to have advocated a sort of "think before you act" ethics rather than conversion to a new way of life.[2] But philosophia could still generally refer to a bios, and do so in ways not derivative of non-bios conceptions, such as attitude attributions (e.g., "loving wisdom") or cognitive-content attributions (e.g., "thinking about the conditions of knowledge").

A particular challenge to thinking about "philosophical ways of life" is deciding on the criteria for one's being philosophical. One criterion might be what we now find common to all cases of philosophy so deemed: for instance, devaluing traditional sources of tradition in the search for knowledge or reflection on the nature of reflection (Adamson 2019; Sassi 2018). But our criteria need not have been the criteria of the Greeks, and so they may not track their understanding of philosophia or the way they differentiated philosophoi from other practitioners. And it is their understanding of and distinctions made about philosophia that could become the object

[1] An argument developed in Moore 2019b.

[2] For the finding and its connection to Delphi, see Robert 1968; Moore 2015, 28–30, and 2019b, 291–97; Verhasselt forthcoming.

of reflection for the Greeks, which could influence their ongoing thinking about philosophia—and thus, arguably, our own.

The evidence from the Greek experience in India, beyond its intrinsic fascinations and unfamiliarity, speaks to these distinctions. Perhaps more starkly than anywhere else in the fourth century we see in it what it means to live a life "philosophically," as a *philosophos*. To be sure, there is other evidence, for example from the middle comic dramatist Alexis and in a fragment of prose comedy in an Oxyrhynchus papyrus, but both, while important, are perhaps overstylized.[3] Plato's dialogues may seem stylized in the other direction; they also have a supremely complex relationship with the ongoing development of the discipline.[4] The historiographical reports about India have unique value in their claim to descriptive neutrality, concerned to report sociological categories rather than exhort or dissuade people to or from any ethical or intellectual commitments. None of this entails an ease of interpretation; the reports exist mainly as Roman-era paraphrases or excerpts of late fourth-century BCE writings, where the later historians do not particularly care about the philosophical status of the philosophoi they discuss. Many pertinent questions remain unanswered, or are hardly even asked. On the upside, new questions get raised, encouraging further research or speculation about philosophy as a way of life. This essay serves, then, as a first entry into and protreptic toward complementing the usual topics of study for "philosophia as a way of life"—the Hellenistic/Socratic school authors and their reception—with such fourth-century writers as Megasthenes, Nearchus, and Onesicritus (cf. Hadot 2002; Cooper 2012).

2. Megasthenes' *Indica* and the Social Class of Philosophoi

After the death of Alexander the Great in 323, his generals continued the job of imperial expansion and consolidation. Seleucus I Nicator (c. 358–281 BCE) sought to secure the tenuous eastern reaches of Macedon and, forgoing conquest there, settled on border negotiations with northern India. As part of his 303 BCE peace settlement with that region's political leader, Chandragupta Maurya, Seleucus (or possibly Sibyrtius, a satrap of western India) sent a Greek named Megasthenes as ambassador. Megasthenes came to write a four-book study of India, the *Indica*.[5] The influence and endurance of that work was so great as to have large parts

[3] Alexis frr. 37, 140, 247 PCG, with discussion of dating in Arnott 2011 and context in Battezzato 2008; *Oxyrhynchus Papyri* 3659, with attribution to the mid-fourth century (Aristotle's *Protrepticus*?) by Hutchinson and Johnson 2018. For both see Moore 2019b, 297–306. A list of abbreviated titles appears in the Appendix below.

[4] See, e.g., Nightingale 1995 and 2004, with qualifications in Moore 2019b, 221–59.

[5] A convenient version of the fragments, based on Jacoby, is Roller 2008. The newest edition is in preparation by Richard Stoneman. For a recent introduction to the man, see Stoneman 2019, 129–85 and passim; see also Karttunen 1989, 96–99, and 1997, 69–93.

relied upon by three major Roman-era historians: Diodorus Siculus (mid-first century BCE), Strabo (end of the first century BCE), and Arrian (mid-second century CE). This influence was earned not only by the eyewitness testimony of Megasthenes and by his extensive reliance on local informants but also by his incisive theoretical structure framed by the leading anthropological, naturalistic, and political theories of his century.[6]

Megasthenes is the earliest Greek author explicitly quoted to refer directly to contemporaneous non-Greeks as participating in philosophia.[7] The verb appears in a cross-cultural comparison quoted by Clement of Alexandria: "Yet everything the ancients said about nature was also said by people philosophizing outside Greece, namely the Brahmins in India and the so-called Ioudaioi [Jews] in Syria."[8] Clement, a Christian apologist, is quoting Megasthenes in partial support of his thesis that Greek philosophia followed, and even derived from, non-Greek philosophia. While this passage does not directly corroborate the derivation thesis (Clement focuses on it in adjacent sentences), it provides a condition for its truth. The distinctive doctrines about the world found in earlier Greek writings are not unique to Greece. Here "philosophizing" involves speaking about nature in a way characteristic enough to allow for the cogency of identifying specifically cross-cultural influence; it is not merely the kind of talk that would occur at any time and any place. The localizing of such talk to a few determinate (and, as it turns out, elite) groups within a region—the Brahmins in India, the Jews in Syria—suggests that these special observations about nature are matters of concerted discussion among dedicated interlocutors, and that they are taught and learned. More significantly, if Clement's point is that the Greeks acquired their philosophical doctrines from thinkers east of the Aegean, the ideas about nature must be abstracted from any culturally determined beliefs, for example those based in scripture or ritual, that would limit their relevance or persuasiveness to foreigners.[9]

This verbatim passage of Megasthenes' work does not speak to philosophizing as a bios by contrast to philosophizing as a purely intellectual, occasional, or morally irrelevant practice—or, anyway, to whatever the

[6] See, e.g., DS 38.1–2. Kosmin 2014, 44–45, argues for the diplomatic and literary shrewdness of Megasthenes; he attempted to describe India so as to construct a model for an autonomous parallel to the Seleucid realm.

[7] There were earlier studies of India and Persia—lands where practitioners who could be recognized as philosophizing lived—namely, in Ctesias of Cnidus's late fifth-century BCE *Indica* and *Persica*, but none of the (very few) fragments from or testimonies about them include anything about philosophia.

[8] Clement *Stromata* 1.72.4, attributed to book 3 of the *Indica*. All translations are my own.

[9] A long history of earlier and later scholars, into the present day, have wondered about non-Greek influences (including Indian) on Greek philosophy, but discoveries one way or the other would not explain why Greeks could call other intellectual traditions philosophia other than that they saw certain familiarities. See Karttunen 1989, 108–21, for an account of some earlier attempts to ground Greek thought in non-Greek thought.

opposed conception might be. It focuses on philosophizing as having or coming to have marked views about nature. So this passage by itself is neutral with respect to our opening question, concerning the Greek conception of philosophia vis-à-vis a way of life. But we have reasons to wonder whether a way of life undergirds the having or sharing of views of nature.

The more capacious and bios-relevant material from Megasthenes about Indian philosophoi comes in the form not of direct quotation but of extensive and usually uncited paraphrase. We find this in the three historians named above, where they include India's history in their respective total histories. We cannot always tell with precision what counts as a paraphrase of Megasthenes (rather than of some other source) and when his terminology gets replaced by later vocabulary (rather than gets quoted verbatim), but comparison across and within the historians provides some reliability. Indeed, an important claim of this essay is that in the paraphrases of Megasthenes about philosophoi the term *philosophoi* appeared in the source (that is, Megasthenes') text. My confidence has a double basis: the fact that Clement quotes Megasthenes to use a *philosoph-* term for certain Indians who talk about nature, and the fact that both Diodorus and Strabo use the vocabulary of philosophoi, and they are more reliable on this matter (for independent reason) than Arrian, who does not.[10] Subsidiary evidence comes from the fact that Aristotle already speaks of Persian Magi in the context of the history of philosophia (*Metaph.* N 1091b10).[11] And writers about India before Megasthenes—the Onesicritus and Nearchus mentioned above, and to be studied below—seem to have gotten close to describing certain Indians as philosophizing.

Megasthenes discussed philosophoi at several points in his *Indica*.[12] The most famous of these points involves him setting philosophoi first in a seven-part (μέρη) social division, following whom (in order of discussion) are to be found the farmers, herdsmen, craftsmen, soldiers, overseers, and advisers/leaders (DS 2.40.1–3; cf. Arr. *Ind.* 11.1–8; Strabo 15.1.39). Megasthenes observes, in the formulation of Diodorus, that the class—or caste—of philosophoi is smaller than the other classes but is superior in

[10] Arrian uses sophistai in place of philosophoi. But he wrote rather later, differs more from Diodorus than Strabo does (suggesting Arrian is the outlier), conflates various sources, and lives at the time of the so-called Second Sophistic, where sophistai has special resonance. Thanks to Duane Roller for discussion of this issue: 2008, comm. on F19b and *per litt.* Karttunen 1997, 56, also takes this position.

[11] See Horky 2009 for the knowledge of Magi in the early Academy, as well as Palmer 2000.

[12] For a general discussion of the material below, see Stoneman (2019, 290–331), who concerns himself especially with the Indian literature that confirms the validity of the accounts by Megasthenes (and his predecessors). I leave the Indian perspective mostly unexplored in this essay, as extraneous to the lexical or conceptual point about the Greek meaning of the term *philosophia*. See Seaford 2016 for a productive comparison of Indian and Greek philosophy, along with the provocative McEvilly 2002.

distinction (ἐπιφανείαι) to all of them.[13] Its members surpass others in their piety and their expertise concerning the afterlife, "the things in Hades."[14] They generally have no official duties, which means that they neither exercise power over others nor have it exercised over them. This liberty, combined with their knowledge, lets them be responsive to private requests for sacrifices for the living and the dead. They do accede to a yearly public request to foretell (προλέγοντες) the coming year's weather, diseases, and other important seasonal variation, thereby allowing the people and the king to prepare for what is to come, in particular by storing up relevant provisions.[15] Year-over-year accuracy of these predictions is ensured internally and with self-control by promises of silence in case one's predictions are shown to have failed, though also by restrictions on non-philosophoi from participating in such predictions. Philosophoi are to be distinguished from the seventh class of the political advisers, those who counsel assemblies on civic affairs, the class from which most magistrates and bureaucrats are drawn.[16]

Who are these philosophoi whom Duane Roller calls "a sort of royal religious advisor" (2008, comm. F19b), and why would Megasthenes call them philosophoi? As far as we know, they have two primary areas of knowledge, connected to the soul and to the cosmos (to use Greek concepts): the rituals conducive to existential flourishing—that is, the tendance of the gods needful for a *eudaimôn* life and death; and the predictions conducive to resource allocation on a local and national scale—that is, the forewarning and assurance of individuals and states against death, illness, and famine. Both areas have practical import and serve the people at large. Their leisure means that their service is never contingent on external matters, never skewed by power dynamics or interrupted by business.[17] We may wonder whether that leisure is also the stuff from which their knowledge of

[13] Arrian differs somewhat from Diodorus in specifying that there is compulsory labor or tithing; only the philosophoi know how to prophesy; and there is no prophesy about private affairs. On the complicated question and scholarly tradition about these groups, see Karttunen 1997, 82–87.

[14] More properly: "being most cherished by the gods and having the most experience about the things in Hades" (ὡς θεοῖς γεγονότες προσφιλέστατοι καὶ περὶ τῶν ἐν Ἅιδου μάλιστ' ἐμπείρως ἔχοντες, 2.40.2).

[15] Strabo 15.1.39 emphasizes that they may present their forecasts in writing; that these observations serve explicitly as advice for the king; and that they take up the matter of the state in general.

[16] DS 2.41.4–5; cf. Arr. *Ind.* 12.6–7. Diodorus says that this seventh group is "the smallest" and "most admired for nobility of birth and *phronêsis*," both of which claims are similar to the claims he made about the philosophoi. The same tension exists in Arrian, who calls the seventh group most eminent in *sophia* and *dikaiosunê*. The ambiguity between the first and seventh classes can probably be blamed on Megasthenes. I suspect this is explained by some overlap between characteristics, especially the propensity to give advice to the ruling person or persons.

[17] Compare Socrates' denial of teaching for pay, Plato *Apology* 19e1 and Xenophon *Memorabilia* 1.6.2.

"the things in Hades" and their predictions are made; Megasthenes seems not to have said so here. It depends on the percentage of their week or year they spend in ritual sacrifice, but the implication is that sacrificing does not occupy all their time. (Egyptian and Chaldaean priests are said to have had time to invent mathematics [see Aristotle *Metaphysics* A 981b24].) How else would they make reliable predictions and know the ritual intricacies, in degrees inaccessible to anybody else, without employing their free time for it? In any event, these philosophoi have their social role in their benefit to others, gain unique skill to perform unique tasks, and help themselves only derivatively—accruing the honor that is their due.

Why would Megasthenes have called these helpful people philosophoi, and what does this say about philosophy as a way of life? The first question is a little tricky to answer. In the Greek context, ritual sacrifice is not a salient task of any philosophos; public prophesy may seem atypical of philosophoi; and political advice is seen mainly as parrhesiastic counter-advice. So perhaps Megasthenes is looking elsewhere, for example to leisure? Maybe so; but in fact the practical differences between Indian and Greek philosophoi may not be so extreme as just suggested. Many Greek philosophers have attributed to them works entitled "On the Things in Hades" (Περὶ τῶν ἐν Ἅιδοῦ) (e.g., Democritus [DL 9.46]; Heraclides Ponticus [DL 5.87]), and the ritual aspect is not foreign at least to Pythagoreans and Empedocleans (Burkert 1972; Kingsley 1995). By the fourth century, the story of Thales's predicting a bumper crop in olives served as a paradigm for philosophical success (Aristotle *Politics* 1 1259a5–19); and Empedocles presents prophesy, with medical insight, as his primary skill.[18] Pythagoras, Parmenides, Protagoras, Anaxagoras, Plato, and Aristotle, among others, were said or thought to have advised cities. Now, any one of these skills alone would not count one a philosophos, since priests generally sacrificed, prophets generally prophesied, and political advisers typically gave political advice. But the union of the skills makes a difference, if the preeminence of one's possession of them also does. Megasthenes presumably judges these people philosophoi because their various activities rely on a nonobvious view of nature at its largest scale, at the level of its and our cycles, both seasonal and psychical, a view acquired during leisure that benefits the public. This would envision being philosophos as a bios, a way of life, to the extent that it is, not strictly because it involves "practices of the self" or "spiritual exercises," as typically discussed in scholarship, but because it integrates (presumably lifelong) learning, cosmic understanding, and one's practical and civic affairs. The investigation by philosophoi into foundational matters brings them to an ever-flowing fountain of skillfulness with worldly relevance.

[18] Empedocles fr. B112 DK/D4 LM (= DL 8.62): οἱ μὲν μαντοσυνέων κεχρημένοι, οἱ δ' ἐπὶ νούσων (l. 9).

The discussion or mention by Megasthenes of philosophoi elsewhere in the *Indica* shows an expanded though still compatible sense of philosophia. He says that in India the philosophoi and *phusikoi* ("naturalists") explain the extensive system of rivers, which often overflow (DS 2.37.6). Some philosophoi inform him, the ambassador-ethnologist, on anthropological matters (Strabo 15.1.57). After rationalizing the Greek gods Dionysus and Heracles as human founders of India, he says that mountain philosophoi sing the praises of the former, while those in the plains venerate the latter.[19] In the context of stories about Alexander's confrontation with the self-immolating Indian practitioner named Calanus (discussed below), Megasthenes claims that Indian philosophoi are generally expected *not* to commit suicide and are judged impetuous if they do.[20] We can see the connections between these references to philosophoi and the canonical one discussed above. Floods are a stereotypically cyclical macro-phenomenon, crucial to agriculture and safety, and a familiar topic for Greek philosophoi (best known from the context of the Nile). This would appear to be a core concern of the forecasting Indian philosophoi. Perhaps phusikoi share this interest but not other interests of the philosophoi. Accurate predictions about the effect of natural events on people would need to involve knowledge of the populations so affected, and thus the anthropological knowledge is not surprising. This leisured class may also simply be those with time to have conversations, or to have noticed, or to be good at communicating with foreign travelers. The piety of philosophoi would explain the hymning of Dionysus and Heracles. Finally, the Calanus story points to a self-control that Megasthenes' remark about the promise of silence already hinted at.

3. Megasthenes and Philosophical Ways of Life

So far we have seen Megasthenes define philosophoi functionally or sociologically, in large part by contrast with other socially crucial groups, not mainly by their daily activities or fundamental personal commitments. This may matter. There is, after all, an ambiguity in the concept "way of life": is one's job, or cultural status, relevant? Why wouldn't it be? Well, some may feel that social position does not go deep enough, that it does not describe a *way* of *living*, only one's socio-institutional functions for a certain number of hours a day. In any event, Megasthenes does also discuss the more personal-level aspects of the bios of these philosophoi. This comes out when Strabo in particular reports Megasthenes' division of philosophoi into two branches: the

[19] Strabo 15.1.58. On Dionysus and Heracles as personages in Indian religion, see Dahlquist 1962; Karttunen 1989, 210–19; Puskás 1990.

[20] Strabo 15.1.68; cf. Arrian *Anabasis* 7.2.2–4. For the question of Indian self-immolation, see Karttunen 1997, 64–67.

Brachmanes and the Garmanes.[21] We might not have expected this division, given the unitary account of the *philosophoi* in the seven-class analysis, but of course nothing prevents finer-grade differentiation. We will be able to integrate the unitary and two-part accounts of philosophoi once we look at the details.

The Brachmanes, Megasthenes says, have won slightly more distinction and have greater doctrinal consistency among themselves than the Garmanes (Strabo 15.1.59). While the Brachmanes are in utero, eloquent men give them and their mothers disciplined advice. After birth the Brachmanes learn from increasingly effective teachers (cf. Plato *Alcibiades* 121b7–122a10; Boyce 1970). For thirty-seven years of their maturity they move to a rural grove and pass a simple, ascetic, and celibate life of study and discussion. They talk about death and orient their training toward it, believing that life reached its apex in the womb and that the true and happy life comes to philosophoi only in death (cf. Plato *Phaedo* 63e–69e). They argue against the possibility that good or bad could really ever happen to someone—which presumably means that they judge desire and fear nugatory. They live by deeds rather than words, following myth in most things (διὰ μύθων τὰ πολλὰ πιστουμένους) and thus, I suppose, not growing anxious about conventional accounts.[22] They believe that the cosmos is spherical, has a beginning and end, and submits to the force and presence of god; they accept diverse first principles but give priority to water; they postulate a fifth superlunary element; they locate Earth at the center of the universe; they theorize about seed and soul; and they propound various myths about the soul's immortality and judgments in Hades. The other branch, the Garmanes, by contrast, includes the Hylobioi, a forest-dwelling (hence their Greek name), bark-wearing, leaves-and-fruits eating (that is, both vegetarian and nonagriculturalist), abstinent, abstemious, and mendicant group.[23] They advise kings, perform prayers, prophesy, are enchanters skilled in the rites and customs of the dead in Hades, and investigate causes (πυνθανομένοις περὶ τῶν αἰτίων) (Strabo 15.1.60).

The description of the Garmanes better matches that of the philosophoi in Megasthenes' social hierarchy, in the focus on sacrifice, advice, and prophecy, though we might not have expected such rusticity! The Brachmanes seem not to live by (publicly oriented) "words," which would seem to prevent their giving weather or existential advice, and in fact they seem not even to live for the success of this world. They apparently spend their time on metaphysical reflection. Like the Garmanes, they perform

[21] For the range of names used by Greeks for Indian intellectuals and the reality behind them, see Karttunen 1997, 55–64.

[22] Cf. Plato *Phaedrus* 229e, in which Socrates explains that he has more important work to do than find the explanatory weaknesses in mythology—namely, to come to know himself.

[23] Strabo emphasizes that these are called philosophoi by remarking that physicians, who are "like *philosophoi* concerning humans" (ὡς περὶ τὸν ἄνθρωπον φιλοσόφους), are also frugal and can practice feats of endurance.

ascetic exercises of self-work; but they seem to do so solely to promote the learning and study necessary for acquiring those abstract views about cosmological and psychological matters. All the same, the philosophoi of the social hierarchy could very well include these two branches. Both branches have been absolved of obligatory labor or production, and both understand something about the world's cycles. It would be sensible to read Megasthenes' claim that philosophoi help with sacrifices and predictions to refer to the philosophoi prepared to do so, namely, the Garmanes; the Brachmanes contribute to their brethren's "distinction" and perhaps some of the theoretical background. Compare the relationship today between hardcore researchers and somewhat broader public intellectuals.

We readily see the connection to philosophia as a way of life. Both groups of philosophoi live deliberately, outside the familiar routines. The Brachmanes undergo a deliberate and concerted education in their youth. Then for the bulk of their lives they live intentionally, separate from the humdrum hassles of the city, practicing desire control, and learning. They unite their theoretical ideas with their embodied practice, replicating, as it were, death in life, acknowledging as evils or hindrances much of what the rest of us pursue and value. They also have views of the cosmos, though Strabo does not report whether Megasthenes reflected on their connection, if any, to their way of life—a notoriously hard connection to draw for any thought-community, even when it is to be central, as it was, for example, for Buddhists, Stoics, and Epicureans. The Garmanes have an equally distinctive practical life. They live a desire-negating life, seeking some precivilizational naturalness, and have an expertise in religious ritual.

The bios of the Brachmanes is more familiarly philosophos: they train themselves on the basis of the results of their study and discussion of transcendental issues. They may justify their views about immortality and normativity, which in turn provide practical guidance on their (reasoned) views about the nature of the universe and human life. Our reports do not link the way of life of the Garmanes so obviously to reasoning, though the linkage obviously exists. They are said to investigate "causes," apparently a shorthand reference to fundamental explanation. Their ability to advise, forecast, and deal with the dead would seem to depend on a broad investigatory knowledge. Their idiosyncratic treatment of desires could be, for sure, just a thing they do; but it is more likely that it represents a principled approach to total self-abnegation, and that they take the position that such self-abnegation contributes to their practical success.

On this survey, then, we see that Megasthenes recognizes philosophoi as those whose distinctive and superior practical life depends on, or at least works in tandem with, theoretical investigation and discussion, on the one hand, and ascetic body work, cessation of or indifference to desires and pangs, on the other hand. Thus Megasthenes sees philosophia as a way of life. But Megasthenes is not our only or earliest source for this view.

4. Before Megasthenes

We saw something awkward or imprecise about the taxonomy of philosophoi, presented monolithically in the seven-class section and in an uneven pair elsewhere. This could have several explanations: selective excerpting of Megasthenes centuries after he wrote; his own imperfect exposition, over a long book, of much unwieldy material; or his zealous application of ill-fitting Greek categories and schemata to unfamiliar speech acts and group actions. An improved analysis of philosophoi in India may come from looking at some of Megasthenes' predecessors in Indian anthropology of philosophy: the so-called Alexander historians, the intellectuals who accompanied the campaign east in the 330s and 320s.

Nearchus grew up with Alexander in Macedon and accompanied him as eventually a fleet commander (for Nearchus, see Kartunnen 1989, 90; Whitby 2012). He wrote about their adventures, and his description of India became a primary source for Arrian's *Indica*. He mostly did not use the term *philosophos* in his extant fragments but seems to refer to the same sociological groupings as Megasthenes does. Nearchus writes of two groups of "naked sophists," gymnosophists, living in the open air.[24] The Brachmanes, he says, are engaged in civic affairs (πολιτεύεσθαι) and act as standing advisers to the kings (παρακολουθεῖν . . . συμβούλους). The other group, which goes unnamed but in which he includes Calanus, whom we have already heard about, studies nature (σκοπεῖν τὰ περὶ τὴν φύσιν). Both groups live an austere lifestyle (διαίτας . . . σκληράς) and let women philosophize with the men (συμφιλοσοφεῖν) (Strabo 15.1.66).

Nearchus thus presents Indian "sophists" from two vantages: externally, as physically naked practitioners of self-work, and internally, as related sects with political and naturalistic interests. Because Strabo, our source for Nearchus, uses the word *sophistai* (sophists) to refer to these practitioners here but philosophoi when reporting Megasthenes' report, apparently about the same people, we should assume that Nearchus in fact (in contrast to Megasthenes) used the word *sophistai*. It is, after all, a good fourth-century Greek word for generic intellectual practitioners.[25] Obviously the term does not refer only to people who teach rhetoric and political savvy to young democratic and aristocratic men. Its semantic breadth allows for its application to advisers, naturalists, and those who direct their efforts at psychosomatic self-improvement. So Megasthenes seems to have taken over from Nearchus his taxonomy and description of a certain set of practitioners and replaced their name *sophistai* with a new one, *philosophoi*, which evidently does not imply a change in meaning. We see an inkling of this conversion already in Nearchus. His remark that men and women "philosophize together" (συμφιλοσοφεῖν) suggests that the verb may have

[24] Arr. *Ind.* 11.7: γυμνοί . . . οἱ σοφισταί.
[25] For fourth-century usage, see Moore forthcoming b.

preceded the noun in its use for various idiosyncratic foreign practitioners of self-improvement or cultural contribution (as Megasthenes' remark about the Syrian Jews quoted above corroborates). Thus Nearchus, if he is writing soon after the death of Alexander, early in the final quarter of the fourth century, will manifest an increasing but not total development of philosophos-group terms in Indian anthropology, a development that is completed in Megasthenes.

This inflection point in the wider application of philosophos-group terms makes a starker appearance in Nearchus's fellow historian Onesicritus, to whose work Nearchus sometimes responds (Strabo 15.1.66; see Whitby 2011). Onesicritus too writes of the Indian sophist named Calanus (Plutarch *Life of Alexander* 65.2; Lucian *Passing of Peregrinus* 25; Strabo 14.1.64). On one occasion he does so while recalling a longer story about his own mission to learn the wisdom (ἀκροασόμενος τῆς σοφίας) of the "sophists" (Strabo 14.1.63–65). While on campaign in India, King Alexander had heard about the highly esteemed naked sophists who "practiced endurance" (καρτερίας ἐπιμελοῖντο) and wanted to know more. He had also heard, however, that they were aloof, indifferent to conventional dynamics of political power. So he sent an envoy, Onesicritus himself. Onesicritus writes that when he journeyed out he found fifteen such sophists in a group a few miles outside the city, holding postures, naked, in searing heat all day. He struck up conversation with one Calanus. Calanus, seeing his interlocutor's elaborate clothing, laughed, and as Onescritus records his response, tells a sort of Myth of the Fall: toil, which is man's lot, punishes his excess and luxury (πλησμονῆς . . . καὶ τρθφῆς); only discipline and the other virtues (σοφρωσύνης τε καὶ τῆς ἄλλης ἀρετῆς) can bring about forgiveness.[26] So Calanus tells Onescritus that they can talk if Onescritus disrobes—that is, literally purifies himself of sartorial excess and luxury. Onescritus hesitates, and this gives Mandanis (otherwise known as Dandanis), the oldest and wisest (σοφώτατος) of the sophists, and (we are told) a critic of Calanus's hypocrisy, a chance to speak. Mandanis says that he praises Onescritus's king, the empire-leading Alexander, for his "desire for wisdom" (ἐπιθυμοίη σοφίας), and that indeed Alexander was "the only one to philosophize in arms" (μόνον . . . αὐτὸν ἐν ὅπλοις φιλοσοφοῦντα). He means that only Alexander desires to learn how to teach his subjects discipline (σωφρονεῖν), a desire presumably inferred from the very fact of Alexander's having sent Onescritus here. And so Mandanis explains what his people do: they eliminate pleasure and pain from their souls; they practice bodily toil distinct from pain and thereby strengthen the mind; and having done so they end disputes and promote useful counsel in both public and private. Onescritus is asked for the Greek

[26] This story originates in Indian myth even if rephrased with Greek concepts, according to Bar-Kochva 2010, 72 n. 94. For the translation of *sôphrosunê* as "discipline," see Moore and Raymond 2019, xxxiv–xxxvii.

equivalents to these Indian sophists; he names Pythagoras, Socrates, and his teacher Diogenes of Sinope. Mandanis avers that those Greek exemplars are not true equivalents; in still preferring convention over nature, they do not live simply or nakedly enough. Mandanis then adds, as a sort of afterword, that he and his like "examine many aspects of nature" (περὶ φύσιν πολλὰ ἐξετάσαι) and forecast the seasonal cycles. They are given gifts whenever they enter the city, and join private dinners for discussion. And they so dislike bodily decrepitude that they prefer suicide through self-immolation to it.

We see in this story two blurrily distinguished perspectives on the sophists, as we have already seen in our later writers. One is a kind of existential or private perspective on the mental and bodily practices of self-work; the other is a kind of theoretical or public perspective on the naturalistic and religious aspects of their beliefs and civic usefulness. The desire modification of the Indian sophists is linked explicitly to an improvement in intellectual competence; both aspects—the conative and the cognitive—are part of a whole way of life. We also see that the linguistic lesson from Onescritus corroborates that from Nearchus. "Sophists" teach "wisdom" but can be said actively "to philosophize." Indeed, there might even be some etymological play linking sophists with philosophy, in Mandanis's remark about Alexander's "desire for wisdom." Such play would not be surprising from Onescritus, who is said to have studied with the intellectually engaged Cynic Diogenes—a view made plausible by the Cynic-sounding speech he attributes to Mandanis and its connections to Pythagoreanism and Socratism.[27] We also see the term *sophistai* linked to "philosophizing," as Alexander's disposition that leads him to learn from such men as Calanus and Mandanis, and this probably prepares the way for Megasthenes to replace the verbal form with the nominal form.

This phenomenon concerning the description of Indian intellectuals has its correlate in descriptions of other foreign intellectuals, and looking at them we may be reminded about the flexibility of the term *philosophia*. We have already seen Megasthenes' brief remark about the Syrian Jews. We get more information from the work of Hecataeus of Abdera, whose study of Egypt appears to have given structural inspiration to Megasthenes' (for Hecataeus, see Lang 2012). (Like Onescritus, Hecataeus studied with

[27] Qualifying Onescritus's relation to Diogenes as simply "an admirer" of the writings is Bar-Kochva (2010, 71), who also argues that he "deliberately described the Indian sages in Cynic guise as a way of bestowing upon the Cynic lifestyle prestige and a glorious antiquity." Even if Onescritus's and (later) Clearchus's anthropologies of Indian philosophers serve as offshore debates about Cynicism, the fact that Greeks were able to call certain actual Indian people philosophoi meaningfully reveals the lexical shift I am addressing here. On Onescritus's Cynicism see Moles 1995, 144–46; Stoneman 1995; Powers 1998; Desmond 2008, 30; Bosman 2007.

men slotted into the Greek philosophical tradition, especially Pyrrho.)[28] In a passage in Diodorus that probably quotes directly from Hecataeus, Hecataeus writes that "the [Egyptian] Thebans say they were the most ancient of people, and were the first to discover *philosophia* and precise astrology" (πρώτοις φιλοσοφίαν τε εὑρῆσθαι καὶ τὴν ἐπ' ἀκριβὲς ἀστρολογίαν, DS 1.50.1).[29] This along with Diodorus's ensuing material suggests that philosophia includes some humanly relevant star study. Diogenes Laertius claims that Hecataeus wrote something multi-parted called "On the Egyptian Philosophy" (Περὶ τῆς τῶν Αἰγυπτίων φιλοσοφίας [DL 1.10]). This exact title is not found elsewhere, but Diogenes says that Hecataeus wrote in it that the Egyptians called the sun and the moon gods, their theory of a bounded and spherical cosmos, the fieriness of the stars and the eclipses of the moon, the details of astrological influence on life on Earth, the discovery of geometry and arithmetic, the immortality and transmigration of the soul, and in general their natural explanations for everything.[30] These topics match almost precisely those found in Megasthenes' doxography of the Brachmanes.[31] What we lack is anything about desire modification or asceticism. Perhaps the Egyptian philosophoi had some degree of it or something else distinctive about the way they lived—apart from the researches—but perhaps not. Perhaps a philosophical bios does not need ostentatious self-abnegation; or perhaps philosophia can be practiced outside a life-embracing bios.

5. Conclusion

On the whole, the Indian philosophoi are taken to be a socially discrete group of people, readily clumped by observers though also internally differentiated. They develop and promulgate their discipline ostensibly through an unusual regime of physical training but also through lecture

[28] Hecataeus was himself called a "philosopher" (*Suda* s.v.; Josephus *Against Apion* 1.183) and "sophist" (Plutarch *Lycurgus* 20.2), and was connected to the Abderan philosophical traditions (Clem. *Strom.* 2.130–34) and the tutelage of Pyrrho (DL 9.69). On the connection between Pyrrho—who appears to have traveled with Alexander to the East—and Indian philosophy, see Bett 2000, 169–78; Kuzminski 2008; Beckwith 2015.

[29] This attribution is cautiously maintained by Burton 1972, 4, 7, 25, 34, and Murray 1970, 146 (but mistakenly denied by Lang 2012, comm. on F 25, because of a typo in representing Murray's chart).

[30] Maybe a chapter of the larger work on Egypt was called, perhaps in excerpted or epitomized form, "On the Egyptian Philosophy," possibly on the grounds that it explicitly spoke of philosophia. Plutarch cites Hecataeus for the claim that Egyptian kings, being priests, drank in the measure set out by sacred texts, but Hecataeus had just stated that the priests forwent wine when they were "philosophizing, learning, and teaching divine matters" (*On Isis and Osiris* 353b). So while Plutarch does not definitely attribute the term "philosophizing" to Hecataeus, it is possible that Hecataeus discusses "philosophizing" in the section Plutarch is reading.

[31] Diogenes (1.9) also says that Hecataeus spoke of the divinities of the *magoi*, perhaps in comparison with those of the Egyptian priests.

and discussion. This discipline has a private function: happiness, or the retreat from suffering. But it also seems to have a public function, though precisely how has not been specified. These philosophoi can forecast seasonal cycles, which is of enormous public benefit; they can perform religious rituals; some may advise civic leaders; and some may investigate nature. Thus philosophia is a way of life, even if not always a well-understood one.

The term *philosophia* is not used for a pursuit just of any person who engages in intellectual or cognitive cultivation, since presumably plenty of Indian people engaged in learning but did not count, either to Indians or Greeks, as "naked sophists" or philosophoi. Nor is it just any person who advances reasons in public deliberation, since the advisers of Megasthenes' seventh social class, who are explicitly differentiated from philosophoi, surely do so as well. If we see anything of the so-called Platonic view of philosophers, those who contemplate the eternal verities, or the Aristotelian, of those who seek out the most fundamental causes, we see it not as a core element but as a peripheral and only occasional one. So we can ask: What led the Greeks to apply a term they had used domestically for a few different kinds of people to a not-exactly-cognate group abroad? More concretely, what justified or occasioned the lexical shift from sophistai in Nearchus and Onescritus to philosophoi in Megasthenes?

A full answer would require its own study. A simple answer seems to be that the term *philosophoi* began, in the early fourth century, to denote groups with a range of intellectual practices, not just people given to quasi-formalized dialectical exchange (as at Gorgias *Helen* 13 and *Dissoi Logoi* 1.1 and 9.1), and certainly not just people with a shared canon and shared dialectical norms—that is, a discipline and an increasingly well-defined set of rationalistic methods. We see hints of these nondialectical, nondisciplinary practices of personal improvement in the fourth-century historian Herodorus's remarks about Heracles in particular: practices of self-work, desire modification, and heroic effort (Herodorus fr. 14; see Moore 2017). We get a notion of the variety in the groups of philosophoi in the apologetics of Isocrates for his own form and the conceptions Socrates imputes to his interlocutors.[32] Thus we can hypothesize a variable conception of philosophoi as self-conscious groups of aspirants to a certain constellation of psychic self-improvement and knowledge discovery. This conception would apply readily to newly encountered groups abroad, as long as some of their practices were familiar as methods of self-work and investigation.

[32] For Isocrates, especially *Against the Sophists*, *Helen* (1–8, 66–67), *Busiris* (1, 17, 42, 49), and *Antidosis* (183, 261–70), see Moore 2019b, 210–17; for Socrates, especially *Apology* and *Theaetetus*, see Peterson 2011; Moore 2019b, 171–93, 223–56.

Appendix

List of Abbreviated Titles

Arr. *Ind.* = Arrian, *Indica.*
DL = Diogenes Laertius, *Lives of the Eminent Philosophers.*
DS = Diodorus Siculus, *Library of History.*
Strabo = Strabo, *Geography.*

References

Adamson, Peter. 2019. "What Was Philosophy?" *New York Review of Books* (June 27).

Arnott, W. Geoffrey. 2011. *Alexis: The Fragments: A Commentary*. Cambridge: Cambridge University Press.

Bar-Kochva, Bezalel. 2010. *The Image of the Jews in Greek Literature: The Hellenistic Period.* Berkeley: University of California Press.

Battezzato, Luigi. 2008. "Pythagorean Comedies from Epicharmus to Alexis." *Aevum antiquum* 8:139–64.

Beckwith, Christopher. 2015. *Greek Buddha: Pyrrho's Encounter with Early Buddhism in Central Asia*. Princeton: Princeton University Press.

Bett, Richard. 2000. *Pyrrho, His Antecedents, and His Legacy*. Oxford: Oxford University Press.

Bosman, Philip. 2007. "King Meets Dog: The Origin of the Meeting Between Alexander and Diogenes." *Acta classica* 50:51–63.

Boyce, Mary. 1970. "Zoroaster the Priest." *Bulletin of the School of Oriental and African Studies* 33:22–38.

Burkert, Walter. 1972. *Lore and Science in Ancient Pythagoreanism*. Cambridge, Mass.: Harvard University Press.

Burton, Anne. 1972. *Diodorus Siculus*. Leiden: Brill.

Cooper, John M. 2012. *Pursuits of Wisdom: Six Ways of Life in Ancient Philosophy from Socrates to Plotinus*. Princeton: Princeton University Press.

Dahlquist, Allan. 1962. *Megasthenes and Indian Religion: A Study in Motives and Types*. Stockholm: Almqvist & Wiksell.

Desmond, William. 2008. *Cynics*. Berkeley: University of California Press.

Hadot, Pierre. 2002. Translated by Michael Chase. *What Is Ancient Philosophy?* Cambridge, Mass.: Harvard University Press.

Horky, Phillip Sidney. 2009. "Persian Cosmos and Greek Philosophy: Plato's Associates and the Zoroastrian Magoi." *Oxford Studies in Ancient Philosophy* 37:47–103.

Hutchinson, D. S., and Monte Ransome Johnson. 2018. "Protreptic and Apotreptic: Aristotle's Dialogue *Protrepticus*." In *When Wisdom Calls: Philosophical Protreptic in Antiquity*, edited by Olga Alieva, Annemaré Kotzé, and Sophie Van der Meeren, 111–54. Turnhout: Brepols.

Karttunen, Klaus. 1989. *India in Early Greek Literature*. Helsinki: Finnish Oriental Society.

________. 1997. *India and the Hellenistic World*. Helsinki: Finnish Oriental Society.

Kingsley, Peter. 1995. *Ancient Philosophy, Mystery and Magic: Empedocles and Pythagorean Tradition*. Oxford: Clarendon Press.

Kosmin, Paul. 2014. *The Land of the Elephant Kings*. Cambridge, Mass.: Harvard University Press.

Kuzminski, Adrian. 2008. *Pyrrhonism: How the Ancient Greeks Reinvented Buddhism*. Lanham, Md.: Lexington Books.

Lang, Philippa. 2012. "Hekataios of Abdera (264)." In *Brill's New Jacoby*. https://referenceworks.brillonline.com/entries/brill-s-new-jacoby/hekataios-264-a264

McEvilley, Thomas. 2002. *The Shape of Ancient Thought: Comparative Studies in Greek and Indian Philosophies*. New York: Allworth Press: School of Visual Arts.

Moles, John. 1995. "The Cynics and Politics." In *Justice and Generosity: Studies in Hellenistic Social and Political Philosophy: Proceedings of the Sixth Symposium Hellenisticum*, edited by André Laks and Malcolm Schofield, 129–58. Cambridge: Cambridge University Press.

Moore, Christopher. 2015. *Socrates and Self-Knowledge*. Cambridge: Cambridge University Press.

________. 2017. "Heracles the Philosopher (Herodorus Fr. 14)." *Classical Quarterly* 67, no. 1:27–48.

________. 2019a. " Aristotle on *Philosophia*." *Metaphilosophy* 50, no. 3:339–60.

________. 2019b. *Calling Philosophers Names: On the Origin of a Discipline*. Princeton: Princeton University Press.

________. Forthcoming a. "Aristotle's Philosophêmata." In *Aristotle's Fragments*, edited by Antonio Pedro Mesquita. Berlin: De Gruyter.

________. Forthcoming b. "The Fourth-Century Reception of the Sophists." In *The Cambridge Companion to the Sophists*, edited by Joshua Billings and Christopher Moore. Cambridge: Cambridge University Press.

Moore, Christopher, and Christopher C. Raymond. 2019. *Plato: Charmides. A Translation with Introduction, Notes, and Analysis*. Indianapolis: Hackett.

Murray, Oswyn. 1970. "Hecataeus of Abdera and Pharaonic Kingship." *Journal of Egyptian Archaeology* 56:141–71.

Nightingale, Andrea. 1995. *Genres in Dialogue: Plato and the Construct of Philosophy*. Cambridge: Cambridge University Press.

________. 2004. *Spectacles of Truth in Classical Greek Philosophy: Theoria in Its Cultural Context*. Cambridge: Cambridge University Press.

Palmer, John A. 2000. "Aristotle on the Ancient Theologians." *Apeiron* 33, no. 3:181–205.

Peterson, Sandra. 2011. *Socrates and Philosophy in the Dialogues of Plato*. Cambridge: Cambridge University Press.

Powers, Nathan. 1998. "Onesicritus, Naked Wise Men, and the Cynics' Alexander." *Syllecta classica* 9, no. 1:70–85.
Puskás, Ildikó. 1990. "Magasthenes and the 'Indian Gods' Herakles and Dionysos." *Mediterranean Studies* 2:39–47.
Robert, Louis. 1968. "De Delphes a l'Oxus: Inscriptions grecques nouvelles de La Bactriane." *Comptes rendus de l'Academie des inscriptions et belles lettres* 112, no. 3:416–57.
Roller, Duane. 2008. "Megathenes (715)." In *Brill's New Jacoby*. https://referenceworks.brillonline.com/entries/brill-s-new-jacoby/megasthenes-715-a715
Sassi, Maria Michela. 2018. *The Beginnings of Philosophy in Greece*. Princeton: Princeton University Press.
Seaford, Richard, ed. 2016. *Universe and Inner Self in Early Indian and Early Greek Thought*. Edinburgh: Edinburgh University Press.
Stoneman, Richard. 1995. "Naked Philosophers: The Brahmans in the Alexander Historians and the Alexander Romance." *Journal of Hellenic Studies* 115:99–114.
________. 2019. *The Greek Experience of India: From Alexander to the Indo-Greeks*. Princeton: Princeton University Press.
Verhasselt, Gertjan. Forthcoming. "The Seven Sages and the Inscription of Aï Khanoum." In *Clearchus of Soli,* Rutgers University Studies in Classical Humanities, edited by David C. Mirhady. New Brunswick: Transaction.
Whitby, Michael. 2011. "Onescritos (134)." In *Brill's New Jacoby*. https://referenceworks.brillonline.com/entries/brill-s-new-jacoby/onesicritos-134-a134
________. 2012. "Nearchos (133)." In *Brill's New Jacoby*. https://referenceworks.brillonline.com/entries/brill-s-new-jacoby/nearchos-133-a133

CHAPTER 2

PHILOSOPHY AND THE GOOD LIFE IN THE *ZHUANGZI*

PENGBO LIU

1. Introduction

Skeptical themes and arguments have been a central topic in contemporary studies of the philosophy of the *Zhuangzi*.[1] Scholars have debated the extent to which Zhuangzi is genuinely a skeptic or a relativist (or both), and if he is, what kind of skeptical stance he adopts: is his skepticism primarily doctrinal (Hansen 2003; Fraser 2009), or therapeutic (Ivanhoe 1993; Schwitzgebel 1996), or interrogative (Wong 2006)? It is not, however, the aim of this essay to take sides in these debates. My interpretation of the *Zhuangzi* only assumes that (1) the text raises serious questions and skeptical arguments that challenge our claims of knowledge about the right way of living, and (2) by way of stories, fables, jokes, aphorisms, and arguments, the text endorses what looks like a positive conception of the good life. These assumptions are substantive, but hardly controversial.[2]

[1] See the essays in Kjellberg and Ivanhoe 1996. For more recent discussions, see Hansen 2003, Wong 2005, Fraser 2009, Chung 2017, and Chiu 2018, among others. I follow the dominant contemporary interpretative approach to the *Zhuangzi* in assuming the text is the work of multiple authors, edited and compiled over many decades. For ease of exposition, I use "Zhuangzi" and "the *Zhuangzi*" interchangeably, but the *Zhuangist* view as I interpret it is, following common practice, mainly based on and reconstructed from the *Inner Chapters* (which are generally recognized as attributable to a single author, probably the historic Zhuangzi) and related material in the *Miscellaneous Chapters* (esp. chaps. 23–27).

[2] For example, these assumptions are compatible with the reading that Zhuangzi is *not,* at the end of the day, a skeptic, despite the skeptical argument he raises and considers.

Philosophy as a Way of Life: Historical, Contemporary, and Pedagogical Perspectives.
Edited by James M. Ambury, Tushar Irani, and Kathleen Wallace.

Published 2021 by John Wiley & Sons Ltd.

My focus in this essay is one particular type of skeptical challenge, which has not, in my opinion, received the attention it deserves. It is the challenge to philosophical disputation, or *bian*. In ancient Chinese, bian has two primary senses: dispute/disputation and discriminate/distinction. These senses are closely related: to dispute about an issue is to try to distinguish the right view about it from the wrong ones. In the East and the West, and in ancient and modern times, disputation is the defining mode or characteristic of philosophy. Philosophers argue *for* their favored view and argue *against* their opponents. While rational argument is perhaps not the *only* thing that makes philosophy what it is (and obviously it is not only the philosophers who argue), it is clearly central to it. Moreover, it is often taken for granted that disputation is critically important for the discovery of truth, which is, after all, the goal of philosophy (or at least one of the main goals).

Zhuangzi, however, is keen on exposing the limitations of philosophical disputation and argument: from his perspective, while these practices may not be totally pointless, their usefulness tends to be exaggerated, and their harms overlooked. I shall call this the *metaphilosophical skepticism* of the *Zhuangzi*.

This essay is, in part, an exposition of metaphilosophical skepticism in the *Zhuangzi*. A second and more ambitious goal is to show how a broadly skeptical outlook is not only compatible with but also supports a positive picture of the good life. The essay proceeds as follows. In the next section, I distinguish three lines of Zhuangist arguments for metaphilosophical skepticism. Then, in section 3, I show that instead of advocating the elimination of philosophy, the *Zhuangzi* can be read as embracing a broader and more inclusive conception of philosophy, the goal of which is to engage us to reflect on our limitations, question things we take for granted, and better appreciate alternative perspectives and possibilities. Philosophy thus understood is pluralistic, in that it is compatible with a variety of methods and approaches: argument and disputation, but also fictions, jokes, paradoxes, spiritual exercises, and so on. Furthermore, as I argue in section 4, this pluralistic metaphilosophy and the Zhuangist conception of the good life are deeply connected: philosophical practices, in this broad, Zhuangist sense, pave the way for a more open-minded, adaptive, and flexible stance that is essential to the Zhuangist way of life.[3] I conclude with an example to illustrate how Zhuangist skeptical philosophy can provide practical guidance in dealing with adversity in life.

[3] Indeed, it may be said that, unlike the Pyrrhonian skeptic, who is known for the ability to construct opposing arguments that are equally compelling, the characteristic ability of the Zhuangist skeptic is the ability to maintain such an epistemic stance with *whatever tools or methods* at hand.

2. A Metaphilosophical Skepticism: Zhuangzi's Criticisms of Disputation

In the *Inner Chapters*, Zhuangzi raises a mix of epistemological, psychological, and conceptual criticisms of disputation. While the considerations underlying these criticisms are related and mutually supportive, each has a somewhat different focus from the others. Hence, it will be worthwhile to discuss them separately.

First, in a widely discussed passage Zhuangzi apparently argues that when two parties are in disagreement, there is no way of knowing who is *really* right (*guo shi*) and who is *really* wrong (*guo fei*). If you and I are in a genuine disagreement, we obviously cannot settle our dispute by ourselves. But others would not help either. An external "judge" who sides with me would naturally disagree with you—but in that case, you would not be converted because you have *already* believed that my side is wrong. Similarly, if the "judge" happens to agree with you, this fact would not change my mind either. The upshot, then, is that we cannot decide who "wins" the debate (2/84–2/90).[4]

This passage reminds many scholars of the famous *unresolvability*, or *undecidability*, argument of the ancient Greek skeptics.[5] According to the skeptics, disputes are unresolvable because, among other things, there is no *nonarbitrary* way to settle a dispute. More precisely, if my opponent asked me to *justify* my claim that P, I have to appeal to another premise, Q; but she of course would reject Q if Q were merely arbitrary. So either I continue to justify Q with yet another premise, in which case the same challenge arises again, or I appeal to P to justify Q, in which case I would be arguing in a circle. Either way, my opponent would remain unconvinced.[6]

This is a plausible interpretation, but it is not clear to me the extent to which Zhuangzi's concern is similar to the Greek skeptics'. Unlike the Greek skeptics, Zhuangzi does not treat the disagreement about X as an argument to establish a skeptical *doctrine* (for example, we do not know X) or to induce a skeptical attitude (for example, suspending judgment about X). Instead, Zhuangzi seems to be more interested in showing the futility of philosophical disputation itself. To see this, it is important to note that the Zhuangist unresolvability argument also admits a less epistemological, but more psychological, interpretation. Take, for example, Zhuangzi's criticism of the Confucian/Mohist dispute. In one passage, Zhuangzi claims that when Confucians and Mohists debate about the correct Way, they each affirm what the other negates, and negates what the other affirms (2/26). On the face of it, however, this

[4] Citations to the *Zhuangzi* give the chapter and line numbers in Zhuangzi 1956.

[5] See, for example, Kjellberg (1994), Hansen (2003), and Fraser (2009). For the classic presentation of the problem, see Sextus Empiricus (2000, 41).

[6] The way I frame the unresolvability argument follows closely what is known as Agrippa's trilemma, but other formulations are also possible. For a helpful discussion of Agrippa's trilemma, see Barnes 1990.

observation seems quite uncontroversial: isn't this exactly what people do when they argue against each other? What is so problematic about this practice? Moreover, doesn't Zhuangzi himself also argue against both Confucians and Mohists?

A close examination of this passage helps to put things in perspective: "The Way is obscured by small completions. Words are obscured by glory and show. So we have the rights and wrongs of the Confucians and the Mohists. Each calls right (*shi*) what the other calls wrong (*fei*) and each calls wrong what the other calls right. But if you want to right their wrongs and wrong their rights, it's better to throw them open to the light" (2/25—27).[7] Several things are noteworthy about this passage. First, Zhuangzi is not criticizing the *content* of the views or arguments of the Confucians and Mohists; rather, he takes issue with what they *do*, that is, *the way* each group disputes with the other. This explains why, although he criticizes the Confucian and Mohist disputers, he does not conclude that they should thereby refrain from regarding their opponents' views as wrong; rather, his suggestion seems to be that there is a better way of doing it, namely, "throwing [our opponents' rights and wrongs] into light." The last phrase is a translation of *ming*, which Angus Graham renders as "illumination." I say more about ming below (section 4), but here the gist of the Zhuangist complaint seems to be that by criticizing each other in the wrong sort of way, the debaters somehow have obscured the *Dao*, or Way. Importantly, the text implicitly contrasts the ideal of ming with disputation, and regards the latter as a symptom of "small completion" (*xiaocheng*) of the Way. Hence, to make sense of Zhuangzi's criticism of the Confucian/Mohist dispute, we need to know why "small completion" is problematic.

Indeed, I believe that considerations about "small completion" give rise to another Zhuangist argument against disputation itself, which I call the *argument from partiality*. Right before the quoted passage, Zhuangzi claims that the distinction between *shi* and *fei*, right and wrong, is the product of *chengxin*, or the completed, or fully formed, heart (2/22). In the classical Chinese tradition, *xin* (commonly translated as "heart-mind") is the organ responsible for both our cognitive *and* our affective abilities. For the *Zhuangzi* in particular, when the heart is "completed," it becomes closed, exclusive, and even dogmatic. Crucially, Zhuangzi contends that *chengxi* is the precondition for judgments of *shi-fei,* or right and wrong (2/22). This point is worth highlighting: it is not that the judgments (of shi-fei) themselves fix and rigidify a distinction, and thereby make one dogmatic; instead, it is that only when one's heart is *already* completed, closed, and partial would one *choose to use* that type of judgment to express one's opinions and preferences. In other words, one's heart is completed, not

[7] All translations of passages from the *Zhuangzi* are by Paul Kjellberg in Ivanhoe and Van Norden 2005, unless otherwise indicated.

because one is committed to a *particular* doctrine of right and wrong, but because one is *disposed to* form or accept such a doctrine, regardless of its content, in a closed-minded and dogmatic way. Therefore, chengxin is content neutral. The implication then is that it is possible to make a shi-fei judgment in a nondogmatic, provisional, and open-minded way (that is, without a completed heart). Indeed, as we have seen, Zhuangzi himself seems to allow certain ways of shi-ing or fei-ing others.

In the *Zhuangzi*, the problem with partiality is primarily epistemic: being attached to a particular dao, or way, one risks overlooking alternative possibilities, which may be equally valid or even better suited for the issue at hand. It also makes one more susceptible to egocentric biases and misunderstanding, imposing one's own ideas on those of others. Interestingly, Zhuangzi seems to think the problem has a *moral* dimension as well: while engaging in (combative and adversarial) debates, people tend to be obsessed with reputation and status (such as being the "winner" of the debate). While this may be an exaggeration, the underlying worry, I think, is not too difficult to appreciate: after all, "right" and "wrong" have strong evaluative connotations, and in practice the evaluation of a *view* easily spills over to the worth of *the person* who holds the view. Hence, in a shi-fei debate one is naturally emotionally invested in, and attached to, one's view (and the side one belongs to). Then the issue, implicitly at least, is no longer merely *what* is right but also *who* is right.

Now the plausibility of this argument depends to a large extent on human psychology. It is not hard to imagine a calm, impartial, *and* open-minded philosopher who is, in debating with others, only interested in uncovering the Truth, but whether we are (or can be) like this is an empirical question that Zhuangzi himself cannot answer.[8] Still, as far as our *actual* philosophical practice is concerned, I think Zhuangzi's points are worth taking seriously, especially if we want to improve the way we do philosophy.

Zhuangzi also has a third and apparently deeper criticism of disputation. It appears deeper in that it stems from a pivotal and perhaps constitutive feature of philosophy itself, namely, the very conceptual apparatus or framework that makes philosophical argument/disputation possible. For this reason, I call this *the argument from conceptual deficiency*.

The text, it seems to me, points toward two interconnected types of deficiency. The first is that in ancient Chinese philosophical disputations evaluative terms such as shi-fei are rigid or absolute. The same is, I think, also largely true of their contemporary counterparts, at least when we apply these evaluative terms to philosophical claims or positions: right and wrong, true and false, justified and unjustified. What is right cannot be

[8] Research of social psychology in recent decades, however, suggests that we are far from this ideal. And indeed one common complaint against contemporary philosophy is its adversarial, combative style.

wrong; what is wrong cannot be right, period.[9] Against this assumption, much of the *Inner Chapters* is devoted to showing the contextual and perspectival dependency of shi-fei judgments: different creatures have different natures and preferences, so what is the right way for one creature may be the wrong way for another; evaluative judgments of the same person often change over time; and so on. Many modern interpreters understand these passages as suggesting that Zhuangzi is a relativist about the right way of life. What is often overlooked in the literature, however, is that Zhuangzi also challenges the shi-fei distinction itself. A notable exception to this trend is Chris Fraser. According to his interpretation (2009, 449), for Zhuangzi, completion, that is, adopting a norm for discriminating shi-fei, is *inherently* deficient in that it inevitably excludes alternative ways of discriminating shi-fei. But this is the case only if the shi-fei distinction is treated as absolute: for if the relevant norm of shi-fei admits variability and flexibility, those who endorse the norm will have no problem recognizing the plurality of *shi*s and *fei*s.

The second kind of conceptual deficiency has to do with the way different views or theories are compared and contrasted: right versus wrong; truth versus falsity; justified versus unjustified; and so on. These dichotomies can help to sharpen one's stance and thereby to clear the ground for debate; but it can also create oversimplified, and often distorting, oppositions. The oversimplification can take many forms. For example, two opposed views may in fact be compatible with each other, or can be made compatible with minor tweaks. Even when they are indeed incompatible in theory, their difference may not matter very much in practice. It is also possible that the "wrong" view contains important insights that are neglected by the "right" view, so that the "right" view can be improved if it is revised to incorporate them. Yet another possibility is that while two views are opposed at a general level, in some contexts one view works better, whereas in other contexts another view is more appropriate: in other words, the problem is not so much of the inherent plausibility of the views disputed but their claims of comprehensiveness or universality. Relatedly, a prominent theme in the *Zhuangzi* is the observation that the world is highly complex, heterogeneous, and constantly changing. Hence, the text is highly skeptical of any attempt to capture all these pluralities and the diversity of the way things are in simplistic, theoretical terms.

The overarching worry, then, is that when philosophical disputation is framed in these rigid and oversimplifying terms, it will be difficult for one side to treat the other side fairly and charitably, and appreciate the merits

[9] Things are a lot more complex today, given the popularity of contextualism and relativism in some circles. So this claim needs to be qualified. Still, at least at a metaphilosophical level, I am not aware of anything contextualist or relativist about the truth (or justification) of a philosophical *theory*.

of their views and perspectives. Consequently, disputers will hardly have the incentive to develop an improved, and more inclusive, view that incorporates insights from both sides.

To recapitulate: in this section I have reviewed three Zhuangist arguments against philosophical disputation. The *unresolvability argument* contends that philosophical disputations are futile because there is no convincing way to settle a dispute; the *argument from partiality* claims that disputers often, if not always, argue from a completed heart, thus cannot adequately appreciate other views or perspectives as they are; the *argument from conceptual deficiency* claims that the conceptual apparatus that frames philosophical disputations cannot do justice to the complexity and inclusiveness of the Dao. Of course, these arguments are not supposed to be independent; indeed, they may complement or reinforce one another. For example, one reason a philosophical debate is irresolvable may well be that the debaters on both sides argue from a partial point of view, argue in a dogmatic fashion, *and* treat their opposition as absolute and nonnegotiable. Likewise, the conceptual apparatus applied in disputation may reinforce partiality: disputers may even become more partial and dogmatic once they adopt oversimplifying conceptual devices to defend their own positions and refute alternatives.

3. Philosophy Beyond Disputation

3.1. Philosophy as a Way of Life

On Pierre Hadot's influential conception of philosophy as a way of life, the task of philosophy is therapeutic: philosophy is, first and foremost, a practice that aims to "transform the whole of the individual's life" (1995, 265), for example, to overcome mental disturbances and attain tranquillity and peacefulness. According to a competing conception, one that is perhaps more familiar and attractive to academic philosophers in the Anglo-American tradition, the philosophical life is a life guided by reasoning and argument (Cooper 2012, 18), as opposed to spiritual exercises (for example, meditation, fasting, prayer, reciting sacred texts, and so forth).

The philosophy of the *Zhuangzi*, unsurprisingly, defies easy classification. On the one hand, it does contain therapeutic elements, and even recommends practices that can be suitably called *spiritual* (the most famous is probably *xinzhai*, or heart-fasting, in the *Renjianshi* chapter). On the other hand, however, the *Zhuangzi* is also vigorously argumentative, and its critiques of other philosophers are often sharp and perceptive. Construing the Zhuangist arguments as *merely* therapeutic seems to imply that they are bad arguments, or, perhaps more precisely, that whether they are cogent arguments is simply irrelevant, and that they are not to be taken seriously qua arguments. Therefore, since I believe that many of the Zhuangist arguments are powerful and should be taken seriously, I find it implausible to view them as *merely* therapeutic.[10]

How, then, can we reconcile these two apparently conflicting images of the *Zhuangzi*? A quick answer, detailed below, is that while Zhuangzi is critical of disputation, his metaphilosophical skepticism is modest: the substance and style of his writings suggest, not the elimination of philosophy, but a broader and more inclusive conception of philosophy, in which disputation and argument assume a valuable but much less central role.

3.2. Toward a New Conception of Philosophy

The stylistic diversity and complexity of the *Zhuangzi* is what makes the text both fascinating and, at times, frustrating. Sometimes making clear sense of an obscure saying or story is painfully difficult, even impossible. But sometimes it is also fun and stimulating. Indeed, some of the greatest works in literature and the arts are so powerful and thought provoking precisely *because* they are ambiguous. Perhaps the obscure passages in the *Zhuangzi* should be read as poems or short stories, not philosophy per se; or, more plausibly I think, they point to a more inclusive conception of philosophy than the kind of philosophy we are used to.

Indeed, in light of his skepticism about disputation, it is natural that Zhuangzi would seek novel ways to convey his messages. In particular, his distrust of the shi-fei discourse makes him deliberately refrain from making strong or definitive assertions. This explains why he often admits his own ignorance and bewilderment, and also why he raises so many questions but rarely answers them definitely. An extreme example is that, at times, Zhuangzi expresses uncertainty about whether what he says is really meaningful: "Now I've said something, but I don't know if what I've said meant anything or not" (2/51).

I believe that there is more to Zhuangzi's prose style than caution or intellectual modesty. The wild imagination and playful, sometimes ecstatic, tone of the text gives the impression that Zhuangzi actually enjoys challenging his readers (and himself) and leaving things open. The text is filled with fantastic stories, paradoxical questions, aphorisms, jokes, and so on. Indeed, it seems that the goal of his writing is not to *articulate* and *defend* his own commitments, or even to *convince* readers of a particular position; instead, it is to *provoke* readers to reflect on and question things that they have otherwise taken for granted, and, importantly, to have fun in such thinking and questioning.

To support this interpretation of the Zhuangist *metaphilosophy*, let us consider a few of the many stylistic and linguistic devices the text uses. For example, the text frequently appeals to what is called "lodged words,"

[10] For reasons of space I cannot do justice to the therapeutic reading of Zhuangzi here. For more critical discussions of this reading, see Hansen 2003, Wong 2005, and Fraser 2009.

yuyan, that is, words attributed to other people or fictional characters: most notoriously, Confucius is sometimes used as a mouthpiece for Zhuangist ideas (e.g., 6/60–74) but is occasionally ridiculed as being stuck in his own limited perspective (e.g., 5/4–31). Second, another distinctive characteristic of the *Zhuangzi* in ancient Chinese philosophy is its extensive use of stories, including fables and parables. These stories are sometimes wildly imaginative and always entertaining. Zhuangzi himself is the protagonist of many such stories. One naturally assumes that he is a spokesperson of Zhuangzist ideas, and an exemplar of the Zhuangist life; however, he is sometimes depicted as being "trapped" in the world of things like everyone else (20/61–65), and in one instance, he is mocked for his narrow-mindedness (by a skeleton, of all things [see 18/22–29]).

Therefore, the text is often *doubly* ambiguous, as the reader is confronted with two interpretative questions: First, what does the story mean? Second, does the story truly reflect or express Zhuangzi's own thought? It is natural, then, that the text of *the Zhuangzi* often lends itself to different interpretations. But it is not just the stories that are ambiguous. When it comes to more expository and argumentative passages, Zhuangzi often employs devices to create a sense of indeterminacy. We have noted that the text raises more questions than answers. But even when a declarative statement (or a positive argument) is made, for example, that something is P, it is often followed by a double question: "Is it really P? Or is it really not-P?" I think this form of questioning suggests that the Zhuangist concern is as much about the subject matter as it is about the very *concept* used to describe it. In other words, Zhuangzi is not just interested in whether the thing is in fact P but also (and perhaps more) in whether it is legitimate or fruitful to think *in terms of* the P-ness of things; that is, to classify things as P and not-P. For example, as we have seen in the case of shi-fei, he challenges the very scheme of distinction because it is (or is often treated as) absolute and rigid.

This interest in challenging our conceptual scheme is also shown in many other paradoxical sayings, such as "the greatest disputation is speechless" (2/59).[11] The underlying concern here, it seems to me, is not whether a concept is sensible or legitimate but whether our assumptions about what falls under the concept are too narrow and dogmatic. Hence, with the paradoxical sayings, Zhuangzi seeks to expand our conceptual repertoire and enable us to entertain new conceptual possibilities. Furthermore, since conceptual distinctions play an important role in guiding our practical life, this exercise can potentially enrich our practices as well.

While obviously much more could be said about the style of *the Zhuangzi*, and the interplay between the style and the substance, the examples above suffice, I think, to show that many of its ambiguities and indeterminacies

[11] These forms of writing style are, according to some interpreters, instances of what Zhuangzi calls *zhiyan*, "goblet words," or "spillover words." For a helpful discussion of zhiyan, see Chiu 2015.

are probably deliberate.[12] I propose, then, that these deliberate maneuvers can be understood in light of a distinctive view of the nature and goal of philosophy. While the *Zhuangzi* has no *explicit* discussion of what philosophy is or should be, the image of philosophy that emerges from the text, through the arguments, questions, jokes, stories, paradoxical sayings, and so forth, is one that is devoted to eliciting the awareness of our own limitations, and to provoking us to entertain and appreciate alternative possibilities (for example, alternative values, conceptual frameworks, ways of life, and the rest), whether or not we endorse them eventually. In short, this is a philosophy that aims to challenge and provoke, as opposed to prove or establish any particular doctrine. This kind of philosophy can be seen as an inquiry, though it is not an inquiry that primarily aims to uncover Reality or Truth but one that seeks to overcome our prejudices and dogmatism and to prepare or reorient us to a broader, and more inclusive, understanding of things (including ourselves).[13]

To put this conception of philosophy in perspective, let us reconsider the contrast, mentioned above, between two competing conceptions of philosophy as a way of life: one highlights the therapeutic and transformative power of philosophy and compares philosophy to spiritual exercises, such as meditation; the other stresses the foundational role of rational argument. Now from the Zhuangist standpoint, these two approaches are in fact compatible. This is because, for all their problems and limitations, argument and disputation, when used in the right way, can still contribute to the main goals of philosophy (understood in the Zhuangist way): negative arguments can expose the inadequacies and partiality of a position and can motivate the advocate of that position to improve or look for better alternatives; positive arguments, even if they cannot fully establish a position, may persuade us to take that position seriously as a viable alternative to our own. On the other hand, however, argument and disputation will assume a much less central place in philosophy thus understood, for the same goals can be achieved, in principle at least, by a story, a joke, a question, and so on.[14] Why limit philosophy to argument and disputation? Indeed, why limit philosophy to words? If, as Zhuangzi seems to believe,

[12] David Wong is right that Zhuangzi "would be highly amused at the scholarly obsession with being right on the meaning of his text" (2005, 91).

[13] Even if philosophy itself does not, or cannot, tell us what the best understanding is. As human beings, perhaps we are always stuck with one kind of limitation or another. This may well be our predicament (20/61–65), but the Zhuangist would confront it with a sense of irony, instead of despair. Cf. Nagel 1971 on the absurd.

[14] As Eric Schwitzgebel writes in a recent blog post: "If an essay, or a parable, or a dialogue, or an aphorism, or a movie engages the reader toward new reflections on fundamental questions about meaning, value, the human condition, the nature of knowledge or art or morality or love or mentality, pushing us out of our settled and conventional ways of thinking, challenging us to explore and reconsider—that's philosophy." ("Science Fiction as Philosophy," *The Splintered Mind*, May 23, 2019, http://schwitzsplinters.blogspot.com/2019/05/science-fiction-as-philosophy.html)

certain spiritual exercises are conducive to the kind of openness that helps us to overcome our prejudices, or to prevent us from forming a "completed heart," then they are surly to be recommended. But just as argument and reasoning can be used in a dogmatic way, so can spiritual exercises. Zhuangzi would not hesitate to call out and laugh at spiritual exercises that only preserve or reinforce dogmatic beliefs, religious or otherwise. In short, it does not matter *what* method or approach we adopt when we do philosophy, but it matters greatly *how* we do it.

4. Life Beyond Shi-Fei

Features of the Zhuangist conception of philosophy are echoed in the Zhuangist way of life, to which we now turn. What matters to the Zhuangist life is the *way* in which one forms, maintains, and acts on one's evaluative attitudes; it has less to do with the exact contents of one's beliefs and actions. Indeed, from the outside, the ideal life may not be that different from an ordinary life, and Zhuangzi himself, in a number of places, seems to recommend *yu zhu yong*, "lodging in the ordinary" (2/36, 2/47).[15] From the inside, however, things are a lot more complicated and interesting, and this is also where his conception of the good life converges with his metaphilosophy.

This ideal way of life is exemplified by the sage (*shengren*), or the true person (*zhenren*). According to the text, the sage does not deem anything simply as shi or fei, nor does he treat the concepts of shi and fei as absolutely opposed (2/29–30). This is partly because he recognizes the perspective dependency of our shi-fei judgments and thus is able to adopt a more inclusive and accommodating stance (2/58)—not unlike the Dao itself, which transcends the rigid shi-fei dichotomy. In this way, the sage occupies the position of the "pivot" of the Dao and achieves the stance of illumination (ming). "[The sage] just goes along with things. What is this is also that, and what is that is also this. That is both right and wrong. This is also both right and wrong. So is there really a this and a that? Or isn't there any this or that? The place where neither this nor that finds its counterpart is called the pivot of the Way. Once the pivot finds its socket it can respond endlessly. What's right is endless. And what's wrong is endless, too. This is why I say it's better to throw them open to the light" (2/29–31). Now it is tempting to read Zhuangzi as claiming that the sage *identifies with* the Dao and abolishes all distinctions, including shi-fei: the Dao is an undifferentiated whole, and thus all distinctions are inevitably partial and biased. Nothing in the text requires this reading, however. The Dao for Zhuangzi is indeed maximally inclusive, but this does not imply that no distinction can be made between things; rather, it is entirely compatible with this conception of the Dao that it accommodates many different

[15] Cf. Sextus Empiricus (2000, I 23–24).

perspectives, and thus many different ways of discriminating shi-fei, although none of the ways has the claim to be absolutely or universally correct. More important, this "eliminativist" interpretation is hardly coherent with Zhuangzi's skepticism about rigid and absolute shi-fei distinctions: for this interpretation implies that abolishing all distinctions, or treating all rights and wrongs as identical, is *the* right attitude to adopt because it conforms to the ultimate Dao. It seems unlikely Zhuangzi would embrace such a dogmatic position.[16]

By contrast, Zhuangzi speaks favorably of *yinshi*, which is translated as "go along with things" (Kjellberg), "'that's it' which goes by circumstances" (Graham), and "going by the rightness of the present 'this'" (Ziporyn 2009). It means, roughly, regarding something as shi in a way that is highly context sensitive, provisional, and fluid. So again, the point here is not *whether* one forms evaluative shi-fei attitudes, or *what* particular things one regards as shi *or* fei, but *how* one forms such attitudes. Indeed, it is hard to see how someone completely devoid of evaluative attitudes, either explicit or implicit, could perform any intentional action at all.[17] As noted above, making evaluative shi-fei judgments is compatible with the Zhuangist ideal of sagehood, provided that they are made in a flexible and nondogmatic way. In particular, the sage's shi-fei judgments show great sensitivity to the perspectives of others: the sage chooses the course of action on the basis of what *fits* the context that involves both parties. This means, in turn, that the sage will seek to accommodate the perspectives of others, including their evaluative judgments, that is, their shi-fei.

This aspect of the Zhuangist sagehood is humorously illustrated by the story of the monkey trainer. "When the monkey trainer was passing out nuts he said, 'You get three in the morning and four at night.' The monkeys were all angry. 'All right,' he said, 'you get four in the morning and three at night.' The monkeys were all pleased. With no loss in name or substance, he made use of their joy and anger because he went along with them. So the sage harmonizes people with right and wrong and rests them on Heaven's wheel. This is called walking two roads" (2/38–40). The monkeys in this story have strong opinions about what is right for them; like the disputers, they are emotionally invested in their opinions. But instead of pointing to their silliness or proving them wrong, the monkey trainer manages to accommodate their opinions without changing the substance.[18] More generally, the idea is that the sage accommodates the perspectives of others and harmonizes with them by "walking two roads." In this way, the sage is able to, in Zhuangzi's characteristically colorful phrase, *make a springtime* with other people and things (5/45).

[16] For similar criticisms, see Fraser (2009, 444–45) and Lai and Chiu (2013, 533–34).

[17] This is analogous to a version of the *apraxia* objection against ancient skepticism that Katja Maria Vogt labels "the Paralysis Challenge." See Vogt 2010.

[18] Perhaps Zhuangzi thinks that a lot of philosophical debates of his time were like this, that is, merely verbal disputes?

The other side of the Zhuangist life is that, released from (rigid conceptions of) shi-fei, the sage attains a state of emotional detachment from, among other things, his own judgments and actions. Recall that one of the Zhuangist criticisms of disputation is that it exploits and reinforces our partiality. All too easily, we become so committed to and emotionally invested in our own views that (whether we admit it or not) we are more interested in proving *we are right* (and *they are wrong*) than listening to others and collaborating with them so as to solve the problem at hand. Besides, being committed to our views in this way makes the debate appear more important than it is really is (and more heated than it needs to be), since now much more is at stake (for example, our reputation, status, self-respect, and the like); this is perhaps why Zhuangzi ridicules his friend and logician Hui Shi for wasting his talents on trivial logical puzzles.

The Zhuangist sage will have none of this. In Zhuangzi's famous metaphor, the sage uses his mind *like a mirror*, without storing or possessing (7/32–33). As I understand it, the metaphor is meant to highlight the way in which the self recedes into the background and assumes a largely *responsive* role: the sage as a responder, not an initiator. While his response to a particular situation is still his, it is not *owned* by him, so to speak.

It is important to note that this form of detachment does not amount to disengagement or passivity: while the sage does not seek to perpetuate any particular view of shi-fei, he does live fully in concrete situations. This could take a lot of attention and effort. While the expressions such as "going along with things" (*yinshi*) and "wandering at ease"(*xiao yao you*) may suggest such a life is easy and carefree, it is not (at least not always). This is because responding properly and fittingly to a particular situation means that we have to attend extremely carefully to, and engage actively with, the complexity and idiosyncrasies of the situation, as is shown in the famous Cook Ding example (3/2–12). Hence, these expressions are best seen as a characterization of the way the sage (1) is maximally open to the diverse experiences that the world has to offer, (2) is undisturbed by challenges and adversities, including death, that he confronts, and therefore (3) is able to be at home in whatever situation he finds himself in. To get a more concrete sense of this kind of life, let us now consider an example: the Zhuangist way of coping with death.

5. Coping with Death: Skeptical Philosophy in Action

The following passage brilliantly exemplifies the distinctive style of Zhuangzi's writing discussed in section 3.2 above; it also illustrates how Zhuangist philosophy might transform our attitude toward death and mortality:

> How do I know that loving life is not a mistake? How do I know that hating death is not like a lost child forgetting its way home? Lady Li was the daughter of the border guard of Ai. When the duke of Jin got her, her tears fell until they

> soaked her collar. But once she reached the royal palace, slept in the king's bed, and ate the meats of his table, she regretted her tears. How do I know that the dead don't regret that they ever longed for life? . . . In the dream, you don't know it's a dream. In the middle of a dream, you may interpret a dream within it. Only after waking do you know it was a dream. Still, there may be an even greater awakening after which you know that this, too, was just a greater dream. But the stupid ones think they are awake and confidently claim to know it. Are they rulers? Are they herdsmen? Really?! Kongzi and you are both dreaming. And in saying you are dreaming, I am dreaming, too. These words might be called a puzzle. (2/78–84)

This passage is attributed to Chang Wuzi, a fictional character. Hence, this is another example of yuyan, "lodged words." To add to the uncertainty of interpretation, before raising his skeptical questions, Chang Wuzi even warned that what he was going to say is *wangyan*, "reckless words."

In any case, it is at least clear that Chang Wuzi (like Zhuangzi himself) is challenging the conventional view that death is bad. The strategy of his challenging is particularly telling. He first entertains the possibility that death may be like a greater awakening and acknowledges that even if this were the case, we would not be in position to know it (for we would all be dreaming). Immediately after this remark, and as if overthrowing what he has just said, Chang Wuzi asserts: "And in saying you are dreaming, I am dreaming, too. These words might be called a puzzle."[19] This is likely yet another strategy Zhuangzi adopts to avoid being committed to any positive view—Zhuangzi, like Chang Wuzi, is too playful for that. It seems that here Zhuangzi is less interested in proposing a revolutionary theory about the value of death and more in engaging readers with alternative possibilities. Perhaps death is not bad at all? Perhaps it is just another awakening? How do we know? Hence, this open-ended style of questioning is perfectly in line with the conception of philosophy in the *Zhuangzi*: a philosophy that aims to make us less prejudiced and more open to alternative possibilities.

At other places, however, the *Zhuangzi* seems to be more affirmative: death and life are on a par, in that they are (1) just parts of the ceaseless process of cosmic transformations (6/46; 6/77–78) and thus (2) our inescapable destiny or fate (5/43–44; 6/20–21).[20] Some scholars interpret these passages as suggesting that one should identify with the objective standpoint of Heaven/Nature (*tian*) or the Dao (Wong 2006, 214), from which life and death alternate just like the four seasons: my birth is a result of transformation (*hua*), and when I die, I will transform into other things. On a more radical version of this reading, there is no *me* as

[19] No wonder he calls his words reckless! It seems as if he will laugh at us if we take his words too seriously.

[20] There are even some complaints that life is burdensome and tiring (6/24), and filled with anxiety and uneasiness (18/5–6).

a separate entity; rather, I am just a part or stage of the continuous cosmic processes. Death, then, is not to be feared and lamented, "because at bottom I am everything and have neither beginning or end" (Graham 2001, 23). Some scholars, on the other hand, read these passages as recommending a philosophical "double vision," that is, we accept the heavenly perspective from which we can question our ordinary attitude toward death, while retaining a human perspective and conforming, at least outwardly, to conventional roles and obligations (Tiwald 2015, 62–44).[21]

While both interpretations contain important insights, neither, I think, is completely satisfactory. My worry, *very* roughly put, is this: the "identifying with the whole" interpretation is in tension with the barrage of skeptical challenges, some of which are cited above, that Zhuangzi raises about our ability to know whether death is good or bad; the idea of double vision is more compatible with these skeptical challenges, but its practical implication is quite unclear: for example, can someone coherently lead such a life, and without constantly falling into some sort of practical paralysis ("Now *which* perspective should I adopt, and *why*?")?

The conception of the good life sketched above suggests an alternative interpretation: the key is not *which* perspective one bases one's evaluative judgments and actions on, or, for that matter, *how many* perspective one can adopt; instead, it is *how* one takes on a perspective and switches between different perspectives. There is no principled reason to limit legitimate evaluative perspectives to just one or two, as long as they are fitting or useful in the context. On this interpretation, when he draws our attention to the place of death in the ceaseless changes of the universe, Zhuangzi is not asserting that this is *the* correct view of death or that we *should* accept death and loss with indifference. Instead, he is trying to get us appreciate a broadened vision that is, when we reflect on it, as compelling as (if not more so) than our conventional view of death. Our problem is not that we fail to appreciate the *ultimate* (in)significance of death or that we do not *really* know whether it is good or bad; rather, it is that, just like the philosophers indulging in disputes, we are preoccupied with a natural but very narrow perspective, to which we adhere closely and emotionally, such that we become blind to alternative ways of understanding death and its relation to life.[22]

If this interpretation is correct, the Zhuangist need not deny that the death of a loved one *is* a loss, and even a significant one. The problem arises when we are preoccupied with the thought that it is *our* loss: that is, when we can see the death only in light of what *we* want or need. This

[21] So, on this interpretation, traditional funeral rites may be compatible with the Zhuangist way of life.

[22] If anything, we have more incentives to adhere closely and emotionally: since it our own lives and the lives of our loved ones that are threatened and deprived by death.

frequently happens when we are attached to our loved ones in a *self-indulgent* way: that is, we value them as the basis for our sense of security in the world, so that we need them for our own sake, not theirs (Wonderly 2016). Interestingly, this Zhuangist diagnosis gains some support from recent psychological studies of grief and resilience, which suggest that most people are in fact quite adaptive to the death of their loved ones. Those who are attached to others in a self-indulgent way, however, are much more likely to have prolonged and pathological grief. In the worst-case scenario, they experience heightened distress, anguish, yearning, and the like, and remain dysfunctional for years.[23]

Moreover, the Zhuangist would also remind us of the varieties of ways to appreciate the value of our loved ones, and ways to *transform* (hua) our relationship after they are gone: pursuing our common interest, carrying on the deceased's wishes, promoting our shared values, and so on. Again, recent empirical literature on the benefits of "continuing bonds" lends support for this idea.[24] While the Zhuangist would in general favor resilience and adaptation, it is important to note that Zhuangist adaptation is not a passive process of *acceptance* but an active and constructive process of *reorganization*. From this perspective, the death of our loved ones is not the end of those relationships but their transformation.

For the Zhuangist, then, there are better and worse ways of responding to loss. Zhuangzi himself, after all, expresses a deep sense of sadness at the grave of his best friend, Hui Shi.[25] To return to the mind-as-mirror metaphor, his suggestion, roughly put, is that we should not "own" the loss but respond to it *as it is*. Some forms of grief and mourning may be inevitable or even appropriate, since the death of a loved one *is* a significant loss; but it is also part of the natural process of change and transformation. After all, self-indulgence or self-centeredness in grieving is not only pernicious to our psychological well-being; more important, it is a failure to value our loved ones as they are, and for their own sake.[26]

6. Conclusion

In this essay, I have developed an interpretation of Zhuangzi's criticisms of philosophical disputation (section 2) and his alternative conception philosophy (section 3). The latter in turn sheds important light on the

[23] For reviews of this literature, see Fraley and Bonanno 2004 and Jerga, Shaver, and Wilkinson 2011.

[24] For recent reviews of this literature, see Field, Gao, and Paderna 2005 and Stroebe, Schut, and Boerner 2010.

[25] The tone of the text suggests that Zhuangzi's sorrow is entirely appropriate, even commendable. For an insightful discussion of this and other related stories in the *Zhuangzi,* see Olberding 2007.

[26] Themes in this section are explored at greater length in my "Attachment, Loss, and Resilience" (Liu, MS).

Zhuangist idea of the good life (section 4) and the Zhuangist attitude toward death (section 5). For the Zhuangist, philosophy is an invitation to reflect and question, and to take neglected, radical, and even unpopular possibilities seriously.[27] It is, in other words, an invitation to the Zhuangist way of life: less self-centered and dogmatic but more flexible, open, and adaptive.

Indeed, there are a number of interesting parallels between this conception of philosophy and the Zhuangist way of life. *Shi* and *fei,* like their English counterparts *right* and *wrong*, are evaluative terms applicable to both a theory and a way of life. A philosophy beyond disputation about shi-fei (of theories) is one that welcomes a variety of methods, approaches, and practices; and a life beyond preoccupation with particular shis or feis (of ways of life) is one that does not indulge in the self but seeks to accommodate others. For the Zhuangist, philosophical reflection is always open-ended, because no matter how hard we try, our views will remain somewhat parochial and biased; for the same reason, we cannot be sure that our way of living is the best (even *for ourselves*). But in both cases, we can come to terms with our limitations, even embrace and make fun of them, and eventually, in Zhuangzi's own words, *wander at ease* within their boundaries.

References

Barnes, Jonathan. 1990. *The Toils of Scepticism.* Cambridge: Cambridge University Press.

Chiu, Wai Wai. 2015. "Goblet Words and Indeterminacy: A Writing Style That Is Free of Commitment." *Frontiers of Philosophy in China* 10, no. 2:255–72.

________. 2018. "Zhuangzi's Knowing-How and Skepticism." *Philosophy East and West* 68, no. 4:1062–84.

Chung, Julianne. 2017. "Taking Skepticism Seriously: How the Zhuang-Zi Can Inform Contemporary Epistemology." *Comparative Philosophy* 8, no. 2:3–29.

Cooper, John M. 2012. *Pursuits of Wisdom: Six Ways of Life in Ancient Philosophy from Socrates to Plotinus.* Princeton: Princeton University Press.

Field, Nigel P., Beryl Gao, and Lisa Paderna. 2005. "Continuing Bonds in Bereavement: An Attachment Theory Based Perspective." *Death Studies* 29, no. 4:277–99.

Fraley, R. Chris, and George A. Bonanno. 2004. "Attachment and Loss: A Test of Three Competing Models on the Association Between Attachment-Related Avoidance and Adaptation to Bereavement." *Personality and Social Psychology Bulletin* 30, no. 7:878–90.

[27] But not, perhaps, *too* seriously.

Fraser, Chris. 2009. "Skepticism and Value in the Zhuāngzi." *International Philosophical Quarterly* 49, no. 4:439–57.

Graham, Angus C. 2001. *Chuang Tzu: The Inner Chapters*. London: Hackett.

Hadot, Pierre. 1995. *Philosophy as a Way of Life*. Edited by Arnold I. Davidson, translated by Michael Chase. Oxford: Blackwell.

Hansen, Chad. 2003. "Guru or Skeptic? Relativistic Skepticism in the Zhuangzi." In *Hiding the World in the World: Uneven Discourses on the Zhuangzi*, edited by Scott Cook, 128–62. Albany: State University of New York Press.

Ivanhoe, Philip J. 1993. "Zhuangzi on Skepticism, Skill, and the Ineffable Dao." *Journal of the American Academy of Religion* 61, no. 4:639–54.

Ivanhoe, Philip J., and Bryan W. Van Norden, eds. 2005. *Readings in Classical Chinese Philosophy*. Indianapolis: Hackett.

Jerga, Angelique M., Phillip R. Shaver, and Ross B. Wilkinson. 2011. "Attachment Insecurities and Identification of At-Risk Individuals Following the Death of a Loved One." *Journal of Social and Personal Relationships* 28, no. 7:891–914.

Kjellberg, Paul. 1994. "Skepticism, Truth, and the Good Life: A Comparison of Zhuangzi and Sextus Empiricus." *Philosophy East and West* 44, no. 1:111–33.

Kjellberg, Paul, and Philip J. Ivanhoe, eds. 1996. *Essays on Skepticism, Relativism, and Ethics in the Zhuangzi*. Albany: State University of New York Press.

Lai, Karyn L., and Wai Wai Chiu. 2013. "*Ming* in the Zhuangzi Neipian: Enlightened Engagement." *Journal of Chinese Philosophy* 40, nos. 3–4:527–43.

Liu, Pengbo. Unpublished. "Attachment, Loss, and Resilience."

Nagel, Thomas. 1971. "The Absurd." *Journal of Philosophy* 68, no. 20:716–27.

Olberding, Amy. 2007. "Sorrow and the Sage: Grief in the Zhuangzi." *Dao* 6, no. 4:339–59.

Schwitzgebel, Eric. 1996. "Zhuangzi's Attitude Toward Language and His Skepticism." In *Essays on Skepticism, Relativism, and Ethics in the Zhuangzi*, edited by Paul Kjellberg and Philip J. Ivanhoe, 68–96. Albany: State University of New York Press.

Sextus Empiricus. 2000. *Outlines of Scepticism*. Edited by Julia Annas and Jonathan Barnes. 2nd edition. New York: Cambridge University Press.

Stroebe, Margaret, Henk Schut, and Kathrin Boerner. 2010. "Continuing Bonds in Adaptation to Bereavement: Toward Theoretical Integration." *Clinical Psychology Review* 30, no. 2:259–68.

Tiwald, Justin. 2015. "Well-Being and Daoism." In *The Routledge Handbook of Philosophy of Well-Being*, edited by Guy Fletcher, 72–85. London: Routledge.

Vogt, Katja. 2010. "Scepticism and Action." In *The Cambridge Companion to Ancient Scepticism*, edited by Richard Bett, 165–80. Cambridge: Cambridge University Press.

Wonderly, Monique Lisa. 2016. "On Being Attached." *Philosophical Studies* 173, no. 1:223–42.

Wong, David. 2005. "Zhuangzi and the Obsession with Being Right." *History of Philosophy Quarterly* 22:99–107.

________. 2006. "The Meaning of Detachment in Daoism, Buddhism, and Stoicism." *Dao* 5, no. 2:207–19.

Zhuangzi. 1956. *Zhuangzi Yinde (A Concordance to Chuang Tzu)*. Harvard-Yenching Institute Sinological Index Series, supplement no. 20. Cambridge, Mass.: Harvard University Press.

Ziporyn, B. 2009. *Zhuangzi: The Essential Writings*. Indianapolis: Hackett.

CHAPTER 3

ESOTERIC CONFUCIANISM, MORAL DILEMMAS, AND FILIAL PIETY

WILLIAM SIN

Two controversial cases in Confucian literature present the demands of filial piety as conflicting with those of justice or impartial ethical considerations. The first is the Case of Concealment: a man finds that his father has stolen a sheep. Should he report the theft to the authorities? Confucius replies that he should *conceal* the matter (*Analects* 13.18).[1] The second is the Case of Evasion: the father of Sage King Shun commits a murder. Should Shun allow the authorities to apprehend his father? Mencius replies that he should protect his father and secretly carry him away (*Mencius* 7A35).[2] A literal—or what I call a *dogmatic*—reading of the texts indicates that both Confucius and Mencius support the value of filial piety over that of justice. Liu Qingping adopts this reading in his works and criticizes Confucianism for promoting corruption at the expense of justice (Liu 2003, 234–50; 2007, 1–19; 2009, 173–88).

In this essay, I provide an alternative reading of the cases, which I call *the liberal reading*. Yes, Confucius and Mencius recommend that agents comply with the demands of filial piety, but this does not prohibit choosing differently in similar circumstances. I argue that the Confucian teachers used these cases as moral dilemmas. Such dilemmas force Confucian students to use a cluster of Confucian virtues, including practical wisdom (*zhi* 智), discretion (*quan* 權), and straight determination (*zhi* 直). The liberal reading views these moral dilemmas as pedagogical tools; like other

[1] The translation I employ is Lau Din-Cheuk's *The Analects* (1979).
[2] The translation I employ is Lau Din-Cheuk's *Mencius* (1970).

Philosophy as a Way of Life: Historical, Contemporary, and Pedagogical Perspectives.
Edited by James M. Ambury, Tushar Irani, and Kathleen Wallace.

Published 2021 by John Wiley & Sons Ltd.

remarks in the *Analects* and *Mencius*, they guide Confucian students in meditative exercises and ultimately transform students' mode of seeing and being (Hadot 1995, 83).

I propose a liberal reading, and adopt an *esoteric* approach, to interpreting Confucian literature. This is because I believe that Confucian teachers used unspoken and intuitive pedagogy to stimulate their students. This differs from *exoteric* approaches, which view readings through systematic and rationalistic elaborations of doctrines. Exotericism and esotericism represent two approaches through which the doctrines of Confucianism can be interpreted (Strauss 1988, 2013; Strauss and Green 1986; Smith 2006). Now, there is much to be said for viewing Confucianism in terms of its exoteric doctrines. We can see this in Liu's interpretation of the Cases of Concealment and Evasion when Liu argues that major forms of special human relationships, especially filial piety, have a supreme moral status. If, however, we examine Confucius's esoteric teaching in the *Analects*, we will interpret and understand the significance of these cases differently.

The objectives of this essay are twofold: first, to analyze the Cases of Concealment and Evasion in *Analects* 13.18 and *Mencius* 7A35 and, second, to explicate the idea of Confucian esotericism and show how Confucian philosophy can be understood as a way of life. The liberal reading opens space for the development of Confucianism as a moral theory that empowers individuality and inspires its followers to live an authentic life rather than a passive, compliant one.

The essay benefits from the works of Pierre Hadot and Leo Strauss. Hadot points out that philosophy, particularly classical philosophy, is an existential choice or way of life that aids an individual's spiritual transformation (2004, 102, 173). Hadot calls this kind of philosophical activity "spiritual exercise" (*askesis*). Though it involves the use of rational and theoretical discourse, it is not bound by them and cannot be reduced to a system of such discourse. Spiritual exercises aim to reshape an individual's way of living and seeing the world. Hadot observes, for example, in Plato's dialogues instances of contradiction, digression, and aporia (perplexity/puzzlement), and he argues that "whether the goal was to console, to cure, or to exhort the audience, the point was always and above all not to communicate to them some ready-made knowledge but to *form* them" (274).[3] Hadot's reading of classical philosophies aligns with ancient Chinese philosophies, especially those of Confucianism and Daoism. There are also cases of contradiction, digression, and aporia in the teachings of Confucius, Mencius, and Zhuangzi. The present essay attempts to demonstrate the connection between Confucian philosophy and Hadot's idea of spiritual exercise. I believe that more can be done in this direction at a later stage.

[3] I am grateful to Kwong Yiu-Fai for helping me sketch Hadot's view here.

Strauss gave esotericism a new meaning, which his predecessors had neglected (Smith 2009, 3). The term "Western esotericism" refers to a subject area within religious studies applied to a range of ideas and currents of mystical nature prior to the end of the eighteenth century (Hanegraaff 2013). In *Persecution and the Art of Writing* (1988) Strauss sees esotericism as a technique that writers used to avoid religious and political persecution. Yet, esotericism per se, when applied to the writing and reading of texts, can be more than a method of concealment and circumvention. Sometimes, in the absence of external oppression, writers still have reasons to write in an encoded way. For they may believe a certain truth would harm humanity (Strauss 1988, 34). In addition, some truths cannot be communicated by scientific method or exoteric means, such as repetition and verification, but may only be revealed as the agent resolves to seek them out and see the truth in "what is singular and nonrepeatable" (Smith 2006, 9). As a result, writers use "brief indication" in their texts, hoping that eager philosophers might get the message even if they live in different times or places (Strauss 1988, 34–35). In the context of this essay, esotericism is regarded as a means of teaching and interpretation that leads to a certain way of life.

The essay is divided into five sections. Sections 1 and 2 outline Confucian ethics and explain the content of esoteric Confucian education. Section 3 introduces the cases of Evasion and Concealment in *Analects* 13.18 and *Mencius* 7A35 and presents some initial analyses in relation to them. Section 4 identifies problems with the dogmatic reading and looks at the pedagogical use of moral dilemmas. Section 5 examines the concept of straightness (*zhi*) with regard to the Case of Concealment. I also sketch the esoteric readings underlying the Cases of Concealment and Evasion. These readings are supported by reference to how Zhu Xi and other traditional Chinese scholars understood the relation between the act of reading and self-cultivation.

1. Confucian Ethics: An Overview

For Confucians, virtue is by nature the appropriateness of the response of an agent toward different individuals in his social circle. Within this circle, Confucians identify five basic relations, viz., relations between minister and monarch, father and child, elder and younger brothers, husband and wife, and friends (*Mencius* 3A4; *Analects* 12.11; *Zhongyong* 1963; Ames 2011, 183–88). Distinct virtues—*relational* virtues—correspond to an agent's performance with regard to these five relations: loyalty to monarch, filial piety to parents, faithfulness to one's elder brother, obedience to husband, and trustfulness to friends.[4] Specific pairs of other virtues also sprout from the relations an agent has to specific others. They include, for instance, the gracefulness of a monarch and the faithfulness of his minister;

[4] See, however, Rosemont and Ames (2009, 49–50, 99–100) on the concern that relational virtues contribute to a male-dominated patriarchy in society.

the kindness of a father and the piety of his child; the friendliness of an elder brother and the respectfulness of his younger brother, and so on.[5]

Three features can be attributed to these relational virtues. First, they constitute the root of the more general virtues, viz., *ren* 仁 (benevolence) and *yi* 義 (righteousness), which represent a more direct, intuitive, and humane feeling that agents have for any fellow creatures. Second, the relational virtues provide the grounds through which the agent conceives his identity and paths by which he would achieve a good life (*Analects* 1.2; *Zhongyong* 1963; Slingerland 2003, 1–2). For example, Mencius states that the way of the sage king is simply to be a good son and a good younger brother (*Mencius* 6B2). And according to *Xiaojing*, the virtue of filial piety begins in the service of an agent to his own parents, continues in his service to his lord, and culminates in distinguishing himself in the world (Rosemont and Ames 2009, 105). Third, the relational virtues connect to each other holistically. If an agent fails to possess any of the specific virtues, he may not possess others either. So, an unfaithful child will fail to build trust with colleagues and friends; neither will he be loyal to his superiors (*Analects* 1.2; *Zhongyong* 1963; *Daxue* 1994; Ni 2008, 47–48; 2018, 14).

Rites or rituals are distinctive features of Confucian ethics (*li* 禮). Although Confucius is agnostic about the existence of supernatural beings (*Analects* 11.12), the overarching aim of his teaching consists in restoring the prestige and rightful practice of rites for the people—which stem from the practice of the ancient sage kings. What role do these rites have in people's lives? In Confucianism, rites can be understood both narrowly and broadly (Shun 1993). In the narrow sense, rites may refer to the content of ceremonies such as funerals and marriages. Although such ceremonies have religious connotations, they should not be the focus of concern (*Analects* 7.21). Yet participants should still act *as if* deities exist (*Analects* 3.12; see also Radice 2017, 188). By doing this, participants will behave seriously and respectfully, which is appropriate for such events. Of course, under such circumstances, it would be difficult for participants to act in a sincere and natural manner (Slingerland 2014, 66–82, 129–37). Mencius remarks that it will be a moral achievement for an adult child to act well at his parents' funerals (*Mencius* 4B13).

In a broader sense, rites refer to the propriety of conduct in people's interactions with others in different hierarchical positions.[6] Accordingly,

[5] According to Keightley (1993; 1990), the emphasis on the importance of role fulfillment constitutes a moral tradition that Confucius and the editors of the *Analects* inherit from earlier times.

[6] *Liji*, "Fang Ji": "The rules of propriety recognize these feelings of men, and lay down definite regulations for them, to serve as dykes for the people" (Legge 1885b, 245–85). Also *Liji*, "Qu Li I": "They are the rules of propriety, that furnish the means of determining (the observances towards) relatives, as near and remote; of settling points which may cause suspicion or doubt; of distinguishing where there should be agreement, and where difference; and of making clear what is right and what is wrong" (Legge 1885a, 62).

the contents of relational virtues coincide with the demands of rites in the broader sense (Rosemont 1991, 91). These ritual prescriptions certainly cannot tell people what to do in all possible situations; people constantly have to reflect on and refine their conduct (e.g., *Analects* 1.15, 1.4, 7.3, 4.17). Confucius also says that people are not passive vessels of rites but active participants who deliver the substance of rites (*Analects* 15.29). As the contents of rites have a long history of practice and refinement, their existence gives practitioners a moral authority over those who act erratically. Rites and their practice constitute a cultural legacy transferred between people of different generations (Kupperman 2002, 46–47; Olberding 2012, 96).

2. Elements of Esotericism in Confucius's Education

To understand his esoteric pedagogy, let us first look at how Confucius makes sense of the idea of "scholarship" (*xue* 學). Learning is essentially about how people improve themselves (*qiuzhuzi* 求諸己) so that they can act according to the demands of virtues. When Confucius explains why Yan Hui, his favorite disciple, is a good learner, he says that Yan never takes his anger out on others or repeats his mistakes (*Analects* 6.3). For those who treat their parents, superiors, and friends virtuously, Zixia 子夏, one of Confucius's disciples, states that these people can rightly be regarded as learned, even if they may not have been formally taught (*Analects* 1.7). In short, for Confucius, the primary concern of learning is not the acquisition of formal knowledge (*Analects* 4.13, 13.5) but rather a person's ability to engage with others justly and skillfully in social life (*Analects*, 6.13).[7] Confucius himself has an ability to demonstrate a personal style through his dealing with everyday affairs (Olberding 2007, 361–62; Kupperman 2002, 42).

Philosophy for Confucius is comparable to what it was for the Stoics, namely, an "exercise" through which individuals obtain an authentic state of life. "In their view," writes Hadot, "philosophy did not consist in teaching an abstract theory—much less in the exegesis of texts—but rather in the art of living. It is a concrete attitude and determinate lifestyle, which engages the whole of existence. The philosophical act is not situated merely on the cognitive level, but on that of the self and of being. It is a progress which causes us to be more fully, and makes us better. It is a conversion

[7] Ni states that the Confucian tradition of *gongfu* master-disciple relationship "starts from the assumption that true knowledge is much more than what words can convey, and it requires much more than the intellect to perceive, to understand, and to appropriate. One's reason must be aided by cultivated intuition, and by the awareness accessible only through diligent practice" (2016, 126-27). I am grateful to Li Chenyang for pointing out the relevance of Ni's ideas to my discussion.

which turns our entire life upside down, changing the life of the person who goes through it" (1995, 83; see also 60, 267–68).[8]

With such a practical approach to learning, how does Confucius teach? His teaching may be divided into *yanjiao* 言教 (teaching through words) and *shenjiao* 身教 (teaching through his own deeds). Both aspects have a characteristic esoteric style: Confucius is often reticent and modest. Not that he cannot talk eloquently, but he despises those who are showy and loud (e.g., *Analects* 1.3, 12.3). He does not even like to engage in arguments with his students and disciples. For instance, in *Analects* 11.25, Zilu 子路 sends a junior learner, Zigao 子羔, to be the steward of the Ji family. Confucius remarks that this will harm Zigao. Zilu replies that one does not have to read books before embarking on a practical task; one can learn by doing—a view that resembles Confucius's own ideas on the importance of practice. Confucius could object to Zilu's argument by distinguishing between situations where formal learning is essential for practice and situations where it is not. But instead of taking this "analytic step," Confucius simply rebukes Zilu for being glib (see also 17.21).

Why does Confucius do this? Perhaps he senses that Zilu has not replied sincerely (e.g., Slingerland 2003, 122). Zilu has used wit to cover up problematic behaviour, a vice that Confucius despises: glibness (*ning* 佞) (*Analects* 1.3, 17.7; cf. 5.5, 11.25, 12.3, 15.4).[9] Here, it is unclear how far Confucius values clarity of argument, or the critical demonstration of truth. But for him truth in demonstration is much less important than truthfulness in persons.[10] Confucius thinks it a primary duty that learners be alert to their moral dispositions: whether they have been faithful to their lords, sincere to their friends, or practice what they have learnt. They should seek moral self-improvement as far as they can; this is more important than the accumulation of knowledge per se.

As Confucius values improvement of character over clarity in demonstration, observers can be confused by his seemingly contradictory remarks. In *Analects* 11.22, timid Ran Qiu 冉求 and hasty Zilu separately ask

[8] See also Aristotle: "It is right, then, to say that a person comes to be just from doing just actions and temperate from doing temperate actions; for no one has the least prospect of becoming good from failing to do them. The many, however, do not do these actions. They take refuge in arguments, thinking that they are doing philosophy, and that this is the way to become excellent people. They are like a sick person who listens attentively to the doctor, but acts on none of his instructions" (*Nicomachean Ethics* 1105b [1999, 22]).

[9] Slingerland writes: "The original Zhou meaning of *ning* was something like 'attractive or noble in speech,' but in giving it the negative sense of 'glibness,' Confucius portrays *ning* as the false, external counterfeit of true, inner 'Goodness'" (2003, 238).

[10] Compare Hadot's representation of Plato: "Dialogue is only possible if the interlocutor has a real desire to dialogue: that is, if he truly wants to discover the truth, desires the Good from the depths of his soul, and agrees to submit to the rational demands of the Logos. His act of faith must correspond to that of Socrates: 'It is because I am convinced of its truth that I am ready, with your help, to inquire into the nature of virtue'" (1995, 93).

whether they should practice what they have learnt. Though their questions are the same, Confucius tells Ran Qiu that he should go ahead and Zilu that he should hold back. As Confucius doesn't elaborate upon his reasoning, unless such elaborations have practical use for his students, we should not take many of Confucius's teachings literally; sometimes there is no single answer concerning what a person should do to improve himself or to flourish.[11]

Let us turn to how Confucius assessed his students' performance. Confucius uses a nonverbal, private, and almost secretive way to appraise them. To understand a person's character, Confucius observes, one must understand "the basis from which he acts, and discover where it is that he feels at ease" (*Analects* 2.10; Slingerland 2003, 11). Take Yan Hui, for example. Confucius states that Yan is an outstanding student because he exemplifies Confucius's ideas in his *private conduct* (*Analects* 2.9). In another case, Confucius remarks that Yan's *heart* did not stray from benevolence for as long as three months, whereas for others the period was only a day or a month (*Analects* 6.7). Without an intimate understanding of their students, teachers cannot make this kind of observation (see also *Analects* 11.23, 11.26).

Confucius states that there is nothing he does that is not shared with his disciples, and that this is his way (*Analects* 7.24). This may show that he does not use esoteric ways to teach his students (Slingerland 2003, 72). But in the text, he also stresses that his actions are open to "a *couple* of disciples" (*ershanzi* 二三子; my emphasis). As regards others, even those from his own village, Confucius acts in a simple and cautious manner, as if he is unable to speak (*Analects* 10.1). On another occasion, he admires the greatness of Heaven (*tian* 天): it does not "speak," and yet seasons rotate and creatures flourish under it. He remarks that he also wishes to say nothing (*Analects* 17.19).[12] Being Confucius's most gifted disciple, Yan Hui remarks that Confucius's way is extremely difficult to follow: "Catching a glimpse of it before me, I then find it suddenly at my back" (*Analects* 9.11; Slingerland 2003, 90).

In short, esotericism is characteristic of Confucius's pedagogy. This does not overrule the times Confucius uses exotericism in his teaching. In chapter 10 of the *Analects*, he demonstrates the proper ways to conduct various basic activities in everyday life, such as eating, sleeping, sitting,

[11] Smith describes Strauss's interpretation of Plato in this way: "Strauss regards Plato not just as a political, but as a politic writer who engaged in the 'esoteric' strategy of giving to each of his interlocutors what is good for them while only faintly tipping his own hand" (2006, 103).

[12] Olberding (2007, 366) states that Confucius's instruction is indirect, and the moral learner who looks to Confucius must become an able reader of the laconic. She adds: "Confucius does not opine. He does not announce in profound fashion the significance of the everyday. Instead, as Jullien observes, the lesson is inconspicuous, 'based on the principle of the Master's minimal intervention' (Jullien 2000, 199)."

bowing, dealing with those who are mourning, behaving inside a temple, and so forth. These traits represent how Confucius carries himself humbly and sincerely in different circumstances. It may be regarded as the part of his "body teaching" that is accessible to, and can be practiced by, any of his followers.[13]

3. Filial Piety: The Supreme Principle?

This section introduces the Cases of Concealment and Evasion from the *Analects* and *Mencius*. I examine Liu Qingping's reading of the significance of these two cases, according to which the principle of filial piety is the supreme moral principle and outweighs considerations of justice and impartial ethical concerns. Call it the dogmatic reading. I discuss its problems and propose an alternative reading in the next section.

In *Analects* 13.18, Confucius replies to the Duke of She about his opinion on the idea of uprightness. Confucius states that an "upright" son should not report his father's theft of a sheep to the authorities; he should conceal his father's wrongdoing. An upright father would do likewise for his son.

> *The Case of Concealment*
>
> The Duke of She said to Confucius, "In our village we have one Straight Body [*Zhigong*直躬].[14] If a father steals a sheep, his son will give evidence against him." Confucius answered, "In our village those who are straight are quite different. Fathers cover up for their sons, and sons cover up for their fathers. In such behavior is straightness to be found as a matter of course." (*Analects* 13.18, Lau 1979, 121; with my modification)

The second case is from *Mencius* 7A35. Mencius's disciple, Tao Ying 桃應, asks a hypothetical question. If Shun's father (Gu Sou 瞽叟), who is blind, commits a murder, should Shun 舜—being the Sage King—excuse him or allow the authorities to apprehend him? Mencius replies that Shun should abdicate the throne and carry him away, living outside the bounds of civil society.

[13] Olberding states that even these ordinary actions of Confucius can carry deep meanings, which are not readily copied or deciphered by outsiders. She says: "Indeed, Confucius's personal style seems to be just the sort that only becomes apparent over long acquaintance and careful observation" (2007, 360–62).

[14] With regard to the meaning of "Zhigong 直躬," there are three possible interpretations. First, it may refer to a straightforward person whose name is Gong (直人名躬) (Brooks and Brooks 1998, 102; Lu 1983, 352). Second, it may refer to a person who has the character of zhi (直身而行) (Huang 1937, 138). Third, "Zhigong" as a whole may be a proper name, with "Zhi" a surname and "Gong" the given name (姓直名躬) (Xiong 2008, 727; Huang 1900, 323). I am grateful to Wong Sun-Tik for clarification of these distinctions.

The Case of Evasion

> Tao Ying asked: "If Shun was Emperor and Gao Yao the judge, what should have been done if the Blind Man killed a man?"
> "The only thing to do is to apprehend him."
> "In that case, would Shun not try to stop it?"
> "How could Shun stop it? Gao Yao had authority for what he did."
> "Then what would Shun have done?"
> "Shun thought of casting aside the Empire as no more than discarding a worn shoe. He would have secretly carried the old man on his back and fled to the edge of the Sea and lived there happily, never giving a thought to the Empire." (*Mencius* 7A35; with my modification)

By Liu's reading, the cases show that Confucianism places filial piety above principles of justice (Liu 2004, 859; 2007, 4–5), and that the Confucian evaluation of actions is determined by its preference for "consanguineous affection." Both the *Analects* and *Mencius* attribute prime status to filial piety: in *Analects* 1.2, You Zi states that being filial and having brotherly respect is the root of a person's character. Mencius also says that the substance of benevolence is serving one's parents, that the substance of righteousness is obedience to one's elder brothers (*Mencius* 4A27), and that the greatest achievement a filial son can attain is to serve his parents and honor them (*Mencius* 4A19; 5A4).

Critics of Liu argue that his dogmatic reading overlooks certain considerations that underlie the Confucian teachers' remarks. First, in the Case of Concealment, Van Norden (2008, 126) notes that when the conversation takes place, the punishment for the theft of sheep was likely to be harsh, such as the amputation of a limb or tattooing "thief" on the criminal's face.[15] Accordingly, the motivation of the adult child's concealment is to protect his father from serious harm. If the punishment for the crime was more lenient, perhaps the balance of considerations would tilt toward the son reporting the event to the authorities.

Second, in the Case of Evasion, Shun's father, Gu Sou, has committed murder. Although Shun evades justice by escaping with him, he does not interfere with the process of prosecution even though he could have done so. On the contrary, before carrying his father away, Shun withdraws from the throne. These actions show that Shun tries to avoid undermining the government's authority (Li 2008, 76).

Third, Huang as well as Rosemont and Ames draw attention to the importance of remonstration in Confucianism when an adult child's parents have acted in a morally problematic way (Huang 2013, 134; Rosemont and Ames 2008, 11). In the Cases of Concealment and Evasion, the adult

[15] On the severity of the penal code with regard to theft during the Chunqiu 春秋 period and the early Han 漢, see also Wang 2011, 415, and Shen 1985, 1398.

children may be acting to create a favorable environment in which they can remonstrate with their parents (Huang 2013, 142–44; Chen 2011, 455). As a result, the act of evading justice or concealing wrongdoing alone cannot fully represent the intention behind the adult children's actions.

4. The Dogmatic Reading and the Pedagogy of Moral Dilemmas

This section explains the pedagogical considerations in the Cases of Concealment and Evasion. In the dogmatic reading, both Confucius and Mencius place filial piety over justice or impartial ethical considerations whenever the two are in conflict. In the liberal reading, however, the Confucian teachers use the two cases as moral dilemmas to stimulate the growth of practical wisdom in students. On this view, the promotion of the five relations, though important, is not dogma for Confucians to comply with in all cases.

The dogmatic reading has problems. For, if it were true, Shun would have a greater range of options to explore: he could issue official immunity to his father and forbid Gao Yao to investigate the murder.[16] There would be no need for Shun to abdicate the throne and escape with his father. So why didn't Mencius mention these options? One explanation is that concerns about justice and the value of the public interest still carry weight. If that is the case, even if filial piety is more important than justice in this context, considerations of justice do not lose all their normative force in affecting people's deliberation.

A similar point can be made with regard to the Case of Concealment. Confucius states that the son covers up (*yin* 隱) for his father and the father covers up for his son. Huang thinks it is better to translate *yin* as "not disclosing," rather than "covering up" or "concealing" (Huang 2013, 144–45). If so, yin refers to an act of omission, which is more passive than the act of covering up or concealing. Confucius could recommend a more active course of action if filial piety absolutely outweighed the considerations of justice and other impartial ethical concerns; the father and son could simply *lie* to the authorities. That Confucius uses an indirect expression to describe the upright person's behavior may show that he is concerned with the value of justice and impartial morality.

In fact, in both cases, it seems to me that the agents are at least morally permitted to act in accordance with the demands of justice and impartial morality. By imposing overriding moral requirements on the agents to protect their parents' interests, however, the dogmatic reading destroys any moral tension in the scenarios (Van Norden 2008, 126–27) and

[16] Liu himself has mentioned the possibility of Shun making this move (2002, 46; 2007, 6). But he only mentions it to show that Shun does not intend to abuse his power. He has not mentioned it as a logical consequence if favoring kinship bonds over the value of justice would be conceived as a moral requirement. See also Li 2008, 76; Angle 2008, 36.

removes the adult children's room for contemplation and deliberation. As it commands agents to follow the rules of hierarchy unquestioningly, the dogmatic reading paves the way for an authoritarian form of Confucianism.

Let us turn to the discussion of moral dilemmas. They refer to situations in which an agent is confronted with incompatible values and moral requirements (Sinnott-Armstrong 1988, chap. 1; see also Nagel 1979, 134–35). There is nothing the agent can do to avoid acting unethically. If the consequences are serious, he would feel distraught no matter what his decision (McConnell 2018). He would feel this way because of his desire to respect multiple moral requirements, which cannot be fulfilled (Smart and Williams 1973, 116; Williams 1981, 74).

An agent trapped in a moral dilemma is aware of the diversity of values that support the incompatible courses of action; he can foresee that he will suffer, from guilt or remorse, for violating a moral obligation in the situation. To decide what to do, an agent must examine his deep commitments and be determined to perform an action of great consequence (cf. Fried 1970, 227; Williams 1981, 17–19). Here, the idea of determination, or straightness (*zhi* 直), is pertinent; I look at Confucius's idea of *zhi* in the next section.

From a pedagogical perspective, the use of dilemmas motivates students and fosters learning (Berlyne 1960). As esoteric teachers, Confucius and Mencius tend not to answer questions directly. Students are expected to do their own inferential thinking after they are stimulated (e.g., *Analects* 7.8, 9.8, 2.15, 15.31). Applying this thought to the Cases of Concealment and Evasion, we see that the demonstrations of the teachers may not preclude the possibility that their students decide differently. What matters may not be what an agent chooses, it may be *how* he comes to a certain decision and how it connects with his preferences.

Using moral dilemmas, the Confucian teachers can lead their students to experience the practical limits of ethical principles. The students have to employ practical wisdom to balance the conflicting concerns of different moral principles (*Analects* 9:30; *Mencius* 4A17, 6B1, 7A26; Van Norden 2008, 128). This involves a process in which students sacrifice and negotiate principles as well as experience guilt and regret, a process through which they develop their own virtues.[17]

[17] Varela describes the nature of practical knowledge, which is different from one's knowledge of abstractions: "The proper units of knowledge are primarily *concrete*, embodied, incorporated, lived; that knowledge is about situatedness; and that the uniqueness of knowledge, its historicity and context, is not a 'noise' concealing an abstract configuration in its true essence. The concrete is not a step toward something else: it is both where we are and how we get to where we will be" (1999, 7).

5. The Liberal Reading, *Zhi*, and Esoteric Confucianism

Liu's explanation of the Cases of Concealment and Evasion consists of an interpretive claim and an empirical claim.[18] The interpretive claim adopts a dogmatic reading; the empirical claim is that people's acceptance of the dogmatic reading has contributed to a culture of corruption among the Chinese people (Liu 2003, 234–50; 2007, 1–19; 2009, 173–88). Now, while I will not dispute Liu's empirical claim, I believe that there is a connection between the dogmatic reading and political authoritarianism.

The promotion of the relational virtues and the assertion of their importance over other values can lead to the oppression of individuality and tighten the authoritarian rule of any regime over its people (King 1985, 62–65, 72–73). Since this interpretation of Confucianism helps to strengthen social order and control, doctrines associated with the dogmatic reading have been favored by political establishments at various times in history (Wei 2003, 51–56, 284–87). In this essay, though I regard the dogmatic reading as part of the exoteric doctrines of Confucianism, I propose the *liberal* reading, which can support the *esoteric* counterpart of Confucianism. The liberal reading emphasizes the importance of the need for individuals to live authentic lives. When facing moral dilemmas, there are a range of reasons that support incompatible options. What individuals need is a determination to commit to *their* values in life: a character trait that is described in the *Analects* as *zhi*, viz., straightness or straightforwardness. Of course, sometimes agents do not yet have a clear idea about what their values are; under such circumstances, I believe that the exercise of *reading* the two cases still enhances virtues and self-understanding.

The Chinese character *zhi*, 直, appears in key places of the text in relation to the Case of Concealment. Look at the case again. The Duke of She boasted before Confucius about the *straightness* of people in his village; if a father steals a sheep, his son will give evidence against him. Hearing this, Confucius replied that people in his village are *straight* in a different way: fathers cover up for their sons and sons cover up for their fathers. In such behavior is *straightness* to be found as a matter of course. Here, the meanings of zhi are expressed differently by the interlocutors.[19] According to the Duke of She, it literally refers to the compliance of an adult child with the demands of justice at the expense of his father's interests. We cannot ask why the adult child in the Duke of She's village should report his father's wrongdoing to the authorities; that an upright person does an upright thing needs no explanation. In Confucius's response, however, zhi is

[18] Sarkissian (forthcoming) makes a distinction between an "interpretative question" and a "normative question." The interpretative question concerns whether Confucianism has emphasized filial piety over impartial values; the normative question concerns whether Confucianism should commit to such a normative preference.

[19] See Huang 2013, 140; Meng 2004, 460; Guo 2011, 6; see also footnote 14 above.

conceived as a feature of a person's character. The act of concealment is something that an upright person will do because this action springs from his deep commitment.

For the Duke of She, an agent reporting his father's wrongdoing is praiseworthy, as he fulfills an ethical expectation even at the expense of his father's interests. But, for Confucius, complying with legal or common-sense ethical rules is just one side of being good. Another side is to seek for truth within oneself and commit to it (*Analects* 2.3), which can be understood as the virtue of straightness. The agent who does not have a straight character either lacks the ability to act well in the critical moment or fails to cognize his fundamental principle in life. The antonym of straightness (*zhi*) is *qu* 曲, which refers to a calculating and insincere character.[20] Confucius has stated that even if a calculating person cheats his way through life, his downfall is inevitable (*Analects* 6.19). By contrast, a straightforward person may sometimes act imprudently (*Mencius* 2A2); yet when he manages to act truly in a critical moment, the meaning of his life is greatly enhanced. Thus, Confucius says: "He has not lived in vain who dies in the evening, having been told about the Way in the morning" (*Analects* 4.8).

In the context of the *Analects*, zhi alone is not sufficient for someone to be a *junzi* (virtuous person), who must acquire both a refinement as well as a truthful native substance in his character (*wenzhibinbin* 文質彬彬) (*Analects* 6.18); a person acting straightly but without propriety can appear rude (*Analects* 8.2); a person should also learn the intricacies of social relationships, otherwise he will be blunt and impatient.[21] Confucius also says, however, that those who are resolute, simple, and *speak little* are close to being benevolent, and if one cannot have moderate persons around oneself for associates, one must turn to the ardent and the overscrupulous (*Analects* 13.27, 13.24).

According to the liberal reading, students' engagement with the Cases of Concealment and Evasion can trigger the growth of virtues. The Confucian teachers bring out the moral dilemmas so that, in order to proceed, students must consult practical wisdom (*zhi* 智), use discretion (*quan* 權), and be determined (*zhi* 直) to make sacrifices; for this is how they can

[20] The person with a mentality of *qu* can be a person with *ressentiment* in the context of modern society. Nietzsche writes: "The man of *ressentiment* . . . loves hiding places, secret paths and back doors, everything covert entices him as his world, his security, his refreshment; he understands how to keep silent, how not to forget, how to wait, how to be provisionally self-deprecating and humble. A race of such men of *ressentiment* is bound to become eventually cleverer than any noble race" (2007, 21).

[21] *Analects* 17.8. In *The Water Margin*, both Li Kui 李逵 and Lu Zhishen 魯智深 cause trouble when they feel indignant. Lu attacks the monks of *Mount Wutai* 五台山, whereas Li indiscriminately butchers ordinary people in *Jiangzhou* 江州 (Shi and Luo 1999, 110–49, 1206–11). They are vivid representations of persons who have *zhixing* but without knowledge about the intricacies of social relationships.

overcome difficulties and complete their lives' mission. This is one way to interpret Confucius's strategy of teaching.

Alternatively, we can read the passage in the light of Confucius's role as an esoteric educator; the Case of Concealment is a tool for Confucian students to engage in spiritual exercise. In his reply to the Duke of She, Confucius uses a set of (mainly) four-syllable expressions: *fuweiziyin, ziweifuyin, zhizaiqizhongyi* (父為子隱, 子為父隱, 直在其中矣). These lines may not be taken literally as an answer to the Duke of She's remark. Their content directly opposes the duke's view and gives rise to a moral dilemma that blocks an agent's rational deliberation. They simultaneously generate a poetic rhythm that allows the agent to recite and enter a contemplative state.[22] Being in this state, a devoted student would attempt to learn the limits of his character and the depths of his commitments in life. He would attempt to connect the basis of his actions to the principle with which he feels at home (*Analects* 2.10, 4.2). This meditative process cannot be reduced to discreet cognitive steps that anyone can comprehend and follow. It is an intuitive and obscure process, also an educational experience.[23]

In ancient China, the act of studying or reading consisted not only of a process of rational inquiry but also of emotive immersion, and of certain bodily engagements, such as the use of the voice in recital. Confucius says, "Knowing the truth is not as good as loving it; loving it is not as good as taking delight in it" (*Analects* 6.20).[24] In the Song period, both Cheng Hao and Zhu Xi remark that one needs to ruminate and savor (*wanwei* 玩味) what one is studying. "Chanting" is a method that Zhu Xi recommends. He lauds the saying of Sima Guang, a well-known minister in North Song: "Books must be chanted. By reciting them and pondering their meanings, readers will be greatly benefited" (Zhu 2002a, 570; my translation; cf. Wu 2013, 87). Zhu also says: "While reading a book, . . . one must recite loudly and clearly; one must make no mistake with any word, must not add any extra word, nor mix up the word order. One should not use artificial means to help with the memorization. . . . There is an old saying: 'After you have read a book a hundred times, its meanings will naturally dawn on

[22] Note Hadot's remark on the emphasis on the "effects of sound" in Greco-Roman antiquity: "And they [written works in Greco-Roman antiquity] were intended to be read aloud, either by a slave reading to his master or by the reader himself, since in antiquity reading customarily meant reading aloud, emphasizing the rhythm of the phrase and the sounds of the words, which the author himself had already experienced when he dictated his work. The ancients were extremely sensitive to these effects of sound" (1995, 62).

[23] Describing Strauss's view of esoteric teaching, Smith says: "Pre-modern thinkers presented a purely edifying teaching that could be grasped by any relatively intelligent reader and another, esoteric teaching wrapped up in enigma, contradiction, and paradox that would have quite another meaning for the philosophers or philosophers-in-training" (2006, 37; see also Strauss 1988, 22–37).

[24] In *Analects* 1.15, Confucius praises Zigong, who responds to Confucius's comment by reciting a poem in *Shi Jing* (*The Poetry*), viz., Wei Feng Qi Ao 衛風淇奧. The poem compares self-cultivation to the craft of polishing.

you'" (Zhu 2002b, 374; my translation).[25] Zhu's strategy of reading echoes what Du Fu famously says in his poem: "In reading I wore out (*puo* 破) ten thousand scrolls, I seemed helped by the gods when using my brush" (Du 2016, 51). Here, the Chinese word *puo* literally means "breaking," as in "breaking a limit" or "breaking through a barrier." How does one "break into" books of literature and classics? This action may involve deliberation and rational analysis, but more importantly reciting and getting acquainted with the books' materials (cf. Yuen 1960, 461).

Let us turn to Mencius's esoteric teaching in the Case of Evasion. Tao Ying asks Mencius: If Shun's father commits a murder, should Shun allow him to be apprehended or should he save him by any means? This question is followed by an exchange between the teacher and his disciple. Mencius initially reiterates the importance that people comply with the established rules of the legal authorities. But Tao Yin is persistent in chasing the trail of argument, which leads to the million-dollar question: What would Shun have done? Mencius then sternly states his view, which practically *opposes* what he said earlier: Shun should save his father and abandon the empire like a worn shoe. This twist in the narrative throws readers into an aporia: How can anyone so readily give up his "empire"—his career and achievements in life? How can anyone, after giving up everything, live cheerfully and happily with his father (as Mencius described)? Now, is Mencius merely talking about the priority of filial piety over impartial ethics?[26] Or is he also guiding his readers in how to live free of the bonds of material attachments? Mencius is famous for promoting the technique of nourishing his great and righteous spirit (*haoranzhiqi* 浩然之氣) (*Mencius* 2A2). I suspect that *reading* this passage would contribute to one's maintenance of this worthy goal. An appropriate response to the passage of the Case of Evasion will consist not just in one's analyzing the layers of its exoteric meanings but in one's reading it and "breaking into" the text as Du Fu says.

In short, with regard to the dilemmas in the Cases of Concealment and Evasion, there is obviously no easy answer to them. The agents facing them must make a judgment and act in accordance with the particular circumstantial features found within their perspectives. We can say that it is because these dilemmas are difficult to deal with that the teachers would prescribe them. These devices may not be meaningful if students will not *use* them to improve their moral standing. From this point of view, Confucius and Mencius prescribe the cases as "formulae" for their students

[25] For a general view of Zhu's understanding of how reading relates to self-cultivation, see Angle and Tiwald 2017, 152–54.

[26] Zhao Qi comments that Shun's great filial virtue "brings glory to his father and enables Shun to abandon the world" (大孝榮父, 遺棄天下) (Jiao 1987, 933; my translation). Zhu Xi states that Shun's action reflects the deep nature of the laws of Heaven and the exact order of human relations" (天理之極, 人倫之至) (2002c, 437–38; my translation). I owe these points to Wong Sun-Tik.

to attain spiritual progress. Hadot's remark on Plato's dialogues is pertinent to our understanding of the Confucian teachers' dialogues:

> All the circles, detours, endless divisions, digressions, and subtleties which make the modern reader of Plato's *Dialogues* so uncomfortable are destined to make ancient readers and interlocutors travel a specific path. Thanks to these detours, "with a great deal of effort, one rubs names, definitions, visions and sensations against one another"; one "spends a long time in the company of these questions"; one "lives with them" until the light blazes forth. Yet one keeps on practicing, since "for reasonable people, the measure of listening to such discussions is the whole of life." . . . What counts is not the solution of a particular problem, but the road travelled to reach it; a road along which the interlocutor, the disciple, and the reader form their thought, and make it more apt to discover the truth by itself. (1995, 92)

In conclusion, the Cases of Concealment and Evasion are two canonical passages in Confucianism, which provide evidence either for the theory's patriarchal oppression of individuality or for the theory's empowerment of individuals to live a truthful and authentic life. In this essay, I have explained a liberal esoteric reading of the cases. I contend that we should regard the two cases as pedagogical tools. As such, they open up a wide space of interpretation of the Confucian doctrines. With regard to the two moral dilemmas, individuals can make spiritual progress through an extended engagement with them. Confucianism would not merely serve regimes by reinforcing the established social and political order; it would provide the materials for individuals to enrich their wisdom and spirituality, and to achieve perfection.

Acknowledgments

This essay has profited from conversation and feedback from many others, especially Kwong Yiu-Fai, Wong Sun-Tik, Choi Wai-Kit, Li King-Wai, and the anonymous reviewers for *Metaphilosophy*. I want to express my special gratitude to Takao Asano, the librarian of Sapporo Municipal Library and Information Center (札幌市図書・情報館), who provided extra facilities for me to prepare this essay on the day of submission.

References

Ames, Roger T. 2011. *Confucian Role Ethics: A Vocabulary*. Hong Kong: Chinese University Press.

The Analects. 1979. Translated by Din-Cheuk Lau. New York: Penguin Books.

Angle, Stephen C. 2008. "No Supreme Principle: Confucianism's Harmonization of Multiple Values." *Dao: A Journal of Comparative Philosophy* 7, no. 1:35–40.

Angle, Stephen C., and Justin Tiwald. 2017. *Neo-Confucianism: A Philosophical Introduction*. Cambridge: Polity Press.

Aristotle. 1999. *Nicomachean Ethics*. Translated and annotated by Terence Irwin. Indianapolis: Hackett.

Berlyne, Daniel E. 1960. *Conflict, Arousal, and Curiosity*. New York: McGraw-Hill.

Brooks, E. Bruce, and A. Taoke Brooks. 1998. *The Original Analects: Saying of Confucius and Its Successors*. New York: Columbia University Press.

Chen, Qiaojian 陳喬見. 2011. "The Private and the Public: Self Rule and Rule by Law 私與公: 自治與法治." In *Collected Works of Confucians: The Criticism of Criticism of Confucian Ethics*《儒家倫理新批判》之批判, edited by Guo Qiyong, 447–92. Hubei: Wuhan Daxue Chubanshe.

"Daxue 大學 (The Great Learning)." 1994. In *Collected Commentaries on the Four Books* 四書章句集註, edited by Zhu Xi, 1–13. Taibei: Da'an Chubanshe.

Du, Fu 杜甫. 2016. *The Poetry of Du Fu*. Edited and translated by Stephen Owen. Berlin: Walter de Gruyter.

Fried, Charles. 1970. *An Anatomy of Values*. Cambridge, Mass.: Harvard University Press.

Guo, Qiyong 郭齊勇. 2011. "On Mutual Disclosure of Wrongdoings Among Family Members, Legal Allowance for Nondisclosure, and Their Implications on Legal Reform Today '親親相隱' '容隱制'及其對當今法治建設的啓廸" In *Collected Works of Confucians: The Criticism of Criticism of Confucian Ethics*《儒家倫理新批判》之批判, edited by Guo Qiyong, 1–23. Hubei: Wuhan Daxue Chubanshe.

Hadot, Pierre. 1995. *Philosophy as a Way of Life*. Edited by Arnold Davidson, translated by Michael Chase. Oxford: Blackwell.

________. 2004. *What Is Ancient Philosophy?* Translated by Michael Chase. Cambridge, Mass.: Harvard University Press.

Hanegraaff, Wouter. J. 2013. *Western Esotericism: A Guide for the Perplexed*. London: Bloomsbury.

Huang, Jinhong 黃錦鋐. 1900. *Xinyi Zhuangzi Duben* 新譯莊子讀本. Taiwan: Sanmin.

Huang, Kan 皇侃. 1937. *Lunyu Jijie Yishu* 論語集解義疏. 4 vols. Shanghai: Shangwu Yinshuguan.

Huang, Yong. 2013. *Confucius: A Guide for the Perplexed*. London: Bloomsbury.

Jiao, Xun 焦循. 1987. *Mengzi Zhengyi* 孟子正義. Beijing: Zhonghua Shuju 中華書局.

Jullien, François. 2000. *Detour and Access: Strategies of Meaning in China and Greece*. Translated by Sophie Hawkes. New York: Zone Books.

Keightley, David. 1990. "Early Civilization in China: Reflections on How It Became Chinese." In *Heritage of China: Contemporary Perspectives on Chinese Civilization*, edited by Paul S. Ropp, 15–54. Berkeley: University of California Press.

________. 1993. "Clean Hands and Shining Helmets: Heroic Action in Early Chinese and Greek Culture." In *Religion and Authority*, edited by Tobin Seiber, 21–45. Ann Arbor: University of Michigan Press.

King, Ambrose Y. C. 1985. "The Individual and the Group in Confucianism: A Relational Perspective." In *Individualism and Holism: Studies in Confucian and Taoist Values*, edited by Donald Munro, 57–84. Ann Arbor: University of Michigan Press.

Kupperman, Joel J. 2002. "Naturalness Revisited: Why Western Philosophers Should Study Confucius." In *Confucius and the Analects: New Essays*, edited by Bryan W. Van Norden, 39–52. New York: Oxford University Press.

Legge, James, trans. 1885a. *Sacred Books of the East*. Vol. 27, part 3. Edited by Friedrich Max Müller. Boston: Adamant Media.

________. 1885b. *Sacred Books of the East*. Vol. 28, part 4. Edited by Friedrich Max Müller. Boston: Adamant Media.

Li, Chenyang. 2008. "Does Confucian Ethics Integrate Care Ethics and Justice Ethics? The Case of Mencius." *Asian Philosophy* 18, no. 1:69–82.

Liu, Qingping 劉清平. 2003. "Filiality Versus Sociality and Individuality: On Confucianism as 'Consanguinitism'." *Philosophy East and West* 53, no. 2:234–50.

________. 劉清平. 2004. "On the Confucian Consanguinism in Confucius and Mencius 論孔孟儒學的血親團體性特徵." In *A Collection of Essays in the Debate on Confucius Ethics* 儒家倫理爭鳴集, edited by Guo Qiyong, 853–87. Wuhan: Hubei Jiaoyu Chubanshe.

________. 劉清平. 2007. "Special Topic: Filial Piety: The Root of Morality or the Source of Corruption?" *Dao: A Journal of Comparative Philosophy* 6, no. 1:1–19.

________. 劉清平. 2009. "To Become a Filial Son, a Loyal Subject, or a Humane Person? On the Confucian Ideas About Humanity." *Asian Philosophy* 19, no. 2:173–88.

Lu, Deming 陸德明. 1983. *Jingdian Shiwen* 經典釋文. Beijing: Zhonghua Shuju.

McConnell, Terrance. 2018. "Moral Dilemmas." In *Stanford Encyclopedia of Philosophy*, edited by Edward N. Zalta (Fall 2018 Edition). Accessed December 24, 2019. https://plato.stanford.edu/archives/fall2018/entries/moral-dilemmas/.

Mencius. 1970. Translated by Din-Cheuk Lau. New York: Penguin Books.

Meng, Peiyuan 蒙培元. 2004. "Human Beings as Emotional Beings人是情感的存在." In *A Collection of Essays in the Debate on Confucius Ethics* 儒家倫理爭鳴集, edited by Guo Qiyong, 455–72. Wuhan: Hubei Jiaoyu Chubanshe.

Nagel, Thomas. 1979. *Mortal Questions*. Cambridge: Cambridge University Press.

Ni, Peimin. 2008. "Do Not Take Confucians as Kantians: Comments on Liu Qingping's Interpretation of Confucian Teachings." *Dao: A Journal of Comparative Philosophy* 7, no. 1:45–49.

________. 2016. *Confucius: The Man and the Way of Gongfu*. London: Rowman and Littlefield.

________. 2018. "Can Bad Guys Have Good *Gongfu*?—A Preliminary Exploration of Gongfu Ethics." *Journal of Chinese Philosophy* 43, nos. 1–2:9–31.

Nietzsche, Friedrich. 2007. *On the Genealogy of Morality*. Translated by Carol Diethe. Cambridge: Cambridge University Press.

Olberding, Amy. 2007. "The Educative Function of Personal Style in the 'Analects'." *Philosophy East and West* 57, no. 3:357–74.

________. 2012. *Moral Exemplars in the Analects: The Good Person Is That*. New York: Routledge.

Radice, Thomas. 2017. "Confucius and Filial Piety." In *A Concise Companion to Confucius*, edited by Paul R. Goldin, 185–207. Oxford: John Wiley and Sons.

Rosemont, Henry, Jr. 1991. "Rights-Bearing Individuals and Role-Bearing Persons." In *Rules Rituals, and Responsibility: Essays Dedicated to Herbert Fingarette*, edited by Mary Bockover, 71–102, La Salle, Ill.: Open Court.

Rosemont, Henry, Jr., and Roger Ames. 2008. "Family Reverence (*xiao* 孝) as the Source of Consummatory Conduct (*ren* 仁)." *Dao: A Journal of Comparative Philosophy* 7, no. 1:9–19.

________. trans. 2009. *The Chinese Classic of Family Reverence: A Philosophical Translation of the Xiaojing*. Honolulu: University of Hawaii Press.

Sarkissian, Hagop. Forthcoming. "Do Filial Values Corrupt? How Can We Know? Clarifying and Assessing the Recent Confucian Debate." *Dao: A Journal of Comparative Philosophy*.

Shen, Jiaben 沈家本. 1985. *Lidai Xingfa Kao* 歷代刑法考 (Investigations into the Punishments and Laws of the Historical Dynasties). 4 vols. Beijing: Zhonghua Shuju.

Shun, Kwong-loi. 1993. "*Jen* and *Li* in the 'Analects'." *Philosophy East and West* 43, no. 3:457–79.

Sinnott-Armstrong, Walter. 1988. *Moral Dilemmas*. Oxford: Basil Blackwell.

Slingerland, Edward, trans. 2003. *Confucius Analects: With Selections from Traditional Commentaries*. Indianapolis: Hackett.

________. 2014. *Trying Not to Try: Ancient China, Modern Science, and the Power of Spontaneity*. New York: Broadway Books.

Smart, John J. C., and Bernard Williams. 1973. *Utilitarianism: For and Against*. Cambridge: Cambridge University Press.

Smith, Steven B. 2006. *Reading Leo Strauss: Politics, Philosophy, Judaism*. Chicago: University of Chicago Press.

_______. 2009. *The Cambridge Companion to Leo Strauss*. Cambridge: Cambridge University Press.

Strauss, Leo. 1988. *Persecution and the Art of Writing*. Chicago: University of Chicago Press.

_______. 2013. *On Tyranny*. Edited by Victor Gourevitch and Michael S. Roth. Chicago: University of Chicago Press.

Strauss, Leo, and Kenneth Green. 1986. "Exoteric Teaching." *Interpretation* 14, no. 1:51–59.

Van Norden, Bryan W. 2008. "On 'Humane Love' and 'Kinship Love'." *Dao: A Journal of Comparative Philosophy* 7, no. 2:125–29.

Varela, Fracisco J. 1999. *Ethical Know-how: Action, Wisdom, and Cognition*. Stanford: Stanford University Press.

Wei, Zhengtong 韋政通. 2003. *Zhongguo Wenhua Gailun* 中國文化概論. Hunan: Yuelu Shushe 嶽麓書社.

Wang, Huaiyu. 2011. "Piety and Individuality Through a Convoluted Path of Rightness: Exploring the Confucian Art of Moral Discretion via Analects 13.18." *Asian Philosophy* 21, no. 4:395–418.

Williams, Bernard. 1981. *Moral Luck: Philosophical Papers, 1973–1980*. Cambridge: Cambridge University Press.

Wu, Yu Bi. 2013. *The Journal of Wu Yubi: The Path to Sagehood*. Translated by Kelleher M. Theresa. Indianapolis: Hackett.

Xiong, Lihui 熊禮匯. 2008. *Xinyi Huainanzi* 新譯淮南子. 2 vols. Taipei: Sanmin.

Yuen, Mei 袁枚. 1960. *Suiyuan Shihua* 隨園詩話. Beijing: Renmin Wenxue Chubanshe 人民文學出版社.

"*Zhongyong* 中庸 (The Doctrine of the Mean)." 1963. In *A Source Book in Chinese Philosophy*, translated and compiled by Wing-Tsit Chan, 97–114. Princeton: Princeton University Press.

Zhu, Xi 朱熹. 2002a. "Sanchao Mingchen Yanhanglu 三朝名臣言行錄." In *Zhuzi Quanshu* 朱子全書, vol. 12, edited by S. Wang 黃書元 and S. Xia 夏秀流, 331–872. Shanghai: Shanghai Guji Chubanshe 上海古籍出版社 and Anhui Jiaoyu Chubanshe 安徽教育出版社.

_______. 2002b. "Tongmeng Xuzhi 童蒙須知." In *Zhuzi Quanshu* 朱子全書, vol. 13, edited by C. Wang 王純 and M. Zheng 鄭明寶, 371–77. Shanghai: Shanghai Guji Chubanshe and Anhui Jiaoyu Chubanshe.

_______. 2002c. "*Mengzi Jizhu* 孟子集注." In *Zhuzi Quanshu* 朱子全書, vol. 6, edited by S. Wang 黃書元 and S. Xia 夏秀流, 242–460. Shanghai: Shanghai Guji Chubanshe and Anhui Jiaoyu Chubanshe.

CHAPTER 4

RENAISSANCE HUMANISM AND PHILOSOPHY AS A WAY OF LIFE

JOHN SELLARS

Historiography of Humanism

In the mid-nineteenth century Ernst Renan proclaimed that what we think of as the Renaissance was fundamentally a literary movement, not a philosophical one.[1] In one form or another this view has proved to be surprisingly persistent. Renan's aim was to defend the Averroist philosophers of the period associated with the University of Padua from the attacks of Petrarch, by dismissing Petrarch as not really a philosopher at all and so in no place to judge the philosophical standing of others. In the process a well-worn division was set up between two cultures, one philosophical and scientific, the other poetic and literary.[2] If there was any serious philosophy going on during the Renaissance, it was, according to Renan, taking place in universities like Padua and was very much a continuation of the medieval Aristotelian tradition.

This attitude was more or less repeated in the twentieth century by Paul Oskar Kristeller, albeit with a few modifications. He also denied any philosophical status to the humanists. He too acknowledged the philosophical seriousness of the ongoing Aristotelian tradition in the universities but was also keen to defend the Platonist philosophy of Marsilio Ficino, on

[1] See Renan 1852, 255. Renan's view was influential for two of the most important figures to write about humanism in the twentieth century, Eugenio Garin and Paul Oskar Kristeller. For the former see Garin 1965, 1–3. Kristeller's relationship with Renan and the contrast between humanism and the universities are discussed in Grendler 2006, 107–11.

[2] See Garin 1965, 1, and also Cassirer, Kristeller, and Randall 1948, 11, where "spiritual Florence" is contrasted with "naturalistic Venice."

Philosophy as a Way of Life: Historical, Contemporary, and Pedagogical Perspectives.
Edited by James M. Ambury, Tushar Irani, and Kathleen Wallace.

Published 2021 by John Wiley & Sons Ltd.

whom he wrote a dissertation.[3] Kristeller presented Ficino as a systematic metaphysician, but the humanists, in his view, were simply the successors of a medieval tradition of rhetoric teaching, combined with a passion for classical learning.[4] Their works had, in his words, "nothing to do with philosophy even in the vaguest possible sense of the term" (Kristeller 1944–45, 354).[5] Thus, Kristeller continued, the humanists were "on the whole neither good nor bad philosophers, but no philosophers at all" (354). He did concede that they had some interests in moral philosophy, but only in an amateurish way. This was in part an attack on the view of his contemporary Eugenio Garin, who saw humanism as a thoroughly philosophical movement that shaped all thought of the period, including the Aristotelian tradition.[6] But for Kristeller the humanists are quite rightly left out of the history of philosophy because what they were primarily engaged in was a literary cultural and educational programme (see, e.g., 1979, 22–23).

A further version of this view has been repeated more recently by a number of historians of philosophy working primarily on medieval philosophy who are keen to stress continuity through the history of philosophy. John Marenbon, for instance, has proposed the idea of a long Middle Ages, drawing on the work of historians such as Jacques Le Goff, in which he stresses the way in which medieval traditions of philosophy continued in the universities right through the Renaissance and into the early modern period.[7] We can see a similar approach in Robert Pasnau's book on metaphysics from the thirteenth to the seventeenth centuries.[8] What this approach tends to do is to stress the continuity of the medieval tradition into and through the Renaissance period, emphasizing the ongoing Aristotelian tradition in the universities but having little to say about humanists active outside those institutions. Pasnau refers to such people as "the so-called Renaissance philosophers," although he is prepared to concede that "it is perhaps too much to say that there is *no* philosophy in authors like Giovanni Pico della Mirandola and Marsilio Ficino."[9] In sum,

[3] Kristeller's dissertation was written in German in 1937 but first published in English, in Kristeller 1943. For discussion of the context in which it was written, including Kristeller's relationship with Heidegger, see Blum 2006.

[4] See Kristeller's introduction in Cassirer, Kristeller, and Randall 1948, 2–3. Note also Kristeller 1944–45, 354–55.

[5] Kristeller 1944–45, 354, with discussion in Pine 2006, 213–16, Witt 2006, 257–59, and more recently Kraye 2016. Later, in Kristeller 1964, 4–5, Kristeller gave a more nuanced assessment, acknowledging that some of the humanists made at least some contribution to philosophy. On the origins on Kristeller's account see Monfasani 2000.

[6] See Garin 1965, 5–7. On the debate between Kristeller and Garin see Celenza 2004, 16–57.

[7] On Le Goff and the idea of a long Middle Ages, see Monfasani 2006, 168–69.

[8] See Marenbon 2013 and Pasnau 2011. For deprecations of the Renaissance by historians of medieval philosophy, note also Étienne Gilson's statement that the Renaissance was not the Middle Ages plus man but the Middle Ages without god, on which see Monfasani 2006, 168.

[9] Pasnau 2011, 419 and 93, respectively. Thus he is grudgingly prepared to acknowledge figures that Kristeller counted as Platonist philosophers but, like him, has no time for any of the humanists.

many historians of philosophy remain sceptical about the philosophical value of what went on in the Renaissance, in particular sceptical about the value of anything we might think of as distinctively "Renaissance," such as the activities of the humanists.[10] Indeed, the push to stress continuity over rigid periodization has inclined some to propose abandoning the category of Renaissance philosophy altogether, arguing that nothing really new or distinctive happened that was not merely a repetition of existing trends in the Middle Ages.[11]

This well-established narrative has been challenged in recent years by a handful of scholars, most notably Christopher Celenza. He has noted that, all too often, standard narratives of the history of philosophy tend to have a Renaissance-sized gap in them in between Ockham and Descartes.[12] He traces this back to the shift in the historiography of philosophy in the eighteenth century, usually associated with Jacob Brucker, that saw a move away from thinking about the history of philosophy in terms of a series of schools and towards a focus on abstract systems of thought.[13] Under the older model, exemplified by Diogenes Laertius and copied right up to the seventeenth century, the history of philosophy was written as a series of lives in which biography and doctrine were recorded side by side. The move away from this model in the late eighteenth century had the effect of marginalizing earlier philosophers whose work didn't neatly fit into the new systematic approach to philosophy. So, Celenza turns to the work of Pierre Hadot for an alternative model with which to reassess previously marginalized figures in the history of philosophy, and he primarily has the Renaissance humanists in mind. Only Hadot's model of philosophy as a way of life, he suggests, can enable us to make philosophical sense of the humanist culture of the long fifteenth century that, he says, "has been written out of the history of philosophy."[14] Although Celenza doesn't mention

[10] See further Nauta 2009, 296 n. 12, with further references, noting that historians of medieval philosophy have often dismissed either humanists or the Renaissance as a whole as superficial and unoriginal.

[11] This is nothing new: Kristeller 1944–45, 347, noted that "certain medievalists have questioned the very existence of the Renaissance and would like to banish the term entirely from the vocabulary of historians."

[12] See Celenza 2013. At 371 Celenza writes, "There is a long caesura in most histories of philosophy between the era of Ockham and that of Descartes." Compare this with Schmitt's working definition of Renaissance philosophy as the period between Ockham and Bacon (Schmitt, Skinner, and Kessler 1988, 5).

[13] See Celenza 2013, 367–69, building on the work of Catana 2008. According to Celenza (372), this shift was first noted by Garin. On this topic see the important historiographical work in Santinello and Blackwell 1993 and, more recently, the studies of Renaissance and early modern philosophical biographies in Baker 2017.

[14] Celenza 2013, 383, drawing on Hadot 1995. See also Celenza 2014, which appeals again to Hadot and challenges the criticisms in Cooper 2012 against Hadot's approach. In a similar spirit, this time taking inspiration from Michel Foucault, see also Zak 2010 and 2014. Foucault was of course himself taking inspiration from Hadot. Ceron 2015 draws on both Hadot and Foucault for similar ends.

it, it is also worth noting the earlier work of Juliusz Domanski, who wrote an account of medieval and Renaissance thought through the lens of Hadot's model.[15]

There has been some pushback against Celenza's proposal. Lodi Nauta has challenged the claim that *all* philosophers during the Renaissance understood philosophy in this way, wanting instead in part to defend what he calls "an argument-centered approach" (2009, 297–98 n. 23). Nauta reads Celenza's position as involving a crude division between premodern philosophers who all saw philosophy as a way of life and modern systematic philosophy arising in the eighteenth century. But as Nauta notes, there is plenty of theoretically oriented metaphysics and epistemology in premodern philosophy and conversely modern proponents of philosophy as a way of life (297–98 n. 23). That seems right: whether it be antiquity, the Renaissance, or more recent times, it would be a mistake to look for metaphilosophical homogeneity in any period.[16] This particularly applies in the case of the Renaissance, and in what follows we shall see examples of metaphilosophical arguments that themselves illustrate the existence of what we might call metaphilosophical pluralism. Not everyone agreed about what they thought philosophy was.

More recently, David Lines has argued that while a few figures in the Renaissance might have thought of philosophy as "a style of life," the majority saw philosophy as a predominantly theoretical enterprise, "an activity of the mind" (2018, 283). Lines's aim is to argue against Kristeller's sharp division between proper philosophers and literary humanists, defending the philosophical standing of at least some humanists by showing that they were playing the same game as everyone else. They too had interests in logic and natural philosophy, Lines argues (295). He does concede, however, that "it is indeed possible to say that some humanists, following Petrarch, saw philosophy . . . as being practical and not necessarily systematic. But [he continues] this was not the default or general position" (295). So, like Nauta, Lines challenges the blanket claim made by Celenza, acknowledging that there may have been a degree of metaphilosophical pluralism in the Renaissance, noting that "definitions of philosophy in the period were eclectic in their sources" (296).

Naturally whether one thinks that thinkers such as the humanists were proper philosophers or not primarily depends on what one thinks philosophy is. Kristeller came out of a broadly Kantian way of thinking about philosophy, although it is worth noting that he also attended lectures by Husserl and Heidegger (see Blum 2006, 21 and 30). His emphasis on

[15] See Domanski 1996, esp. 102–14, later drawn on by Hadot himself in Hadot 2002, 262–63.

[16] Nauta's criticism of Celenza parallels one of Cooper's criticisms of Hadot, namely, that it would be a mistake to make global claims about how philosophy was conceived in any particular period. See further Cooper 2012, 24–26, and, earlier, Sellars 2003, 33–36, and Zeyl 2003.

systematic, theoretical philosophy prioritized Aristotelianism and Platonism, both conceived in not uncontroversial ways. More recent historians of philosophy trained within the analytic tradition also inevitably bring with them their own presuppositions about what philosophy is, as of course does everyone else. My claim is that many of the negative assessments of the philosophical standing of humanists from the Renaissance are the product of assumptions about what philosophy is, sometimes held explicitly but often remaining implicit. There are a number of loosely related points I should like to make. First, following Celenza, we ought to pay attention to how individual thinkers conceived philosophy, in order to understand them on their own terms (see Celenza 2013, 376). Second, we also need to acknowledge that in every period there have been debates about what philosophy is, and it is not obvious that in any period everyone straightforwardly agreed on this. That's not what philosophers do. So, following Nauta and Lines, it would be a mistake to claim metaphilosophical homogeneity in any period, including the Renaissance. Third, we also need to pay attention to the sources drawn on by thinkers. In the case of Ficino, for example, understanding his idea of philosophy will require paying some attention to the conception of philosophy in Plotinus and the later Neoplatonists, which is itself a contested issue.[17] In the case of Petrarch, for instance, we need to pay attention to the ancient philosophers that he was reading, not least Cicero and Seneca. If we can accept that some humanists, based on their close study of philosophers such as Cicero and Seneca, embraced an ancient conception of philosophy understood as way of life, then it becomes possible to reassess a number of things they were doing that in the past were dismissed as mere literary activities, such as writing letters of consolation or producing biographies of philosophers. Suddenly, a much larger proportion of their work starts to look like philosophy, when approached through this lens.

In what follows I want to look at three cases where we see thinkers in the Renaissance engaged in metaphilosophical reflection, often in dialogue with ancient material that expresses views about the nature of philosophy. I want to show that some of these thinkers *did* see themselves as philosophers, and their sense of what it meant to be a philosopher was shaped by ancient models of philosophy as a way of life. I do not want to argue that

[17] Compare, for instance, the more existential interpretation in Hadot 1993 (first published in 1963) with the more analytic one in Emilsson 2017. See in particular the review of the latter by Luc Brisson (2018), where he writes: "This book is impeccable from a material, pedagogical, and academic viewpoint. However, it describes a Plotinus with the features of a contemporary philosophy professor living and working in a high-level university. He is an intellectual, interested essentially in epistemology and ethics, in their anthropological, cognitive, and logical dimensions. This book provides an image of Plotinus that corresponds to the standard modern interpretation, in line with neo-Kantianism . . . . Such an approach is not questionable in itself, but it is reductionist. It must be repeated: for Plotinus, philosophy is a way of life."

everyone in the Renaissance was really practising philosophy as a way of life, but I do hope to show that some did conceive of what they were doing in this way, and these are figures often overlooked or ignored by too many narratives of the history of philosophy. The idea of philosophy as a way of life, then, enables us to reassess positively the philosophical standing of a number of the figures from this period.

Petrarch

The first Renaissance text to consider is Petrarch's work *On His Own Ignorance*, dating from 1367.[18] This might be described as a polemic against contemporary Aristotelian philosophy, although not necessarily against Aristotle himself, as Petrarch is keen to stress that Aristotle's modern followers do not do their hero justice.[19] In particular it is a defence against charges brought by contemporary Aristotelians that Petrarch himself possessed no great learning, which is to say that he was not sufficiently knowledgeable about Scholastic philosophy. Accordingly, he was not a proper philosopher and so not qualified to contribute to philosophical debates. Echoing Plato's *Apology of Socrates*, the response by Petrarch is to admit freely his own ignorance but also to draw attention to the ignorance of his accusers.[20] While his Scholastically minded opponents ridicule Petrarch both for his limited knowledge of and lack of interest in Aristotle, Petrarch responds by decrying their unthinking commitment to the words of the Stagirite. This is something Petrarch finds faintly ridiculous, writing: "I certainly believe that Aristotle was a great man who knew much, but he was human and could well be ignorant of some things, even of a great many things."[21] Implicit here is the charge that these self-proclaimed philosophers take their uncritical admiration to such extremes that they effectively give up independent thought altogether. Consequently it is *they* who do not deserve the title of philosopher.[22]

[18] The full title is *De sui ipsius et multorum ignorantia* (hereafter shortened to *De ignorantia*). I have used the critical edition (by Hankins) in Marsh 2003, which also contains a facing translation. Note also the earlier translation in Cassirer, Kristeller, and Randall 1948, 47–133. There is a helpful discussion of the background to the text by Kennedy 2009; note also Rummel 1995, 30–35. This was one of the texts that exercised Renan (1852, 265–68).

[19] See *De ignorantia* 11 (Marsh 2003, 233): "They deviate and depart so far from their master."

[20] See *De ignorantia* 48 (Marsh 2003, 265). The discussion is clearly based on personal exchanges, and Petrarch describes himself participating in philosophical discussions with his detractors. His critics were four men from Venice, on whom see Kennedy 2009, 264–65. On the wider context see Kristeller 1952.

[21] *De ignorantia* 49 (Marsh 2003, 265): *Ego uero magnum quendam uirum ac multiscium Aristotilem, sed fuisse hominem, et idcirco aliqua, imo et multa nescire potuisse arbitror.*

[22] Whether this is a fair account of the Scholastic philosophers of his day is another matter; it may well accurately reflect some of his own encounters even if it can hardly stand as a fair generalization of late medieval philosophy as a whole.

One of the most striking features of Petrarch's polemic is its attack on Aristotle's *Nicomachean Ethics*. Despite making a point of distinguishing between contemporary followers of Aristotle and the man himself, Petrarch still has little positive to say about Aristotle's most famous ethical work. He claims that Aristotle knew nothing of true happiness. In part this is simply due to the fact that Aristotle was a pagan and so ignores what Petrarch the Christian takes to be necessary conditions for true happiness, namely, faith and belief in an immortal soul.[23] Petrarch of course acknowledges that Aristotle was writing before the true light of Christianity had come to shine, but even so the flaw remains. Petrarch goes on to characterize himself as first and foremost a Christian rather than a philosopher, although at the same time he denies the label of philosopher to his opponents as well.[24] He goes on to praise his principal intellectual hero, Cicero, and discusses passages from Cicero's philosophical books in some detail. This need not concern us here, and indeed Petrarch himself acknowledges it as a detour from his main topic, which he goes on to characterize as the question whether one ought to follow Aristotle. His answer is a resounding no.[25] There are, he suggests, two types of philosopher: those who are philosophers only in name, who tell many lies, and those who are true philosophers and speak only the truth. Both Plato and Aristotle fall into the former group.[26] Presumably only a Christian philosopher, Augustine perhaps, can count as a true philosopher for Petrarch. Cicero is saved thanks to his cautious scepticism.

Petrarch's real argument against the *Nicomachean Ethics*, however, is that it fails to deliver on what it promises, namely, teaching one how to become good.[27] Reading Aristotle might make one more learned but it will not make one better, he says.[28] The *Nicomachean Ethics* lays out what virtue is, indicates how to define it, and teaches one much in the realm of ethical theory, but it lacks the necessary punch to set its readers on the path to virtue. For that readers would do better turning to Cicero or Seneca, or even to a poet like Horace, whose maxims are far more memorable than anything Aristotle wrote.[29] Petrarch goes on to cite Socrates as the inspiration behind this Latin tradition of philosophical moralizing that he champions, and he

[23] See *De ignorantia* 49–50 (Marsh 2003, 265–67). It is worth noting that Petrarch was arguing against Averroist interpreters of Aristotle who would have denied that Aristotle was committed to a belief in an individual immortal soul.

[24] See *De ignorantia* 52 (Marsh 2003, 269).

[25] See *De ignorantia* 101 (Marsh 2003, 311).

[26] See *De ignorantia* 103 (Marsh 2003, 311). Later Petrarch offers a more positive assessment of Plato; see ibid. 114 (Marsh 2003, 321–23).

[27] See *De ignorantia* 107 (Marsh 2003, 315).

[28] Ibid.

[29] This issue of memorability is closely related to the assimilation and digestion of philosophical ideas outlined by Seneca (e.g., *Ep.* 2.2–4) and discussed by Petrarch in his *Secretum*. On this see Zak 2014. On the role of assimilation in philosophy as a way of life see Sellars 2003, 121–22.

thinks Aristotle openly hostile to this ultimately Socratic approach to philosophy. This impression was due to a misreading of a passage in Aristotle, thanks to Petrarch's reliance on one of the older Latin translations of the *Metaphysics* (which renders Aristotle's remark that Socrates was "busy with ethics" but uninterested in the study of nature as saying that Socrates was a "peddler of morality").[30] Even so, the misreading is instructive for us, for it shows that Petrarch's natural assumption was to see Aristotle and Socrates opposed to one another on the issue of the purpose of philosophy. What Petrarch proposes, in place of what he takes to be Aristotle's theoretical approach to philosophy, is a more practical approach focused on self-transformation. He writes, "The true moral philosophers and valuable teachers of virtues are those whose first and last purpose is to make their students and readers good."[31] These true moral philosophers are primarily Latin authors inspired by the Hellenistic philosophical schools, with Socrates standing in the background as the ultimate source of inspiration. The goal of philosophy, for Petrarch, is not to know virtue but to acquire it.[32] His own knowledge of Socrates was thin to say the least, and Petrarch never had an opportunity to read the *Apology*, but even so there is what we might call a discernible Socratic spirit in his work.[33]

Petrarch's text is complex and may be seen to be doing a number of different things at once. For present purposes the key point to note is that Aristotle's *Nicomachean Ethics* is rejected because, despite its opening promise, it is seen as a work primarily concerned with ethical knowledge rather than practical self-transformation. This makes it clear that the contrast at work here is not one between moral philosophy and the rest but rather one between two conceptions of what philosophy as such is for. It is also worth noting that, despite his polemics against his Scholastic contemporaries, for Petrarch philosophy remains in a sense a handmaiden to theology. To be more precise we should say that the philosophical life is an aid to and preparation for the religious life. Even so, the metaphilosophical claim is fairly clear: philosophy is an activity devoted to living well, and

[30] See *De ignorantia* 108 (Marsh 2003, 317), referring to *Metaph.* 1.6, 987b1–2. Petrarch quotes from one of the older translations of the *Metaphysics* (either by James of Venice (*AL* 25, 1–1a, 21), the "translatio media" (*AL* 25, 2, 21), or by William of Moerbeke (*AL* 25, 3.2, 28), which at 987b1–2 have Aristotle call Socrates a "peddler of morality" (*circa moralia negotiantem*). This is the famous passage where Aristotle reports that Socrates was busy (πραγματεύομαι) with ethics but uninterested in the study of nature. While those three Latin versions all have *negotiante*, the "translatio vetus" (*AL* 25, 1–1a, 104, an anonymous revision of James's version) and Cardinal Bessarion's much later version (Bekker 1831–70, vol. 3, 484) have (the more accurate) *tractante* and *tractaret*, respectively. For the relevant *AL* texts see Vuillemin-Diem 1970, 1976, 1995.

[31] *De ignorantia* 110 (Marsh 2003, 317): *Hi sunt ergo ueri philosophi morales et uirtutum utiles magistri, quorum prima et ultima intentio est bonum facere auditorem ac lectorem.*

[32] *De ignorantia* 111 (Marsh 2003, 319).

[33] On Petrarch's limited knowledge of Socrates see Trinkaus 1979, 7–11. His "Socraticism" probably came primarily via Cicero, whose references to Socrates are examined in Glucker 1997.

this conception of philosophy is a Socratic one that is presented as an alternative to the theoretically oriented Aristotelian tradition of his day.[34]

Leonardo Bruni

A number of the metaphilosophical themes that Petrarch introduces are taken up and developed by Leonardo Bruni in the next century. Like Petrarch, Bruni thinks that the study of ancient authors is ultimately motivated by a desire for guidance on how to live. He also shares with Petrarch the view that it is possible to extract such guidance from a wide range of ancient authors. In his *On the Study of Literature*, written in 1424, Bruni gives top priority to religious literature and, like Petrarch, singles out Augustine for special mention.[35] After that comes moral philosophy, described as the art of living well (*bene vivendum*). Bruni refers to the doctrines of Epicurus, Zeno, and also Aristotle, presenting all of them as offering valuable guidance for life.[36] Just as Petrarch had suggested that further moral guidance might be found in the work of poets such as Horace, Bruni too goes on to suggest that ancient historians, orators, and poets all offer useful moral lessons.[37]

For present purposes two points are worth noting. The first is that Bruni sees a certain type of moral philosophy as something that offers us guidance on how to live and, moreover, as something we read (along with some other types of literature) for the sake of that guidance rather than anything else. As he puts it elsewhere, all these humanities disciplines are "related to life and behaviour" (*pertinent ad vitam et mores*) and "try to produce good men" (*faciendum virum bonum*).[38] Bruni makes these points as part of an attempt to define what he famously calls *studia humanitatis* rather than to define philosophy alone, but it is clear that he sees a certain type of philosophy as part of this wider educational project.

This idea that philosophy might contribute to a project of trying to live well echoes the description of Socrates' mission in the *Apology*. This was a text that (unlike Petrarch) Bruni knew well, having translated it into LaThompsontin himself.[39] We find further echoes of Socrates in Bruni's

[34] On Petrarch's conception of philosophy as "care of the soul" see further Zak 2010, 79–120.

[35] The full title is *De studiis et litteris liber ad Baptistam de Malatestis*. Text in Baron 1928, 5–19, Viti 1996, 248–78, and Kallendorf 2002, 92–124. Translations in Griffiths, Hankins, and Thompson 1987, 240–51, and Kallendorf 2002, 93–125. In what follows I rely on the text in Kallendorf. The reference to Augustine is in sec. 15 (Kallendorf 2002, 107).

[36] *De studiis et litteris* 16 (Kallendorf 2002, 107).

[37] *De studiis et litteris* 18–21 (Kallendorf 2002, 109–13).

[38] See the *Letter to Niccolo Strozzi* (*Epistulae* 6.6), text in Mehus 1741, vol. 2, 48–51, translated in Griffiths, Hankins, and Thompson 1987, 251–53.

[39] See Griffiths, Hankins, and 1987, 261. Bruni's translation of the Apology was probably completed in 1424 and printed just once, in 1475 (see STC ip00775000), soon to be eclipsed by the publication of Ficino's translations of all of Plato (first printed in 1484). See further Hankins 1990, vol. 2, 383, 739.

own *Introduction to Moral Philosophy*.[40] In the opening line of this work Bruni stresses that his central concern is not with mere living but rather with living well (*bene vivendi*), echoing one of Socrates' most famous sayings in the *Crito*, a text that Bruni translated into Latin twice.[41] Dismissing natural philosophy as the mere accumulation of knowledge with no practical use, Bruni champions moral philosophy, which he says involves paying attention to ourselves and to what is properly our own, again echoing Socrates' concern in the *Apology* with taking care of oneself.[42] The distinction here is plain: it is one between philosophy conceived as knowledge of Nature versus philosophy conceived as an art of living. Bruni's conception of philosophy is thus strikingly Socratic. This ought not to come as a great surprise given that Bruni translated both the *Apology* and the *Crito*, and so had intimate knowledge of Plato's account of Socrates.

The second point worth noting is that, unlike Petrarch, in *On the Study of Literature* Bruni includes Aristotle alongside the Epicureans and Stoics as an ancient philosopher who offers guidance on how to live. He also turns to Aristotle in his *Introduction to Moral Philosophy*, discussing Aristotle's account of the highest good alongside the accounts of the Hellenistic schools, all of whom are seen to be contributing to the ultimately Socratic project of learning how to live well. Indeed, Bruni's account of moral philosophy is structured by the argument in book 1 of the *Nicomachean Ethics*: thus the first topic to discuss is whether there is a highest good to which all human actions point.[43] Aristotle's discussion of intrinsic and instrumental goods that seemed to leave Petrarch so cold is an essential part of Bruni's Socratic project. He follows this with an account of the Stoic conception of the highest good, virtue, and seeks to minimize the distance between the Peripatetic and Stoic positions in a manner reminiscent of Antiochus as recounted by Cicero in book 5 of *De finibus*.

[40] *Isagogicon moralis disciplinae*: text in Baron 1928, 20–41, and Viti 1996, 200–240; translation in Griffiths, Hankins, and Thompson 1987, 267–82.

[41] See *Isagogicon* (Baron 1928, 20; Griffiths, Hankins, and Thompson 1987, 267): *Si ut vivendi . . . sic etiam bene vivendi cura nobis esset, infinitos paene labores, quibus stultitia aestuat humana, tamquam superfluos et insanos fugiendos longe omittendosque putaremus*. Compare with *Crito* 48b: ὅτι οὐ τὸ ζῆν περὶπλείστου ποιητέον ἀλλὰ τὸ εὖ ζῆν ("the really important thing is not to live but to live well"). In Bruni's first translation of the *Crito* into Latin this passage reads: *erat enim quod vivere non plurimi faciendum sit sed bene vivere* (Berti 1983, 173); in the second: *quod vivere ipsum non multi faciendum est sed bene vivere* (ibid., 214).

[42] See *Isagogicon* (Baron 1928, 21; Griffiths, Hankins, and Thompson 1987, 268): *At vero haec altera philosophia tota (ut ita dixerim) de re nostra est. Itaque qui huius cognitione omissa physicae iutendunt, ii alienum quodammodo negotium agere videntur, suum omittere*. Compare with *Apology* 29d–e, 30a–b: "Are you not ashamed that you give your attention to acquiring as much money as possible, and similarly with reputation and honour, and give no attention or thought to truth and understanding and the perfection of your soul?" and "For I spend all my time going about trying to persuade you, young and old, to make your first and chief concern not for your bodies or for your possessions, but for the highest welfare of your souls."

[43] Compare *Isagogicon* (Griffiths, Hankins, and Thompson 1987, 269) with *Eth. Nic.* 1.1.

It is clear that Bruni shares Petrarch's broadly Socratic conception of philosophy as an activity devoted to living well. Bruni also downplays the value of pursuing theoretical knowledge that has no direct impact on one's ability to attain happiness. Where they differ is that Bruni sees Aristotle's ethical works as offering a contribution to this broadly Socratic project. This no doubt reflects his detailed knowledge of the *Nicomachean Ethics*, which, like the *Apology* and the *Crito*, Bruni also translated into Latin, combined with his lack of familiarity with the *Metaphysics* (see Griffiths, Hankins, and Thompson 1987, 267), where Aristotle places theoretical knowledge centre stage.[44] Indeed, in his own biography of Aristotle, written to counteract what he thought was the negative image presented in the biography in Diogenes Laertius, which was in the process of being translated into Latin by Ambrogio Traversari, Bruni presented Aristotle as a master of rhetoric and eloquence, focusing on his works in ethics, politics, rhetoric, and poetics, while barely mentioning the theoretical works that were central to the Scholastic reception of Aristotle.[45] Bruni's Aristotle was a humanist.

Giovanni Pico della Mirandola

While Petrarch was openly scathing about the Scholastic approach to philosophy, in the text we have just considered Bruni was more or less silent. For a more positive engagement with the Scholastic tradition we must turn to another humanist, working a little later: Giovanni Pico della Mirandola.

In 1485 Pico wrote a letter to the humanist Ermolao Barbaro in which he defended the Scholastic approach to philosophy.[46] The defence is written as an example of how Scholastic philosophers might defend themselves from the criticisms of humanistic rhetoricians rather than as an explicit statement of Pico's own views. Indeed, at the very end of the letter Pico distances himself from the views he has just offered, although it is unclear whether this is merely for the benefit of the recipient (see Garin 1952, 822; Fallico and Shapiro 1967, 117). But regardless of Pico's own view, the letter makes some interesting points.

The principal aim of the letter is to defend Scholastic philosophers against the charge that they write barbarous, clumsy Latin. Pico responds by insisting that the task of philosophy is to try to uncover the nature of

[44] Bruni's translation of *Eth. Nic.* was first published in Strasbourg sometime before 1469 (see ISTC ia00983000). The preface is translated in Griffiths, Hankins, and Thompson 1987, 213–17. For further information, see Lines 2002, 483–84.

[45] Bruni's *Vita Aristotelis* is printed in Baron 1928, 41–49 (not in full), in Düring 1957, 168–78, and Viti 1996, 501–29 (with Italian translation). It is translated into English, with a useful introduction, in Griffiths, Hankins, and Thompson 1987, 283–92. For studies see Fryde 1988, Ianziti 2002, and (a revised version of the last) Ianziti 2012, 147–66.

[46] Text in Garin 1952, 804–22; translation in Fallico and Shapiro 1967, 105–17. For further discussion see Breen 1952; Kraye 2008; Lines 2018, 286–89; note also, more briefly, Rummel 1995, 45–46; Kraye 1996, 145–46.

things and that its search for truth requires a subtle and cautious use of language that is not always attractive. Echoing the well-worn Platonic distinction between the philosopher and the sophist, Pico contrasts the Scholastic philosopher's commitment to the truth with the rhetorician's ease with lies and deceit (Garin 1952, 808; Fallico and Shapiro 1967, 107). The true philosopher is uninterested in show and adornment: "Nothing is more foreign to philosophy than that which smacks of ostentatiousness or vulgar display."[47] What is striking here, though, is that Pico does not restrict this to the philosopher's use of language; it applies also to the philosopher's life: "The tastes of the man-of-the-world, whether in food or in discourse, differ from those of the philosopher who indulges in such things only as necessity demands. If the former neglected such things, he would soon lose his status, while if the latter sought such things, he would no longer be a philosopher."[48] Anyone, Pico continues, can impress people with fine words, but that is not the principal goal of the philosopher, who would happily express himself through actions alone if possible. Citing the Roman Stoic Musonius Rufus, Pico suggests that anyone talking only to impress others is no philosopher at all.[49] Instead, three things identify the true philosopher: his way of life, the truth of what he says, and the seriousness with which he speaks.[50] It is striking that the first in this list is the philosopher's way of life.[51]

It is not clear to what extent Pico himself shared the view that he articulates. His argument seems to be primarily against eloquence unguided by wisdom, which he says is like "a sword in the hands of a madman" (*gladius in furentis manu*) (Garin 1952, 820; Fallico and Shapiro 1967, 116), rather than an argument against eloquence as such, and the letter concludes by praising its recipient Barbaro as an eloquent philosopher. What is most interesting in the present context, however, is not the debate about the relative merits of philosophy and rhetoric but rather the conception of philosophy that Pico develops along the way. It is clear that Pico sees the philosopher as someone devoted to uncovering the truth about the nature of things, and in this he follows the definition of philosophy that goes back

[47] Garin 1952, 810; Fallico and Shapiro 1967, 109: *Nihil esse diversum magis ab institutio philosophi quacumque in re, quam quod luxum aut fastum aliqua ex parte sapit.*

[48] Ibid.: *Omnino non eadem ratio civilis habitus et philosophici, sicut neque mensae neque sermonis; utitur his philosophus dumtaxat ad necessitatem, utitur civilis homo etiam ad gratiam, quam et hic, si neglexerit, non civilis, et ille, si affectaverit, non erit philosophus.*

[49] Ibid. See Musonius Rufus fr. 49 (Hense 1905, 130–31), from Aulus Gellius, *Noctes Atticae* 5.1.

[50] Garin 1952, 816; Fallico and Shapiro 1967, 113: *Tribus maxime persuadetur, vita dicentis, veritate rei, sobrietate orationis.*

[51] Lines 2018, 287, claims that Pico was uninterested in the idea of philosophy conceived as the pursuit of a good life; instead his primary concern was with the search for truth, *veritas*, "which has a clearly speculative valence." Lines goes on to acknowledge, however, that "the contemplative *life* is in view here" (my emphasis).

to Aristotle's *Metaphysics*.[52] But he is also keen to stress that what the philosopher believes will have an impact on his way of life and that philosophers as a group share a distinctive way of life unlike that of ordinary people, reflecting their disinterest in worldly affairs. Pico cites Socrates and Pythagoras as role models here, but Aristotle's conception of the contemplative life fits very neatly with what Pico is trying to say. Indeed, Pico sees the pursuit of truth as the primary characteristic of the philosopher, "whose sole purpose," he writes, "is to know and to demonstrate the truth to others."[53] This is a pursuit so all-consuming that it cannot but have an impact on and express itself in the philosopher's way of life. In this sense, Pico outlines a thoroughly Aristotelian view, in contrast to Petrarch and Bruni, both of whom embrace a more Socratic conception of philosophy. Pico's Aristotle, however, also shares something in common with Hadot's portrait of Aristotle as a philosopher primarily concerned with how to live, for as we have seen it is the philosopher's way of life that occupies first place in Pico's list of the three defining characteristics of the true philosopher.[54] In both cases the activity of philosophy cannot but transform the practitioner's way of life.

Conclusions

We have seen three different humanists reflecting on the nature of philosophy. Petrarch proposed a broadly Socratic conception of philosophy as a way of life, learned second-hand from Latin authors such as Cicero and Seneca. Bruni proposed a syncretic conception of philosophy as a way of life, drawing on Socrates, the Stoics, and Aristotle's ethics. Pico offered an Aristotelian image of a philosophical life, in which the pursuit of knowledge remained central, reflecting his admiration for the virtues of Scholasticism. All three prioritized the claim that the task of philosophy was fundamentally one concerned with the transformation of one's way of life.

As we saw at the beginning, Kristeller famously dismissed the humanists as not really philosophers at all. Later he suggested that they had an interest in moral philosophy but not much else. More recently, Jill Kraye and David Lines have challenged that view, by pointing to examples of humanists who paid attention to topics in logic and physics (see Kraye 2016 and Lines 2018). Kraye has argued that humanism ought better to be understood as a particular approach to texts that might be applied to philosophical texts of all types, or none. It was primarily concerned with

[52] See Aristotle, *Metaph.* 1.1, 981a30–b6; see also 982a1–3 and 993b19–21.

[53] Garin 1952, 808; Fallico and Shapiro 1967, 108: *Cuius studium omne in cognoscenda et demonstranda ceteris veritate versatur.*

[54] See Hadot 2002, 77–90, for Hadot's account of Aristotle as a philosopher primarily motivated by the desire to live a contemplative life.

establishing an accurate text and understanding it within its historical context, rather than being solely focused on the validity and consistency of arguments (see Kraye 2016, 21).

I have tried to argue here that the three humanists discussed above, working in the light of their careful attention to ancient texts, took up a conception of philosophy that they found in those works, one that is quite different from those that many modern historians of philosophy hold, whether implicitly or explicitly. What they found in Cicero, Seneca, Plato, the Neoplatonists, and, depending on one's point of view, Aristotle was an image of philosophy as an activity devoted to self-transformation that would, in turn, shape one's way of life. This shaped their own understanding of philosophy and what it meant to be a philosopher. By paying attention to their own metaphilosophical reflections and commitments, then, we can see that they do indeed deserve to be counted as philosophers.

Appendix

List of Abbreviations

AL	*Aristoteles Latinus*
Ep.	*Epistulae/Letters* (Seneca)
Eth. Nic.	*Ethica Nicomachea/Nicomachean Ethics* (Aristotle)
ISTC	Incunabula Short Title Catalogue (online at http://istc.bl.uk)
Metaph.	*Metaphysica/Metaphysics* (Aristotle)

References

Baker, P. 2017. *Biography, Historiography, and Modes of Philosophizing: The Tradition of Collective Biography in Early Modern Europe*. Leiden: Brill.

Baron, H. 1928. *Leonardo Bruni, Humanistisch-Philosophische Schriften*. Leipzig: Teubner.

Bekker, I. 1831–70. *Aristotelis Opera*. 5 vols. Berlin: George Reimer.

Berti, E. 1983. *Il Critone Latino di Leonardo Bruni e di Rinuccio Aretino*. Florence: Leo S. Olschki.

Blum, P.R. 2006. "The Young Paul Oskar Kristeller as a Philosopher." In *Kristeller Reconsidered: Essays on His Life and Scholarship*, edited by J. Monfasani, 19–38. New York: Italica Press.

Breen, Q. 1952. "Giovanni Pico della Mirandola on the Conflict of Philosophy and Rhetoric." *Journal of the History of Ideas* 13:384–412.

Brisson, L. 2018. Review of Emilsson 2017. *Notre Dame Philosophical Reviews* 2018.02.02. Online at https://ndpr.nd.edu/news/plotinus/

Cassirer, E., P. O. Kristeller, and J. H. Randall. 1948. *The Renaissance Philosophy of Man*. Chicago: University of Chicago Press.

Catana, L. 2008. *The Historiographical Concept "System of Philosophy": Its Origin, Nature, Influence and Legitimacy*. Leiden: Brill.
Celenza, C. 2004. *The Lost Italian Renaissance: Humanists, Historians, and Latin's Legacy*. Baltimore: Johns Hopkins University Press.
________. 2013. "What Counted as Philosophy in the Italian Renaissance? The History of Philosophy, the History of Science, and Styles of Life." *Critical Inquiry* 39:367–401.
________. 2014. "Ideas in Context and the Idea of Renaissance Philosophy." *Journal of the History of Ideas* 75:653–66.
Ceron, A. 2015. "Leon Battista Alberti's Care of the Self as Medicine of the Mind: A First Glance at *Theogenius*, *Profugiorum ab erumna libri III,* and Two Related *Intercenales*." *Journal of Early Modern Studies* 4:9–36.
Cooper, J. M. 2012. *Pursuits of Wisdom: Six Ways of Life in Ancient Philosophy from Socrates to Plotinus*. Princeton: Princeton University Press.
Domanski, J. 1996. *La philosophie, théorie ou manière de vivre? Les controverses de l'Antiquité à la Renaissance*. Fribourg: Éditions Universitaires Fribourg Suisse.
Düring, I. 1957. *Aristotle in the Ancient Biographical Tradition*. Göteborg: Elanders.
Emilsson, E. K. 2017. *Plotinus*. Abingdon: Routledge.
Fallico, A. B. and H. Shapiro. 1967. *Renaissance Philosophy, Volume 1: The Italian Philosophers*. New York: The Modern Library.
Fryde, E. 1988. "The First Humanistic Life of Aristotle: The 'Vita Aristotelis' of Leonardo Bruni." In *Florence and Italy: Renaissance Studies in Honour of Nicolai Rubinstein*, edited by P. Denley and C. Elam, 285–96. London: Westfield College.
Garin, E. 1952. *Prosatori Latini del Quattrocento*. Milan: Riccardo Ricciardi.
________. 1965. *Italian Humanism: Philosophy and Civic Life in the Renaissance*. Oxford: Basil Blackwell.
Glucker, J. 1997. "Socrates in the Academic Books and Other Ciceronian Works." In *Assent and Argument: Studies in Cicero's Academic Books*, edited by B. Inwood and J. Mansfeld, 58–88. Leiden: Brill.
Grendler, P. F. 2006. "Paul Oskar Kristeller on Renaissance Universities." In *Kristeller Reconsidered: Essays on His Life and Scholarship*, edited by J. Monfasani, 89–130. New York: Italica Press.
Griffiths, G., J. Hankins, and D. Thompson. 1987. *The Humanism of Leonardo Bruni: Selected Texts*. Binghamton, N.Y.: Medieval and Renaissance Texts and Studies.
Hadot, P. 1993. *Plotinus or The Simplicity of Vision*. Chicago: University of Chicago Press.
________. 1995. *Philosophy as a Way of Life*. Oxford: Blackwell.

_______. 2002. *What Is Ancient Philosophy?* Cambridge, Mass.: Harvard University Press.
Hankins, J. 1990. *Plato in the Italian Renaissance*. 2 vols. Leiden: Brill.
Hense, O. 1905. *C. Musonii Rufi Reliquiae*. Leipzig: Teubner.
Ianziti, G. 2002. "Leonardo Bruni and Biography: The *Vita Aristotelis*." *Renaissance Quarterly* 55:805–32.
_______. 2012. *Writing History on the Renaissance: Leonardo Bruni and the Uses of the Past*. Cambridge, Mass.: Harvard University Press.
ISTC. Incunabula Short Title Catalogue. Online at http://istc.bl.uk/
Kallendorf, C. W. 2002. *Humanist Educational Treatises*. Cambridge, Mass.: Harvard University Press.
Kennedy, W. J. 2009. "The Economy of Invective and a Man in the Middle: *De sui ipsius et multorum ignorantia*." In *Petrarch: A Critical Guide to the Complete Works*, edited by V. Kirkham and A. Maggi, 263–73. Chicago: University of Chicago Press.
Kraye, J. 1996. "Philologists and Philosophers." In *The Cambridge Companion to Renaissance Humanism*, edited by J. Kraye, 142–60. Cambridge: Cambridge University Press.
_______. 2008. "Pico on the Relationship of Rhetoric and Philosophy." In *Pico della Mirandola: New Essays*, edited by M. V. Dougherty, 13–36. New York: Cambridge University Press.
_______. 2016. "Beyond Moral Philosophy: Renaissance Humanism and the Philosophical Canon." *Rinascimento* 56:3–22.
Kristeller, P. O. 1943. *The Philosophy of Marsilio Ficino*. New York: Columbia University Press.
_______. 1944–45. "Humanism and Scholasticism in the Italian Renaissance." *Byzantion* 17:346–74.
_______. 1952. "Petrarch's 'Averroists': A Note on the History of Aristotelianiam in Venice, Padua, and Bologna." *Bibliothèque d'humanisme et Renaissance* 14:59–65.
_______. 1964. *Eight Philosophers of the Italian Renaissance*. Stanford: Stanford University Press.
_______. 1979. *Renaissance Thought and Its Sources*. New York: Columbia University Press.
Lines, D. A. 2002. *Aristotle's Ethics in the Italian Renaissance (ca. 1300–1650)*. Leiden: Brill.
_______. 2018. "Defining Philosophy in Fifteenth-Century Humanism: Four Case Studies." In *Et Amicorum: Essays on Renaissance Humanism and Philosophy*, edited by A. Ossa-Richardson and M. Meserve, 281–97. Leiden: Brill.
Marenbon, J. 2013. *Continuity and Innovation in Medieval and Modern Philosophy*. Oxford: Oxford University Press for the British Academy.
Marsh, D., ed. and trans. 2003. *Francesco Petrarca, Invectives*. Cambridge, Mass.: Harvard University Press.

Mehus, L. 1741. *Leonardo Bruni, Epistolarum Libri VIII*. 2 vols. Florence: Bernardi Paperini.

Monfasani, J. 2000. "Toward the Genesis of the Kristeller Thesis of Renaissance Humanism: Four Bibliographical Notes." *Renaissance Quarterly* 54:1156–73.

________. 2006. "The Renaisssance as the Concluding Phase of the Middle Ages." *Bullettino dell'Istituto storico italiano per il medio evo* 108:165–85.

Nauta, L. 2009. *In Defense of Common Sense: Lorenzo Valla's Humanist Critique of Scholastic Philosophy*. Cambridge, Mass.: Harvard University Press.

Pasnau, R. 2011. *Metaphysical Themes, 1274–1671*. Oxford: Clarendon Press.

Pine, M. L. 2006. "Paul Oskar Kristeller on Renaissance Scholasticism." In *Kristeller Reconsidered: Essays on His Life and Scholarship*, edited by J. Monfasani, 213–21. New York: Italica Press.

Renan, E. 1852. *Averroes et l'averroïsme*. Paris: Auguste Durand.

Rummel, E. 1995. *The Humanist-Scholastic Debate in the Renaissance and Reformation*. Cambridge, Mass.: Harvard University Press.

Santinello, G., Blackwell, C. W. (Eds.) 1993. *Models of the History of Philosophy I: From Its Origins in the Renaissance to the "Historia Philosophica."* Dordrecht: Kluwer.

Schmitt, C. B., Q. Skinner, and E. Kessler. 1988. *The Cambridge History of Renaissance Philosophy*. Cambridge: Cambridge University Press.

Sellars, J. 2003. *The Art of Living: The Stoics on the Nature and Function of Philosophy*. Aldershot: Ashgate.

Trinkaus, C. 1979. *The Poet as Philosopher: Petrarch and the Formation of Renaissance Consciousness*. New Haven: Yale University Press.

Viti, P. 1996. *Leonardo Bruni, Opere Letterarie e Politiche*. Turin: Unione Tipografico-Editrice.

Vuillemin-Diem, G. 1970. *Aristoteles Latinus 25, 1–1a: Metaphysica, Translatio Iacobi sive "Vetustissima" et Translatio Composita sive "Vetus."* Brussels: Desclée de Brouwer.

________. 1976. *Aristoteles Latinus 25, 2: Metaphysica, Translatio Anonyma sive "Media."* Leiden: Brill.

________. 1995. *Aristoteles Latinus 25, 3: Metaphysica, Recensio et Translatio Guillelmi de Moerbeka*. 2 vols. Leiden: Brill.

Witt, R. G. 2006. "The Humanism of Paul Oskar Kristeller." In *Kristeller Reconsidered: Essays on His Life and Scholarship*, edited by J. Monfasani, 257–67. New York: Italica Press.

Zak, G. 2010. *Petrarch's Humanism and the Care of the Self*. Cambridge: Cambridge University Press.

________. 2014. "Humanism as a Way of Life: Leon Battista Alberti and the Legacy of Petrarch." *I Tatti Studies in the Italian Renaissance* 17:217–40.

Zeyl, D. 2003. Review of Hadot 2002. *Notre Dame Philosophical Reviews* 2003.06.09. Online at https://ndpr.nd.edu/news/23663-what-is-ancient-philosophy/

CHAPTER 5

CARTESIAN PHILOSOPHY AS SPIRITUAL PRACTICE

JOSEPH I. BREIDENSTEIN JR.

1. Introduction

Although the image of Descartes meditating in his stove-heated room has become emblematic of academia's alienation from everyday life, Descartes himself conveys a more practical approach to philosophy in the preface to the French edition of *Principles of Philosophy*: "To live without philosophizing is tantamount to living with one's eyes closed[, and] . . . in order to live according to a standard and to find our way in this life, we need philosophy even more than we need our eyes in order to walk straight" (Descartes 2015, 125). It is by considering Cartesian philosophy as a whole that we can reconcile its theoretical and practical aspects, as well as understand Cartesian philosophy as a spiritual practice. Descartes illustrates the holistic nature of his philosophy when he writes, "The whole of philosophy is like a tree, the roots of which are metaphysics and the trunk physics, while the branches that grow from the trunk are all the other sciences" (2015, 131). Vance G. Morgan also suggests that Cartesian philosophy is a continually evolving organism: "It is hard to imagine that Descartes seriously thought that metaphysics and the physical sciences would ever come to a state of definitive completion" (1994, 24), and, in fact, this dynamic aspect of Cartesian philosophy is a direct consequence of the mutual irreducibility of Descartes's primary notions.

Descartes maintained that all knowledge is based on the three primary notions of soul, body, and the union of soul and body, each of which can only be understood on its own terms by its own particular faculty (2015,

Philosophy as a Way of Life: Historical, Contemporary, and Pedagogical Perspectives.
Edited by James M. Ambury, Tushar Irani, and Kathleen Wallace.

Published 2021 by John Wiley & Sons Ltd.

4–7). Whereas the soul "is conceived only by the pure intellect," the body can be known most readily by "the intellect aided by the imagination," and the union of soul and body is only known clearly by the senses because, even with the aid of imagination, it remains inherently obscure to the intellect (2015, 9). The mutual irreducibility of these notions ensures the dynamism of Cartesian philosophy by demonstrating its dependence on imagination and sensation as sources of knowledge that continually escape the confines of any exclusively intellectual system. While several commentators have suggested that the primary notions of soul and body may more plausibly be understood as conceptual abstractions, they still uphold the intellectual irreducibility of the third primary notion, and it seems to be this irreducible significance of sensation that incited Descartes to approach philosophy as a spiritual practice (see Alanen 2003, 71; Brown and de Sousa 2003, 170).

This is because sensation plays an essential role in what Morgan refers to as "the crowning achievement" of Descartes's philosophical system, namely, Descartes's ethics (1994, 23). Descartes describes ethics as "the ultimate degree of wisdom," which "presupposes a comprehensive knowledge of the other sciences" (2015, 131), and he demonstrates the ethical significance of sensation when he writes that "the conduct of our life depends entirely on our senses" (1988, 57). That is, Descartes could not rely on the intellect alone in order to promote the most important part of his philosophy. Instead, he suggests that we practice philosophy as a way to utilize our intellect and imagination so as to cultivate noble forms of sensation. In this essay, I both demonstrate the spiritual nature of Cartesian ethics and explain the primacy of ethics (and hence of spirituality) for Descartes's approach to philosophy in general. I conclude by describing the role of temporality in Cartesian ethics and addressing several objections.

1

Morgan conveys how Cartesianism could be interpreted as a paradigmatic instance of academic introspection and isolation when he notes that, for Descartes, "the source of human knowledge is not the known object of knowledge but is the knowing subject itself" (1994, 14). The objects of knowledge are unified by the subject's understanding because the subject carries within itself the principles of unity, namely, rationality and innate ideas. That is, for Descartes, all human beings are capable of acquiring knowledge because each person's soul possesses, a priori, both the natural light of rationality that enables the person to distinguish truth from falsity and the innate seeds of wisdom that serve as the subject matter to which the natural light is applied. The goal, however, of applying rationality to our innate ideas is "to help the knower develop an internal sense of truth in general," which is useful both for intellectual investigations and for guiding one's behavior (Morgan 1994, 21). In fact, Descartes maintains that "the true function of reason is to examine the real value of all the goods whose acquisition seems to depend in some way on our own behavior, so that we shall never fail to direct all our efforts to the attempt to attain those that are in truth the most desirable" (2015, 45). Descartes's metaphysics itself necessitates that this sense of truth not be confined to intellectual speculation alone because, while metaphysical knowledge is deduced from the primary notion of the soul and its innate ideas, the human being itself falls under the third primary notion of union. In other words, the metaphysical constitution of the human being itself necessitates a distinction between metaphysical (intellectual) certainty and moral (sensible) certainty (Morgan 1994, 67), and, in doing so, it entails that the sense for truth extend from intellectual theory to ethical practice. Descartes is clear that the method of doubt "is to be restricted only to the contemplation of the truth" (2015, *Principles,* § 3), because absolute certainty cannot be attained outside metaphysical speculation. One may only attain a probabilistic degree of certainty concerning the things that pertain to sensation, and the intellect can only contribute to this indirectly by cultivating a sense of truth in general.

According to Descartes, "the true use of our reason in the conduct of our life consists purely in dispassionately weighing and considering the value of all perfections" so as to attain "true knowledge of the good" (2015, 36, 47). In order to help Princess Elisabeth both develop her sense of truth and use it in a practically efficacious way, Descartes provided four metaphysical truths, the contemplation of which was supposed to make her sufficiently circumspect.

The first truth is that there is an infallible and infinitely perfect god on whom everything in the world depends. Descartes tells Elisabeth that knowing that God is the ultimate cause of everything that happens "teaches us to take in good part whatever happens to us," so much so that "we can even find joy in our afflictions" (2015, 49). The second useful truth is that our soul continues to exist without the body and "is capable of enjoying an infinity of contentments that cannot be experienced in this life." There are distinct intellectual emotions that "are produced in the soul by the soul itself" (2015, *Passions,* art. 147), which are both primarily responsible for our well-being in this life and, if they are founded on true knowledge, can be as immortal as the soul itself (Descartes 2015, 47).[1] Descartes maintained that contemplating such a blissful immortality can help us dispassionately employ our rationality in this world insofar as it "prevents us from fearing death, and so loosens our attachment to the things of this world" (2015, 49–50). Third, in order to further loosen her worldly

[1] "That the pleasure of the soul in which happiness consists is not inseparable from physical cheerfulness and ease" is evident from the pleasure we derive from engaging in physical exercises. The reason the soul finds pleasure in such exercises is that "they make it aware of its strength or skill, or some other perfection of the body to which it is attached" (Descartes 2015, 56).

attachments, Descartes writes that Elisabeth should form a proper judgment of God's works and come to terms with the vast extent and inherent goodness of the universe. By thinking that "there is always more good than evil in this life" because "there is no evil from which one cannot derive some advantage, provided one has good sense" (2015, 32, 71), one can cultivate the kind of generous perspective that would facilitate dispassionate and rational evaluation. The final useful truth is that, even though each of us is an individual with his or her own distinct interests, "we cannot exist on our own [since] . . . each of us is, in fact, part of the universe" (2015, 50). In light of this universal connectivity, "we should always put the interests of the whole of which we are a part above those peculiar to ourselves" (2015, 50) and find contentment in our inherent connections to each other.[2]

His prescription of these four truths to Elisabeth indicates that Descartes saw intellectual theorizing as being both practically and spiritually significant insofar as it cultivates one's sense of truth and can be used to develop a worldview that helps one contend with the inevitable difficulties of worldly existence. While the other-worldly aspects of Descartes's spirituality (that is, the belief in God and immortality) may be met with suspicion by many contemporary readers, the this-worldly aspects (that is, the overall goodness of the world and one's intimate connection to it) provide us with a more palatable form of spirituality that understands that what we think about the world influences how we feel about and act within it. Before further defending spirituality as an important aspect of Cartesian ethics, however, I would like to discuss how his fourth useful truth both entails the ethical imperative to act on behalf of others and explains how one's community may inhibit one from doing so.

In the *Meditations*, Descartes writes that the mind understands when it "turns itself in some way towards itself and gazes on one of the ideas that are contained within itself" (2008, 52). Error arises when one misuses one's infinite free will by extending it beyond one's finite intellect so that one either assents to or denies matters that one does not clearly and distinctly understand (2008, 41–42). In order to avoid intellectual error one should restrict assent to those ideas that one clearly and distinctly perceives. The fact that the activity of willing depends on one's intellectual, emotional, and perceptual capacities, however, means that the development of one's will is an inescapably embodied and communal enterprise.[3]

[2] Descartes puts forth a physical basis for this metaphysical truth in *The World* where he writes that the parts of matter "are all in contact with each other on all sides without there being any vacuum between them" (Descartes 2003, 106). For more on Descartes's physics, see Garber 1992.

[3] Descartes argues that the will is only able to either affirm or deny when the intellect presents something to it for affirmation or denial (2008, 41), and Morgan specifies that "the activity of the soul is in a very real sense dependent upon and limited by its perceptions" and passions: "The soul is able to act in only as many ways as it is capable of being acted upon" (1994, 161–62).

Descartes emphasizes the embodied nature of interpersonal relations and maintains that we must become aware of the intellectual limitations that result from them. The prejudices that people acquire in childhood are the prime causes of error because they often obscure people's clear and distinct perceptions (2015, *Principles,* §§ 50, 71), and they are difficult to overcome because they are not merely thought of intellectually but also lived physically: "There is such a close connection between our soul and our body that the thoughts that accompanied certain movements of the body, at the very beginning of our lives, are still accompanying them" (2015, 74). Furthermore, it is not just that what one thinks but also how one feels that is influenced by one's social environment. "To see one is esteemed by others is a reason to esteem oneself" (2015, *Passions,* art. 204), and, "although the people is a very bad judge, yet . . . we cannot live without it, and it matters to us to be esteemed by it" (art. 206). It is in this way that the use of one's will in intellectual speculation can be inhibited by societal prejudices and evaluations, and, while the prescription by Descartes of the four useful truths may be symptomatic of a metaphysical form of optimism, this is balanced by his realistic pessimism concerning people in general as well as the unique difficulties that philosophically minded individuals have to face: "People with commonplace and mediocre minds, being similar to those they have to deal with, see further into their intentions and succeed more easily in their undertakings than those of the more lofty intelligence" (2015, 65).

For Descartes, the prejudicial inertia of mediocre ways of thinking and feeling is broken by the production of noble souls. Although we are all equal insofar as each of us possesses free will, reason, and innate ideas, Descartes finds it easy to believe that God has placed souls of various degrees of nobility within different bodies (2015, *Passions,* art. 161). As Morgan has observed, this distinction between different qualities of soul "is crucial to the development of Cartesian ethics" (1994, 33 n. 25) because it explains how individual shortcomings and communal prejudices may be overcome. Also, while Morgan describes nobility of soul in terms of the quality of intellect or the manner in which intellect interacts with the passions (1994, 98, 203), Paul Hoffman's discussion of the different kinds of strength of soul further emphasizes the role that willpower has to play in this interaction (2003, 283). Descartes's characterization of weak souls as allowing themselves to be continually carried away by momentary passions (2015, *Passions,* art. 48) may be more accurately interpreted, argues Hoffman, as a form of laziness rather than weakness (2003, 284). This underscores how important Descartes thought it was that people not only have the right values but also possess the resoluteness to consistently adhere to them, and, while he writes of noble souls as being created by God, he nevertheless insists that they can be produced here on earth because "a good upbringing can do much to counter the shortcomings a person is born with" (2015, *Passions,* art. 161). Although the inequalities and contingencies of life make it impossible for every person to cultivate virtue by practicing philosophy, those whose souls have benefited from either an auspicious birth or a noble upbringing have a duty to assist those who are less fortunate in developing their own intelligence and willpower (Morgan 1994, 204). It is in this way that Cartesian philosophy is as much a communal practice as it is an intellectual discipline.

In sum, Cartesian ethics is a spiritual practice in the sense that it is an endeavor to ennoble peoples' souls that employs the contemplation of spiritual ideas. Now that I have described the significance of the soul's intellect and will as they pertain to this process, I turn to Descartes's second primary notion, namely, the body. By discussing the role of habit and imagination in Cartesian ethics, I clarify how people can cultivate a sense of truth in the form of intellectual emotions as well as begin to address the significance of temporality.

2

As Lisa Shapiro has noted, time itself differentiates between metaphysical theorizing and ethical practice: "The difference between matters of the true and matters of the good is the amount of time we can afford to spend reaching our decision" (1999, 274 n. 30). In order to avoid the kind of irresolution that results from methodical doubt's encroachment into the ethical realm, Descartes created a provisional morality in chapter 3 of the *Discourse on Method*, the first maxim of which is to obey the laws and customs of one's own country and to guide one's behavior "by the most moderate and least excessive views that are generally accepted in practice by the most sensible people" (2003, 19). Since the only thing that is certain about this life is that we will inevitably have to act regardless of our uncertainty, philosophy must provide people with techniques that enable them to cope with the uncertainty of the world, and, although his admonition to obey the customs of one's community may appear to contradict his concern with overcoming societal prejudices, this is not the case.[4] Descartes specifically emphasized that one should seek guidance from one's community cautiously and judiciously: "To discover what [people] really believed, I should pay more attention to what they did than what they said" because "there are few people who are willing to express everything they believe," and "many do not know what they themselves believe" (2003, 19). The cultivation of a *sense* of truth is particularly important in this regard because "it is better in this sphere [of civic life] to govern oneself by experience rather than reason, since one rarely has to deal with people who are perfectly rational" (2015, 76).

[4] Morgan notes that the appearance of an "unreflective social conformism" in Descartes's first maxim is due to the fact that "the Cartesian enterprise is not aimed at external reform, but rather at the transformation of individual knowledge" (1994, 45).

Although one must avoid being unduly obstinate in one's views, Descartes's second maxim is that once one decides to act, one must "be as firm and resolute as possible" and even follow doubtful views as if they were certain (2003, 20).[5] One should have a consistent resolution to always act according to the advice of reason so that one is never led astray by either one's passions (2015, 35) or the uncertainty that attends the temporal limitations of making a decision: "Whenever we are unable to identify the most true opinions, we should follow the most probable" and "think about them subsequently no longer as doubtful" (2003, 20). The significance of this maxim is that it enables one to avoid feeling regret, and Descartes relates that following this maxim has freed him "from all the regrets and remorse that usually disturb the consciences of weak and wavering minds." The reason for this is that "it is not in human nature to know everything, or always to judge as well on the spur of the moment as when we have plenty of time for deliberation" (2015, 55). One has reason to feel regretful only if one acts against one's conscience, but not if one has failed to consider better alternatives, because such consideration was precluded by the necessity for action. For Descartes, pursuing virtue consists precisely in this firm resolution to follow probability as if it were certainty.[6]

The third and final maxim is "to try always to overcome [oneself] rather than fortune" by changing one's desires and getting used to believing that "there is nothing that is completely within our control apart from our thoughts" (Descartes 2003, 20). Keeping one's limitations in mind accustoms one to not desiring things that are outside one's control, and this, in turn, enables one to properly channel one's energy toward goals that are actually attainable. Whereas the second maxim protects one from the burden of regret, this maxim protects one from the discontentment that attends unfulfilled desires, and according to Descartes, "nothing can prevent us from being content but desire, and regret or repentance." It is in this way that "virtue alone is sufficient to bring us contentment in this life," and this is itself significant because without the prospect of becoming content, people are unlikely to try and become virtuous: "Virtue, which is the target, does not appear very desirable when it appears by itself; and contentment, the prize, cannot be won, unless you follow virtue" (2015, 42).

There are several things to note about Descartes's provisional ethics. The first is that, unlike the method of doubt, which Descartes employed to discover metaphysical certainty only after he was able to distance himself

[5] "It would be a major lapse of common sense if, because I approved of something at one time, I was still obliged to consider it good subsequently when, perhaps, it may have ceased to be good" (Descartes 2003, 20).

[6] "Whosoever has lived in such a manner that his conscience cannot reproach him for ever having failed to do all those things that he has judged best (which is what I mean here by 'pursuing virtue') receives thereby a satisfaction that has so much power to make him happy that the most violent surges of passion are never strong enough to trouble the tranquility of his soul" (Descartes 2015, *Passions*, art. 148).

from any practical concerns, Cartesian ethics admonishes us to create our own certainty in the sphere of civic life. Second, Cartesian ethics is primarily an ethics of form and not of content: given the uncontrollable nature of the external world, Descartes defines virtue in terms of the form of an action, as the firm resolution to act according to reason, and not in terms of the consequences of actions, which may be influenced by forces beyond one's control (Morgan 1994, 109). Third, Descartes specifies the necessary content of his ethics when he writes that "strength of soul is not sufficient without knowledge of the truth" (2015, *Passions,* art. 49). Since "vice is typically the result of ignorance" (2015, *Passions,* art. 160), the certainty one creates in practical life can only be virtuous if it is based on sound theoretical knowledge. It is by using the will properly in intellectual speculation so that it assents only to clear and distinct ideas that people can acquire knowledge that, in turn, enables them to properly examine their values, thereby overcoming societal prejudices. In this way, the cultivation of a sense of truth is simultaneously a cultivation of nobility of soul, but the final thing to note about Cartesian ethics is that even this combination of will and intellect is insufficient: "Besides the knowledge of the truth, habit is also essential if we are to be always disposed to judge correctly" (Descartes 2015, 51). One needs will, knowledge, and *practice* in order to become virtuous because, for Descartes, virtues are "habits in the soul that dispose it to certain thoughts" (2015, *Passions,* art. 161). The importance of habit becomes clear when we take into consideration the significance of the passions for Cartesian ethics.[7]

Passion is both the primary incentive and the greatest obstacle to becoming virtuous because it is that which both "make[s] for all that is good or bad in this life" (Descartes 2015, *Passions,* art. 212) and disposes people to make improper judgments by misrepresenting its objects (2015, 46). Descartes turns to habit in the form of the association principle so as to utilize the passions in the pursuit of virtue: "The principle on which everything I have written about [the passions] is based [is] . . . that there is so close a union between our soul and our body that when we have once linked some bodily action with some thought, then in the future, whenever one of the two presents itself to us, the other will as well" (2015, *Passions,* art. 136). Just as a connection to one's community can be both the source of an ethical imperative and an obstacle to fulfilling it, the union of mind and body is both the source of one's prejudices as well as the means for overcoming them. Although Descartes held the most common first cause of the passions to be the neural activity of the pineal gland (2015, *Passions,* art. 51), the key to his ethical utilization of the passions is the endeavor to

[7] Descartes "claims that the moral issues concerning the passions are not his primary interest" and that he opts for approaching the passions not as a moral philosopher but 'en physician', as a physicist" (Brown 1999, 216). Lilli Alanen, however, provides an explanation of why Descartes would downplay his moral interest in the passions when she notes that he did "not want to get involved in writing, publicly, about ethical matters" (2004, 210).

make them arise directly from the soul. One cultivates such intellectual emotions by critically examining one's values (Brown 2002, 270) so as to form more rational associations that, over time, can reform one's psychological as well as physiological habits: "Our passions cannot be directly aroused or banished by the action of our will; but they can be indirectly, by the representation of things that are habitually associated with the passions we want to have, and that are contrary to those we wish to reject" (Descartes 2015, *Passions,* art. 45). In fact, knowledge of this process is itself "very useful to anyone as an encouragement to concentrate on regulating his passions" and indicates that "even those who have the weakest souls could acquire a very absolute command of all their passions, if one were to take the trouble to train them and guide them properly" (2015, *Passions,* art. 50). Nevertheless, in keeping with the dynamism of Cartesian philosophy, Morgan is right to emphasize that, however rational the new habits may be, they must be continually reviewed and adjusted because, if they are not, "the possibility of moral growth stimulated by increased knowledge is removed" (1994, 192).

Whereas the intellect serves a primarily critical role in this process, the imagination functions constructively by helping one incorporate rational evaluations into one's own physical being. It is able to do this because, in contrast to the intellect's indirect influence, the imagination directly influences the body. In the *Meditations,* Descartes defined imagination as "a certain application of the knowing faculty to a body intimately present to that faculty" (2008, 51), and he wrote to Elisabeth that "when the soul uses its will [in imagination] to apply itself to some thought that is not only intelligible, but imaginable, this thought makes a new impression in the brain" (2015, 57). These statements indicate the two distinct ways in which imagination is applied to the body. On the one hand, it considers things that are not just intelligible, like a mathematical proof, but also imaginable, like one's own body or any other corporeal object. On the other hand, by considering such things, the imagination creates new impressions in the brain that would not follow from the consideration of intellectual abstractions. However slight the physical influence of the imagination may be, the fact that it is more viscerally efficacious than the intellect ensures its value as a means by which one can utilize the passions. It is with the help of the imagination that ideas such as the four useful truths can begin to manifest psychologically and physiologically as new associations or dispositions.

Besides being the means by which more rational values are incorporated, the body's epistemic contribution also indirectly facilitates the soul's moral development. According to Amélie Oksenberg Rorty, it is the body itself that makes philosophical inquiry possible by contributing information unattainable through intellectual speculation alone. The body serves as "the medium and the messenger by which the imperial will realizes many of its operations," such as retrieving memories and determining which data are relevant, and it is also the means by which we acquire data about such things as "the motion of physical objects" that "cannot be specified by the intellect alone" (Rorty 1992, 372, 375). Just as the intellect can indirectly influence one's passions through the association principle, the body can indirectly contribute to one's understanding of the soul by providing such extra-intellectual data: "Nothing at all can cause us to know something other than our mind without at the same time bringing us, much more certainly, to knowledge of our own mind" (Descartes 2015, *Principles,* § 11).

Rorty summarizes the epistemic significance of the body with the statement "find a healthy body type and you'll find a reliable perceiver [of data]" (1992, 377), and I argue that the body possesses a similar ethical significance, for Descartes, in the sense that having a healthy affective disposition is essential for being able to uphold one's values within the uncertainty of real life: "The utility of the passions consists purely in this: that they fortify and preserve thoughts in the soul that are good for it to retain, and which otherwise could be easily effaced" (Descartes 2015, *Passions,* art. 74). Considering the intellectual limitations of everyday life, however, there still remains the problem of how, without adequate time for deliberation, one is to discern which thoughts are good for one to retain. This is where the third faculty comes into play. Sensation is the application of a body to the cognitive faculty, and, according to Descartes, "sensory perceptions . . . were specifically given by nature for signifying to the mind what things are beneficial or harmful to the composite of which the mind is part" (2008, 59). That is, to go along with his distinction between theoretical and moral certainty, Descartes provides what Annette Baier has referred to as "a double standard of intellectual distinctness," according to which the impressions that guide our actions are as distinct to the senses as they are confused to the intellect (1985, 76). Just as healthy passions enable one to grasp and retain thoughts that are good for the soul, healthy sensations enable one to discern which thoughts should be retained and hence which habits should be cultivated. As we shall see, it is one's sense of time that intimates the direction of one's intellectual, ethical, and spiritual development.

3

Just as the realm of Descartes's provisional morality is delineated by the constraints of time, how one relates to the different modes of time is an integral part of the experience of nobility. While we have already seen how being resolute can help one cultivate a sense of contentment regarding the past, one's capacity for resoluteness itself depends on one's relation to the present. Passions can cause regret to the extent that they dispose, but not determine, one to act contrarily to one's conscience, and "the most general and easy remedy for all the excesses of passion" is, when one is stirred by them, to "be alert, and remember that whatever presents itself to the imagination tends to deceive the soul" (Descartes 2015, *Passions*, art. 211).

Although many circumstances require immediate action, if possible, when one is overcome by passions one should try to refrain from either pursuing actions or making judgments at that time and instead direct one's attention to considering alternative perspectives. Although Descartes admits to Elisabeth that "it is virtually impossible to withstand the initial turmoil that new misfortunes bring about in us" (2015, 32), in *The Passions of the Soul* he nevertheless intimates that practice can make a difference in such situations. "There is no human wisdom capable of withstanding [the passions] if one is not sufficiently prepared" (2015, *Passions,* art. 211), and developing a habit of remaining alert and circumspect in the midst of present conflict is one such form of preparation.

Furthermore, developing such a sense of past contentment and present circumspection is itself dependent on one's relation to the future. Descartes argued that the principal utility of moral philosophy consists in the regulation of desire because "passions cannot induce us to perform any action except through the agency of the desire they arouse" (2015, *Passions,* art. 144), and he maintained that desire disposes the soul, "with reference to the future, [towards] those things it represents to it as beneficial" (art. 86). It is by striving to have one's desires reflect one's knowledge of the truth that one is able to feel confident about the future, or the direction of one's life, and this, in turn, helps one remain circumspect in the face of present challenges. Such confidence, or strength of soul, enables people to "feel a satisfaction in themselves at everything that befalls them, even the most distressing and unbearable events," because these are seen as providing them with opportunities for exercising their strength (Descartes 2015, 25).

Desire renders "all the senses more acute and all parts of the body more mobile" (Descartes 2015, *Passions,* art. 101), and, through its rationalization, one cultivates a sense for the truly good. For Descartes, the ability to rationalize one's desire depends on one's capacity for wonderment, which is itself distinguished by the fact that it does not seem to produce any changes in the heart or blood. "In wonderment, the soul is suddenly taken by surprise, which causes it to consider attentively the objects that it finds rare and extraordinary" (art. 70), and, accordingly, wonder "is focused not on good or bad but only on the knowledge of the thing that has given rise to it." That is, it is as a passion for knowledge itself that wonder drives the rationalization of one's other passions. Nevertheless, just as desire can become unhealthy when it is based on falsehood, wonder can become harmful when it is excessive because it then habituates one to a state of "blind curiosity," which distorts reason by having one remain fixed on the superficial appearances of things without acquiring any further knowledge (arts. 75, 76, and 78). In order for wonderment to be a healthy sensation, it needs to be driven by desire because, whereas wonderment rationalizes desire by inculcating in one the desire for knowledge, desire, in turn, protects one from excessive wonderment by driving one to fulfill the desire for knowledge. The only remedy against excessive wonderment is "to acquire a knowledge of many things" (art. 76).

Through the mutual development of desire and wonder, one develops the healthy affective disposition that characterizes a noble soul. That nobility may be understood as a form of health is suggested in two ways. First, Descartes maintained that he knew of no thought more conducive to the preservation of one's health than a firm conviction of one's own strength or the "architecture" of one's body (2015, 20), and it certainly seems that the kind of strength of soul that he associates with nobility can also function in a similar way. Second, he writes that "those who are noble . . . [v]alue nothing more highly than doing good to other human beings, for the sake of which they regard their own interests as unimportant" (2015, *Passions,* art. 156). If a noble soul's concern for humanity may be described as love, and the feeling of love is indeed "beneficial for the health" (art. 97), then nobility of soul is certainly a healthy condition.[8] Speculative as these conclusions may be, they nevertheless offer an explanation for why Descartes held ethics in such high esteem, namely, that it grounds his physics and metaphysics. On an individual level, Cartesian ethics admonished one to cultivate the kind of healthy disposition that facilitates the reliable perception of data, and, on a societal level, an individual's own cultivation of virtue helps promote a healthier cultural environment where collective prejudices are less likely to inhibit metaphysical speculation. In other words, just as ethical practice is grounded in the physiology of the imagination and the metaphysics of the intellect, ethics in turns grounds metaphysics and physics by promoting bodily and communal health. Finally, the superior status and spiritual nature of Cartesian ethics enables us to interpret Cartesian philosophy in general as a spiritual practice whereby one may utilize all branches of knowledge so as to both ennoble one's own soul by embodying spiritual truths and help others contend with the inevitable obstacles of daily life.

4

In conclusion, I would like to address three problems that might be put forth against Cartesian ethics. First, Cartesian ethics may appear to be in tension with metaphysics insofar as Descartes portrays the latter as an inherently unhealthy enterprise. He relates that he himself only spends "very few hours per year" in thoughts "that occupy the intellect alone" (2015, 9) and even admonishes Elisabeth to "avoid any kind of serious meditation on intellectual matters" (29). His comment, however, that

[8] Descartes also acknowledges the benefits of negative emotions, however: "With respect to the body, love and joy are more conducive to health but sadness and hatred more conducive to survival" because while the former promote circulation of blood and digestion, in terms of survival, "it is better to avoid harmful things than obtain goods one can live without" (Brown 2006, 176–77). See also Descartes 2015, *Passions,* arts. 97–98, 102–3, 108, and 137.

metaphysical speculation would be harmful because it inhibits the understanding from attending to "the functions of the imagination and the senses" (9), and his advice to Elisabeth that "intellectual diversions, which others would find very burdensome, may sometimes enable you to relax" (33), indicate how this conflict can be overcome. While metaphysical speculation can be harmful if it excludes imagination and sensation and is taken too seriously, when it is done in coordination with the other faculties and in a detached manner, it can prove to be beneficial for individual and collective health. Second, Elisabeth is correct to question the practical efficacy of the four useful truths that Descartes prescribes to her because it seems intuitive that just thinking about them is not enough to make one feel better about the terrible things that happen in life.[9] Again, however, it must be kept in mind that, for Descartes, intellectual endeavors should not be undertaken in isolation from imagination and sense perception. Spiritual ideas appear inefficacious in bringing about a dispositional change only if they are assumed to do all of the work, but when they are accompanied by proper habits and sensations, such ideas can become efficacious. Finally, Descartes's concept of the noble soul may seem to be an unrealistic or unattainable ideal. Thinking about it in this way, however, is inconsistent with the dynamic nature of Descartes's own philosophy, according to which there is always room for growth. If one's body plays a significant role in becoming noble and is itself continually subject to external forces, then it seems plausible to read Descartes's view of nobility as articulating a kind of experience that comes and goes rather than an ultimate state of being. It is a state of being content with the past, circumspect in the present, and confident about future, and, as a passion of the soul, it is an experience of the eternal within the temporal that one cultivates so that it may, one hopes, become a habitual disposition.

Acknowledgments

I would like to thank Mark Smith and an anonymous reviewer for their insightful advice on earlier drafts of this essay.

References

Alanen, Lilli. 2003. *Descartes' Concept of Mind.* Cambridge, Mass.: Harvard University Press.

________. 2004. "Descartes and Elisabeth: A Philosophical Dialogue?" In *Feminist Reflections on the History of Philosophy*, edited by Lilli Alanen and Charlotte Witt, 193–218. Dordrecht: Kluwer Academic.

[9] In response to Descartes's discussion of the effects that thinking about God's perfection is supposed to have, Elisabeth insists that she "cannot consider the harmful incidents that befall [those close to her] in any other light than that of evil" (Descartes 2015, 27).

Baier, Annette. 1985. *Postures of the Mind*. Minneapolis: University of Minnesota Press.

Brown, Deborah J. 1999. "What Was New in the *Passions* of 1649?" *Acta Philosophica Fennica* 64:211–31.

________. 2002. "The Rationality of Cartesian Passions." In *Emotions and Choice from Boethius to Descartes*, edited by Henrik Lagerlung and Mikko Yrjönsuuri, 259–78. Dordrecht: Kluwer Academic.

________. 2006. *Descartes and the Passionate Mind*. Cambridge: Cambridge University Press.

Brown, Deborah J., and Ronald de Sousa. 2003. "Descartes on the Unity of the Self and the Passions." In *Passions and Virtue in Descartes*, edited by Byron Williston and André Gombay, 153–74. Amherst, N.Y.: Humanity Books.

Descartes, René. 1988. *Descartes: Selected Philosophical Writings*. Translated by John Cottingham, Robert Stoothoff, and Dugald Murdoch. Cambridge: University of Cambridge Press.

________. 2003. *Discourse on Method and Related Writings*. Translated by Desmond M. Clarke. London: Penguin Books.

________. 2008. *Meditations on First Philosophy: With Selections from Objection and Replies*. Translated by Michael Moriarty. Oxford: Oxford University Press.

________. 2015. *The Passions of the Soul and Other Late Philosophical Writings*. Translated by Michael Moriarty. Oxford: Oxford University Press.

Garber, Daniel. 1992. "Descartes' Physics." In *The Cambridge Companion to Descartes*, edited by John Cottingham, 286–334. Cambridge: Cambridge University Press.

Hoffman, Paul. 2003. "The Passions and Freedom of Will." In *Passions and Virtue in Descartes*, edited by Byron Williston and André Gombay, 261–300. Amherst, N.Y.: Humanity Books.

Morgan, Vance G. 1994. *Foundations of Cartesian Ethics*. Atlantic Highlands, N. J.: Humanities Press International.

Rorty, Amélie Oksenburg. 1992. "Descartes on Thinking with the Body." In *The Cambridge Companion to Descartes*, edited by John Cottingham, 371–92. Cambridge: Cambridge University Press.

Shapiro, Lisa. 1999. "Cartesian Generosity." *Acta Philosophica Fennica* 64:249–76.

CHAPTER 6

LEIBNIZ'S PHILOSOPHY AS A WAY OF LIFE?

PAUL LODGE

In a 2012 review of Lloyd Strickland's *Leibniz and the Two Sophies* (LTS), which is a selection of Leibniz's correspondences with Electress Sophia of Hanover and her daughter Sophia Charlotte, queen in Prussia, I made the following observations:

> As Strickland rightly points out, the correspondence has one very important dimension. . . . For nowhere else in Leibniz's corpus do we find Leibniz as concerned to press the practical importance of his conclusions about the nature of reality and the proper conception of our relation to God. The contentment that should arise from believing in the justice of a God who has created us as members of the best of all possible worlds is clearly offered as a way of life rather than as an abstract theory. There may well be a PhD thesis or book in the waiting for someone who works closely with these texts and others to explore Leibniz's philosophy as way of life. (Lodge 2012, 181)

Since 2012, I have written papers on Leibniz's views on damnation and mysticism, Leibniz's ultimate justification for the principle of sufficient reason, and most recently an introduction to Leibniz's book the *Theodicy* (see Lodge 2015; 2017; 2018; forthcoming). A recurrent theme in these essays has been that a proper understanding of Leibniz's views requires a focus on Leibniz's practical concerns. None of them, however, is a direct engagement with my suggestion in my 2012 review that someone explore Leibniz's philosophy as a way of life, nor do I know of a place where that

Philosophy as a Way of Life: Historical, Contemporary, and Pedagogical Perspectives.
Edited by James M. Ambury, Tushar Irani, and Kathleen Wallace.

Published 2021 by John Wiley & Sons Ltd.

line of thought has been explored independently of my suggestion. This essay is an initial step in that direction.

While I didn't mention Pierre Hadot (1922–2010) explicitly in my review, the choice of language was not accidental. I had read *Philosophy as a Way of Life* (Hadot 2002) not long before I wrote it. Furthermore, in a way that clearly resonates with others who encounter that book for the first time, it had left me with the sense of having been given a phrase with which to express something obvious and yet seemingly novel, namely, that there is a philosophical way of living, and that we should regard at least some of the "great philosophers" as having conceived of their lives in that way and as having attempted to make that way of living available to others.

Hadot's own focus was mainly on philosophers of antiquity. But Hadot also gives voice to his sense that much of what passed for philosophy during his professional lifetime was not of this kind. While this is clearly an oversimplification, it also has an air of truth, at least when we restrict our attention to much of the Anglophone philosophy that has been produced since the beginning of the twentieth century. Furthermore, I think it is hard to deny that this has cast an unhelpful shadow over the way in which the work of some figures in the history of modern philosophy has been taken up during that time. And it is my contention that Leibniz has been one of the primary victims.

My main concern in this essay is to make a preliminary case for the thesis that Leibniz conceived of his philosophy as a way of life. I include brief discussions of a number of the central components of that philosophy. I do not spell out the Leibnizian way of life out in any detail, since I do not yet have those details organized in the right way. In part encouraged by a referee for this collection, however, who noted that the essay "offers a surprising and potentially illuminating central proposal," it seems to me that the public provision of a manifesto and initial road map at this point is a worthwhile endeavour.

I begin by saying something more about why I think the essay might be seen to make "a surprising . . . proposal." Then I provide a summary of Hadot's account of what it is for philosophy to be a way of life. With Hadot's account in place, the remainder of the essay offers a sketch of how Leibniz measures up against Hadot's criteria. It may be that some readers will be a little disappointed by the lack of detail at this point, but I hope that the essay will prove valuable for most.

While the expression "philosophy as a way of life" now has a life of its own, it seems to me that it is worth starting my road map with Hadot. This is partly because he remains a relatively obscure thinker, and I think it is worth trying to expose his ideas to a wider audience. But, more important, Hadot provides a detailed set of criteria that give concrete expression to the generic sense that one can live philosophically. And these criteria allow the existential elements in Leibniz's philosophy to come readily into view.

It may be that these criteria will serve as a ladder that can be thrown away if the manifesto is taken up. Indeed, it may also be the case that consideration of Leibniz's philosophy as a way of life in Hadot's sense will lead to a rethinking of the adequacy of Hadot's account. Nonetheless, I think it is a useful ladder for now.

1. Common Conceptions of Leibniz's Philosophy

The bulk of this essay is concerned with Hadot and the positive case for thinking of Leibniz's philosophy as a way of life. I want to begin, however, by returning to the apparent novelty of this claim and reflect a little on why it gives this appearance. The comments like those from my referee are still somewhat unexpected to me. The reaction I have received from colleagues and students, however, when suggesting that Leibniz's philosophy has existential concerns at its heart has often been one of surprise as well. Indeed, when presenting a version of the present essay at a recent history of philosophy conference, around half of the audience raised their hands when I asked whether this was their reaction.[1]

Just why people are surprised is unclear. It could be that some think of Leibniz as the kind of grandiose thinker who falls foul of Kierkegaard's accusation: "In relation to their systems, most systematisers are like a man who builds an enormous castle and lives in a shack beside it" (1938, 156). I suspect, however, that the explanation is often more mundane, namely, the fact that Leibniz is not generally regarded as someone who engaged with ethics in his philosophy at all. And the reasons for this are easier to discern.

Exposure to Leibniz's philosophy, in the Anglophone world at least, is usually available only in the context of university courses in early modern philosophy that are devoted to issues in "theoretical philosophy," that is, metaphysics, epistemology, and logic broadly construed. This is, in turn, an artefact of the fact that the history of ethics and the history of political philosophy are generally taught separately from the history of theoretical philosophy, and the fact that Leibniz never made his way into the mainstream conception of the canon in the history of ethics and political philosophy.[2] Furthermore, the fact that Leibniz's practical philosophy has been largely absent from the classroom has had a knock-on effect, namely, that the standard collections to which those taking courses on Leibniz have access are ones in which pieces concerned with metaphysics, epistemology, and logic predominate—here I am thinking primarily of the collections

[1] Hadot himself suggests that there are figures in the modern era who "rediscovered . . . some of the existential aspects of ancient philosophy" (PWL 271). Even he misses out Leibniz, however. Among seventeenth- and eighteenth-century philosophers, Descartes and Spinoza are the only ones he mentions (271).

[2] It is interesting to note, however, that John Rawls's course at Harvard, which was later published as *Lectures on the History of Moral Philosophy*, included a lengthy discussion of Leibniz (Rawls 2000, 104–42).

edited by G. H. R. Parkinson (PW) and by Roger Ariew and Daniel Garber (AG).[3]

It does not take much effort to see that this lens is highly distorting. Two of Leibniz's most famous pieces both have as their denouement an account of what the good life consists in (see the *Discourse on Metaphysics,* secs. 35–37 [A VI iv, 1584–88/AG 66–68], and *Monadology,* secs. 82–90 [GP VI, 621–22/AG 223–24]); and works such as the *Theodicy* are saturated with ethical concerns (Lodge forthcoming). Moreover, in another of Leibniz's major writings—*New Essays on Human Understanding*—which is a dialogue between characters representing the views of Locke and Leibniz, respectively, Theophilus (the stand-in for Leibniz) declares: "You had more to do with speculative philosophers, while I was more inclined towards moral questions" (NE 71). Finally, ethical concerns come to the fore in other collections of Leibniz's writings, including *Leibniz: Philosophical Papers and Letters* (L), the general selection used by more advanced students, *Leibniz: Political Writings* (POL), and *Leibniz on God and Religion* (LGR). But first impressions are crucial, of course.

Another potential obstacle to conceiving of Leibniz in the Hadot mould comes in the form that appeared in an essay by a graduate student that I read recently, which included a sentence that began: "As a Christian. . . ." While hard evidence might be difficult to locate, my sense is that, to the extent that most people entertain thoughts about the more practical sides of his thought, they take Leibniz to be little more than an apologist for a version of Christianity. Indeed, scholars such as C. W. Russell in the nineteenth century and Maria Rosa Antognazza in the twenty-first have sought to argue explicitly for such a view (see Russell 1841, 429, and Antognazza 2007).

It is an interesting question whether there is really any problem with the idea that Christianity could be a philosophical way of life. Hadot himself gives reasons for thinking that there is a tension, although he is willing to talk of Christian philosophy. In a move that might surprise some readers, however, he does not locate this in the fact that Christianity involves "the explanation of sacred texts" or the fact that it is "based on revelation" (2002, 240). This is because he contends that "within Greek philosophy as well, there existed an entire tradition of systematic theology inaugurated by Plato's *Timaeus* and the tenth book of the *Laws,* and developed in book twelve of Aristotle's *Metaphysics*" and that "this tradition distinguished the various sources of revelation and the different modes of action of divine reality" (240). Instead he draws attention to the fact that, unlike philosophical ways of life, Christian life—the paradigmatic form of which for Hadot is monastic life—"always presupposed the help and grace of God, as well as the fundamental disposition of humility" (248). Christianity does not rely solely on human therapeutic techniques for its transformation of human

[3] A list of abbreviations of primary works is provided in the References section below.

nature. It may well involve techniques for the "renunciation of one's will" (248), but this can only yield the *hope* of salvic transformation. The transformation itself also requires divine intervention that is essentially mediated by a relationship with Jesus. How might this fit with Leibniz?

A full case for my view would be an essay unto itself. Popular conceptions notwithstanding, however, the writings of Leibniz suggest an interpretation that would circumvent any perceived tension between his Christianity and regarding his philosophy as a way of life. For according this interpretation Leibniz wasn't a Christian in any conventional sense at all—at least towards the end of his life.[4]

Let me for now briefly outline some of the key pieces of evidence for this claim. One is biographical, namely, the fact that Leibniz had earned the nickname "Glaubenichts" ("believes in nothing") in his hometown of Hanover by the time he died, partly due to his infrequent attendance at his local Lutheran church (see LGR 10 n. 46). A second consideration arises when one notices that the *Monadology*, a late work that gives the appearance of being a résumé of Leibniz's philosophy, speaks openly of God, but does not include any mention of Jesus, in the closing sections, which are concerned with moral and political issues (see secs. 84–90, GP VI, 621–22/AG 223–25). But more striking is the preface to Leibniz's 1710 publication, the *Theodicy.*

Leibniz begins the preface with the claim that "sound piety," which he also calls "light and virtue," though not widespread, is something that has been "imitated" in the "formularies of belief and ceremonies" of religion. He goes on to express positive views about Moses, before referring to "Jesus Christ, divine founder of the purest and most enlightened religion" (GP VI, 25/H 49). All that Jesus is said to have done, however, is to have successfully propagated to the masses the truth of an essential dogma of the religion that Leibniz favours, namely, the dogma of personal immortality. Along with a monotheism that ascribed the traditional attributes of omnipotence, omniscience, and omnibenevolence to the ground of reality, Leibniz suggests that immortality was already taught esoterically among some adherents to Judaism. Jesus is said to be "divine" (GP VI, 25/H 49), but there is no talk of the incarnation, and it is tempting to see the word "divine" as indicating nothing more than the fact that Jesus's life, like Moses's, was a special gift from God.

Of course, it is not the case that theological commitments disappear from Leibniz's philosophy. Indeed, the *Theodicy* is in part an extended

[4]A number of scholars have tried to make the case that Leibniz was not a Christian in quite different ways. For example, see Macdonald Ross (1993), Brown (2001), Hunt (2003), Coudert (1995). The difficulty of determining the basis for making the assessment was brought home to me in conversation with the Leibniz scholar Robert Adams, who noted that at the founding of the Society for Christian Philosophers it was ultimately decided that what was required to count as a Christian philosopher was simply that one self-identify as a "follower of Jesus."

argument that allows one to take seriously the claim that the universe was created by a God whose nature comprises the traditional attributes. But this is all a matter of natural theology rather than revelation (Lodge forthcoming). And, as we have seen Hadot point out, a commitment to a form of theism leaves Leibniz happily in the company of many other philosophers who were clearly not Christians.

2. Hadot's Conception of Philosophy as a Way of Life

I want to turn next to the ideas that are involved in the conception of philosophy as a way of life that is particular to Hadot's work. Given that Hadot discusses elements of this conception across numerous writings, this is not a straightforward task. A key source is the essay entitled "Philosophy as a Way of Life" in the volume of translations of Hadot's writings that appeared in English under that title. But the themes of that essay are repeated many times elsewhere. A proper account would therefore require more careful exploration of Hadot's writings than I shall be able to undertake here. But for present purposes, I take the essay "Philosophy as a Way of Life" (which I refer to as "PWL" to distinguish it from Hadot's thesis) as the canonical statement of Hadot's view and draw on his other writings only occasionally.

2.1. Philosophy as a Way of Life: An Outline

PWL begins with a long quote from Philo of Alexandria's *On the Special Laws*, which dates from around the beginning of the Common Era. According to Hadot, "one of the fundamental aspects of philosophy in the Hellenistic and Roman eras comes clearly to the forefront [in this work]. During this period, philosophy was a *way of life*" (PWL 265). Hadot goes on to suggest that "for the ancients, the mere word *philosophia*—the love of wisdom—was enough to express this conception of philosophy" (265), fleshing this conception out, along with examples from figures from various philosophical schools, as follows: "This is not only to say that [philosophy] was a specific type of moral conduct. . . . Rather it means that philosophy was a mode of existing-in-the-world, which had to be practiced at each instant, and the goal of which was to transform the whole of the individual's life" (265). We can see four elements in Hadot's characterization of Hellenistic and Roman philosophy here. It

1. is a "type of moral conduct";
2. is a "mode of existing-in-the-world";
3. must be "practised at each instant"; and
4. "has a goal," namely, "to transform the whole of an individual's life" (265).

Soon after Hadot adds a fifth:

5. "[philosophy] presented itself as a therapeutic, intended to cure mankind's anguish" (265–66).

And in order to complete the picture, Hadot also characterises wisdom itself—as opposed to the love of wisdom—as having the following three features. It

6. brings "peace of mind (*ataraxia*)" (PWL 265);
7. brings "inner freedom (*autarkeia*)" (265), later glossed as "that state in which the ego depends only on itself" (266); and
8. brings "a cosmic consciousness" (265–66), later glossed as "the consciousness that we are part of the cosmos and consequent dilation of our self throughout the infinity of universal nature" (266).

2.2. Philosophy and Discourse About Philosophy

With his conception of philosophy as a way of life in place, Hadot adds another distinction that is central to his work, which he attributes to the Stoics, namely, the distinction between "discourse about philosophy" and "philosophy itself" (PWL 266). On Hadot's reading, for the Stoics "the parts of philosophy—physics, ethics, and logic—were not, in fact, parts of philosophy itself, but rather parts of philosophical *discourse*" (266–67). The key issue here is: "[W]hen it comes to teaching philosophy, it is necessary to set forth a theory of logic, a theory of physics, and a theory of ethics. . . . But philosophy itself—that is, the philosophical way of life—is no longer a theory divided into parts, but a unitary act which consists in *living* logic, physics, and ethics" (267). It is natural to wonder at this point how one should conceive of the relationship between the teaching and living of philosophy, and how one might move from understanding the content of philosophical discourse to living it. Hadot himself asks the rhetorical question: "Does the philosophical life, then, consist only in the application, at every moment, of well-studied theorems, in order to resolve life's problems?" (268). The answer is, perhaps unsurprisingly, no. More precisely, we are told: "As a matter of fact, when we reflect on what the philosophical life implies, we realise that there is an abyss between philosophical theory and philosophizing as living action. To take a similar case: it may seem as though artists, in their creative activity, do nothing but apply rules, but there is an immeasurable distance between artistic creation and the abstract theory of art" (268). With philosophy the goal "is to transform ourselves" rather than "the mere creation of a work of art" (268). Nonetheless, Hadot wants us to understand the role of theory and practice as analogous. While he does not quite put it this way, the thought seems to be as follows: In both cases one begins by being taught the rules; this is followed by a process of internalising the rules through practice, and the eventual outcome is creating art/living in a way that accords with the rules but does not depend on attempting to self-consciously follow them.

2.3. Spiritual Exercises

At this point in PWL the final piece in Hadot's picture comes into view, namely, the claim that the philosophy of the schools of the ancient world involved the use of "spiritual exercises" (PWL 269). Hadot does not elaborate on this idea much in PWL. It is, however, explored at length in other essays, including "Spiritual Exercises" and "Ancient Spiritual Exercises and 'Christian Philosophy,'" which both appear in the *Philosophy as a Way of Life* volume (in Hadot 1995, 79–144), and "Philosophy and Philosophical Discourse," which is in the volume *What Is Ancient Philosophy?* (2002, 172–233).[5]

In "Philosophical Discourse as Spiritual Exercises," an interview with Arnold Davidson from 2001, Hadot makes the following remark: "I would define *spiritual exercises* as voluntary, personal practices meant to bring about a transformation of the individual, a transformation of the self" (Hadot 2009, 87). As we learn in the introduction to *What Is Ancient Philosophy?* Hadot suggests that the scope of these practices is wider than one might otherwise imagine: "By [spiritual exercises], I mean practices which could be physical, as in dietary regimes, or discursive, as in dialogue and meditation, or intuitive, as in contemplation. . . . The philosophy teacher's discourse could also assume the form of a spiritual exercise, if the discourse were presented in such a way that the auditor, reader, or interlocutor, could make spiritual progress and transform himself within" (2002, 6). Hadot expands on his understanding of the expression "spiritual practice" at length in the essays mentioned above, with examples from various figures and traditions in Greek and Roman philosophy. Furthermore, in the essay "Philosophy and Philosophical Discourse" he provides a complex account that divides the exercises into three broad categories with subdivisions according to the aspects of the philosophical life that they are supposed to enhance. But again, given my present purposes, I shall rest with this basic outline.

3. Leibniz's Conception of Philosophy

I want now to turn to issues that are more directly related to the overall case I want to make, beginning with what Leibniz himself has to say about the nature of philosophy.

[5]Hadot's suggestion that such exercises were constitutive of ancient philosophy has proved contentious. I shall not enter the debate on the issue here, however. For critical discussion, see Cooper (2013, 19–23).

Unfortunately, Leibniz does not use the term "philosophy" in such a way that its meaning is made transparent. He regularly refers to people as "philosophers," but not in such a way that it is evident why they all fall under this category. And while Leibniz often employs the noun "philosophy," the term is used in such a way that it appears to mean little more than whatever is done by the people whom he calls "philosophers." Thus, although there is a sense in which Leibniz thinks philosophy is a "mode of existing-in-the-world," it clearly does not bring with it the kind of commitments that Hadot demands.

In one of his most prominent journal publications, the "New System" from 1695, Leibniz observes: "In philosophy we must try to give reasons by showing how things are brought about by divine wisdom, but in conformity with the notion of the subject in question" (GP IV, 483–84/AG 143), and the idea that philosophy is connected with the use of reason is present in other writings. For example, in the *Theodicy,* where Leibniz expounds at length on the relation between faith and reason, he presents a "thesis" that he claims "philosophy establishes no less than revelation" (part 1, sec. 115/H 186) and another thesis that is described as "purely philosophic, that is, recognizable by the light of natural reason" (part 1, sec. 114/H 185). Thus, it seems that Leibniz regards philosophy as a discipline that employs human reason.

Leibniz also offers, however, a conception of wisdom throughout his writings, which helps flesh things out more, namely, that wisdom is "the science of happiness" (see, e.g., A VI iv, 2798/LGR 138; LTS 167, 169; GP III, 387/L 422; L 425), or as he qualifies it in an essay usually referred to as "On Wisdom," wisdom is "that science which teaches us to achieve happiness" (GP VII, 86/L 425). Given this, I would like to suggest that there is something in Leibniz's writing that could plausibly be regarded as constituting his view of what it is to be a philosopher, or "lover of wisdom," which can be equated with being a pursuer of the knowledge of happiness through the use of reason.

With this account in place, there is more that can be said. "Happiness," which is on at least one occasion equated with "tranquillity of the soul" (A VI iii, 668/LST 166), receives a somewhat equivocal treatment, but there is a common theme. Thus it is said to be a "a lasting state of pleasure" (LST 167), "durable joy" (A VI iv, 2798/LGR 138), or "a state of permanent joy" (GP VII, 86/L 425), where "joy" is understood to be "a pleasure which the soul feels in itself" (GP VII, 86/L 425); or, in a more detailed account, "an impression *of pleasures*, that is a sense of present pleasures, a recollection of past pleasures and a hope of future pleasures" (A VI iv, 2798/LGR 138). Finally, "pleasure" is a state that is intentional and consists in "the feeling of a perfection or an excellence, whether in ourselves or something else" (GP VII, 86/L 425; also see A VI iv, 2798/LGR 138), though Leibniz is also willing to admit a more sophisticated kind of pleasure, which involves not just a feeling but also "knowledge of perfection" (LST 167).

These quotes might seem to suggest a rather implausible view, on which happiness involves a constant positive feeling. But another passage from "On Wisdom" is a little more nuanced and can probably be regarded as employing Leibniz's considered view: "The happy man does not, it is true, feel this joy at every instant for he sometimes rests from his contemplation, and usually also turns his thoughts to practical affairs. But it is enough that he is in a *state* to feel joy whenever he wishes to think of it and that at other times there is a joyousness in his actions and his nature which arises from this" (GP VII, 86/L 425).

The considerations above suggest that Leibniz took the philosopher to be a person concerned with the kinds of things that are at the heart of philosophy as Hadot conceives it. But it still leaves us at some distance from an account of Leibniz's view of philosophy that satisfies the criteria for Leibniz regarding it as a way of life in Hadot's sense. In the rest of this essay I consider, in turn, whether Leibniz is one who simply provides what Hadot calls "discourse about philosophy," how his views square with the criteria that I isolated in Hadot's work, and whether there is any scope for thinking that Leibniz recommended spiritual exercises.

4. Leibniz, Philosophy, and Philosophical Discourse

We have seen that Hadot wants to distinguish philosophy from what he calls "philosophical discourse," where the latter is something that makes theoretical claims about philosophical matters independently of a concern with what it would be to live out a life that internalised those claims. Hadot's view is that much Western philosophy from the Middle Ages onwards should be regarded as a form of philosophical discourse, and there is still a question of whether what Leibniz wrote is merely philosophical discourse.

Prima facie evidence to the contrary comes from one of the earliest of Leibniz's writings, the *Dissertation on the Combinatorial Art* of 1666, in which Leibniz suggests that theory and praxis should not be conceived independently (see A VI i, 229). Indeed, the slogan "theoria cum praxi" has been presented as a motto that Leibniz himself adopted.[6] But, of course, such a slogan is consistent with a more modern conception of the way in which theories might be related to human activity, namely, as instrumentally valuable accounts of the nature of reality. While this is not entirely divorced from the living of a good life, it clearly lacks the kind of existential immediacy that Hadot intends. This is not all we have to go on, however.

One interesting line of thinking, which I shall only mention in passing here, is connected with an argument put forward by Ansgar Lyssy in "'Theoria cum Praxi' Revisited—Leibniz on 'Dangerous' Philosophers"

[6] For example, the Third International Leibniz-Kongress in 1977 was entitled "Theoria cum praxi."

(2016). Lyssy traces the ways in which Leibniz took the theoretical writings of others such as Hobbes and Spinoza to pose a threat on the grounds that problematic modes of life would follow for those who took the claims seriously. The critique that Leibniz offers here implies that there might be better writings to be had, namely, his own, where better is to be cashed out in terms of a preferred mode of existing.

We also find more direct evidence of the way in which the reflections Leibniz offers on the doctrines he presents is accompanied by reflections on a living out of those ideas. In the *Theodicy* and elsewhere, he provides explicit comparisons between his goals and the kind of tranquillity that is the aim of Stoicism, and claims superiority (see Rutherford 2001). But I also want to mention two other striking examples.

The first appears in conjunction with Leibniz's conception of substance in the *New Essays*. "It should be borne in mind that matter, understood as a complete being . . . is nothing but an aggregate or the result of one; and that any real aggregate presupposes simple substances or real unities. If one also bears in mind what constitutes the nature of those real entities, namely perception and its consequences, one is transported into another world, so to speak: from having existed entirely amongst the phenomena of the senses, one comes to occupy the intelligible world of substances" (NE 378). I return to the details of Leibniz's metaphysical claims here later. For now, I simply want to draw attention to the fact that the passage includes the suggestion that exposure to theoretical consideration of the nature of matter and substances will lead the persons using those concepts to come to understand themselves as a substance so conceived. And the kind of understanding that is at issue is articulated in terms of "occupying [a] world" in which one falls under the theoretical concept.

The second piece of evidence draws primarily on the preface to the *Theodicy*. Here Leibniz presents his conception of justice as wise charity and combines it with the claim that the wisest charity is that which is directed towards God, given that God is the most perfect being and thus the most liable to generate happiness in those who love him. Crucial in all of this is the additional doctrine that we ourselves have an innate idea of God. For, in so far as we have the idea of God, we are intentionally directed toward God's perfection and have at least the potential to love God (see GP VI, 26–27/H 50–51). In another piece, "On the True Mystical Theology," Leibniz makes it clear that the enlivening of this idea as we become aware of it will bring love of its object (see LGR 80–84). And in the preface to the *Theodicy* he draws explicit attention to the existential significance of this:

> This kind of love gives birth to that pleasure in good actions which highlights virtue, and, returning all to God as to the centre, transports the human to the divine. For in doing one's duty, in obeying reason, one carries out the orders of the Supreme Reason. One directs all one's intentions to the common good, which is no different to the glory of God; one finds that there is no greater individual

interest than to take up the common interest, and one gains satisfaction for oneself by taking pleasure in the acquisition of true benefits for men. Whether one succeeds or not, one is content with what happens, being resigned to the will of God and knowing that what he wills is best. (GP VI, 27–28/H 51–52)[7]

Interesting as they are, I don't want to dwell on the content of these claims here. My reason for presenting them in this section is that they again show Leibniz offering his views not as philosophical discourse but to be lived in the sense that Hadot suggests was true of Stoic logic, physics, and ethics.

5. Leibniz and Hadot's Conception of Philosophy as a Way of Life

Earlier in this essay, I sketched my understanding of Hadot's particular conception of philosophy as a way of life. I want now to reflect on the extent to which Leibniz's views fall under that conception, partly by drawing on the resources I have presented above.

As I have interpreted Hadot, the word "philosophy" carries with it a number of connotations—eight in total. On the assumption that Leibniz is offering more than philosophical discourse, what we have seen so far allows us to tick off some of Hadot's criteria. I am going to set aside criterion (7) above, that is, the claim that philosophy brings "inner freedom" (PWL 266). While I think what Leibniz says satisfies this criterion, the complications that attend the notion of freedom that he favours render the task of showing this impossible given current space constraints.[8] It is worth noting, however, that Leibniz would not agree with Hadot's suggestion that freedom is "that state in which the ego depends only on itself" (266). But a preliminary case for the remaining criteria seems manageable.

Leibniz's philosophy can surely be said to "ha[ve] a goal," namely, to deliver knowledge of happiness, and there is no obvious reason to think this goal is not intended to "transform the whole of an individual's life" (PWL 265). Thus, it satisfies criterion (4). In addition, the conception of happiness that Leibniz offers makes it clear that philosophy is supposed to bring (6) "peace of mind (*ataraxia*)" (265), and it looks as though this suffices for regarding Leibniz as having a conception of philosophy that satisfies Hadot's criterion (5), according to which philosophy is "a therapeutic, intended to cure mankind's anguish" (265–66).

Leibniz's writings also seem to provide evidence for (1), that his philosophy is a "type of moral conduct" (PWL 265) and (2) is a "mode of existing-in-the-world" (PWL 265). Consider an observation that Leibniz makes in

[7] While the *Theodicy* dates from 1710, more condensed statements of the same kinds of ideas can be found much earlier in Leibniz's career, e.g., in the *Confessio Philosophi*, which was written in 1672–73 (see A VI iii, 141/CP 89).

[8] For a useful introduction to Leibniz's views on human freedom, see Jolley (2005, chap. 5); and see Seidler (1985) for a discussion that presents many texts that would be required for a proper treatment of this issue.

the preface to his *Codex Juris Gentium*, a collection of medieval writings that he published in 1693 designed to support claims of the Holy Roman Empire against the French. After defining "Right" as "a kind of moral power" and "obligation" as "moral necessity," Leibniz adds: "[B]y *moral* . . . I mean something equivalent to natural for a good man" (GP III, 386/L 421). This allows us to see that, for Leibniz, philosophy is a "type of moral conduct." The quick version of why this is the case is to be found via the way that Leibniz characterizes justice, the virtue that constitutes what it is to be "a good man." Throughout his writings, including the preface to the *Codex Juris Gentium*, Leibniz tells us that "we define justice . . . as the charity of the wise man" (GP III, 386/L 421; also see A VI iv, 2798/LGR 137; LST 163). Thus, to be good and to be one who has successfully pursued wisdom are coextensive, and to be a philosopher one must also be a good person, or one who engages in moral conduct. On the assumption that this is the case, (2) follows. For wisdom, as component of justice, is a "mode of existing-in-the-world" (PWL 265).

To address (8) properly, that is, the claim that philosophy brings "a cosmic consciousness" (PWL 265–66), or "the consciousness that we are part of the cosmos and consequent dilation of our self throughout the infinity of universal nature" (266), would require a detailed exploration of Leibniz's anthropology and cosmology. For now, I want to make two points. Earlier in the essay, I introduced a passage from the *New Essays* as evidence that Leibniz is in the business of providing not just philosophical discourse but also a "lived physics." Part of what that passage suggests is that when understanding ourselves properly, we come to inhabit the conception of ourselves as entities whose nature includes "perception and its consequences" (NE 378). There is much more to be said here, but Leibniz is committed to the idea that for substances to perceive is for them to "express" the entire universe from a unique perspective. And while he does not think that what is expressed can ever be transparently available to any of us, he does hold that we can come to understand that we are in such a state.[9] In other words, we acquire a kind of cosmic consciousness.

The issue of "dilation" is addressed in a piece that has come to be called "Leibniz's philosophical dream." Here Leibniz describes a process of being guided to enlightenment through the power of reason, which includes the following characterization of the perception of an enlightened rational being, along with some of its consequences:

> I saw at a distance what I only wanted to consider in general; yet when I studied some spot in a determined way, it at once grew and I needed no other telescopic vision than my own attention to see it as though it were next to me. This gave me a marvelous pleasure and emboldened me to say to my guide: "Mighty spirit—for I cannot doubt that you are of the number of those celestial figures who

[9] For a helpful discussion of this thesis see Sleigh (1990, 170–80).

make up the court surrounding the sovereign of the universe—since you have wanted to clarify so my eyes, will you do as much for my mind?" It seemed to me that he smiled at this speech and took pleasure in hearing of my desire. "Your wish is granted," he said to me, "since you hold wisdom above the pleasure of those vain spectacles the world presents to your eyes. However, you will lose nothing that is substantial in those same spectacles. You will see everything with eyes clarified in a completely different way. Your understanding being fortified from above, it will discover everywhere the brilliant illumination of the divine author of things.[10]

This leaves (3), the claim that philosophy must be "practised at each instant." Evidence for this is harder to find. Leibniz does suggest at one point that wisdom is "to be studied above everything else" (LST 167). But the only place I have discovered in which there is a direct indication of something like the need for ongoing pursuit of wisdom is a letter to André Morrell from 1696. Here Leibniz has drawn attention to the work of Friedrich von Spee. Leibniz often recommended Spee's book *Güldenes Tugend-Buch* (Cologne, 1646) as a manual which would help people acquire the virtue of "true piety," from which love of God above all things follows, and which is equivalent to Leibniz's conception of justice as wise charity. In this letter he also mentions with approval the fact that Spee "even proposes a nice method for praising God at all moments" (LST 155).[11] While nothing more is said here about what it is to praise, there is scope for thinking that to praise God requires one to be philosophical in the extended sense that has emerged through consideration of the relation between Leibniz's views and Hadot's criteria. But even if this account of criterion (3) is too tenuous, I hope that I have made a plausible case for thinking that most of what Hadot implies when he offers his summary of what philosophy as a way of life comprises can be thought to apply to Leibniz's work.

6. Leibniz and Spiritual Exercises

I want to end by turning to the other element that Hadot emphasises when he suggests that ancient philosophy was a way of life, namely, the employment of "spiritual exercises" (PWL 269). As we saw, Hadot has in mind practices that individuals engage in for the sake of their own transformation. But he also allows that philosophical discourse presented by a teacher in a form that could be used by individuals on their own might do this job.

On Hadot's view, spiritual exercises were undertaken by people who were either living in philosophical communities that embraced a particular

[10] The translation is Donald Rutherford's. See http://philosophyfaculty.ucsd.edu/faculty/rutherford/Leibniz/translations/Dream.pdf

[11] As Irene Backus notes, Leibniz also provided extracts from Spee's *Güldenes Tugend-Buch* to Electress Sophia along with a letter that probably dates from autumn 1697 in which he provides accounts of his key ethical concepts (A I xiv, 54–60/LTS 175–81). See https://ndpr.nd.edu/news/leibniz-and-the-two-sophies-the-philosophical-correspondence/

tradition or committed followers of a given philosophy in Hadot's sense of the term "philosophy." No such devotion to the philosophy of Leibniz existed during his lifetime, and while there are eighteenth-century philosophers who are sometimes identified as Leibnizian, such as Christian Wolff, they do not seem to have been exemplars of the kind Hadot intends. The very thing that alerted me to the possible connections between Leibniz and Hadot seems relevant here, however, namely, the kind of interactions that Leibniz had with Electress Sophia and Queen Sophia Charlotte, as well as with others with whom he met and corresponded. There is again much more work to be done on these issues, including further exploration of hundreds of pieces of correspondence, but I want to point to two things here.

The first is the analysis that we find in Lloyd Strickland's introduction to the correspondence between Leibniz and "the two Sophies." Strickland notes that Leibniz focuses much of the philosophical elements of his letters on two issues: (1) his conception of substance and (2) the material that forms the central ethical components of his *Theodicy*, which Strickland refers to as Leibniz's "philosophy of contentment" (LTS 45). As Strickland points out, Leibniz draws his correspondents' attention to those of his ideas that, if taken up in a lived way, would enable virtue and the happiness that accompanies it. But it is the mode of presentation that is of particular interest, since the letters also contain repeated pithy accounts of the key philosophical concepts in accordance with which the Leibnizian way of life would need to be lived. Furthermore, as Strickland notes, these elements of Leibniz's philosophy are by no means restricted to this correspondence. Strickland points to writings that I have already cited, such as "On Wisdom," but a particularly interesting example is found in an unpublished piece from the late 1670s, from which I have quoted liberally above. This appears in another volume of Strickland's translations, *Leibniz on God and Religion*, where Strickland gives it the title "Aphorisms Concerning Happiness, Wisdom, Charity and Justice" (LGR 137). It consists of a series of definitions of terms that are central to Leibniz's ethics, such as "justice," "charity," "wisdom," "happiness," 'pleasure," and "joy," followed by a series of short propositions concerning God's will and similarly short "theorems concerning wisdom and happiness" (LGR 138–40). The form of writing that we find here is such that the central claims could easily be digested and remembered by anyone whom Leibniz managed to convert to his way of philosophizing.

I don't know of a place in which Leibniz explicitly advocates anything like the repetition and internalization of these kinds of concepts and claims by individual people, although it doesn't seem to be much of a stretch of the imagination to think that he would have hoped that they would have received attention as something quite removed from a set of theoretical claims. Other evidence of his commitment to something like Hadot's spiritual practices can, however, be found in writings in which Leibniz offers suggestions for how we might go about securing virtuous actions.

Among these, the chapter in the *New Essays* concerned with freedom is a particularly perspicuous case. After noting that we have the requisite ideas innately, that is, those of "God, virtue, and happiness" (NE 186), Leibniz suggests that the kind of knowledge we have of them "cannot influence us" and that "something livelier is needed if we are to be moved" (186). We are then given a number of suggestions as to how these ideas might gain the force they need. While the "first step would have to be in education" (NE 187), Leibniz offers another route for "a grown man who missed this" (187), namely, that when "in a good frame of mind he ought to make himself laws and rules for the future, and then carry them out strictly, drawing himself away—abruptly or gradually, depending on the nature of the case—from situations which are capable of corrupting him" (NE 187). He then proceeds to offer some more concrete examples:

> A lover will be cured by a voyage undertaken just for that purpose; a period of seclusion will stop us from keeping company with people who confirm some bad disposition in us. Francisco Borgia, the General of the Jesuits, who has at last been canonized, was given to drinking heavily when he was a member of fashionable society; when he was considering withdrawing from the world, he retrenched gradually to almost nothing, by each day letting a drop of wax fall into the flagon which he was accustomed to drinking dry. To dangerous interests we will oppose innocent ones like farming or gardening; we will avoid idleness, will collect curiosities, both natural and artificial, will carry out experiments and inquiries, will take up some compelling occupation if we do not already have one, or engage in useful and agreeable conversation or reading. (187)

Later in the same chapter, Leibniz turns to another strategy that it appears may still be required by those who have been educated well by others or by themselves. Here the issues concern situations in which inclinations towards just activity might be overwhelmed by more immediate passions.

> [W]hat is required is that the mind be prepared in advance, and be already stepping from thought to thought, so that it will not be too much held up when the path becomes slippery and treacherous. It helps with this if one accustoms oneself in general to touching on certain topics only in passing, the better to preserve one's freedom of mind. Best of all, we should become accustomed to proceeding methodically and sticking to sequences of thoughts for which reason, rather than chance (i.e. insensible and fortuitous impressions), provides the thread. It helps with this if one becomes accustomed to withdrawing into oneself occasionally, rising above the hubbub of present impressions—as it were getting away from one's own situation and asking oneself "Why am I here?", "Where am I going?", "How far have I come?", or saying "I must come to the point, I must set to work!" (NE 196)

In fact, the *New Essays* are by no means unique in this regard. Michael Seidler suggests that although "Leibniz's remarks on this subject are scattered and unsystematic, when gathered they comprise an informal program of practical moral advice that . . . reflects the psychic therapy [*Seelenleitung*] offered by Seneca and his Neostoic disciples" (1985, 24). And Seidler's article provides a useful compendium of examples from across Leibniz's career (see 1985, 25–33; also see Jorati 2017, chap. 6). *Pace* Seidler, though, there is at least one place in which we find a systematic outline of what is described as a "sensible means to arouse one daily" if one is "concerned with [one's] salvation" (A VI iv, 2276/D 191).

The piece in question, which dates from 1679–81, is a fictional dialogue entitled "Conversation Between Father Emery the Hermit and the Marquis of Pinese, Minister of Savoy, Which Has Yielded a Remarkable Change in the Minister's Life, or Dialogue About the Application One Must Have for One's Salvation" (A VI iv, 2245–83/D 169–200). Towards the end of this piece, the character of Father Emery provides the character of the Marquis of Pinese with seven rules that he should follow, the elaboration of which includes such things as: "look for a study companion" (2276/191); "prepare a written project that will serve as a rule for the rest of one's life, which will thereby be reduced to a few major maxims one should always have in sight" (2277/191); "examine oneself every day about the standing of one's project in order to verify what one has missed and what one has achieved" (2277/192); "keep a record of everything that may be useful" by having "a diary notebook of passed things, a reminder-notebook of future things or things to do, handy sheets of paper for writing down quickly whatever memorable thing pops up in reading, in conversation, in work, or in meditation" (2277/192); and "one must look for all imaginable skills in order to moderate the passions, which can disturb the use of reason" (2277/192). At one point, Leibniz adds that it would "be practical to have an Enchiridion or handbook, where the most important pieces of knowledge we need would be marked" (2277/192), even suggesting that "since there are things one must know by heart, one could assure this by means of verse—for which purpose the burlesque would be particularly appropriate" (2277/192). The "Conversation" provides a schema for spiritual exercises rather than a set of spiritual exercises. Nevertheless, it shows us that, albeit in the context of a fictional dialogue, Leibniz was committed to the idea of a regimen of spiritual exercises. And with such a schema in mind, we are well placed to use the more disparate material to construct a more detailed account of the kinds of spiritual exercises that were part of Leibniz's philosophy conceived as a way of life.

7. Conclusion

As I noted at the beginning of this essay, my intentions have been to provide an initial road map for further elaboration of what it would be to conceive of Leibniz's philosophy as a way of life. My hope is that, by looking at Leibniz through the lens of Hadot's work, I have shown that there are reasons for thinking that such an approach might be productive—whether Hadot himself is ultimately the most useful guide or not.

But I want to end with two further reflections. Although I have focussed on Leibniz, I also hope the discussion might encourage people to consider the extent to which it might be illuminating to think similarly about more recent philosophers whose work is not usually taken to be existentially motivated. How does the philosophy of W. V. O. Quine or David Lewis, for example, look if understood as "a way of life"? And what should our attitude be towards philosophers whose work cannot be conceived in such a way?

Finally, while I have not spelled out the content of Leibniz's views in enough detail at this point, I want to suggest that reflection on what it would be to have a lived version of those views might provide the basis for developing a neo-Leibnizian approach to twenty-first-century life. Leibniz himself might well have welcomed such an attempt, given the recent emergence of a cottage industry in guides to living a Stoic existence of the kind that he vehemently opposed.[12] But one can only wonder what kinds of opposing strategies he might have endorsed on noticing resources available to his Stoic opponents, such as the webpage https://dailystoic.com/, which features the work of Ryan Holiday along with the opportunity to buy merchandise like the memento mori signet ring and a variety of medallions, pendants, and prints of sages.

Acknowledgments

Many thanks for helpful comments on an earlier version of this essay go to Bob Adams, Åsne Grøgaard, Julia Jorati, Jeff McDonough, Katherine O'Donnell, Paul Solman, and audiences at University College Dublin, and the conference *Philosophy as a Way of Life in the History of Philosophy* at King's College London. I would also like to thank my brother Richard for the copy of *Philosophy as a Way of Life* that introduced me to the work of Pierre Hadot in the first place.

References

Abbreviations of Primary Texts

A: *Samtliche Schriften und Briefe*, edited by Deutsche Akademie der Wissenschaften. 8 series, each divided into multiple volumes. Berlin: Akademie, 1923–. Cited by series, volume, and page.

AG: *Leibniz: Philosophical Writings*. Edited and translated by R. Ariew and D. Garber. Indianapolis: Hackett, 1989.

12 The authors of these books range from academics such as William Irvine (2009), John Sellars (2019), and Massimo Pigliucci (2017), through those without such affiliations, such as Ryan Holiday and Stephen Hanselman (2016) and Nils Salzgeber (2019).

D: G. W. *Leibniz: The Art of Controversies*. Edited and translated by M. Dascal with Q. Racionero and A. Cardoso. Dordrecht: Springer, 2008.

GP: *Die philosophischen Schriften von Gottfried Wilhelm Leibniz*. Edited by C. I. Gerhardt. 7 vols. Berlin: Weidman, 1875–90. Reprinted Hildesheim: Olms, 1978. Cited by volume and page.

H: *Theodicy*. Translated by E. Huggard. Indianapolis: Open Court, 1985. Cited by part and section, other than the preface, where references to GP are employed.

L: *Gottfried Wilhelm Leibniz: Philosophical Papers and Letters*. 2nd edition. Edited and translated by L. Loemker. Dordrecht: Reidel, 1969.

LGR: *Leibniz on God and Religion*. Edited and translated by L. Strickland. London: Bloomsbury, 2016.

LST: *The Shorter Leibniz Texts*. Edited and translated by L. Strickland. London: Continuum, 2006.

LTS: *Leibniz and the Two Sophies*. Edited and translated by L. Strickland. Toronto: Centre for Reformation and Renaissance Studies, 2011.

NE: *New Essays on Human Understanding*. 2nd edition. Translated by P. Remnant and J. Bennett. Cambridge: Cambridge University Press, 1996. Page numbers from NE are identical with those in A VI, of which it is a partial translation.

POL: *Leibniz: Political Writings*. 2nd edition. Edited and translated by P. Riley. Cambridge: Cambridge University Press, 1988.

PW: *Gottfried Wilhelm Leibniz: Philosophical Writings*. Edited by G. H. R. Parkinson, translated by M. Morris and G. H. R. Parkinson. Everyman: London, 1973.

Secondary Texts

Antognazza, M. R. 2007. *Leibniz on the Trinity and Incarnation*. New Haven: Yale University Press.

Brown, S. 2001. "The Regularization of Providence in Post-Cartesian Philosophy." In *Religion, Reason, and Nature in Early Modern Europe*, edited by R. Crocker, 1–16. Dordrecht: Kluwer.

Cooper, J. 2013. *Pursuits of Wisdom*. Princeton: Princeton University Press.

Coudert, A. 1995. *Leibniz and the Kabbalah*. Dordrecht: Kluwer.

Hadot, P. 1995. *Philosophy as a Way of Life*. Oxford: Blackwell.

________. 2002. *What Is Ancient Philosophy?* Cambridge, Mass.: Harvard University Press.

________. 2009. *The Present Alone Is Our Happiness*. Palo Alto, Calif.: Stanford University Press.

Holiday, R., and S. Hanselman. 2016. *The Daily Stoic: 366 Meditations on Wisdom, Perseverance, and the Art of Living: Featuring New Translations of Seneca, Epictetus, and Marcus Aurelius*. London: Profile Books.

Hunt, S. D. 2003. *Controversy in Marketing Theory: For Reason, Realism, Truth and Objectivity*. New York: M. E. Sharpe.

Irvine, W. 2009. *A Guide to the Good Life: The Ancient Art of Stoic Joy*. Oxford: Oxford University Press.

Jolley, N. 2005. *Leibniz*. London: Routledge.

Jorati, J. 2017. *Leibniz on Causation and Agency*. Cambridge: Cambridge University Press.

Kiergegaard, S. 1938. *Journals of Søren Kierkegaard*. Translated by A. Dru. Oxford: Oxford University Press.

Lodge, P. 2012. Review of *Leibniz and the Two Sophies: The Philosophical Correspondence*, edited and translated by Lloyd Strickland. *Leibniz Review* 22:179–90.

Lodge, P. 2015. "True and False Mysticism in Leibniz." *Leibniz Review* 25:55–87.

Lodge, P. 2017. "Eternal Punishment, Universal Salvation and Pragmatic Theology in Leibniz." In *Universal Genius: Tercentenary Essays on the Philosophy and Science of G. W. Leibniz*, edited by L. Strickland et al., 301–24. London: Palgrave Macmillan.

Lodge, P. 2018. "Leibniz on the 'Justification' for the Principle of Sufficient Reason (Mainly) in the Correspondence with Clarke." *Logical Analysis and History of Philosophy* 21:69–91.

Lodge, P. Forthcoming. "The Theodicy." In *G. W. Leibniz: Key Philosophical Writings*, edited by P. Lodge and L. Strickland. Oxford: Oxford University Press.

Lyssy, A. 2016. "'Theoria cum Praxi' Revisited: Leibniz on 'Dangerous' Philosophers." In *Für unser Glück oder das Glück Anderer: Vorträge des X. Internationalen Leibniz-Kongresses*, edited by W. Li et al., 113–24. Hildesheim: Olms.

Macdonald Ross, G. 1993. "Leibniz and the Origin of Things." In *Leibniz and Adam*, edited by M. Dascal and E. Yakira, 241–57. Tel Aviv: University Publishing Projects.

Pigliucci, M. 2017. *How to Be a Stoic: Ancient Wisdom for Modern Living*. London: Rider Books.

Rawls, J. 2000. *Lectures on the History of Moral Philosophy*. Edited by B. Hermann. Cambridge, Mass.: Harvard University Press.

Russell, C. W. 1841. "Protestant Evidence of Catholicity." *Dublin Review* 10:394–429.

Rutherford, D. 2001. "Leibniz and the Stoics: The Consolation of Theodicy." In *The Problem of Evil in Early Modern Philosophy*, edited by E. Kramer and M. J. Latzer, 138–64. Toronto: University of Toronto Press.

Salzgeber, J. 2019. *The Little Book of Stoicism: Timeless Wisdom to Gain Resilience, Confidence, and Calmness*. E-book available from Amazon.

Seidler, M. 1985. "Freedom and Moral Therapy in Leibniz." *Studia Leibnitiana* XVII, no. 1:15–35.

Sellars, J. 2019. *Lessons in Stoicism*. London: Allen and Lane.

Sleigh, R. C., Jr. 1990. *Leibniz and Arnauld: A Study of Their Correspondence*. New Haven: Yale University Press.

CHAPTER 7

PHILOSOPHY AS A FEMINIST SPIRITUALITY AND CRITICAL PRACTICE FOR MARY ASTELL

SIMONE WEBB

Introduction

There has hitherto been insufficient attention paid to how gender might inflect and affect philosophy as a way of life. Initial questions that spring to mind include: Are philosophical ways of life implicitly gendered? Do women face obstacles to practising philosophical modes of living? Is the philosophical existence desirable for women? Are there specific ways in which women might want to practise philosophy? Can philosophical modes of living function in feminist ways?

It's the last of these questions that I hope to shed some light on in this essay. By looking at how the early modern feminist philosopher Mary Astell (1666–1731) presents philosophy as a practice that can benefit women specifically, suffering as they do from the detrimental effects of sexist societies, I aim to address the potential use of philosophical practice as feminist activity.

My understanding of "philosophy as a way of life" is broad, drawing primarily not from Pierre Hadot (1922–2010) but instead from the later work of Michel Foucault (1926–1984) on practices of the self, care of the self, and philosophy as a spirituality and critical practice. I interpret "philosophy as a way of life" broadly to encompass multiple modes of philosophy beyond rational argumentative discourse, particularly those modes that have a transformative effect on the self.

My contention is that Astell presents philosophy and philosophical thinking as a practice that transforms the woman who undertakes it: a

Philosophy as a Way of Life: Historical, Contemporary, and Pedagogical Perspectives.
Edited by James M. Ambury, Tushar Irani, and Kathleen Wallace.

Published 2021 by John Wiley & Sons Ltd.

practice that forms part of a set of exercises aimed at the care and development of women's selves. She provides a gendered perspective on philosophical modes of living, showing how women stand in greater need of philosophical practices, how they require certain conditions in order to practice philosophy, and how philosophy can function as a Foucauldian-style "critique" of misogynistic conventions. Philosophy for Astell, I argue, acts to challenge structures of sexist domination as well as addressing internalised prejudices against women in a way that contributes to women's freedom and autonomy.

I first introduce Astell and her major philosophical works and positions. Then I touch briefly on the relationship between Hadot and Foucault, and the conception of philosophy as a way of life that I am using. I identify four key elements of Foucault's model of philosophy and spend the bulk of the article reading Astell's texts in light of these elements, showing how they relate to her feminist project. I conclude by returning to the question of gender and philosophy as a way of life, addressing concerns about the use of philosophy as a feminist practice.

Mary Astell

Mary Astell was an English philosopher, theologian, political pamphleteer, and feminist. She is best known for her two-part feminist philosophical treatise *A Serious Proposal to the Ladies* (1694, 1697), as well as her biting critique of the marital state in *Some Reflections upon Marriage* (1700). Between the two parts of *A Serious Proposal,* she published her correspondence with the English Malebranchean John Norris (1657–1712), *Letters Concerning the Love of God* (1695), while her magnum opus may be considered to be *The Christian Religion as Profess'd by a Daughter of the Church of England* (1705). In addition, she wrote several more overtly political tracts targeting specific events of the day.

Astell's philosophy can be broadly characterised as rationalist and Cartesian, with strong Platonist elements and drawing heavily too on Nicolas Malebranche and the Port Royal logic. Astell positions herself explicitly against John Locke throughout her oeuvre, and also against Locke's friend and fellow philosopher Damaris Masham (1678/9–1708)—although unintentionally in the latter case, as she believed one of Masham's treatises to be Locke's handiwork. Her work is highly situated in, and perhaps inextricable from, an Anglican Christian framework. It is worth noting that Astell was conversant with the same classical traditions from which Hadot and Foucault draw, her published and unpublished writing both containing knowledgeable references to Stoicism and Epicureanism.[1]

[1] See, for instance, references to Cato's "Stoical Principles" (Astell 1996, 63), a critique of "Stoical Apathy" in *Letters Concerning the Love of God* (Astell and Norris 1695, 130), the "Epicurism" of right Christian living (Astell 1717, 251), and "Good Christians indeed being the truest *Epicures*" (Astell 2002b, 221).

By drawing her into philosophy as a way of life, then, I am situating her in a philosophical tradition originating in ancient philosophical schools.

Astell was labelled "the first English feminist" by Bridget Hill in the 1980s, and the question of the extent and the nature of Astell's feminism has recurred in secondary scholarship. What is incontrovertible, however, is that Astell provides a systematic analysis of how women are disadvantaged by sexist social structures and habits: what she terms "custom." She's not especially concerned, however, with the material disadvantages or political rights that women lack. The problem she identifies instead is that women are inhibited from constituting themselves as ethical, virtuous subjects: their very selves are warped and damaged by custom. This renders them subject to certain vices to a greater degree than men: vanity, for instance, and pride. *A Serious Proposal* is dedicated both to explicating Astell's analysis of the condition of women and to proposing solutions. Astell's solution is twofold: first, an all-female educational and religious institute in which women will be separated from men's predation and the detrimental effects of social custom; second, a comprehensive intellectual and spiritual regimen that individual women can follow at home for their self-development and transformation.

Foucault and Hadot

The relationship between Foucault's work on practices of the self, philosophy as spirituality, and the care of the self and Hadot's work on philosophy as a way of life has been well documented (see, e.g., Hadot 1995, 206–13, Banicki 2012, Testa 2016, and Sellars forthcoming). Understandings of Foucault's account of philosophy vary: Foucault has been interpreted as advocating philosophy as a way of life, in line with Hadot's thought, which is constituted *by* certain practices; on the other hand, Foucault's conception of philosophy has also been understood as *itself* a practice, one of many possible "technologies of the self." It is not my intention here to go into detail regarding the similarities and differences between Hadot and Foucault: instead, I intend to take from each the notion of philosophy as either *being* or *incorporating* certain practices; as something beyond what Hadot terms philosophical "discourse." My focus, however, is on Foucault's late work. This is roughly speaking from the latter two volumes of the *History of Sexuality* onwards and includes many interviews and lectures. The most significant for my purposes are "The Ethics of the Concern of the Self as a Practice of Freedom" (1997a) and *The Hermeneutics of the Subject* (2005).

In the late 1970s, stimulated partly by his engagement with ancient philosophy and Hadot's work, Foucault began to reconceptualise philosophy as something that could be a vital component of self-transformation and an ethical, political existence. This was a shift from his previous, more disparaging views about philosophy, which, according to Ladelle McWhorter,

Foucault saw as having "little if any value in contemporary society" (McWhorter 2016, 23). There are four key aspects of his new understanding of "philosophy" that I want to highlight. Firstly, philosophy's role as a "practice of the self." Secondly, philosophy as a "spirituality" on Foucault's understanding of the term. Thirdly, philosophy as "critique," an unknotting of the world around us and our own selves. Finally, the relationship between philosophy and freedom, and philosophy's role as a "freedom practice."

By situating Astell's writing in Foucault's framework, I am not retroactively imposing Foucault's conception of philosophy on a seventeenth-century woman's texts. Foucault engages closely with historical philosophical traditions—largely ancient and early Christian, but including the early modern period at times—to build his model of what philosophy has been and can be. I am arguing that Astell participates in a historical tradition that Foucault identifies and should be understood in relation to other philosophers and writers of Astell's period who also engaged with that tradition in varying degrees. While Astell is particularly notable for her gendering of the practices and ideas involved, she is not uniquely or unexpectedly anticipating Foucault: rather, she is part of the very philosophical tradition from which he draws his material for analysis.

Care of the Self

Before we address the practice of philosophy in Foucault and Astell, it is worth situating both thinkers in relation to a broader ethical picture drawn from Foucault's later body of work: one centring on the care of the self.

"No solicitude in the adornation of your selves is discommended, provided you employ your care about that which is really your *self*" (2002a, 52–53), Astell advises female readers in the opening pages of *A Serious Proposal to the Ladies*. In antiquity, Foucault argues, "we have . . . an entire ethics revolving around the care of the self; this is what gives ancient ethics its particular form" (1997a, 285). The care of the self is a central theme in Foucault's later thought: not only is the third volume of *The History of Sexuality* entitled *The Care of the Self*, the concept appears and reappears throughout the many interviews, lectures, and essays that constitute Foucault's last body of work. Foucault interprets ancient—and to some extent early Christian—ethical culture as centring on caring for the self.

Ethics for Foucault concerns "the way in which individuals are urged to constitute themselves as subjects of moral conduct," and a history of ethics is thus concerned with "the models proposed for setting up and developing relationships with the self, for self-reflection, self-knowledge, self-examination, for the decipherment of the self by oneself, for the transformations that one seeks to accomplish with oneself as object" (1985, 29). In the moralities with which Foucault is most concerned, the "forms of relations with the self" (30) are the central focus: these are ethics-oriented, as opposed to code-oriented, moralities.

In some of these ethics-oriented moralities Foucault identifies the *care* of the self as the key *way* in which the self relates to itself, most prominently in the morality of the ancient Western world. From "the fifth century B.C." through "Greek, Hellenistic and Roman philosophy, as well as Christian spirituality," roughly speaking ending in early Christian asceticism, Foucault identifies "a body of work defining a way of being, a standpoint, forms of reflection, and practices" (1985, 11) that constitute the "event in thought" (9) of care of the self. An ethics that centres the care of the self is one that advocates an attention to and concern for the *self* first and foremost, as opposed to other things that might seem worthy of attention. Its aim is to transform and work on the self to a certain end.

Astell's concern that women should turn their attention on their "own Minds" (2002a, 52) and "Souls" (54) is a recurring motif in *A Serious Proposal*. From the first page, Astell directs women towards the benefits to their selves of what she is about to propose: "Its aim is to fix that Beauty, . . . which Nature with all the helps of Art cannot secure: . . . An obliging Design, which wou'd procure them inward Beauty, to whom Nature has unkindly denied the outward; and not permit those Ladies who have comely Bodies, to tarnish their Glory with deformed Souls. . . . Not suffer you to take up with the low thought of distinguishing your selves by any thing that is not truly valuable" (51).

While Astell refers to the "Vertue" of women at the beginning of the text, the ethical emphasis here is entirely on their *selves* rather than their duties or concern for others or to a set of moral rules. Surely, she writes, "you cannot be so unkind to your selves, as to refuse your *real* interest" (2002a, 52). Indeed, as far as *other* people are concerned, she explicitly criticises giving too much attention to them in one respect at least. It is degrading to women, she suggests, to be concerned with "attract[ing] the eyes of men. We value *them* too much, and our *selves* too little, if we place any part of our worth in their Opinion" (55). Women better spend their time working on and improving their own selves than on endeavouring to be pleasing to "vain insignificant men" (56). *A Serious Proposal* is oriented from the beginning, then, to persuading women to be concerned for their selves—and this is expressed as a gendered concern. Women are advised to take *genuine* care of their selves *rather than* to turn their attention towards men's opinions and desires.

The orientation towards the self as an ethical concern is not limited to *A Serious Proposal*'s opening sallies. Part I's concluding passages reinforce the message of the opening pages by exhorting female readers to "a sort of Bravery and Greatness of Soul" that "consists in living up to the dignity of our Natures" (2002a, 111). A "wise and good woman," says Astell, is "she who chiefly attends the *one thing needful*, the *good part which shall not be taken from her*" (112): in other words, her self. We should note here that

Astell presents the self as an appropriate object of chief concern, not as a supplementary or transitional matter.

The introduction to part II of *A Serious Proposal* consists of "a farther Perswasive to the Ladies To endeavour the Improvement of their Minds" (2002b, 119), urging readers with even greater vigour towards work on the self. If "it is not worth while to procure such a temper of mind as will make us happy in all Conditions, there's *nothing* worth our Thoughts and Care [my italics]" (121), Astell writes: the attention the reader should give to her own mind is evidently paramount. As in the beginning of part I, Astell makes no reference to moral codes or duties to those around us. She instead expects her readers to be "fill'd with a laudable Ambition to brighten and enlarge your Souls" (122), and the remainder of part II of *A Serious Proposal* is devoted to providing such readers with the means for doing so.

On my interpretation of her body of work, then, Astell too puts forward an ethic of care for the self. This is not the place to develop further details of that reading, but I shall argue in what follows that Astell *genders* care for the self in illuminating ways. On her account, women are in greater need of care of the self than men, due to the damaging effects of sexist "custom" on their selves. They also require, or at least would find highly beneficial, separation from men and the rest of society in order to practise care of the self effectively. This is the context in which Astell's use of philosophy should be seen: one in which she is diagnosing, and providing a regimen to cure, problems affecting women's selves specifically. Philosophy is a fundamental component of this cure.

Philosophy as Practice

Practices—or technologies—of the self are the things individuals do that "permit [them] to effect by their own means or with the help of others a certain number of operations on their own bodies and souls, thoughts, conduct, and way of being, so as to transform themselves" (Foucault 1988). They are things the self does in order to work on itself, techniques that are not invented by the individual but drawn from previously existing models. These can be practices of freedom, a way for the subject to resist or oppose domination, but they need not be: techniques of the self can also be a way for the self to impose pernicious discipline on itself. Foucault partly drew this concept from Hadot's notion of "spiritual exercises." The resemblance is clear: Hadot writes that "in these exercises, it is thought which, as it were, takes itself as its own subject-matter, and seeks to modify itself" (1995, 82).

On Foucault's account, philosophy *is* clearly a practice of the self. What, Foucault asks, "is philosophy today . . . if it is not the critical work that *thought brings to bear on itself*? [my italics]" (1985, 8–9). Elsewhere he refers to philosophy as "all the work that has been done . . . to become other than what one is" (1997b, 327). In both formulations, philosophy is presented as a reflexive practice that transforms and alters the self that undertakes it.

There is a recognition throughout Astell scholarship that philosophy for Astell is not inert but has practical impact on the lives and existence of those who undertake it: it serves as a way for women to work on their selves. Alice Sowaal describes philosophy as functioning for Astell's ideal reader as "the tool that will lead her to develop her perfections" (2007, 239), while William Kolbrener refers to Astell's "philosophical method for the overcoming of imagination [and] passion" (2007, 56). Jacqueline Broad too is at pains to urge that "her [Astell's] philosophy was purposively designed to bring about changes in the practical lives of women" (2015, 23). Where the scholarship perhaps falls short is in recognising that Astell's philosophy not just as something that, through its arguments, can lead women to certain conclusions that assist them in development but as being *in itself* a transformative practice. This is its spiritual role, which I will outline after giving an example of how philosophical thought functions as a practice for Astell.

One of the passages most clearly demonstrating the role of philosophical thought as a transformative practice of the self can be found in part II of *A Serious Proposal*. Astell is advising her readers on the way to obtain the "most desirable Temper" (2002b, 209), with "a Sagacity of Understanding to discern readily what is best, but likewise with such a Regularity of Will, as makes it even Hate and Abhor all evil ways" (209). To become as wise and self-controlled as Astell deems ideal, she recommends attempting to do so "somewhat . . . by way of Meditation and somewhat by way of Exercise" (210). The meditation she goes on to discuss consists of a rational consideration of several philosophical topics and their connection to each other. The subjects are "our own Nature, the Nature of Material Beings, and the Nature of GOD" (210). Astell begins by advising readers to "consider what we Are, that Humane Nature consists in the Union of a Rational Soul with a Mortal Body, that the Body very often Clogs the Mind in its noblest Operations" (210). From this dualist foundation, she goes on to remind us that we are "united in some measure to all who bear a Human Form" (210) and encourages us to "consider what are the proper Duties and Enjoyments of such a nature as ours" (210). If we meditated on all these things, Astell argues, and "were we so far at least Philosophers, as to be able to pass a due estimate on material Beings" and "not to prize them above their real value," then "we shou'd not be long in discerning the good effects" (210). She expounds these good effects at length, considering each topic in turn.

By considering the arguments for dualism, "we shou'd be convinc'd that the Body is the Instrument of the Mind and no more, that it is of much Inferior Nature, and therefore ought to be . . . ready on all occasions to serve the Mind" (2002b, 210). It is through philosophical activity, then, that women will "learn what is *truly* to love our selves [my italics]" (211): not to "pamper our Bodies" (211) but instead to subdue them to our minds. By considering our unity with a greater whole and our connectedness to each other, we will realise that we can never benefit ourselves by harming others. Finally, by noting that "we do not find intire Felicity in our selves, but . . . are conscious of many wants which must be supply'd elsewhere" (212), we will be led to consider where those wants will be met, realise that it will not be in material beings, and instead be led to "that infinite Good which alone can satisfie us" (212): God. Once we start contemplating the divine appropriately, we will find ourselves transformed. "All our Passions will be Charm'd, and every Inclination attracted!" (213). In this passage, then, Astell presents philosophical activity—as the rational following of arguments on a topic—as something that leads us to unity with our ultimate good. Following the arguments given is no mere cognitive process but something that transforms our very way of being.

We also find Astell using philosophy in this passage to contribute to the care of the self. It is by considering dualist arguments, after all, that women will understand what care for the self *really* consists in; that while "Self-Love as it is usually understood has a very ill Character and is the Root of Evil, yet rightly apply'd it is Natural and Necessary" (2002b, 211). As I have already observed, Foucault draws a close connection between care of the self and philosophy, particularly in antiquity, where, on the one hand, philosophy functions *as* a set of principles and practices enabling care of the self and, on the other hand, taking care of oneself is a precondition for the rational, philosophical life. If we read Astell as proposing an ethics of care of the self for women, then philosophy contributes to that care of the self in two ways: first, by providing women with the tools to understand what the self really is and what it means to care for it, and secondly by being *in itself* transformative.

By using philosophy to show women what it really means to care for the self, Astell is challenging the effects of sexist custom, which teaches women that caring for the self consists in adorning the body for the sake of male attention. Astell instead insists that we should "pride ourselves in something more excellent than the invention of a Fashion: And not entertain such a degrading thought of our own *worth*, as to imagine that our Souls were given us only for the service of our Bodies, and that the best improvement we can make of these, is to attract the eyes of men" (2002b, 55). This is a comment that may, perhaps, resonate with women today.

So, among the practices of the self that Astell advocates in *A Serious Proposal* are techniques of rational thought and reflection that contribute to self-transformation and care of the self. It is these practices that focus on the use of reason and systematic reflection that I am identifying as philosophical practices of the self, and they form a key part—although not the only part—of Astell's regimen for women.

Philosophy as Spirituality

Foucault identifies philosophy as, in some historical moments, belonging to a particular subset of practices of the self: the ethos or collection of practices he calls "spirituality." Foucault understands by spirituality "the subject's attainment of a certain mode of being and the transformations that the subject must carry out on itself to attain this mode of being" (1997a, 294). Not all practices of the self constitute a spirituality, nor are all conceptions and modes of philosophy spiritual, but certainly for Foucault philosophy *has been* intertwined with spirituality. This relationship too is linked back to care of the self, with Foucault asserting that "spirituality and philosophy were identical or nearly identical in ancient spirituality. In any case, philosophy's most important preoccupation centered around the self, with knowledge [*connaissance*] of the world . . . serving, most often, to support care of the self" (294). We can say, then, that for Foucault philosophy is a practice of the self that has historically been a spiritual practice aimed at caring for the self. I contend that a similar relationship between philosophy, care of the self, and spirituality is discernible in Astell's writing.

Foucauldian spirituality has three major characteristics, all of which are visible in *A Serious Proposal.* First, it "postulates that the truth is never given to the subject by right" (Foucault 2005, 15); instead, the subject must be transformed or altered in some way to attain the truth. Secondly, there must be "a work of the self on the self, an elaboration of the self by the self, a progressive transformation of the self by the self for which one takes responsibility in a long labor of ascesis" (16). Finally, "the truth is not just what is given to the subject, as reward for the act of knowledge" (16): rather, the truth itself, once attained, has further transformative effects on the subject. Prior to what he terms "the Cartesian moment," Foucault suggests, philosophy and spirituality were inextricable: following this moment, the tradition of philosophy as purely cognitive activity, separate and separable from spirituality, emerged.[2] In Foucault's own work, however, a spiritual dimension—particularly the work of the self on the self—is reincorporated into philosophical practice. In Astell too, I argue, philosophy as a process of rational thought is at the same time a spirituality, possessing Foucault's three characteristics.

First, then, I must demonstrate that on the account Astell provides, her subject cannot access truth before being transformed. Admittedly, Astell proposes that "there are some degrees of Knowledge necessary before there can be *any* Human Acts" (2002b, 129); merely by virtue of possessing rationality a human being will also possess "the Rudiments of Knowledge" (128). There are some components of the truth, then, that the subject does have right of access to inherently, merely by being a human subject. For instance, the principle "*That we ought as much as we can to endeavour the Perfecting of our Beings, and that we be as happy as possibly we may*" (129). Further access to the truth, however, is cloudy. When the subject, starting

[2] Foucault himself acknowledged the crudeness of the phrase "Cartesian moment," and Descartes's own spiritual philosophy has been commented on: see Cottingham 2006.

from that principle, goes on to ask *how* to perfect her being and become happy, "Our Reason is at first too weak, and afterwards too often too much sophisticated to return a proper Answer" (129). Without further work of the right kind, the subject cannot get further than the initial self-evident principle. There are, in other words, conditions to knowledge.

Furthermore, these conditions in Astell are not of the sort Foucault identifies in Cartesian philosophy: "These are all conditions that are either intrinsic to knowledge or extrinsic to the act of knowledge, but which do not concern the subject in his being" (Foucault, 2005, 18). Astell's conditions, on the contrary, relate to the soul's purity: "Any eminent degree of Knowledge, especially of Mortal and Divine Knowledge . . . can never be obtain'd without considerable degrees of Purity" (2002b, 131). It is only by tackling "the Corruption of the Heart" (130), Astell proposes, that we can access truth: "The more Pure we are the clearer will our Knowledge be" (131). The first characteristic of spirituality is thus evidently fulfilled in *A Serious Proposal*.

Secondly, there is the ascesis: a set of exercises designed at transforming the subject so that it can access the truth. Astell challenges her readers at the beginning of part II: "Is it the difficulty of attaining the Bravery of the Mind, the Labour and Cost that keeps you from making a purchase of it?" (2002b, 121). Later, she identifies the purpose of our life in this world as being "to pass our Probation, to Prepare our selves and be Candidates for Eternal Happiness," something that can only be achieved "by Labour and Industry" (132). To free ourselves from prejudice and custom, which act as fetters to the understanding and the will, respectively, we must put in "a good deal of Time and Pains, of Thought and Watchfulness to the rooting out of ill-habits, to the fortifying our Minds against foolish Customs" (141). This work by ourselves on ourselves is emphasised by Astell as necessary to gain the purity of heart and clarity of understanding needed to access the truth. It is the "best Method for Improvement" (142), the details of this work that women need to enact on their selves in order to become able to access truth, which Astell spends the bulk of part II of *A Serious Proposal* elaborating. As well as the philosophical practices that I have already described, Astell's ascesis for women includes practices of meditation, emotional control, improving conversations with friends, self-knowledge, and reading appropriate books in the right way (155–56, 162, 210).

The final characteristic of spirituality is its recursivity; the truth must further transform the subject who has already been transformed in order to access it. This too is explicit in Astell's conception of knowledge: "When we have procur'd a competent measure of both [knowledge and purity], they mutually assist each other; the more Pure we are the clearer will our Knowledge be, and the more we Know, the more we shall Purify" (2002b, 131). It is plain from this that the attainment of truth rebounds to modify the subject's soul further. Gaining knowledge, Astell argues, is "Instrumental . . . to the Salvation of our Souls. . . . A Great deal of Good will be omitted, and very much Evil, or Imperfection at least, stick to us" if we don't undergo "Meditation and the helps that study affords" (200) to access the truth.

Platonist influences are of course at play here. The Christian neo-Platonist Simon Patrick (1626–1707), for instance, was "convinced that a properly cultivated spirituality could offer a form of contemplative reunion with God" (Wilde 2013, 157), drawing on Plotinus as an expert on spiritual techniques that could facilitate this. John Norris, with whom Astell corresponded in their *Letters Concerning the Love of God,* had connections with the school of philosophers known as the Cambridge Platonists, who believed that "all the philosophical schools had arrived at truths which could be amalgamated with Christian teachings into a single, complete, and correct system" (Astell and Norris 1695, 37). In a Platonic framework, "[i]n order to ascend . . . and finally be united with the divine, the human being must become purer and more knowing" (12). Sarah Apetrei situates Astell in "the second generation of English Platonists" who "took refuge in the more spiritualist and ascetical aspects of their tradition" (2010, 105); the reference to spirituality and ascetics resonates, of course, with Foucault's concerns in the history of philosophy.

In addition to Christian Platonist influences, the philosophical method that Astell proposes for women to learn to think properly is drawn from Cartesian methods generally and the Cartesian-influenced *Port-Royal Logic* in particular. Her method as such and her advocacy of philosophy as a means to transform the character, are by no means unique: in the work of Henry More (1614–1687) and Nicolas Malebranche (1638–1715), in particular, we find close parallels.

In his *Account of Virtue* (1690), we find More undertaking a project extremely similar to Astell's. The "Work in Hand, was an honest Intention to excite the Minds of Men unto Virtue," he writes in the epistle to the reader. More himself acknowledges his debt both to "what *Des-Cartes* in his *Definitions* of the *Passions* had done before him" and to "many of the Ancients," citing throughout his book the work of Stoic philosophers such as Marcus Aurelius and Epictetus. Like Astell's, More's Christian Platonism is evident throughout: "What Rational Creature is there, but must acknowledge, That Virtue has a participation with the Divine Nature?" More, then, like Astell, is embedded in a Christian Platonist framework that also draws from Stoic texts and, later, Cartesianism.

Malebranche, too, whom Astell repeatedly acknowledges as an influence, insists that philosophy should be appropriately transformative when read in the right way. He criticises, for instance, those readers of Descartes who "read his works as fictions and romances, which are read for diversion and not meditated upon for instruction" (1997, 13). The very intended aim of *The Search After Truth*, for Malebranche, is to "render the mind as perfect as it can naturally be, by supplying the help necessary to extend its scope and make it more attentive and by laying down the rules that it must observe" (408). Like Astell, Malebranche explicitly intends his readers to take up his method and apply it to themselves, becoming intellectually and ethically transformed as a result. John Norris, with whom Astell corresponded, was a close follower of Malebranche and the main transmitter of his ideas into English philosophy.

Throughout the early modern period philosophy is presented at many further instances as a route to self-transformation and constitution as an ethical subject: a practice of the self, in Foucault's terms. Thus Astell's project is far from unique, and it simply provides another example of the mode of philosophy that Foucault identifies in the history of philosophy, and that continues more richly in the early modern period than he explicitly acknowledges. Astell, however, links philosophy as a transformative practice to women in particular. It's her use of philosophy as a *feminist* practice which I want to address further.

Philosophy for Astell is a spiritual practice that both requires and enables self-transformation. Thus far, this may not sound specifically feminist in nature: Astell happens to be advocating philosophical exercises to women, but the practices themselves seem to be gender neutral. She is, however, advocating such practices to women in the face of social obstruction and disapprobation, in a context where they are prevented from accessing the knowledge and education in thinking well that Astell judges vital to becoming an ethical, virtuous subject. Women, she says, are disproportionately left uncultivated and their intellect left untrained. "Boys have much Time and Pains, Care and Cost bestow'd on their Education, Girls have little or none" (1996, 28), she states baldly. "Were the Men as much neglected, and as little care taken to cultivate and improve them, perhaps they wou'd be so far from surpassing those whom they now dispise, that they themselves wou'd sink into the greatest stupidity and brutality" (2002a, 57). A spiritual philosophical practice, then, can have feminist value in its resistance to the sexist structures and effects of an oppressive society, enabling women to care for the self, which custom has damaged and warped.

Her envisioning of her practices as resistance is at its most evident in the introduction by Astell to part II of *A Serious Proposal*. Here, she does her best to convince her female readers of the value of attaining wisdom, which is linked to the rejection of masculine domination: "I dare say you understand your own interest too well to neglect it so grossly and have a greater share of sense, whatever some Men affirm, than to be content to be kept any longer under their Tyranny in Ignorance and Folly, since it is in your Power to regain your Freedom, if you please but t'endeavour it" (2002b, 121). On Astell's account, the most concerning effects of misogynistic social custom and male domination are on women's ethical selves: they are rendered foolish, prone to folly and vice, with their passions left unchecked by their reason. The most important mode of resistance, then, is for women "to be absolute Monarchs in [their] own Bosoms" (234). Even though women aren't given the same education as men, Astell thinks, they are still capable of educating *themselves*. Ideally, this would take place in a communal all-female setting as described in the first part of *A Serious Proposal*; in the meantime, however, Astell's purpose in the second part is "to lay down . . . some more minute Directions" (126) for women to follow. By following such instructions, women will improve their selves, become virtuous and wise subjects, and thus be able to resist the pernicious effects of mainstream society.

It may be useful also to link Astell's philosophical spirituality to the mystical slant that characterized much seventeenth-century feminism according to Apetrei. This "mystical principle, which emphasized subjective knowledge, or an inward encounter with spiritual guidance, above the authority mediated by texts and customs" (Apetrei 2010, 128–29), enabled women to resist the purported authority of biblical texts or "knowledge and authority as mediated by men" (150). By situating Astell's spirituality in the context of Christian mysticism as well as a philosophical spiritual tradition, it is possible to see how the notion of the individual subject attaining transformation through access to divine truth can function as feminist resistance against a particular mode of religious subjugation of women.

Philosophy as Critique

Philosophy for Foucault is inextricable from "critique": "The task of philosophy as a critical analysis of our world is something that is more and more important" (2002, 336). Critique in this context is a particular ethos or attitude that "simultaneously problematizes man's relation to the present, man's historical mode of being, and the constitution of the self as an autonomous subject" (Foucault 1983). Through critique we can uncover the contingency of aspects of our world that are presented to us as given and necessary, and thus we can open up possibilities for doing otherwise than we believe we are able. While it's not Foucault's primary concern, we can immediately see the link to gendered structures and conventions that are presented to us as given, which a philosophical critique can be of use in challenging.

The critical function of philosophy is not a purely outward-facing concern, however, something wholly distinct from its role as practice of the self. Philosophy's task of working out how "to think differently, instead of legitimating what is already known" (Foucault 1985, 9), is at the same time a task that implicates the subject who undertakes it. The critique of the present moment entails the "displacement and detachment of frameworks of thinking, the changing of received values and all the work that has been done to think otherwise, *to do something else, to become other than what one is*—that, too, is philosophy [my italics]" (Foucault 1997b, 327). This transformation of the self who undertakes philosophy, the becoming other than what one is, can of course be linked back to philosophy as spirituality.

"'Tis true, thro' Want of Learning, and of that Superior Genius which Men as Men lay claim to, she [the author] was ignorant of the *Natural Inferiority* of our Sex, which our Masters lay down as a Self-Evident and Fundamental Truth" (1996, 9), Astell writes at the beginning of *Reflections upon Marriage*. She goes on to assert that the only way to demonstrate a case satisfactorily is "not by *Affirming*, but by *Proving*, so that every one may see with their *own* Eyes, and Judge according to the best of their *own* Understandings" (10), insisting on a female reader's, or "reflector"'s, "Natural Right of Judging for her self" (10) concerning what is right. Astell is insisting, it seems, on the rejection of supposed self-evident truths about women, instead advocating that women should use their own intellectual capabilities to establish the truth. For Astell and Foucault alike, philosophy functions as a way to dislodge what is presented as truth and to find alternative truths or modes of living. For Astell, this use of philosophy specifically comes into play regarding accepted "truths" about women and their moral and intellectual capacities.

Beyond the use of philosophy to dismantle and challenge custom, Astell advocates critique as a personal practice, as a means for women to think themselves differently.[3] This is a direct consequence of philosophy's role as social critique: as Sowaal identifies, Astell in *A Serious Proposal* presents strategies that will "displace the WDN [Women's Defective Nature] Prejudice, or at least provide tools to critique the customs that perpetuate it" (2007, 238). On Sowaal's interpretation, "Astell reveals that women are gripped by a skeptical predicament" borne of "societal prejudice and custom," which is pervasive and pernicious, causing "confusion and paralysis" (238). This sceptical predicament is the Women's Defective Nature Prejudice, the "prejudice that women 'naturally' have 'feminine vices'" and that "a woman's vice follows from the nature that women have, a nature that is defective" (231). It's precisely through the use of philosophical arguments that one tackles this confusion and paralysis, allowing women to exist differently in the world.

"As Prejudice fetters the Understanding so does Custom manacle the Will, which scarce knows how to divert from a Track which the generality around it take" (2002b, 139), Astell writes. Here, as elsewhere, she explicitly connects social context and individual constraint. Custom, she argues, "enslaves the very Souls of Men" (140). Custom functions to the specific

[3] "Thinking themselves differently" is a phrasing drawn from Foucault's ethics, and the surrounding literature, that is not the same as "thinking *about* themselves differently." Rather, for Foucault, thinking in a new way is itself to *be* in a new way, to become a different person via the very act of thinking. Subjects constitute and create themselves by the practices they undertake, which can be practices of thought. So, on my interpretation of Astell, women who think themselves differently are altering their own subjectivities by their philosophical practices.

detriment of women's selves: for Astell, prejudice and custom are gendered social effects that affect women's very beings in a variety of negative ways. To "Conquer the Prejudices of Education, Authority and Custom," however, requires more than "a Generous Resolution and Courageous Industry" (140). Instead, it takes work, and we must "attempt . . . the most prudent Method" (140). A large part of this method, as elaborated in *A Serious Proposal*, involves learning to think and argue clearly.

Throughout *A Serious Proposal*, Astell contrasts accepted models of femininity and womanhood with the qualities of which she deems women capable. She attacks the vices and defects that she admits many women suffer from: vanity, folly, ignorance, a tendency to "be Proud and Petulent, Delicate and Fantastick, Humorous and Inconstant" (2002a, 61). As I discussed earlier, and as Sowaal emphasises, one of Astell's key moves is to reject the claim that "Women are *naturally* incapable of acting Prudently, or that they are necessarily determined to folly [my italics]" (58). Contrary to much popular opinion, Astell insists, "Women need not take up with mean things, since . . . they are capable of the best" (59). This challenge to customary understandings of womanhood is explicitly philosophical on her account: she challenges those who would bar women from self-improvement and education either to "take up *his* Paradox, who said *That Women have no Souls*; which at this time a day, when they are allow'd to Brutes, wou'd be as unphilosophical as it is unmannerly; or else let them permit us to cultivate and improve them" (81). The claim that women are soulless, that they are not capable of improvement and development, is one that Astell identifies as not in accordance with philosophical reason.[4] As Sowaal addresses in her essay on Astell's method, Astell is not primarily attempting to persuade *men* to change their opinion on women's capabilities: rather, by challenging customary beliefs and prejudices regarding women's nature, she is setting her female readers on the path to self-transformation and improvement—a path that will be further facilitated by her "strategies that displace the WDN Prejudice" (Sowaal 2007, 238). In other words, Astell is enabling women to become and to *be* different from how they may have accepted themselves as being.

A Serious Proposal works to assist women in thinking and doing "otherwise," to displace and transform their frameworks of thinking, and to become other than what they were, through the critical use of philosophical reason. By challenging and interrogating the limits of our world as it is given to us, Foucault claims, we can thus open up a space to exist differently within that world. Astell precisely challenges the limits of her readers' world, showing her readers the irrationality of customary prejudices concerning women.

[4]The "soulless" claim is a satirical exaggeration of less extreme claims held about women at the time: the view that women had no souls was not seriously advanced in Astell's period.

Philosophy as Freedom Practice

Foucault links the critical component of philosophy to a resistance to oppression and domination. "In its critical aspect," he asserts, "philosophy is that which calls into question domination at every level and in every form in which it exists, whether political, economic, sexual, institutional or what have you" (1997a, 300–301). This "critical function of philosophy," he goes on to say, "derives from the Socratic injunction 'Take care of yourself,' in other words 'Make freedom your foundation, through the mastery of yourself'" (301). In this interview, Foucault establishes the care of, the ethic of, the self, as a "freedom practice": "What is ethics, if not the . . . conscious [*reflechie*] practice of freedom?" (284).

For Astell too, the practice of philosophy—situated as part of a regimen for care of the self—can at the same time be a way for women to practise freedom. First, as Sowaal explains, the philosophical critique of social custom facilitates women in the realisation that their faults and vices are not intrinsic to their being women but rather inculcated by extrinsic factors. This opens up the possibility of their self-transformation and no longer being subject to, and slaves to, the same vices and passions as before. "Why," Astell asks her readers at the beginning of part II of *A Serious Proposal*, "shou'd we not assert our Liberty, and not suffer every Trifler to impose a Yoke of Impertinent Customs on us?" (2002b, 120). Custom functions as a restraint on women's practice of freedom: the use of philosophy challenges custom—and domination—thus permitting women to assert, to practise, their liberty.

Secondly, the practice of philosophy as rational reflection itself works to transform women. Astell draws an explicit connection between rational thought and female freedom. "Why won't you begin to think, and no longer dream away your Time in a wretched incogitancy?" she inquires of her female readers, soon going on to ask, "Can you be in Love with servitude and folly?" (2002b, 120). By clarifying their ideas, she argues, women can avoid making false judgements and simply concurring with custom. If we merely accept "Customs and the Observations we make on the Practice of such" as the source of our ideas, they are likely to be "very fallacious and many times opposite to the Dictates of Reason" (170). If instead we reason appropriately and "make right use of our Faculties," we will "certainly be Enlighten'd, and cannot miss of obtaining as much Truth" (175) as we are capable of receiving.

By being led by the love of truth rather than by passions, worldly interests, or self-love, women will have internal liberty in the sense of "living life in accordance with the deeper interests of the true self" (Broad 2015, 173) and will avoid the efforts of "a Designing Person" (2002b, 187) who "seems to have an Intention to reduce us to the vilest Slavery, the Captivation of our Understandings" (188). While we need different and supplementary exercises to provide us with a "Regularity of Will" (209), rational and logical reflection helps us to "Disengage our selves from all our former Prejudices, from our Opinions of Names, Authorities, Customs and the like" (133), all of which "Contract our Souls[,] . . . hinder the free range of our Thoughts and confine them only to that particular track which these have taken, and in a word, erect a Tyranny over our free born Souls" (133). Philosophical practice, on Astell's account, aligns us with reason, which "wills that we shou'd think again, and not form our Conclusions . . . till we can honestly say, that we have with out Prejudice or Prepossession view'd the matter in Debate on all sides . . . only determined by Truth it self" (135). By using philosophical reflection, then, women can place themselves at a distance from ordinary ways of thinking and conventions, and from prejudices that serve to keep them inhibited. They provide themselves with the ability to question those prejudices and to form opinions based on reason instead.

As Broad explains, for Astell "freedom of the will . . . does not guarantee that the agent herself is free. A free agent must also have the capacity for reason and *independence of judgment*" (Broad 2015, 172). This is precisely what Astell's female reader can develop through the use of philosophy. Broad draws a connection between Astell's advocacy of inner liberty and modern feminist accounts of autonomy, such as that given by Marilyn Friedman. She argues that "Astell would agree with Friedman that true liberty is a matter of living life in accordance with the deeper interests of the true self—interests that have been carefully considered through a process of proper self-reflection" (173–74) and that "like Friedman, she urges women to embrace their capacity for self-determination in order to overcome oppressive gender practices of their time" (174). I would add to Broad's point that Astell specifically uses the practice of philosophy to foster women's autonomy in this way. We can also understand philosophy, then, as something that challenges and resists domination, and that can be of particular use for women.

Philosophy and Feminism

I've argued for a picture in which philosophy functions for Astell as a spiritual practice that transforms women in the face of social restrictions, liberating them from the prejudices inculcated by sexist custom and facilitating their autonomy. Drawing on Astell might point us towards ways in which philosophical practices or ways of life can be feminist tools of self-transformation and social critique.

This mode of philosophy has been seen as inimical to feminism, however. Astell's inward focus is potentially at odds with a feminist grappling with the world around us, a concerted collective effort to change society for the better. This is illustrated most starkly in *Some Reflections upon Marriage*, in which Astell encourages women trapped in bad marriages to use them as opportunities to exercise and cultivate their virtue. "If any

Woman think her self Injur'd," she writes, "she has a Remedy in reserve . . . the Exercise and Improvement of her Vertue here, and the Reward of it hereafter" (1996, 80). There is a worry that philosophical practices of the *self* might contribute to passivity in the face of injustice and domination. Sowaal has highlighted this concern in Astell, writing that "Astell's view seems to promote passivity in women . . . according to Astell, women are not to actively protest the current institutional systems, but rather they should ignore society and meditate solitarily" (2017, 180).

I want to suggest, however, that we can understand Astell as proposing strategically useful practices, including philosophy, for women to undertake *given* the state of society in which they find themselves. She is sceptical regarding the possibility for collective female action but nonetheless shows an awareness of the oppression of women as a group, beyond the individual warping of women's selves. This comes through especially clearly in *Some Reflections upon Marriage*. Astell refers to a "Tyrannous Domination which Nature never meant," which "render[s] useless if not hurtful, the Industry and Understandings of half Mankind" and bids a sarcastic "Adieu" to "the Liberties not of this or that Nation or Region only, but of the Moiety of Mankind!" (1996, 31). Here, she links the oppression or freedom of nations with that of women, clearly conceiving of women as a collective: the "moiety," or half, of humanity. The "Custom of the World has put Women, generally speaking, into a State of Subjection" (10), she observes. Famously, she compares this subjugation with slavery: "How much soever Arbitrary Power may be dislik'd on a Throne," she bitterly points out, "not *Milton* himself wou'd cry up Liberty to poor *Female Slaves*, or plead for the Lawfulness of Resisting a Private Tyranny" (46–47). Her most known quote is probably the aphorism "If *all Men are born free*, how is it that all Women are born slaves?" (18), which she goes on to elaborate: "As they must be if the being subjected to the *inconstant, uncertain, unknown, arbitrary Will* of Men, be the *perfect Condition of Slavery?*" (18–19). The strength with which she draws this comparison seems to imply the moral righteousness of resistance: "Patience and Submission are the only Comforts that are left to a poor People, who groan under Tyranny, *unless* they are strong enough to break the Yoke, to Depose and Abdicate, which I doubt wou'd not be allow'd of here [my italics]" (46). The issue here concerning collective resistance doesn't appear to be Astell's disapproval: it appears instead to be Astell's (not unwarranted) pessimism regarding a group's ability to do so.

Indeed, despite her noted claim that "we mean not to intrench on any of [men's] lawful privileges" (2002b, 233) and her remark that "Women have no business with the Pulpit, the Bar or *St. Stephens Chapel*" (196) (the latter a metonym for the Houses of Parliament), Astell does in fact comment in passing on the possibility of organised political action by women as a class. In *Some Reflections upon Marriage,* she writes: "I do not propose this to prevent a Rebellion, for Women are not so well united as to form an

Insurrection" (1996, 29). In this passage, the implication is that Astell's aversion to communal political action on the part of women is due less to disapproval and more to a pessimism concerning its practicality. She is seemingly cynical about women's abilities to engage in collective action, writing with biting sarcasm that they "are for the most part wise enough to Love their Chains, and to discern how very becomingly they set" (29). In light of this passage, then, we might again want to read Astell's emphasis on individual women's self-development as a practical response to the difficulty in uniting women in insurrection. If Astell is right that women "have a Spice of Masculine Ambition, every one wou'd lead, and none will Follow" (29), then an individual woman who wants to make a change is likely to have more success in cultivating her self or the selves of other individual friends than she is in collective feminist action. Despite her pessimism about collective action, there is a sense in which Astell offers hope: rather than despairing at the perhaps insurmountable challenge of uniting communities of women to rise up against sexist domination, individual women can do something active and concrete as they care for and work on their selves and those of their friends.

It's worth noting, too, that Astell's conception of the self doesn't emerge as the "atomized" self that Foucault has (unfairly, I would argue) been criticized for holding. Rather, as Joanne Myers shows in her comparison of Astell with Damaris Masham, despite Astell's caution regarding love for beings other than God, Astell's texts nonetheless "imagine the self as bound to and sometimes even indistinguishable from others" (2013, 535). On Myers's account, Astell "[stresses] participation and dependence as key features of the self" (543). This dependence is linked particularly to friendship between women, linking back to her recognition of women as a distinct oppressed group. The best kind of friendship between women, Astell writes, is characterised by "the greatest usefulness, the most refin'd and disinteress'd Benevolence, a love that thinks nothing within the bounds of Power and Duty, too much to do or suffer for its Beloved; And makes no distinction betwixt its Friend and its self" (2002a, 99). The love of real friendship, then, erodes the boundaries between selves. Astell's concern is not *just* for individual women who seek self-development: rather, those individual women are connected to and dependent upon others. Astell's very advocacy, in part I of *A Serious Proposal*, of a separate communal educational space for women points to an understanding of the value of solidarity and community.

By practising philosophy, women can transform their selves, access truth, and critique custom in a way that further aids their own development—and, crucially, this can be done *whether or not* society also changes, and regardless of the presence or absence of organised opposition to sexist structures. All that's required, on Astell's account, is time, solitude, and advice on philosophical method (although Astell admits that many women will struggle to find the first two of these). Philosophical practices of the self are not antithetical to a collective feminist politics, I suggest, but complementary to it.

Conclusion

It's the notion of finding contemporary value in the feminist practice of philosophy offered by Astell that I want to conclude with. This is not to say, of course, that we should want to take up her regimen wholesale: much about her stance on a variety of subjects may be troubling to modern feminists. Foucault warns us, in reference to retrieving elements of ancient morality for contemporary use, that "you can't find the solution of a problem in the solution of another problem raised at another moment by other people" (1997c, 256). He does, nonetheless, want to point towards similarities between the moralities, and the philosophies, of the past and those of the present moment. For Foucault, "all of Greek experience can be taken up in nearly the same manner by each time taking into account differences of context and by indicating those aspects of the experience which could perhaps be salvaged" (1990, 249). Notwithstanding the differences of experience and in social structure between women in Britain, for instance, today and Mary Astell writing at the end of the seventeenth century, there are nonetheless aspects to be salvaged. Today too we witness and experience women's selves being affected and damaged in various ways by the powerful forces of a misogynistic society.

I want to suggest tentatively that women here, now, might find the use of philosophical reflection of value as a tool to unpick internalised beliefs about our own nature, to challenge what is presented to us as given, to care for our selves, and to practise freedom. Astell's work reminds us that our concern as feminists should not be simply for what women, as the selves they already are, are inhibited from doing or forced to do, or how they are treated. Instead, their very *selves* are detrimentally affected by social "custom." Philosophical reflection has the potential to complement externally directed activism. While it is not possible here to present a full picture of how that might look, we can see how some of Astell's own examples might be relevant for us today.

Astell draws attention to how women are deceived by custom into believing that their worth lies solely in men's attraction to them. As a result of this, they value their bodies too highly, concerning themselves primarily with fashion and their external beauty, neglecting their ethical and intellectual capacities. Philosophical activity, however, can provide women with an understanding of what's *really* important: not their physical appearance or ability to attract men but their ethical subjectivity. Many women today are absorbed in concerns similar to those addressed by Astell. It seems conceivable that philosophical reflection could help women, in the face of pervasive societal conditioning, to unpick their beliefs about—for instance—bodily worth. Taking weight and body size as an example—one that I have wrestled with personally—philosophical reflection could plausibly help women detach themselves from an obsession with weight loss and thinness: both due to explicit arguments on the topic and due to the refocusing of attention on intellectual concerns.

Feminist philosophical reflection could occur either in group settings or in an individual context. Regarding philosophy as a group activity, I am drawing from my experiences volunteering with the Stuart Low Trust Philosophy Forum, a philosophy discussion group aimed at vulnerable adults in London. Many participants report benefits for their well-being and sense of self. Perhaps we can envision (and even put into practice) such a group philosophical practice aimed exclusively at women, in a reimagining of Astell's project.

References

Apetrei, Sarah. 2010. *Women, Feminism and Religion in Early Enlightenment England.* Cambridge: Cambridge University Press.

Astell, Mary. 1717. *The Christian Religion, as Profess'd by a Daughter of the Church of England.* Printed by W. B. for R. Wilkin, at the King's-Head in St. Paul's-Church-Yard. Eighteenth Century Collections Online. While it would of course have been preferable to be able to cite Jacqueline Broad's modern scholarly edition of *The Christian Religion* (2013), I have not found it possible to obtain a copy in the United Kingdom. This sadly indicates one of the problems that remains when studying early modern women philosophers: even where scholarly editions of texts exist, they are not always accessible to readers.

________. 1996. *Some Reflections upon Marriage*. In *Political Writings,* edited by Patricia Springborg. Cambridge: Cambridge University Press.

________. 2002a. *A Serious Proposal to the Ladies: Parts I and II. Part I.* Edited by Patricia Springborg. Peterborough, Ont.: Broadview Press.

________. 2002b. *A Serious Proposal to the Ladies: Parts I and II. Part II.* Edited by Patricia Springborg. Peterborough, Ont.: Broadview Press.

Astell, Mary, and John Norris. 1695. *Letters Concerning the Love of God.* London: Printed for S. Manship and R. Wilkin. Early English Books Online.

Banicki, Konrad. 2012. "Therapeutic Arguments, Spiritual Exercises, or the Care of the Self: Martha Nussbaum, Pierre Hadot and Michel Foucault on Ancient Philosophy." *Ethical Perspectives* 22, no. 4:601–34. https://doi.org/10.2143/EP.

Broad, Jacqueline. 2015. *The Philosophy of Mary Astell: An Early Modern Theory of Virtue*. Oxford: Oxford University Press. http://www.oxfordscholarship.com.libproxy.ucl.ac.uk/view/10.1093/acprof:oso/9780198716815.001.0001/acprof-9780198716815.

Cottingham, John. 2006. "Descartes as Sage: Spiritual Askesis in Cartesian Philosophy." In *The Philosopher in Early Modern Europe: The Nature of a Contested Identity*. Edited by Ian Hunter, Stephen Gaukroger, and Conal Condren, 182–201. Cambridge: Cambridge University Press.

Foucault, Michel. 1983. "What Is Enlightenment?" In *The Foucault Reader*, edited by Paul Rabinow, 32–50. New York: Pantheon Books. https://doi.org/10.4324/9780203070468.

________. 1985. *The History of Sexuality, Volume 2: The Use of Pleasure*. New York: Pantheon Books. https://soth.alexanderstreet.com/cgi-bin/asp/philo/soth/sourceidx.pl?&sourceid=S10021786.

________. 1988. "Technologies of the Self." In *Technologies of the Self: A Seminar with Michel Foucault*, edited by Luther H. Martin, Huck Gutman, and Patrick H. Hutton, 16–49. Amherst: University of Massachusets Press. https://foucault.info/doc/documents/foucault-technologiesofself-en-html.

________. 1990. *Politics Philosophy Culture: Interviews and Other Writings, 1977–1984*. Edited by Lawrence D. Kritzman. London: Routledge. https://doi.org/10.3817/0677032152.

________. 1997a. "The Ethics of the Concern of the Self as a Practice of Freedom." In *Ethics: Subjectivity and Truth*, edited by Paul Rabinow, 281–301. New York: New Press.

________. 1997b. "The Masked Philosopher." In *Ethics: Subjectivity and Truth*, edited by Paul Rabinow, 321–27. New York: New Press.

________. 1997c. "On the Genealogy of Ethics." In *Ethics: Subjectivity and Truth*, edited by Paul Rabinow, 253–80. New York: New Press.

________. 2002. "The Subject and Power." In *Power: Essential Works of Foucault, 1954–1984*, volume 3, edited by James D. Faubion, 326–48. London: Penguin Books.

________. 2005. *The Hermeneutics of the Subject: Lectures at the Collège de France, 1981–2*. Edited by Frédéric Gros. New York: Picador.

Hadot, Pierre. 1995. *Philosophy as a Way of Life: Spiritual Exercises from Socrates to Foucault*. Edited by Arnold I. Davidson. Malden, Mass.: Blackwell.

Kolbrener, William. 2007. "Astell's 'Design of Friendship' in *Letters* and *A Serious Proposal, Part I*." In *Mary Astell: Reason, Gender, Faith*, edited by William Kolbrener and Michal Michelson, 49–64. Aldershot: Ashgate.

Malebranche, Nicolas. 1997. *The Search After Truth*. Edited by Thomas M. Lennon and Paul J. Olscamp. Cambridge: Cambridge University Press.

McWhorter, Ladelle. 2016. "The Abolition of Philosophy." In *Active Intolerance: Michel Foucault, the Prisons Information Group, and the Future of Abolition*, edited by Perry Zurn and Andrew Dilts, 23–40. London: Palgrave Macmillan.

More, Henry. 1690. *An Account of Virtue: or Dr. Henry More's Abridgement of Morals, Put into English*. London: Printed for Benj. Tooke. Early English Books Online.

Myers, Joanne E. 2013. "Enthusiastic Improvement: Mary Astell and Damaris Masham on Sociability." *Hypatia* 28, no. 3:533–50. https://doi.org/10.1111/j.1527-2001.2012.01294.x.

Sellars, John. Forthcoming. "Self or Cosmos: Foucault Versus Hadot." In *The Late Foucault: Ethical and Political Questions*, edited by Marta Faustino and Gianfranco Ferraro. London: Bloomsbury.

Sowaal, Alice. 2007. "Mary Astell's Serious Proposal: Mind, Method, and Custom." *Philosophy Compass* 2, no. 2:227–43. https://doi.org/10.1111/j.1747-9991.2007.00071.x.

________. 2017. "Mary Astell on Liberty." In *Women and Liberty, 1600–1800: Philosophical Essays*, edited by Jacqueline Broad and Karen Detlefsen, 178–94. Oxford Scholarship Online. http://www.oxfordscholarship.com.libproxy.ucl.ac.uk/view/10.1093/oso/9780198810261.001.0001/oso-9780198810261-chapter-12.

Testa, Federico. 2016. "Towards a History of Philosophical Practices in Michel Foucault and Pierre Hadot." *Pli*, special volume: 168–90.

Wilde, Cornelia. 2013. *Friendship, Love, and Letters: Ideals and Practices of Seraphic Friendship in Seventeenth-Century England.* Heidelberg: Universitätsverlag Winter.

CHAPTER 8

NIETZSCHE AND UNAMUNO ON *CONATUS* AND THE AGAPEIC WAY OF LIFE

ALBERTO OYA

1. Introduction

Those familiar with the philosophical works of Nietzsche and Unamuno will probably be surprised at the possibility of there being a philosophically relevant connection between the two. They seem to be engaged in two completely different and even opposite philosophical projects: Nietzsche defended the claim that a Christian way of life was something typical of sick and decadent people, while Unamuno, by appealing to our (according to Unamuno, natural) longing for an endless existence, aimed to offer a natural, nonevidential foundation for religious faith.

The truth is, however, that Unamuno's defense of religious faith can be read as a response to Nietzsche's claim that a Christian, agapeic way of life is something life-denying, contrary to our healthy, natural constitution. In fact, as I show here, Unamuno explicitly favored this reading. In doing so, he was probably motivated by the thought that all his reasoning starts from a metaphysical assumption similar to that of Nietzsche—that is, a modified version of Spinoza's *conatus*, or striving, construed not only in terms of self-preservation but also in terms of increase of power. Whereas Nietzsche claimed that a Christian, agapeic way of life is something antinatural insofar as it goes against the natural tendency to increase one's own power, Unamuno responded by arguing that an agapeic way of life is precisely a direct consequence of this natural tendency.

Philosophy as a Way of Life: Historical, Contemporary, and Pedagogical Perspectives.
Edited by James M. Ambury, Tushar Irani, and Kathleen Wallace.

Published 2021 by John Wiley & Sons Ltd.

Unfortunately, the connection between these two authors has received very little serious attention from scholars. It is true that some studies have attempted to compare them by following a somewhat rigorous, systematic approach (see, e.g., Gómez 2010), but they are more like biographical studies, aiming not to directly analyze the philosophical connections between Nietzsche and Unamuno but rather to explore the similarities and differences between their intellectual environments.

If we turn to the few studies that aim to focus on the philosophical connections between Nietzsche and Unamuno, however, the situation is disappointing. Among them we can find some quite astonishing claims, such as that Unamuno purposely misread Nietzsche, that "Unamuno did not know Nietzsche well because he did not want to know him; perhaps he was afraid to discover a more logical way than his own to live the radical doubt that overwhelmed him. But this path would lead him to the abyss, a danger of which he was well aware" (Gónzalez Urbano 1986, 16).[1] Similarly, Wirtz claims: "It is possible that in reality Nietzsche and Unamuno would have understood each other very well, if Unamuno had been able to overcome his human weakness and accept the death of God" (2013, 513).[2] I cannot see what the philosophical relevance of these kinds of unjustified psychological claims may be: in fact, they seem to be nothing more than an ad hoc denial, not only of Unamuno's philosophical capacities, but also of his sincerity. I hope we shall all agree that these sorts of affirmations are entirely irrelevant in serious philosophical reflection.

The aim of this essay, then, is to try to fill this gap in the literature by pointing out the philosophical relevance of Unamuno's attempt to provide a natural foundation for religious faith when assessing Nietzsche's criticisms of carrying out a Christian, agapeic way of life. In doing this, we must bear in mind that neither Nietzsche nor Unamuno was, strictly speaking, worried about the legitimacy of a religious way of life as something grounded in the truth of the factual belief that God exists; rather, what is at stake for both authors is whether engaging in a religious way of life is legitimated (or not) as being something consistent (or inconsistent) with our natural (and hence inalienable) inclinations. Unamuno's philosophical relevance consists in offering a Christian understanding of an agapeic way of life that, far from being life-denying in the way Nietzsche understood Christianity to be life-denying, aims to be life-affirming, in the sense of it being a direct consequence of what, according to both Nietzsche and Unamuno, is our most basic and natural inclination.

[1] My translation. The Spanish text reads: "Unamuno no conoció bien a Nietzsche porque no quería conocerle; sintió quizá miedo de descubrir una vía más lógica que la suya propia para vivir la duda radical que lo embargaba. Pero esta vía le conduciría al abismo, y él era conciente de ese peligro."

[2] My translation. The Spanish text reads: "Es posible que en realidad Nietzsche y Unamuno se hubieran entendido muy bien, si Unamuno hubiese podido superar su debilidad humana y aceptar la muerte de Dios."

2. Spinoza's Conatus

As I noted above, Unamuno sees his position as being a successful response to Nietzsche insofar as he takes it as being the right implication of their shared starting point. This common claim that seems to be at the basis of all their philosophical reasoning is a modified version of Spinoza's conatus.

The doctrine of conatus is first stated in the sixth proposition of the third part of the *Ethics*, where Spinoza claims: "Each thing, as far as it can by its own power, strives to persevere in its being" (1985, 498).

This striving (*conatus* in the original Latin text) for self-preservation is taken to be the basic motivational force behind all of an individual's endeavors. It should not, however, be understood teleologically, as a conscious effort toward an end but rather be understood as a natural tendency (as an *appetite*, in Spinoza's terminology) that constitutes "the actual essence" of all "singular things" (Spinoza 1985, 499)—that is, something that all singular things are led to because of their own nature. This is why Spinoza adds the clause "as far as it can by its own power": by this, he is restricting this conatus, or striving, to things acting out of inertia, as it were, by their own nature and without any kind of external intervention.

It is also important to emphasize that although Spinoza accepts that complex, conscious individuals like human beings can become aware of this conatus (by which it ceases to be an appetite and becomes a desire), Spinoza's conatus is a metaphysical claim of universal application that refers not only to conscious beings but to all singular things. The most common reading among Spinoza scholars of "singular things" understands the term as referring to all those sets of physical particles that have a certain form that is differentiable from other sets of physical particles (see, e.g., Nadler 2006, 138–40; Bennett 1984, 232). That is: not only do conscious beings like humans or complex animals strive to persevere in their being, so equally do plants and rocks.

3. Nietzsche on Conatus: The Will to Power

Nietzsche claimed that all living beings aim, as their most basic natural inclination, toward the increase of their power. He called this natural tendency "the will to power." The importance of this claim in Nietzsche's philosophy is evident, since it is what led him to proclaim the ideal of the overman (*Übermensch*) and its related claim that we should aim to affirm the eternal recurrence of everything. As we shall see, the will to power is also what is behind Nietzsche's criticisms of leading a Christian, agapeic way of life.

As is often noted, Nietzsche's formulation of the will to power did not arise from the void but emerged from a critical interaction with Spinoza's claim that all singular things naturally strive to persevere in their being (see, e.g., Look 2001; Grosse Wiesmann 2013; Ioan 2017). In fact, Nietzsche himself acknowledged his admiration for Spinoza's philosophical views in a letter to Overbeck dated July 1881, in which he goes on to confess: "I am utterly amazed, utterly enchanted. I have a *precursor*, and what a precursor! I hardly knew Spinoza: that I should have turned to him just *now*, was inspired by 'instinct.' . . . Even though the divergencies are admittedly tremendous, they are due more to the difference in time, culture, and science. *In summa*: my lonesomeness, which, as on very high mountains, often made it hard for me to breathe and made my blood rush out, is now at least a twosomeness. Strange" (1976, 92).

This does not mean, of course, that Nietzsche accepted Spinoza's literal formulation of conatus. Like Spinoza's conatus, Nietzsche's will to power should be understood as a natural tendency; but, in contrast to Spinoza's conatus, Nietzsche's will to power does not seem to apply to all singular things (that is, whether conscious or not) but seems to apply *only* to biological living organisms. A more important difference is that Nietzsche read Spinoza's conatus as making a claim about self-preservation, whereas the will to power is explicitly formulated not in terms of self-preservation but in terms of increase of power. This last point is an important difference because, according to Nietzsche, self-preservation and increase of power are two completely different, even mutually exclusive, things. He clearly states these two points in his *Thus Spoke Zarathustra*: "Where I found the living, there I found will to power; and even in the will of those who serve I found the will to be master. . . . Indeed, the truth was not hit by him who shot at it with the word of the 'will to existence': that will does not exist. For, what does not exist cannot will; but what is in existence, how could that still want existence? Only where there is life is there also will: not will to life but—thus I teach you—will to power" (1976, 227–28).

It is important to emphasize that this seeking towards the increase of one's own power is not an ethical, normative claim but, as I have just said, a natural tendency present in all of us, which is why any attempt to go against it would be an antinatural action amounting to an unsuccessful attempt at self-deception by pretending to deny one's own nature. Unsuccessful because, being natural, this seeking of ours cannot be completely silenced and will in the end be reexpressed in other, more indirect forms—which is precisely one of the core claims behind Nietzsche's thesis of the "transvaluation" defended in *On the Genealogy of Morals*: "These weak people—some day or other *they* too intend to be strong, there is no doubt of that, some day *their* 'kingdom' too shall come—they term it 'the kingdom of God,' of course, as aforesaid: for one is very humble in all things!" (1989, 48).

We should not, then, attempt to act against our own natural constitution but rather attempt to affirm life as what it is and to affirm ourselves as what we are—thereby "becoming what we are." As far as I am aware, Nietzsche himself does not explicitly offer a systematic account of how we are to understand this affirmation. It is clear, however, that affirming life involves at least our willingness to accept (probably not necessarily as a factual claim but just as a thought experiment, as an "if") the idea of the eternal recurrence of the same, which Nietzsche does not hesitate to refer to in *Ecce Homo* as "the highest formulation of affirmation that is at all attainable" (1989, 295). It is through our willingness to embrace the possibility of the eternal recurrence that we come to actively affirm, and not merely resign ourselves to, our whole singularity. In contrast with "the last man," who cowardly evades both reality and his own nature, thereby making "everything small" (1976, 129), Nietzsche's ideal of the overman embodies this sort of affirmative attitude toward life and oneself.

Even without entering into a detailed account of Nietzsche's notion of the will to power, it is easy to see that the claim that all living beings naturally aim at the increase of their own power is precisely what is behind Nietzsche's ferocious criticism of the Christian call to follow an agapeic way of life. Throughout all his texts, but perhaps in a more systematic way in *On the Genealogy of Morals*, Nietzsche constantly emphasizes that the will to power is inconsistent with following a Christian, agapeic way of life. Christian values, Nietzsche says, constitute a diminishment of the individual's power insofar as they imply not an affirmation but a denial of this earthly life. And since the aim to increase one's own power is a natural tendency present in all living beings, the way of life defended by Christianity is something antinatural, given to sick and decadent people. To illustrate this point, take the following extract from *The Antichrist*, where Nietzsche explicitly states that his denial of Christianity is not due to the lack of evidence for forming the belief that the Christian God actually exists but due to the fact that the sort of values associated with this God go against our natural healthy constitution:

> That we find no God—either in history or in nature or behind nature—is not what differentiates *us*, but that we experience what has been reversed as God, not as "godlike" but as miserable, as absurd, as harmful, not merely as an error but as a *crime against life*. We deny God as God. If one were to *prove* this God of the Christians to us, we should be even less able to believe in him. In a formula: *deus, qualem Paulus creavit, dei negatio*. . . . Nobody is free to become a Christian: one is not "converted" to Christianity—one has to be sick enough for it. We others who have the *courage* to be healthy and also to despise—how may we despise a religion which taught men to misunderstand the body! which does not want to get rid of superstitious belief in souls! which turns insufficient nourishment into something "meritorious"! which fights health as a kind of enemy, devil, temptation! which fancies that one can carry around a "perfect soul" in a cadaver of a body, and which therefore found it necessary to concoct a new conception of "perfection"—a pale, sickly, idiotic-enthusiastic character, so-called "holiness." . . . At the bottom of Christianity is the rancor of the sick, instinct directed *against* the healthy, *against* health itself. Everything that has turned out well, everything that is proud and prankish, beauty above all, hurts its ears and eyes. (1976, 627–34)

4. Unamuno on Conatus: The Natural Appetite for an Endless Existence

In his major philosophical work, *Del sentimiento trágico de la vida en los hombres y en los pueblos* (Unamuno 1966a) (*The Tragic Sense of Life in Men and Nations*) (Unamuno 1972), Unamuno, despite starting from a similar assumption, defended a view completely opposite from Nietzsche's. Starting too from the metaphysical claim that all existent beings naturally and primarily aim not only at their own self-preservation but also at the increase of their power (from which follows, according to Unamuno, that all existent beings naturally seek an endless existence), Unamuno aimed to offer a natural, nonevidential foundation for religious faith (that is, religious faith is justified not because we are justified in believing that the proposition that God exists is true but because it is something we are naturally led to).

It is important to emphasize that Unamuno's argument does not rely on the psychological claim that we all, as an empirical fact, have the desire for an endless existence; what Unamuno's argument requires is the stronger, metaphysical claim that the most basic natural inclination of all singular things (not only conscious beings like us) is to seek an endless existence. This is what enables Unamuno to conclude that religious faith is a direct consequence of our own nature. Furthermore, this is what explains why, according to Unamuno, we cannot stop seeking an endless existence even if we lack any evidential support to believe that it will occur.

Unamuno's explicit endorsement of Spinoza's argument for conatus (Unamuno 1972, 3–10 [1966a, 109–13]), with the important caveat that what really follows from that argument is not (at least, not only) a natural tendency toward self-preservation but a natural tendency toward the increase of one's own power (Unamuno 1972, 227–28 [1966a, 232]), clearly illustrates why Unamuno regarded his defence of religious faith as starting from the same metaphysical claim as Nietzsche's reasoning. It is the acceptance of this natural tendency that led Unamuno to claim that all singular things naturally seek an endless existence. This seeking, which he refers to as the "hambre de inmortalidad" ("hunger for immortality"), is nothing but the affirmation of this, our earthly life, and the expression of the (alleged) natural inclination to increase one's own power: if we despised and denied the value of this earthly life, then it would make no sense to want it to be eternal. This point is nicely illustrated in one of Unamuno's letters to Ilundáin: "The obsession with death comes from the plenitude of life, and those of us that have it is because we feel that life overflows us, and because it overflows us we want it never to end" (qtd. Fernández González 1997, 375).[3]

[3] My translation. The Spanish text reads: "La obsesión de la muerte viene de plenitud de vida, la tenemos los que sentimos que la vida nos desborda, y porque nos desborda la queremos inacabable."

Unamuno's reasoning for defending the lawfulness of religious faith starts with the recognition that all the evidence we have goes against the possibility of our enjoying an endless existence. Earthly death seems inevitable, and philosophical arguments for human immortality are beside the point because the kind of immortality they aim to demonstrate fails to secure the preservation of our own individuality: it is not the endless existence of our soul that we seek but the endless existence of us as the individuals we are here and now, the immortality of the "hombre de carne y hueso" ("man of flesh and bone").

According to Unamuno, the only way in which our *appetite* for an endless existence could be satisfied would be through the intervention of (the Christian) God, the One who announces his salvation through the resurrection of all the dead. The problem is, however, that we lack any evidential justification for forming the belief that this God exists. Arguments from natural theology fail because they assume that God is akin to a nonobservable scientific theoretical entity to be established through abductive reasoning as being the best explanation of some worldly event. But this, Unamuno says, is an erroneous theological conception: God, by saving us from annihilation, gives the world an ultimate meaning and purpose, but accepting the existence of God does not help us to explain why a given fact has occurred or why the world is such or such a way.

This situation is what Unamuno called "el sentimiento trágico de la vida" (usually translated in English as "the tragic sense of life," although I think it would be more accurate to translate it as "the tragic feeling of life"); that is, the struggle ("agonía") between our wanting an endless existence (and so, derivatively, our wanting God to exist) and our lack of evidential justification for believing that God exists (and so, our lack of evidential justification for believing that we shall enjoy an endless existence).

Since our seeking an endless existence is nothing more than the expression of our natural tendency to increase our own power, the sentimiento trágico de la vida is not a theoretical, intellectual conflict but an emotional one, something we intimately feel—which is why Unamuno calls it "sentimiento" ("feeling"). On the other hand, the conflict is "trágico" ("tragic") because it is irresolvable: we cannot override our lack of evidential justification by voluntarily forming the belief that God exists (or that God does not exist) because our beliefs aim at truth (that is, we cannot believe that P without believing that P is true), and neither can we suspend our judgment and resign ourselves to doubt, since this would amount to silencing our most basic natural inclination.

Our incapacity to solve this conflict causes us a sort of anguish. This spiritual suffering, however, is something desirable in itself, since it is precisely from this spiritual suffering that religious faith emerges.

As soon as we realize that this seeking an endless existence is of universal application, we become aware that all singular things in the world share with us our tragic and anguished condition. Faced with this, we cannot but come to commiserate with and love the whole world. And, Unamuno says, since only living, conscious beings suffer, to claim that the entire world suffers as we do is tantamount to adopting a religious understanding of the world, of seeing the world as a sort of personal conscious being.

In its practical, ethical sense, this religious understanding of the world is translated in an attempt, through the practice of charity, to liberate ourselves and the entire world from the anguished situation in which we all live. To cultivate charity is, Unamuno says, to act in such a way as to lovingly give ourselves over to the spiritual care of others. An illustration in plain terms of this kind of loving, agapeic way of life that Unamuno's religious faith involves can be found in his short novel *San Manuel Bueno, mártir* (Unamuno 1967) (*Saint Manuel Bueno, Martyr*) (Unamuno 1976). This is the story of the fictional character Manuel Bueno, a Spanish Catholic priest who, suffering from the struggle of the sentimiento trágico de la vida, and therefore being unable to come to form the belief that God does actually exist despite his wanting it to be so, devotes his entire life to a loving and generous caring of his people, leading to his posthumous sanctification. While in this novel Unamuno uses the character of a Catholic priest, probably so as to emphasize his contention that his notion of religious faith is the original Christian conception, the one historically announced by Jesus Christ and defended by early Christians, it is important to emphasize that neither Unamuno's charity nor the kind of religious understanding of the world that results from our becoming aware that all singular things in the world share with us the same tragic and anguished condition involves any mystical, transcendental faculty. This sort of agapeic giving of ourselves over to the whole world that Unamuno calls for can be put into practice in every moment of our daily, worldly life—a point Unamuno illustrates with his example of the shoemaker:

> Here behold one type of shoemaker, living off making shoes, but doing it with the minimum workmanship needed to keep his clientele. Then you have this other shoemaker, living on a rather different spiritual plane, for he is possessed by the instinct of workmanship, and out of pride of self or as a point of honor works to earn the reputation as best shoemaker in town, or in Christendom, even if this renown will not earn him any more money or more clientele, but only more renown and prestige. But there is a still higher degree of moral perfection as concerns the office of shoemaker, and that is for the shoemaker to work in order to become for his fellow townsmen the one and only shoemaker, the one who makes their footwear so well that they will miss him when he "dies on them," and not merely "dies," and they will all feel that he ought not to have died at all; and this will come about because he made their footwear in the thought of sparing them from thinking of their feet when they could be thinking of higher things, of the highest truths; in short, he made their footwear with love in his heart for them and for God in them—he made their footwear religiously. . . . By making shoes, and precisely because one makes them, one can gain the kingdom of heaven, providing that as shoemaker one strives to be perfect, just as our Father in heaven is perfect. (1972, 296–301)

Another illustration of this agapeic way of life that Unamuno refers to can be found, he says, in the biblical testimony about the life and works of Jesus Christ: "And the Christ who gave Himself entirely to His brothers in humanity with total self-abnegation is the model for our action" (1972, 292). Unamuno's comments here respond to his already mentioned contention that his position was not an unorthodox one but in fact amounted to a return to the original Christian conception of religious faith. It should be emphasized, however, that his claim that the figure of Jesus Christ embodied this kind of agapeic way of life does not mean that Unamuno saw this lovingly giving ourselves over to the whole world as being justified on theological grounds, because that was the way of life announced by Jesus Christ. As I said before, his reasoning neither presupposes nor aims to end up justifying the truth of any theological or religious statement. Unamuno's reasoning has no factual, cognitive content—and this is so because it does not rely on any given state of affairs of the world, on the fact that the world is in such a way and not in another, but relies on our own natural constitution. Unamuno's agapeic way of life is taken to be our subjective, completely human idiosyncratic reaction to our most basic and natural inclination, and, as such, it does not depend on any given state of affairs of the world completely independent of our own nature.

In short, Unamuno's reasoning is exclusively focused on the concrete subject, the hombre de carne y hueso, and what emerges from him. And this reasoning aims to be of universal application given that we all share the same natural condition—that is, that we are all the same kind of subjects, since we all naturally and primarily seek for an increase of our own power. As I pointed out, Unamuno's contention is not to justify the *truth* of any religious or theological statement but to show that our immersion in a religious, agapeic way of life, despite being a subjective, nonevidentially grounded reaction, is nonetheless legitimated given its foundation in our own natural human constitution. It is in this sense that Unamuno's reasoning amounts to an affirmation of the concrete self, the individual of carne y hueso: we are moved to commiserate with and love the whole entire world by assuming and acting in accordance with our own natural condition, by affirming, and not merely resigning ourselves to, the irresoluble and intimate struggle that according to Unamuno we all naturally suffer from, given our incapacity to secure our attainment of an endless existence—and here it should be noted again that this struggle we are assumed to suffer from, the sentimiento trágico de la vida, emerges as a consequence of our seeking an endless existence, which according to Unamuno is nothing more than the expression of our (alleged) most basic and natural inclination toward the increase of our own power. In Unamuno's words,

> Spiritual love for oneself, the compassion one feels for oneself, may perhaps be called egotism, but nothing could be more opposed to common ordinary egotism. For, from this love or compassion for yourself, from this intense despair,

> from the knowledge that just as before you were born you did not exist so after you die you will be no more, you go on to feel compassion for—that is, to love—all your fellow beings and brothers in this world of appearance, those wretched shadows who file by, going from nothingness to nothingness, mere sparks of consciousness shining for a moment in the infinite and eternal darkness. And from feeling compassion for other men, for those akin to you, beginning with those most akin to you, for those you live among, you go on to feel compassion for everyone alive, and perhaps even for that which does not live but merely exists. That distant star shining up there in the night will one day be extinguished and turn to dust and cease shining and existing. And as with the one star, so it will be with the whole of the starry sky. Poor sky! . . . And thus you will come to feel compassion for all things: you will feel universal love. (1972, 151–53)

It is here, in the conception of charity Unamuno offers us, that his criticism of Nietzsche becomes even more evident. Charity, engaging ourselves in an agapeic way of life, far from being a loss of our own individuality, is the expression of the aforementioned natural inclination: it is through the practice of charity that we come to *feel ourselves* as being part of others, and so we *somehow* surpass our own individuality without ceasing to be the individuals we are here and now. Although it may appear paradoxical at first sight, it is on account of this active affirmation of ourselves in our incapacity to secure our endless existence—that is, to attain the ultimate satisfaction of our selfish, egoistical motivation to increase our own power—that, according to Unamuno, we are moved to adopt a generous and loving agapeic way of life. And it is precisely through this lovingly giving of ourselves over to the whole world that we come to feel that egoistical motivation satisfied. This is what explains Unamuno's claim that "love is consolation in desolation, it is the only remedy against death, since it is death's sister" (1972, 146). That Unamuno takes charity to be an increase of the individual's power is clear from what he says in chapter 11 of *Del sentimiento trágico de la vida en los hombres y en los pueblos*:

> He who does not lose his life shall not find it. Give yourself then to others, but in order to give yourself to them, first master them. For it is not possible to master without being mastered. Everyone nourishes himself upon the flesh he devours. In order to master your neighbor you must know him and love him. By attempting to impose my ideas upon him I become the recipient of his. To love my neighbor is to wish he may be like me, that he may be another I: that is to say, it is to wish I may be he, it is to wish to obliterate the division between him and me, to suppress its evil. My endeavor to impose myself upon another, to be and live in him and by him, to make him mine, which is the same as making my self his, is what gives religious meaning to our collectivity, to human solidarity. . . . The highest precept which arises from the love of God, and the basis for all morality, is this: yield yourself up entirely, hand over your spirit so that it may be saved, so that it may be made eternal. Such is the meaningful sacrifice of life. And yielding oneself assumes, I repeat, an imposition of oneself. True religious morality is essentially aggressive, ever ready to launch an invasion. . . . And

> there is no other way of being all else but by giving oneself to all, and when all shall be all in all, all will be in each one of us. The apocatastasis is more than a mystical dream: it is a norm of action, it is a beacon for high deeds. And from here springs the invasive, overmastering, aggressive, inquisitorial ethic, if you will. For true charity is a species of invasion: it consists in forcing my spirit upon other spirits, in offering them my suffering as nutriment and consolation for their own sufferings, in arousing their unrest, in whetting their hunger for God by my hunger for God. . . . All men should strive to impose themselves upon one another, to give their spirits up to one another, to leave their seals on one another's souls. (1972, 302–7)

Unamuno was, of course, well aware that his defense of religious faith amounted to a response to Nietzsche's denial of a Christian, agapeic way of life as something life-denying, something inconsistent with our most basic and natural inclination to increase our own power. In fact, it seems reasonable to say that when defending his conception of charity Unamuno was directly arguing against Nietzsche. Immediately after the quotes given above, Unamuno, although he does not mention the name of Nietzsche, explicitly denies Nietzsche's claim that Christianity is a morality of slaves: "It gives one pause to recall the argument that Christian morality is the morality of slaves. Who said so? The anarchists! It is anarchism itself, indeed, which is the morality of slaves: only the slave hymns anarchic liberty. *Anarchism: No! Panarchism: Yes!* In short: No! to the creed of 'Neither God nor Master' Yes! to the creed of 'Everyone a God! Everyone a Master!': all men striving to become gods, all striving to become immortal, and doing so by mastering all others" (Unamuno 1972, 307–8).

Contrary to what Nietzsche says, then, Unamuno is claiming that our natural tendency to increase our own power does not in any way imply the decadent and sickly view of the Christian, agapeic way of life. It is just the opposite. We are constituted in such a way that we naturally aim at the increase of our own power, and this is precisely why, Unamuno says, we are naturally led to living a Christian, agapeic way of life. Unamuno's religious faith amounts to an affirmation of life, an increase of one's own power, because it is through our agapeic giving of ourselves over to the whole world that we come to feel in communion with the entire world, feeling thereby that we come to surpass our own individuality without losing our own personal identity, without ceasing to be the individuals of carne y hueso we are here and now. What is natural for us, then, is to give ourselves to the spiritual care of others and to enter into a loving relation with the whole world.

This helps us understand Unamuno's criticism of Nietzsche in his short paper "Uebermensch." In it, Unamuno says that Nietzsche's proposal is a "philosophy—if it is that—of the weak who want to become strong and pretend to be so, and who persistently attempt to make others believe they are strong to see if in this way they convince themselves that they really are, a philosophy of the poor bourgeois tired of being treated as good people who want to appear as barbarous" (1966b, 1368).[4] Nietzsche's ideal of the Übermensch is antinatural, according to Unamuno, since it amounts to a denial of our own human nature, the humanity of the hombre de carne y hueso. In fact, it is also insincere, says Unamuno, since no matter what we do we cannot change our natural condition. This is why we should not attempt to overcome what we are now but attempt to assume our natural condition and act in accordance with it. Our ideal, says Unamuno, should not be the Nietszchean Übermensch, who deceives himself by trying to silence his own natural anguished condition; rather, our ideal should be to assume and affirm our own nature (that is, the sentimiento trágico de la vida) by making it the foundation of our acting (that is, the practice of charity). In short, our ideal should be not the Nietzschean Übermensch but Don Quijote, who "knew how to be poor and be defeated":

> When one aspires to be an over-man, then one is unsure that he is a man, fully and truly a man, a real man. . . . Now, poor *Übermensch* cannot backtrack. He has spent so many years bragging and making his eagle cackle, that now he has no choice but to act the hero. And being a natural-born hero—*der geborener Held*—which is the worst thing that can happen. Being a natural-born hero must be one of the most compromising things in the world. As compromising as being a prophet. Demonstrating acquired science is something that is within many people's reach, but demonstrating infused science is something quite different. And the natural-born hero must have infused, nonacquired courage. For the simple, modest man, nothing more than a man, courage is usually the art of hiding fear, but the over-man, the natural-born hero, must not know fear. What if he knows fear? And what if he knows faintness? The most terrible thing that can happen to a people is that they not be prepared for defeat. The greatness of Don Quijote was that he knew how to be poor and be defeated. (Unamuno 1966b, 1369)[5]

[4] My translation. The Spanish text reads: "Filosofía—si es que lo es—de débiles que quieren hacerse fuertes y fingen serlo y se empeñan en hacer creer a los demás que lo son para ver si así se convencen a sí mismos de que lo sean, filosofía de pobres burgueses que hartos de oírse tratar de buenas gentes quieren aparecer bárbaros."

[5] My translation. The Spanish text reads: "Cuando se aspira a sobre-hombre es que no se está seguro de ser hombre, hombre entero y verdadero, todo un hombre. . . . Ahora el pobrecito *Uebermensch* no puede volverse atrás. Ha estado tantos años soltando baladronadas y haciendo que su águila cacaree, que ahora tiene que hacer el héroe por fuerza. Y el héroe nato—*der geborener Held*—que es lo peor. Hacer de héroe nato debe de ser una de las cosas más comprometidas del mundo. Tan comprometido como hacer de profeta. Demostrar ciencia adquirida es algo que está al alcance de mucha gente, pero demostrar ciencia infusa ya es otra cosa. Y el héroe nato ha de tener valor infuso y no valor adquirido. Para el modesto hombre sencillo, no más que hombre, el valor suele ser el arte de ocultar el miedo, pero el sobrehombre, el héroe nato, no puede conocer el miedo. ¿Y si lo conoce? ¿Y si conoce el desfallecimiento? Lo más terrible que le puede pasar a un pueblo es que no se le prepare también para la derrota. La grandeza de Don Quijote es que supo ser pobre y ser vencido."

5. Conclusion

The aim of this essay is to comment on Unamuno's criticism of Nietzsche by pointing out the philosophical relevance of Unamuno's attempt to provide a natural foundation for religious faith when assessing Nietzsche's criticisms of a Christian, agapeic way of life. Unamuno argued that, far from being life-denying as Nietzsche claimed, our lovingly, agapeic giving of ourselves over to the whole world constitutes an affirmation of ourselves and our (alleged) natural tendency to increase our own power. Unamuno's reasoning is philosophically relevant insofar as, in spite of prima facie appearances, it relies on a metaphysical assumption similar to Nietzsche's, thus aiming to appease all those who agree with Nietzsche about the claim that our most basic and natural inclination is to increase our own power.

As we have seen, Nietzsche regarded the attempt to follow a Christian, agapeic way of life as being nothing more than a cowardly, insincere attempt to evade oneself. Thus, for example, in "On Love of the Neighbor" from *Thus Spoke Zarathustra*, Nietzsche writes: "You flee to your neighbor from yourselves and would like to make a virtue out of that: but I see through your 'selflessness.' The *you* is older than the *I*; the *you* has been pronounced holy, but not yet the *I*; so man crowds towards his neighbor" (Nietzsche 1976, 172).

Unamuno agrees with Nietzsche that each of us should affirm himself or herself, the concrete *I*. Contrary to Nietzsche, however, Unamuno argues that affirming ourselves in our most natural egotism, in our selfish motivation to satisfy our most basic and natural inclination to increase our own power, is precisely what moves us to a generous, loving giving of ourselves over to the whole world: "This *egotism* is the only true cure for *egoism* or spiritual avarice, the vice of keeping and saving oneself for oneself rather than striving to make oneself eternal by giving oneself" (1972, 310).

Ultimately, Unamuno's point is that carrying out an agapeic way of life, commiserating with and lovingly giving oneself to the whole world, does not constitute a diminishment of one's own power but is rather the only way to increase it. It is only through the agapeic giving of ourselves that we come to feel in communion with the whole world while preserving our own singularity, while continuing to be the same individuals we are here and now. According to Unamuno, then, an agapeic way of life is not merely consistent with human nature but an affirmation of it, the expression of our most basic inclination to increase our own power.

References

Bennett, Jonathan. 1984. *A Study of Spinoza's Ethics*. Indianapolis: Hackett.

Fernández González, Ángel. 1997. "Nueva lectura de 'Diario íntimo' de Unamuno." *Cuadernos Cátedra Miguel de Unamuno* 32:369–77.

Gómez, Michael A. 2010. "Unamuno, Nietzsche and Religious Modernism: Affinities and Complexities Concerning the View of Faith." *Anales de la literatura española contemporánea* 35, no. 1:223–56.

González Urbano, Eulalia. 1986. "Visión trágica de la filosofía: Unamuno y Nietzsche." *Logos: Anales del seminario de metafísica* 21:13–39.
Grosse Wiesmann, Hannah. 2013. "Spinoza's Conatus and Nietzsche's Will to Power: Self-Preservation vs. Increase of Power?" *Acta Universitatis Carolinae: Interpretationes: Studia philosophica europeana* 3, no. 2:49–61.
Ioan, Razvan. 2017. "A Case of 'Consumption': Nietzsche's Diagnosis of Spinoza." *Nietzsche-Studien* 46, no. 1:1–27.
Look, Brandon. 2001. "'Becoming Who One Is' in Spinoza and Nietzsche." *Iyyun* 50:327–38.
Nadler, Steven M. 2006. *Spinoza's Ethics: An Introduction*. New York: Cambridge University Press.
Nietzsche, Friedrich. 1976. *The Portable Nietzsche*. Edited and translated by Walter Kaufmann. New York: Penguin Books.
________. 1989. *On the Genealogy of Morals and Ecce Homo*. Edited and translated by Walter Kaufmann. New York: Vintage Books.
Spinoza, Benedictus. 1985. *Ethics: Demonstrated in Geometrical Order and Divided into Five Parts*. In *The Collected Works of Spinoza*, edited and translated by E. M. Curley, 408–617. Princeton: Princeton University Press.
Unamuno, Miguel de. 1966a. *Del sentimiento trágico de la vida en los hombres y en los pueblos*. In Miguel de Unamuno: *Obras completas*, vol. VII: *Meditaciones y ensayos espirituales*, edited by Manuel García Blanco, 109–302. Madrid: Escelicer.
________. 1966b. "Uebermensch." In Miguel de Unamuno: *Obras completas*, vol. IV: *La raza y la lengua*, edited by Manuel García Blanco, 1367–69. Madrid: Escelicer.
________. 1967. *San Manuel Bueno, mártir*. In Miguel de Unamuno: *Obras completas*, vol. II: *Novelas*, edited by Manuel García Blanco, 1127–54. Madrid: Escelicer.
Unamuno, Miguel de. 1972. *The Tragic Sense of Life in Men and Nations*. In *The Selected Works of Miguel de Unamuno*, vol. 4, edited and translated by Anthony Kerrigan, 3–358. Princeton: Princeton University Press.
________. 1976. *Saint Manuel Bueno, Martyr*. In *The Selected Works of Miguel de Unamuno*, vol. 7, edited and translated by Anthony Kerrigan, 135–80. Princeton: Princeton University Press.
Wirtz, Wiebke. 2013. "¿Don Quijote como superhombre? La influencia de la filosofía de Nietzsche en la obra de Unamuno." In *"Festina Lente": Actas del II Congreso internacional jóvenes investigadores siglo de oro (JSO 2012)*, edited by Carlos Mata Induráin, Adrián J. Sáez, and Ana Zúniga Lacruz, 503–15. Pamplona: Servicio de Publicaciones de la Universidad de Navarra.

CHAPTER 9

WAYS OF DISCOURSE AND WAYS OF LIFE

PLATO ON THE CONFLICT BETWEEN POETRY AND PHILOSOPHY

I-KAI JENG

1. Introduction

What Plato calls the "quarrel between philosophy and poetry" (*Republic* 607b5–6) ultimately concerns two opposed views of the best life.[1] Philosophy stands for the life led, guided, and ruled by reason and knowledge. It is initially unclear, however, what conception of the good life poetry stands for.

A working definition of poetry may be extracted from the *Republic* sections 601a4–b4 and 603c5–9: poetry portrays humans in action and their assessments of their actions in spoken, metered language, perhaps accompanied by music. In short, poetry is a medium of communication with a certain subject matter: human action and responses to those actions. In books II–III, poetry is regarded as neutral, and its quality is determined by the moral standard it upholds. In other words, in those books poetry is not bound up with a determinate conception of a way of life; it all depends on the stories it tells. But in book X, poetry becomes itself bad: virtually all its

[1] "Best" is meant in both its ethical and its nonethical sense. I will also speak of "the good life" or "the ideal life" and similar expressions to express the same idea. Stephanus page citations are from the *Republic* by Slings 2003. Translations from the Greek are my own.

Philosophy as a Way of Life: Historical, Contemporary, and Pedagogical Perspectives.
Edited by James M. Ambury, Tushar Irani, and Kathleen Wallace.

Published 2021 by John Wiley & Sons Ltd.

stories corrupt the soul. Poetry is no longer neutral and carries a conception of the good life.[2]

The present essay focuses on book X because it presents the more challenging view. By framing that critique as the "quarrel between philosophy and poetry," Plato is simultaneously defending and demarcating the life of philosophy through what he sees as its rival. As Susan B. Levin remarks, "Since Plato's praise of philosophy and its denunciations of its rivals transpire alongside one another, one might anticipate—rightly—that his challenges to the latter would emphasize their shortcomings with respect to this condition" (2001, 142). In other words, the defects of poetry are selected to bring philosophy into relief and justify it.

As the title of my essay indicates, Plato's confrontation with poetry also has much to do with the issue of logos, understood in the widest sense of "discourse." While the discursive character of poetry is evident at first sight, Plato also reveals it to be bound up with a way of life. Book X implies that discursive modes are not innocent and have bearings on how one lives. As Myles Burnyeat comments, "Style . . . springs from, and expresses, the character of a person's soul" (1997, 218). Stylistic, "aesthetic" differences always have ethical import for Plato (Ferrari 1989, 118; Murray 1996, 4).

My essay is divided into three sections. I first discuss a pivotal passage (602c4–606c1) which contends that poetry weakens our ability to reason. Since that discussion explicitly contrasts poetry with rational speech, it provides a first characterization of how philosophic discourse contrasts with poetic discourse. Building upon this, section 3 develops the rivalry through two other passages (604e1–605a6; 601b9–602c2): the philosophic life versus the poetic life emerges as a contrast between the ideals of "unity" versus "freedom," which in turn lead to a number of ways their respective modes of discourse contrast with each other. Poetry's endorsement of freedom explains why it is associated with democracy and tyranny in books VIII–IX. The democratic way of life is one of freedom, while the tyrannical life is the undesirable outcome of pursuing freedom to the extreme. The quarrel, however, is not a simple opposition: while philosophy opposes the life that poetry stands for, in another sense it also needs it for its own purposes. Section 4 takes up this issue to show Plato's complex stance toward poetry.

[2] There is controversy concerning the relation of books II–III to book X. A major issue of contention surrounds 595a5: does *mimēsis* there indicate a shift of meaning in the two discussions? Ferrari 1989, Burnyeat 1997, and Dorter 2006 argue for compatibility; Annas 1981 and Halliwell 2005 consider the two passages to be at odds with each other; Nehamas 1999 and Pappas 2003 adopt a somewhat middle position.

2. The Discourse of Emotions and the Discourse of Measurement

The main point of sections 602c4–606c1 is that *poetry harms our ability to measure through its power to console.*[3] By contrast, philosophic discourse does not console but assesses the significance of our experience and actions. The contrast here exhibits philosophic discourse as *logismos*, calculation or measurement.[4]

The objections to poetry in book X mostly follow the analogy with the painter. Socrates, as a rule, analyzes some defect of the painter in each objection and then argues that this defect applies to the poet as well. The aspect of painting Socrates analyzes in our target passage concerns how the size and shape of things appear. A large object observed from a distance and a small one observed up close can appear equal in size (602c7–8). To know their real size, one needs geometry to compare and measure the two (d6–7), and the power to employ geometry belongs to reason (e1–3). But the appearance that two objects are the same in size is not thereby dispelled (e4–6). Even after being measured, the two do not suddenly appear in their real size to the observer's eyes. The only difference is that now the observer has learned to not take appearances for granted. Socrates, applying the principle of noncontradiction in 436b9–c2, infers that the soul's power to perceive appearance and its power to measure are not identical (602e8–603a3). The power to measure belongs to reason, while the power to perceive appearance belongs to a lowly (*phaulos*: 603a7, b5) part of the soul.[5]

The painter has expertise concerning how things appear and uses this knowledge to create perspectival illusions. In doing so, the painter paralyzes reason. Being dazzled by the painting, the viewer's nonrational part of the soul is excited. And Socrates earlier suggested that when pleasures flow through one part of a person's soul, that person becomes less interested in the pleasures that occur through the activity of other parts (485d6–e2). This assumption is, I think, at work in the argument examined here as well. As the viewer is charmed by the beautiful illusions of the

[3] Poetry's power to harm is stated in strong language. In 595b5, Socrates speaks of "mutilation (*lōbē*) of thought," a word with strong ethical connotations, suggesting poetry's harm to be of a transgressive kind. In 605b4–5 Socrates says that poetry "destroys" (*apollusi*) calculation.

[4] *Logos* and *logismos* are sometimes used interchangeably, referring to the rational part of the tripartite soul. For example, in 605c7 *logos* becomes *logismōi* in d4. Translating *logismos* as "calculation" may be too narrow, but I shall for the most part follow this common translation.

[5] Scholars debate what this lowly part is: appetite, spiritedness, or both? Some even think there is a bipartite analysis of the soul in book X that has nothing to do with the tripartite model in earlier books (e.g., Nehamas 1999, 265–66; Belfiore 1983, 52–54). For my purposes, all that Plato requires is that the soul is *divided* between how things appear and how they are.

painting, the part of his soul that accesses appearances is charged, and the power and motivation to calculate is weakened.[6]

What are the analogous effects in poetry?[7] The painter creates illusory appearances in space; the poet recreates how pleasure and pain are experienced in time. Recall that poetry is defined as imitation of actions and the assessments by the agents of their actions (603c4–9). A person in action finds it difficult to *homonoētikōs diakeitai*, "keep his mind in a harmonious, steady disposition" (603c10). This is because actions occur in time, which involves uncertainty and exposes our vulnerability. All these disturbances have something to do with how pleasures and pains are experienced in time. Just as a small object can appear big up close, the present pleasures or pains expected in the imminent future "loom large." They look "bigger" than they actually are. And when one reacts to them as they appear instead of as they really are, one suffers a disturbance, *tarachē*, that unsettles the soul as the same pleasures and pains become larger and smaller as time passes by (602c12).[8] This is what happens to a virtuous father who lost his son (603e4–10). His reason resists the pain of loss and tries to "push it away," while emotion (*pathos*) "drags him toward the pains" (604a9–10), that is, makes them appear closer in the temporal distance. The pain appears more intense and greater than it actually is.

As in visual illusions, *the father's experience is already distorted* without poetry. What poetry does is reinforce this distortion and thereby weaken reason. Suppose the father had initially been in a steady, neutral state with respect to feelings of pleasure and pain. Losing his son brings him to a negative state. The poet sings of stories involving characters undergoing similar losses and vocalizes the grief that the father would indulge in only when alone (604a1–5). The pain of the father appears more real through the vivid force of poetry. He now "does not recognize greater and less, but thinks the same things sometimes big and sometimes small" (605b7–c2). That is, his reason can no longer discern the true "size" of pleasures and pains, but he goes along with appearances when charmed and moved by the poet.

But poetry can affect its audience in more ways than this. At this point, Socrates turns to "the greatest charge" against poetry: it can injure "even the best among us" (605c9), namely, the *epieikēs* (equitable or decent: 603e4, 605c6), a word emphasizing the self-restraint and balance of the

[6] As Plato uses the masculine for third-person pronouns when speaking generally, this essay follows suit for stylistic purposes, but such use is of course neutral with respect to gender.

[7] Several commentators dismiss the analogy rather prematurely (e.g., Annas 1981, 337–39; Nehamas 1999; Dorter 2006, 320–21). But the opening remark of Socrates in this passage, "let us not just trust the likelihood (*tōi eikoti*) from painting" (603b10–c1), implies that the analogy is more strictly applied than before, since he will now explain the effects of poetry on its own terms (603c5–606d8) to confirm the analogy.

[8] Murray (1996, 213) notes that *tarachē* is also used in 444b6–7 to refer to forms of wickedness. See my discussion of unity and plurality in the next section.

good person. I suggest that Socrates is now turning to discuss virtuous people who have not suffered recent grief like the father in the previous example.[9] In other words, Socrates now proceeds to argue that even for someone who does not "misperceive" pleasure and pain, poetry can still be corruptive.

Virtuous people enjoy seeing heroes lamenting; they sympathize with them (605d2). Their sympathy for sorrow moves them into a negative state; but the enjoyment itself is a positive state, and they move back from that negative state. In other words, virtuous people experience in poetry what is called a deceptive pleasure in book IX (584e–585a). This movement that the soul experiences means that it will appear as a pleasure greater than it actually is (see Burnyeat 1997, 226). There is a second deception as well. Poetry encourages the audience to accept pleasures and pains as they appear by imitating them *in a public setting*.[10] Outside the theater, "the best of us" take pride in exercising restraint. But poetry makes these characters express their feelings freely and presents them as heroes. This is bad precisely because poetry is enjoyable, and there is a tendency to approve what we enjoy. Plato indicates this tendency by constantly putting the words *chairein* (enjoy) and *epainein* (praise, approve) in close proximity in this passage (605d3–4, e5, 606a7, b3). Poetry therefore cannot possibly be good: it creates a double standard in society, the public equivalent of a conflicted soul.

To summarize, poetry creates a mixture of incorrectly felt pleasure and pain and makes the wrong estimations seem true by rendering them publicly acceptable. In doing so, it weakens the soul's reason and the city's power to guide citizens rationally. Its effect is pervasive: it corrupts even the virtuous ones, whether they themselves are already suffering from illusory experiences of pleasure and pain or not.

Socrates' argument rests on three premises. First, human life is full of uncertainties. Things happen "like the falling of dice" (604c5–6). Hence we are prone to be disturbed and unsettled. Second, just as the power of painting lies in knowledge of how color, shape, and the interplay of shadow and light affect perceptual experience, the power of poetry lies in knowledge of how rhythm, harmony, and melody produce or enhance appearances of pleasure and pain (601a8–b8, 607a5–6). Finally, what affects our souls never has a merely localizable effect. What we enjoy in the theater will eventually spread into or infect our attitude and actions outside it

[9] Belfiore (1983, 56) is mistaken, I think, in holding that *epieikēs* refers to "ordinary people" like us. Socrates' critique of poetry in book X appears to be arranged in such a way that it becomes progressively more damning: first the poets deceive only children and those who are childlike (598c2); then they deceive a good father who has recently been unsettled by a misfortune; finally they deceive even "the best among us."

[10] On the importance of the public character of poetry in ancient Greece, see Burnyeat (1997, 244).

(on "infection," see Halliwell 1986, 149; Murray 1996, 226). Poetic language is the discursive expression of emotions and desires. Such language is at odds with the language of reason.

This passage explicitly contrasts poetic with philosophic discourse. The latter occurs as the voice of "law and reason" (604a9–b7). It responds to the grieving father as follows. First, one does not know whether something that is judged bad now will not turn out to be a gain later. Second, dwelling in the past accomplishes nothing. In other words, besides the tendency to value the present more than the past and the future, there is a tendency to treat past pains and efforts as more important than they are, which creates, among other things, attachments to unworthy things (see also 330b8–c6) or the desire for revenge. "Law and reason" urge us to examine instead what can be done to make things right or better (604c10–11). Third, human affairs are not worthy of great seriousness. Seen from the perspective of the eternal, the difference between dying prematurely and dying old is negligible. These three remarks are meant to prepare one for the final claim that what one really needs is not consolation but deliberation (*bouleuesthai*, 604c5), that is, calm reasoning about what to do next.

This speech is unsentimental and harsh. It surely does not "console" in any ordinary sense of the word. Poetic discourse lends voice to the father's pain; instead of echoing that pain, philosophic discourse adopts a "fighting" or "distancing" stance against it. If our experience is distorted by the temporal distance in which we encounter pleasure and pain, philosophic discourse attempts to correct that distortion by urging one to take those temporal effects into consideration. All three claims aim to "pull one out" from wallowing in pain. First, the father is urged to see things not from the present perspective but from imagined past and future ones. He is reminded that "the falling of the dice" can work both ways. The second claim turns our mental gaze toward what is up to us to change the situation. The final claim develops this to the extreme: it asks the father to adopt an *impersonal* view of human life. Human life is only well lived when it can be viewed from the perspective of eternity or something that transcends the human. All these three, then, aim at "neutralizing" the distorting effects that time has on our experience, and thus they restore the proper evaluation of pleasures and pains.

There is much to be said about what the speech of law and reason implies about philosophy. There is more to come in the next section, but here I emphasize one feature: in resisting the tendency to take human experience for granted, philosophic speech reflects that urge to locate the perspective of individual human beings in the context of ever-larger wholes. Poetic discourse, in narrowly focusing on human life, tends to present its limited and partial perspective as comprehensive and absolute. This distortion ultimately divides the community. On a social level, poetry eventually creates a city in which "pleasure and pain become the two kings instead of law and reason—the latter being what always seems the best to the community (*koinēi*)" (607a6–7). The dual verb *basileuseton* emphasizes how pleasure and pain, as opposites and giving opposing orders, create the potential for confusion and unrest. The life of reason is, by contrast, to be on the side of the community. It thinks about the whole. Reason is different from spiritedness and desire because it has the ability to "care about the community (*koinēi*) of all" parts of the soul (589b4–5). Anger only thinks about satisfying its own vengeful urge; desire aims at the present enjoyment or avoidance of pain. Neither tends to the whole soul as reason does. Philosophic discourse directs one's attention to the whole, to how the parts fit together, because that is the concern of the philosophic life. At the level of the individual, reason focuses on not weakening its hold over the other two parts. At the level of the city, reason cares about the whole of the community and therefore has its approval. This is why Socrates constantly mentions reason together with law in this critique: law is what holds communities together and is in this sense reason's ally.

3. Oneness and Freedom, Truth and Creativity

The above contrast between emotion-oriented and whole-oriented speech already intimates how each is bound up with different ways of life. Poetry stands on the side of the individual in presenting human life as it is experienced, while philosophy stands on the side of the community and urges a perspective that resists taking human experience for granted. In order to better bring out the connection between discourse and life, however, let me explore two other critiques of poetry in book X, both of which revolve around the claim that *poetic discourse values change and variety for their own sake*:

(1) Poetry looks for character types that are easily affected by external change. According to Socrates, poetry is the kind of medium most suitable for representing such matters. It is instinctively attracted by the "dramatic" or the "theatrical," the singular events, actions, and transformations, instead of the mundane, the repetitive, or the expected. Poets look for settings and themes that are atypical, that stand out, that are heroic or shocking.

Socrates presents this power of poetry as its *limitation*. Its power to represent change and the dramatic has a reverse side: it is unsuitable for presenting virtuous character. "The irritable part (*aganaktētikon*) [in us] has imitations that are numerous and many-colored (*poikilēn*), but the wise (*phronimon*) and *quiet character, remaining pretty much always itself like itself, is neither easy to imitate* nor easy to comprehend when imitated" (604e1–4, emphasis added). Poetry can imitate those who suffer from internal conflict, since such conflict can show up in a variety of forms, satisfying the poet's need for variation and change: reason against spiritedness, reason against desire, spiritedness against desire, desires fighting among themselves. The virtuous person, however, is "quiet" and not easily disturbed by what happens to him. He remains who he is over time; he is at rest. His wisdom allows him to be secure about the principles he adopts in life, and therefore his mind remains in a balanced and peaceful state (again cf. *homonoētikōs* 603c11).[11]

(2) A second aspect to this urge toward change and variety, one that tends to be less noticed, concerns the poets' pride in their innovative power, their ability to come up with new ways to say new things. Plato is aware of this urge on the poet's part.[12] He indirectly points this out when setting up the triad user-maker-painter to criticize the poet. There is the horseman, who uses reins on his horses; the cobbler who makes the reins for him; and the painter who paints horsemen using reins (601c7–13). Knowledge of something requires the genuine grasp of the *use* of that thing; therefore the horseman knows reins and can distinguish the good ones from the bad (d4–7). The cobbler consults and follows the horseman's feedback and advice (in Socrates' words, the horseman "becomes the cobbler's messenger [*angelos*]" [d9]) to improve on his designs, making reins that are better and more useful. He makes good ones only under the guidance of the horseman; therefore he has only right belief (*orthēn pistin*, 601e7) about the reins. The painter is the lowest in epistemic rank: he is ignorant, because he indiscriminately paints good and bad reins beautifully—visual pleasure is here divorced from benefit or usefulness (602a4–6). Analogously, the poet is ignorant of the moral qualities, that is, "in what way each [character] is bad or good (*ponēron ē chrēston*)" (602b2), and represents them beautifully without concern for how their representations might benefit or harm the city.

Unlike the cobbler, the painter does not consult anyone higher in epistemic rank when painting the reins of a horse. More generally, this indicates that imitative arts, poetry included, differ from ordinary crafts in an important way. Ordinary crafts are oriented toward daily life; their products serve (*hupēretōsin*, 601e1–2) certain functions and tasks, and these functions set limits to their practice. A carpenter, for example, can introduce innovations to table design; but all of them should at least enhance or not impede the usefulness of the table. The painter, by contrast, is not regulated in this way; he is emancipated from the use and function of tables. Similarly, poets can create characters who disregard what people in comparable situations in real life do and consider. They are licensed to be

[11] Halliwell (2002, 83) also notes that the inability of poetry to portray the virtuous person is an important reason for criticizing it. According to Halliwell, Plato initiated a long tradition of thinkers who have offered their own versions of this idea (see 2002, 83 n. 26). I would add to Halliwell's list Kierkegaard, whose Judge Williams similarly argues that a truly meaningful and happy marriage is not "portrayable artistically" (Kierkegaard 1987, 134–36, 138–39).

[12] The contest of poets seems essential also to how Greek poets understood their own activity. Aristophanes, for example, habitually boasts of his own creativity (for example, in *Clouds* 560–2) and depicts a fictional contest between Aeschylus and Euripides where one issue they fight about is which of the two is more innovative (*Frogs*, esp. 939–47).

playful. When Socrates charges that poets create imitations that "are mere play and not serious" (602b7–8), he is emphasizing their ignorance of important things in life. From the poet's point of view, however, this accusation is no accusation at all but a reason why poetry is attractive. Its purpose-free character values playfulness and creativity as worthy of pursuing (Halliwell 1986, 132).

Socrates considers seeking innovation and change for their own sake as bad. If something is in its best possible state, change is only change for the worse (381b10–c1). Suppose that one poet depicted virtuous behavior in a beneficial way. The drive for change means that the next poet will always attempt something different, either to depict the virtuous person in a different, possibly negative, light, or to tell stories about less virtuous or vicious characters. And we are back to the point implied in (1): the poets will sooner or later present less than ideal characters as desirable. Since the best city is by definition the best state that human society can be in, any change encouraged by poets would be change for the worse.

These two considerations further show how the quarrel between poetry and philosophy is in a crucial sense a clash of ideals and values. Their opposing views about the role of speech in life can be understood as an extension of that quarrel about values. As the quote above from 604e1–4 suggests, Socrates' ideal life is characterized by rest and harmony. Rest, because the good person does not suffer from conflict, which is the source of change. The good life is the wise life, and wisdom is reason exercising its function of tending to the whole, arranging one's life in light of a more comprehensive point of view. Hence there is harmony as well. The person with a wise character characterized in 604e1–4 is the stand-in for the philosophic life in this discussion. His wise character is said to be "always itself like itself." This suggests that Socrates' vision of the good life is maintaining and *keeping one's unity and integrity through time* (Halliwell 2002, 92).

If maintaining unity in time is a desirable goal, then truth and rational control are desirable as well. One should seek truth because falsehoods or deceptions sooner or later upset one and create occasions for being unsettled. As we have seen, to be deceived concerning pleasures and pains means that the same pleasure will sometimes appear great and at other times small, and one will be confused and find it difficult to keep one's psychic integrity intact. Therefore, only by figuring out the true significance of pleasures and pains through calculation can one remain undisturbed. Rational control becomes important as well, because, to repeat, pleasures and pains do not stop appearing distorted to humans even after they are calculated. This means that the tendency for the soul to become at odds with itself is forever present. No matter how virtuous one is, one is never so unperturbed as to be wholly unresponsive (603e8–10). Therefore the speech of "law and reason" must check those tendencies from developing beyond control. This means that the good life is not one of doing whatever one likes. The best life exercises self-restraint; the person is willing or prepared to even do violence to one's baser impulses ("to *violently* [*biai*] hold down . . . the desire to weep and shed tears," 606a3–4, emphasis added). Freedom is not an absolute value for the philosophic life.

The character of philosophic discourse follows from the need for truth and rational restraint. I explained in the previous section why philosophic discourse resists life as experienced. Here it can be added that, unlike the variety and change distinctive of poetry, philosophic discourse tends to be repetitive and uniform, not unlike the psychic and communal integrity sought by the philosopher. Philosophic discourse is repetitive partly because the incorrigible distortion that is a feature in human experience means that the battle against the loss of unity will be constant. As Socrates puts it, whenever they hear poetry, philosophers say: "We will *sing* this argument we have just now put forward like an *incantation* (*epōidēn*) so as to take care from falling again into that childish love characteristic of the many" (608a3–5, emphasis added).[13] In other words, Socrates advises that the argument in book X had better be almost religiously chanted over and over again to truly protect one against the seductions of emotions and desires. If the restraint is not to be always violent, then the repetitive use of gentle persuasion in this form is unavoidable.

And philosophic discourse is uniform because the philosopher does not create new and different kinds of discourse for novelty's sake. Since he engages in conversation for the sake of truth, once he possesses truth about some important matter, he will stop seeking change. Instead he will recollect and revisit such matters, constantly examining the same issues with the same kinds of orientations and arguments. For people who are rather hostile to such a way of speaking, such discourse sounds like a broken record. Alcibiades remarks on this in the *Symposium* section 221e5–6. Further, both Callicles and Hippias, on separate occasions, complain that Socrates says the same things all the time. But for Socrates, this is how speeches serious about life should be. Therefore, on both occasions his response to each is the same: he not only says the same things, he always says them about the same topics (*Gorgias* 490e9–491a3; Xenophon *Memorabilia* IV.4.5–7). Philosophic speech seeks truth and is repetitive for the sake of resisting emotions. Truth seeking and repetition are both meant to achieve that ideal of attaining oneness in time.

Poetry does not, perhaps, see this oneness in time as worthy of pursuing. Socrates might think poetry defective because it cannot portray the goodness of being one—such a state is too undramatic. But from its own point of view poetry could respond that Socrates' ideal does not lead to a life well lived. To borrow Callicles' complaint about the person who desires very little and is moderate, such a view of life seems to make "stones and corpses . . . the happiest" (*Gorgias* 492e5–6).

[13] This passage is slightly revised from Reeve's revised edition of Grube.

Unlike philosophy, poetry embraces *freedom* as its ideal. Like the ideal of oneness, freedom is an attempt to overcome the vulnerability of being human in time. It is the vision of doing what one wishes without constraints. One can see this first in the poet's very desire to create poems. The creative act, emancipated from the needs and exigencies of everyday life, expresses that enjoyment of freedom, that desire to live without restraints. The principle of creativity can be understood as a result of endorsing freedom as an ideal. Second, one also sees the ideal of freedom lurking in poetry's effect on the audience. It was noted in the previous section that poetry, by weakening reason, encourages the rule of pleasure and pain. And pursuing what appears pleasant and avoiding what appears painful is to experience oneself as the agent and actor of one's own actions. To act and react as feelings come and go is felt as exercising freedom, especially freedom from law and the dictates of reason.

This in turn indicates an important aspect of poetic discourse. It would seem that, given its need to innovate, poetic discourse is indifferent to truth, which contrasts with philosophic discourse. But in fact this is only half of the story. Seeking freedom *from law* means that poetic speech pays attention to what law prohibits or represses. From the point of view of poetry, the emotions and desires suppressed by law belong to a fuller sense of what it means to be human. Therefore poetry brings them to light by lending them a metrical, musical shape. Unspoken and repressed desires become the poet's sources of inspiration. In this sense, then, poetic discourse still has some relation to truth: it wishes to reveal the desires of the soul without the restraints of law.[14] There is still a difference, however. While the philosopher seeks the truth that achieves ever-higher degrees of integration (with his whole soul, community, the cosmos), the poet seeks the kind of truth that alienates instead of restoring harmony or integrity.

This sheds light on why the *Republic* suggests a connection between poetry and the democratic and tyrannical soul in books VIII and IX. Socrates claims that whenever poets are powerful and honored, cities sooner or later transform into democracy or tyranny, the two worst regimes in Socrates' classification. These two regimes, and their corresponding ways of life, are the least honored in the best city and are the most removed from it. Democracy and poetry are connected because democracy and the democratic person live by the principle of freedom (557b4–6). This could be said to be a hedonistic lifestyle. But this is not the hedonism that aims to maximize one's pleasures and minimize one's pains over time; even this sort of hedonism is too "rational" and constraining for the democratic

[14] That the quarrel concerns the issue of truth is indicated by several occurrences of *alēthēs* and its cognates throughout book X. Socrates says he respects Homer, but the truth about him must be told (595c2). Poetry is inferior in its distance from truth—from reality and the nature of virtue (597e7, 600e6). Finally, poems that demonstrate their benefits to the best city will be readmitted into it as "the best and truest" poetry (608a1–2).

type. Nor does the democratic person seek to distinguish "true" from "deceptive" pleasures and pains as more enlightened hedonists might do. As Socrates describes it, a democratic person merely "gratifies day by day whatever chance desire falls upon him" (561c7). This is the hedonism of the carpe diem type. There is no calculation: such a person drinks when he likes, abstains from alcohol when he likes; he works out when it suits his fancy, he lies at home if he feels like it. He even dabbles in philosophy every now and then (d3). He leads a carefree and utterly nonserious life. Since there is no single goal in life that arranges and orders his activities, there is no part of his soul that rules, it is *anarchos* (558c2). The democratic person lives by a single principle, but no unity of the soul results from it. The democratic soul seems to have the least unity: by letting every desire randomly rule as each comes and goes, it is multicolored (*poikilon*, echoing the texture of poetic discourse) and contains a variety of characters (e3–4).[15] Socrates admits, not without irony, that such a life is "sweet, free, and blessed" (561d7–8).

The philosophic life attempts to see further ahead in time to maintain one's integrity; the democratic life gives up trying altogether. It goes with the flow. It was mentioned before that seen from the point of view of poetry, Socrates' accusation of poetry as "mere play" is no accusation at all but precisely its point. The same can be said of Socrates' association of poetry with children or childish desires. Section 608a5, quoted above, characterizes the passion for poetry as childish. And in the beginning of book X Socrates says that only children or the foolish succumb to the seductions of imitative arts (598c2). But again, the philosopher's accusation can be precisely the point of the poetic-democratic ideal of freedom. To follow one's impulses, to feel unrepressed by law or rules, to freely create and destroy, to not look ahead, to lack seriousness, are what it means to become childlike (see Hadot 1995, 273).[16]

Socrates does not think that such a carefree, childlike hedonism is sustainable, however. The excessive pursuit of freedom ultimately subverts it and leads to the most wretched form of slavery, where the better element, reason, is ruled by the worst, the ever-growing uncontrollable passions and desires (577d1–5, 579d10–e3). This is the tyrannical life. The philosophic life is characterized by awareness of truth and the whole. It is wakeful, and the desires that occur only in dreams are kept there by the philosopher. The

[15] As Halliwell notes, this word can also mean "heterogeneous, constantly shifting" (2002, 94), which further accentuates the contrast with the unity and calmness of the philosophic soul.

[16] Halliwell (2005, 329–30, and 2002, 106–13) identifies the way of life implied in poetry as "the tragic worldview," which sees death as the greatest evil and treats human life as immensely valuable. But such a view assumes that tragedy, not poetry in general, is Plato's real target, an assumption only partly borne out by the text. By contrast, my thesis that poetry upholds the ideal of freedom better explains why it is associated with democracy and tyranny in the text.

tyrannical life, however, turns everything upside down, parallel to what the poets do to the soul, letting pleasure and pain rule over reason. Even if the poets do not praise or endorse the tyrannical life, what the poets present in logos, the tyrannical person or the tyrant does in *ergon*. The poets only depict lawless desires; but, emboldened by the public display of those desires onstage, the tyrannical soul seeks to live and act on them. His open pursuit of lawless desires makes his life a waking nightmare (574e2–3, 576b4).

Moreover, the poet exposes the savage desires that fracture the soul. The tyrannical person lives the slavish life of ever satisfying the insatiable desires. At his worst, he becomes a tyrant and enslaves his own community. The city then exists only to serve the private desires in his fragmentary and restless soul—the exact subversion of the life of the philosopher-king, who lives a unified and orderly life in service of the common good of his community. Whereas a democratic life is marked by freedom and sweetness, there is no redeeming feature in the tyrannical soul.

4. The Inner Need of Philosophy for Poetry

So far I have emphasized the opposition between philosophy and poetry. But Plato throughout the *Republic* hints also at the need for a subtler understanding of the relationship between the two. Despite the criticisms in book X, Socrates concludes that if poets themselves or lovers of poets can offer a defense of poetry, showing that it is not only pleasant but also beneficial to the regimes and human life, then we will listen with good will. For we surely will profit if it should come to light as not only pleasant but also beneficial (607d9–e2). In other words, he is willing to reconsider his position if poetry's intimate. connection with pleasure does not exclude it from benefiting us. Socrates' use of the plural "regimes" is noteworthy. On the one hand, it draws attention to the possibility that, even if poetry is only of extremely limited value in the best city, it might be beneficial in less ideal cities. On the other hand, since "regime" is also used to refer to the order in one's soul (both in the immediate context and before: 591e1, 608b1), Socrates might also be suggesting that the effects of poetry are not simply corruptive for certain types of souls. In short, the quarrel is far from having been definitively concluded. Drawing from the hint indicated by the expression "regimes and human life," I shall now document three ways in which poetry is indispensable for philosophy's own project as a way of life.

(1) In the best city, poetry is necessary for early education. In the case of potential guardians taught at an early age, poetry (along with gymnastics) is necessary for molding their character so that they become receptive to rational speech and painstaking mental studies later on. Furthermore, near the end of his critique in book X, Socrates remarks that only "hymns of gods and praises of good people" (607a3–4) will remain in the best city. I take him to mean that even for the actual adult guardians and the other two classes, poetry that solemnly (this is what I take to be the import of

"hymns") honors perfect beings and depicts virtuous humans as role models remains necessary.

Burnyeat (1997, 276–79) is in this sense quite right: there will be no lack of imitative arts and poetry in particular in the best city. In both these cases, poetry is necessary because the rational powers of its audience, namely, the young men and the class of craftsmen, are not mature or outstanding. If poetry speaks to the nonrational parts of the soul, the management of the best city needs poetry to guide the less rational people toward virtuous conduct. If poetry left to its own devices generates a harmful view of life and enfeebles the audience's reason, poetry regulated and guided by philosophy can be beneficial and even create a sense of unity for the city.

These uses, however, compel poetry to act against its own nature. Poetry is more suitable for portraying less virtuous people; in the best city, philosophers guide poets to praise virtuous people, precisely those characters that are difficult to portray in the poetic medium. Its natural tendency toward change and variety remains suppressed in the best city (see Halliwell 2005, 313; Murray 1996, 15; Griswold 1981, 141). The next two uses, however, indicate the need of philosophy for poetry precisely for poetry's natural (*pephuke*, 605a2–3) tendency toward variety.

(2) Outside the best city, poetry appears necessary. According to Socrates, people usually have not sufficiently reflected on the true nature of human experience. Philosophy is designed to awaken them. This means that the philosopher has an interest in changing his interlocutor's very mode of living (a reflection of his care for the community). Plato variously names this change "protreptic" (*protreptikos*), "conversion" (*periagōgē*), or "soul guiding" (*psychagōgia*). A certain "force" is required to accomplish such an awakening. More specifically, a protreptic discourse must make its audience realize that it is talking about *themselves*, that it is calling *them* to change their ways of living. But philosophic discourse, as characterized above, is not always suitable for this. I have remarked how alienating the speech of "law and reason" might sound to the father. Its disregard of the father's grief can be counterproductive. By contrast, poetry has that unique power to grip its audience in a personal way, making the audience members recognize themselves in the characters, as the father recognizes a similar sorrow in the suffering hero. And poetry's power to discern the desires hidden deep within souls is something philosophers must make use of, in order to truly engage their audience. To the extent that philosophical speeches are addressed to potential philosophers, they cannot be effective without poetry.

(3) Finally, even without the need to transform others, the philosophic life, as it is lived in less ideal cities and regimes, needs poetry. In recounting the myth of Er, Socrates tells Glaucon that "all the danger for a human being" lies in the need to neglect everything else and study attentively and studiously how to properly rank the relative goodness of each way of life.

Studying different lives and correctly evaluating and comparing them are absolutely essential to avoid foolishly choosing tyranny in the afterlife (618b7–e3). Let me demythologize Socrates' speech as follows. In order to maintain the unity of the philosophic life outside the best city, the philosopher has to face and respond to challenges coming from other claims about how one should live. To fail to defend the philosophic life constitutes a double failure: a failure of the rule of reason, and the loss of the original integrity of the soul, which, now unsettled by objections, becomes divided. What Socrates means here, at the very least, is that a successful defense is not forthcoming if one does not study other ways of life and fully comprehend their merits and demerits.[17]

And here philosophy needs poetry, precisely because of its power to discover the variety of desires hidden in the human soul. By focusing on experience and repressed desires in human life, poetry presents a vast number of human possibilities (excepting the virtuous life). The philosopher needs to study the lives portrayed in poetry to defend his own, despite the dangers that he is exposing himself to. The beginning and end of book VIII reflect the philosopher's ambiguous need for and rejection of poetry. Book VIII ends, as I mentioned before, with Socrates noting the kinship between poetry and democracy or tyranny, thus anticipating his rejection of poetry in book X. But that very book also begins the study of degenerate regimes and souls with Socrates praying to the Muses, as if he himself were a Homer who needs inspiration to tell the story (545d7–8). This gesture is a telling sign that Socrates needs the help of poetry to investigate less ideal ways of life. This, I think, partly explains why examination of the relative ranking of lives is said to involve "all the danger for a human being" (618b7–8). The danger or risk is, How can the philosopher use poetry to study other lives without succumbing to its charms and weakening his reason?

5. Conclusion

According to Plato, poetry presents the world as it is experienced. In doing so, it also endorses the ideal of freedom and the pursuit of momentary pleasures as the good life. Poets, both through their own pursuit of creativity and through the stories they tell, weaken reason and encourage their audiences to act upon their desires and emotions. Poetic discourse is about finding a voice for emotions, whether lawful or not; and about seeking innovation and change for their own sake. Philosophy opposes this. Its point of departure is that human experience distorts reality, and truth matters. Philosophic discourse therefore distances itself from experience in search of a truth that one can constantly live by and repeat through time.

[17] As Cooper (2007, 28–32) remarks, it is a distinctive feature of the Socratic conception of philosophic life that the defense of it is part of what it means to live that life.

And it claims that only such discourse is good because it comes from reason, the only human faculty that tends to the whole. The life of philosophy seeks truth to keep one's integrity within time, to make one at home in one's community and the cosmos. Philosophic discourse stands apart from life in order to become a beneficial part of it.

The consideration of philosophy's need of poetry, however, finally complicates this picture somewhat. Philosophical discourse urges us to look at things impersonally, and yet it attempts to get us involved personally. As opposed to poetry, philosophy is the language of calculation and deliberation, akin to mathematical, scientific discourse. But its need for poetry means that its discursive mode cannot be *completely* scientific or mathematical. Perhaps the opposition of philosophy to poetry and its need for it require philosophic discourse to blend the poetic and the scientific into something reducible to neither.

Acknowledgments

This essay is part of a project funded by the Ministry of Science and Technology, Taiwan (project number 107-2410-H-002-251-MY2). An earlier draft of the essay was read at the National Taiwan University–University of Scranton 2019 Joint Workshop, and I am grateful to Andrew Lazella for his comments. I also wish to thank Tushar Irani and an anonymous reviewer for their constructive comments.

References

Annas, Julia. 1981. *An Introduction to Plato's* Republic. Oxford: Oxford University Press.

Belfiore, Elizabeth. 1983. "Plato's Greatest Charge Against Poetry." *Canadian Journal of Philosophy* suppl. 9:39–62.

Burnyeat, Myles. 1997. *Culture and Society in Plato's* Republic. Salt Lake City: University of Utah Press.

Cooper, John M. 2007. "Socrates and Philosophy as a Way of Life." In *Maieusis: Essays in Ancient Philosophy in Honour of Myles Burnyeat*, edited by Dominic Scott, 20–43. Oxford: Oxford University Press.

Dorter, Kenneth. 2006. *The Transformation of Plato's* Republic. Lanham, Md.: Lexington Books.

Ferrari, G. R. F. 1989. "Plato and Poetry." In *The Cambridge History of Literary Criticism*, vol. 1, edited by George A. Kennedy, 92–148. Cambridge: Cambridge University Press.

Griswold, Charles L. 1981. "The Ideas and the Criticism of Poetry in Plato's *Republic*, Book 10." *Journal of the History of Philosophy* 19, no. 2:135–50.

Hadot, Pierre. 1995. *Philosophy as a Way of Life: Spiritual Exercises from Socrates to Foucault*. Edited with an introduction by Arnold I. Davidson, translated by Michael Chase. Oxford: Blackwell.

Halliwell, Stephen. 1986. *Plato: Republic 10: Translation and Commentary*. Liverpool: Liverpool University Press.
________. 2002. *The Aesthetics of Mimesis: Ancient Texts and Modern Problems*. Princeton: Princeton University Press.
________. 2005. "The *Republic*'s Two Critiques of Poetry." In *Platon Politeia*, edited by Otfried Höffe, 313–32. Berlin: Akademie.
Kierkegaard, Søren. 1987. *Either/Or*. Part II. Edited and translated by Howard V. Hong and Edna H. Hong. Princeton: Princeton University Press.
Levin, Susan B. 2001. *The Ancient Quarrel Between Philosophy and Poetry Revisited: Plato and the Greek Literary Tradition*. Oxford: Oxford University Press.
Murray, Penelope. 1996. *Plato on Poetry*. Cambridge: Cambridge University Press.
Nehamas, Alexander. 1999 [1982]. "Plato on Imitation and Poetry in Republic X." In *Virtues of Authenticity: Essays on Plato and Socrates*, 251–78. Princeton: Princeton University Press. Originally in *Plato on Beauty, Wisdom, and the Arts*, edited by J. Moravcsik and P. Temko, 47–78. Totowa, N.J.: Rowman and Littlefield, 1982.
Pappas, Nickolas. 2003. *Routledge Philosophy Guidebook to Plato and the* Republic. 2nd edition. London: Routledge.
Slings, S. R. 2003. *Platonis* Rempvblicam. Oxford: Oxford University Press.

CHAPTER 10

STOICISM AND ITS TELOS

INSIGHTS FROM MICHEL FOUCAULT

ROBIN WEISS

Although the interpretation of Stoicism advanced by Foucault is deservedly famous, the most frequent criticism of his work is that he fundamentally misunderstands the end, or telos, toward which Stoic life is directed and hence fundamentally mischaracterizes the end toward which Stoic philosophy, as a way of life, is directed. In his research, Foucault comes across one way in which several Stoics prefer to articulate the telos, one that can arguably be placed alongside a long list of other definitions of the telos favored by different Stoics down through the centuries: some of them said the end consisted in living in accord with "virtue" (*aretê*), some in living "consistently" (*homologumenôs*), some in living "in harmony with nature" (*kata phusin*), and some in a "smooth flow of life" (*euroia biou*).[1] Although scholars have long set out to show how these various formulations are consistent with one another (Long 1967, Rist 1977, Brennan 2005), they have taken little interest in showing that the formulation discovered by Foucault is consistent with the rest. Regrettably, Foucault himself does not explain how his account is consistent with standard accounts.

That is the task of the present essay. In what follows, I try to show, not only that Foucault's most direct statements regarding the telos are broadly consistent with the Stoics', but also that Foucault's primary claim about the telos can be directly inferred from some basic Stoic principles.

[1] Stob. *Ecl.* 6a30: SVF 3.16: LS 63B; *Diog.* 7.87–88: SVF 3.4, 2.555: LS 63C. A list of abbreviated titles is given in the Appendix below.

Philosophy as a Way of Life: Historical, Contemporary, and Pedagogical Perspectives.
Edited by James M. Ambury, Tushar Irani, and Kathleen Wallace.

Published 2021 by John Wiley & Sons Ltd.

My contention is that Stoics would themselves accept that this claim constitutes an accurate description of the Stoic telos—in the sense that what Foucault has in mind *constitutes* the Stoic telos in whole or in part. Once the connection between Foucault's account and standard accounts of the telos is made clear, we can see that Foucault provides an illuminating interpretation of an often overlooked aspect of Stoic thought about the telos.

I begin by examining some of the most explicit statements Foucault makes about the Stoic telos. I then show how his claims can be justified within the framework of Stoicism, especially the framework of Stoic physics, whose authority he is often thought to reject. Finally, I close by answering some objections to the thesis that he has accurately characterized the Stoic telos. Here, I argue that his account is compatible with existing accounts and is not easily dismissed as reductive. I show that, far from being reductive, Foucault's account is, if anything, much *less* reductive than many contemporary accounts.

Foucault on the Telos

In order to understand his conception of the Stoic telos, one must understand the interpretation Foucault offers of a few passages from Seneca's fifty-second letter and *De tranquilitate*. In the latter, Serenus complains to Seneca that the moment he resolves on a course of action, seeking public office, for instance, he abandons course. And no sooner does he quit public life than he wishes to return to it. Give me some remedy, he begs Seneca, "to bring this vacillation of mine to a standstill" (*quo hunc fluctuationem meam sistas; De tranquilitate* 1.17).[2] Serenus's condition, which is characterized by persistent vacillation, regret, and changes of heart, is *stultitia*. Serenus is a *stultus*, and of his kind, Foucault says this: "The *stultus* wants several things at once, and these are divergent without being contradictory. So he does not want one thing and one thing absolutely. The *stultus* wants something and at the same time regrets it. Thus the *stultus* wants glory and, at the same time, regrets not living a peaceful, voluptuous life, etcetera. Third, the *stultus* is someone who wills, but he also wills with inertia, lazily, and his willing is constantly interrupted and changes its objective" (2005, 133). The discussion of stultitia by Foucault arguably marks the high point of his 1981–1982 lecture course at the Collège de France. From about this point onward, Foucault will understand the eradication of stultitia as Stoicism's telos.[3] Foucault is originally led to this conclusion because his primary interest is in Stoic pedagogy. In this context, he finds the teacher's

[2] All translations from classical texts are my own unless otherwise noted, in which case page numbers are cited for the English translations used.

[3] Foucault observes that stultitia is a recurrent theme, "a kind of commonplace in Stoicism, starting especially with Posidonius" (2005, 131).

primary task is to correct stultitia. Foucault then argues, introducing passages from Seneca to this end, that the philosophic life is defined in opposition to stultitia: philosophy "has to deal with *stultitia* as its raw material, if you like, and its objective is to escape from it" (2005, 131).

For Foucault, stultitia encompasses many forms of "mental restlessness and irresolution." But "the consequence and the principle" of them all is that the stultus "is unable to will properly" (2005, 132). In short, stultitia is a disorder of the will.

Foucault argues that the will is corrupted in this way insofar as it is "determined" by false beliefs or misleading impressions. He tends to think of these as *external* causes of action, since they are usually imposed on the subject by society or by events outside the subject's control. Here, he explains, the individual's will is not "absolute" in the sense of being unconditionally and necessarily determined in a certain direction (that is, by the individual's consistent and unalterable desires). Rather, the individual's will is effected by the intrusion of extraneous beliefs or ways of imagining the world, which become contingent causes of the subject's action (that is, they are not forced upon the subject by necessity but result by chance). Hence the behavior that results is itself contingent, or at least more contingent by comparison with other forms of action. Foucault puts the point rather crudely—and we may question his choice of words—when he says the individual's will is not "absolute" in the sense that it would have "always" been as it was but was rather "determined by this or that event, this or that representation" (2005, 132).[4] The details are vague, but the general point is clear: the subject does not will something unconditionally or necessarily but wills it accidentally, conditional upon the intrusion of a contingent factor, which might have been avoided.

As a consequence of this, Foucault explains, the individual tends to will the wrong things. These things are willed wrongly, from Foucault's point of view, precisely because they are not willed "always" and "absolutely." As a further consequence of the will's determination by changeable, accidental causes, which are themselves subject to contingent events, the will often abandons its original object with time, or eventually attaches itself to new objects. Hence, the will of the individual is not directed simply at one object—"he does not want one thing and only one thing absolutely." Rather, from a certain point of view, the will is always potentially directed toward at least two objects: it desires both X and *not*-X. Finally, the will wills lazily, hesitatingly, vacillatingly, while constantly interrupting itself and shifting its aim (2005, 133).

[4] Foucault is, however, loosely quoting Seneca. The term "absolute" is taken from a passage in Seneca's letters, in which Seneca states that, as long as we are afflicted by stultitia, "we do not will freely (*libere*), without qualification (*absolute*), or always (*semper*)" (*Ep.* 52.1).

Thus does Foucault describe stultitia—the condition he characterizes as the Stoic's goal to avoid. Later, his assertion that Stoic philosophy's end is to remove stultitia will form the basis for his subsequent claim, reasserted throughout the 1981–1982 lecture course, that Stoicism is characterized by an attempt to establish a "relationship of self to self" (2005, 127). I shall reserve discussion of this point until the end of this essay. Suffice it to say, Foucault means the Stoic is especially consumed by the task of keeping watch over himself—his own thoughts, beliefs, imaginings, and impulses—to ensure that *he*, the subject, is always in control of himself and his own actions. The assertion by Foucault that the removal of stultitia is the Stoic telos also forms the basis of his claim that the Stoic's aim is to become a "subject" in the truest sense of the word (2005, 127).[5] Delaying a full explanation of this remark until later, we can safely summarize this to mean that the Stoic's goal is to become an *autonomous* subject, an autonomous subject primarily in the sense of a subject whose actions are minimally determined by factors external to the subject, especially factors whose effects can be avoided. I shall not attempt to defend all these claims in detail. The important point is that the assessment of these more expansive—and controversial—claims hinges upon the prior assessment of the claim that the telos is the eradication of stultitia, which I *will* attempt to defend.

For the purposes of the present essay, let us define stultitia as the inability to pursue an end without vacillation, hesitation, or regret. Let us, by contrast, define the condition opposite to stultitia as *constantia*, the ability to work consistently toward the aim on which one has decided without changing one's mind, or reversing one's decision. For ease of reference, let us call this "consistency of will."

The Truth in Foucault's Analysis

I would now like to argue that, despite being phrased in terms somewhat foreign to the Stoic way of thinking, Foucault's interpretation correctly characterizes the Stoic telos, by pointing to that which constitutes it. At least, Foucault's interpretation cannot simply be rejected on the grounds that it omits explicit mention of those things in terms of which the telos is usually defined, such as nature, virtue, and reason.

Foucault claims that the Stoic telos is the removal of stultitia. Lest we think that he makes too much of stultitia, several passages attest to the prevalence of this theme in early as well as late Stoic thought, which he traces back as far as Posidonius, but for which clear precedents exist in

[5] Stultitia is introduced to provide evidence for this claim. When the topic is put forward, Foucault is arguing that a student of Stoicism "has to replace the non-subject with the status of subject, defined by the fullness of the self's relationship to the self." He then shows, quoting Seneca's fifty-second letter, that a teacher is necessary to complete this process, and that the teacher will accomplish this by correcting the student's stultitia (2005, 129).

early Stoicism. To quote just a few passages besides those Foucault cites, some define vice in terms of stultitia:

> The worthless man, however, having no experience of correct use, does everything badly, acting in accord with his disposition, easily changing his mind and in the grip of regret over every matter (*eumetaptôs ôn kai par' ekasta metameleiai sunechomenos*). Regret is pain at things that have been done, as having been done wrongly by oneself, a passion of the soul which creates unhappiness and is quarrelsome. To the extent that the person in a state of regret feels sorrow at the occurrences, he is annoyed with himself as having been responsible for them. (Stob. *Ecl.* 11i15, 1999, 79, cf. 11m19)

Some passages define virtue in terms of constantia, in a tradition that arguably goes back to the founder of Stoicism.[6] "A disposition and power of the governing principle of the soul, brought into being by reason, or rather, reason itself consistent, firm, and unwavering" (*homologoumenon kai bebaion kai ametaptôn to hupotithentai*; Plutarch, *De virtute morali* 441c: LS 61B).[7] And some passages describe those great moral exemplars, the gods, as possessing absolute constantia and lacking stultitia:

> "Furthermore, it is necessary to affirm this too concerning the gods, and that they are immutable and fixed in their judgments, so as never to depart from their initial decision. For changelessness and firmness too was one of the virtues, and it is reasonable that this provides among them the stability and immobility of what they have once decided" (Stobaeus, *Anthology* 1.3.53, in Hierocles 2009, 63).

These are just a few examples. To the scholar of Stoicism, Foucault's discussion of stultitia should also bring to mind several passages in which it is explicitly stated that the telos is attained with the removal of changes of mind. A glance at Stobaeus shows that the Stoic sage, the one person who can rightly claim to have completely achieved the telos, will never have second thoughts: "Nor does he change his mind in any way, nor alter his opinion, nor is he led astray" (*oude metaballesthai de kat' oudena proton, oude metatithesthai, oude sphallesthai;* Stob. *Ecl.* 11m5).[8] His opposite,

[6] Perhaps it was also to a virtue like this that Zeno, the founder of Stoicism, referred when he originally defined the telos as living *homologumenôs*, "in agreement," or "in harmony," without further qualification. It may also be to the removal of stultitia that Zeno refers when he says that people who live not in agreement but in conflict (*machomenôs*) are unhappy (Stob. *Ecl.* 6a34: SVF 1.179).

[7] The same meaning may be conveyed by several definitions of virtue, which define it as "a consistent character" (*diathesin homologoumenên; Diog.* 7.89: SVF 3.39: LS 61A), one characterized by the ability to form judgments that are consistent with each other over the length or duration of one's whole life (*pantos tou biou, peri holon ton bion, in tota vita; Diog.* 7.89; Stob. *Ecl.* 5b1; cf. Cicero, *De finibus bonorum et malorum* 5.66; *Tusc.* 4.29). These and similar definitions of virtue are examined further below.

[8] The passage is quoted *in extenso* below.

meanwhile, the foolish man, can be found "easily changing his mind and in the grip of regret over each thing" (*eumetaptôs ôn kai par' ekasta metameleiai sunechomenos;* Stob. *Ecl.* 11i15; cf. 11m19, quoted above). And several passages associate vice with stultitia, in one or all of its expressions: (1) vacillation prior to action; (2) changing one's mind while executing an action; and (3) regretting an action after it has been carried out.[9] The evidence is such that one must at least concede that these passages refer to a kind of internal consistency achieved by the virtuous, which is, at a minimum, one precondition for attaining the telos, and which reliably manifests itself in the absence of stultitia.[10] On a superficial reading, therefore, there is enough evidence to support the preliminary hypothesis that the Stoic telos is closely associated with, and is attained coincident with, the removal of stultitia.

Let us begin, however, with Foucault's more surprising observation that the elimination of contingent causes is such an important part of achieving the telos that an individual will fall short of the telos as long as that individual's will is determined by contingent causes. Although the oblique reference to contingent causes is out of place in the context of Stoicism—the Stoics use different terminology—this claim has some truth to it, as a brief look at Stoic physics will demonstrate.

According to Stoic physics, an object's movement is the effect of at least two causes: the cause that *acts* and the cause that is *acted upon*. More specifically, there is the nature of the cause that acts and the nature of the cause that is acted upon. The effect that results from the interaction of these two natures is necessary and unavoidable.[11] Applied to human action, this means that the action of an individual is determined by his or her human nature, and the nature of an external cause that acts upon the

[9] Vacillation is arguably the defining characteristic of vice, because the ignorant man is characterized by having impulses that are *akatastatous kai ptoiôideis*, "unsettled and flighty" (Stob. *Ecl.* 5b13). Vacillation is also considered a sure sign that one has already erred in thought, if not yet in deed (Cicero, *De officiis* 1.30). Cicero testifies that the wise man *suis stare iudiciis*, "stands by his own decisions" (*Tusc.* 5.81–82, trans. LS 63M). Indeed, the abandonment of one's ends is frequently identified with vice, as when Menelaus is singled out as a paradigm of vice because he abandons his intention to kill Helen (Galen, *De placitis Hippocratis et Platonis* 4.6.7: SVF 3.473). As for regret, Cicero reports that it "is a particular characteristic of the wise man that he does nothing which he could regret (*nihil quod poenitere possit facere*), nothing against his will, but that he does everything honorably, consistently seriously, and rightly" (*Tusc.* 5.81–82, LS 63M, 1987, 397).

[10] One example of a scholar who, while hostile to the thesis defended here, concedes this point is Tad Brennan (2005, 141). This point is discussed at further length below, along with the objection that the consistency in question is a mere byproduct of the telos, rather than constitutive of the telos itself.

[11] Events are determined "through the proper nature of each of the existing things" (*dia tês oikeias phuseôs;* Alex. *Fat.* 183.3). For "it is in accordance with their proper nature that they do everything they do in accordance with fate" (Alex. *Fat.* 189.20–22; cf. *Nat. hom.* 106.10–11).

subject, typically a perceptible object that arouses pursuit or aversion.[12] Now, in the case of a human being, the acting cause—or in the Stoics' terms, "antecedent cause"—should be an object that produces a *katalêptic* impression, a katalêptic impression being one that is so clear that it removes from the subject's mind all possibility of its falsehood.[13] Therefore, the object that gives rise to a katalêptic impression acts upon the subject as a necessary cause, causing the subject to assent to the impression. The Stoics even describe the subject's mind as irresistibly "compelled" to assent.[14] Provided the impression contains a certain content, this will in turn necessarily cause the subject to pursue or avoid the object in question.[15] Hence, the *individual's action should be determined by necessary causes.*[16]

If, however, the subject were to assent to a non-katalêptic impression arising from an object, then he or she would be assenting in a way that is *not* necessarily determined by that object. Here, the object does *not* necessarily give rise to an impression that necessarily causes assent; assent *can* be refused. So the assent is *not* necessitated by an antecedent cause. In other words, the individual *is* affected by an object, but in an accidental and contingent manner. (Notice that the Stoics do not explicitly employ the language of "contingency," although they do describe the effect as *non*-necessary.)[17] Further, if the subject acts upon such an impression, then his or her pursuit or avoidance of the object will also be contingent and accidental. *Hence the Stoics' apparent rejection of all contingent action.*

[12] Alexander of Aphrodisias faults the Stoics for holding this view of an individual's action: "They [the Stoics] maintain, their nature is of such a kind, and it is in accordance with their proper nature that they do everything they do in accordance with fate, as it is for heavy things to fall downwards" (Alex. *Fat.* 189.20–22). By his account, the Stoics seem to identify fate not just with the effect of external causes on the human being but with the way human nature is necessarily affected by external causes. Fate, Alexander says, "acts through the proper nature of each of the existing things" (Alex. *Fat.* 183.3).

[13] The katalêpsis "is one which is true and of such a kind that it could not turn out to be false." *Math.* 7.1.152.

[14] The katalêptic impression almost "pulls us by the hair" to assent. *Math.* 7.1.257. See also: *Math.* 7.252; *Acad.* 2.38, *Acad.* 2.77, 2.18, 2.38.

[15] Nemesius states that the impulse is necessary. "But if exercising an impulse, too, follows from necessity, it is clear that those things that happen by impulse, too, will happen in accordance with fate, if they also happen by us and in accordance with our nature, i.e. [in accordance with] impulse and *krisis.*" *Nat. hom.* 106. See further Susanne Bobzien (1998, 376–78).

[16] As is explained below, this kind of necessity does not of course rule out moral responsibility, following Ricardo Salles's compatibilist interpretation (2005, 61–63). This is clearly corroborated by Cleanthes: "Nor is any deed done on earth, god, without your offices . . . save what bad men do in their folly" (Cleanthes, *Hymn to Zeus* 122.11–21: LS 54I: SVF I. 537, 1987, 326). See further Epictetus and Seneca (Epictetus, *Enchiridion* 53; *Dis.* 2.23.42, 2.22.95, *Dis.* 4.1.131, 4.4.34; *Ep.*107.11).

[17] Hence, for example, Cicero's claim that emotions such as love have "nothing either natural or necessary about them" (*aut naturale aut necessarium; Tusc.* 4.60). They are also described as voluntary (*Acad.* 1.5.38; *Noct. Att.* 19.1, LS 65Y). On Stoic conceptions of necessity see Sharples 1975.

From this perspective, it would be absolutely correct for Foucault to assert the existence of a connection between potentially misleading impressions and contingent causes: potentially misleading impressions *are* contingent causes. What's more, an individual's will is contingent *because* it is determined by potentially misleading impressions, and therefore anyone who accepts potentially misleading impressions allows his or her behavior to be determined by contingent causes. Foucault accurately states that, in cases such as this, the "will"—to use his words—cannot be considered "necessary," because, as we can now see, this "will" could easily *not* have existed (that is, it could have been avoided if the subject had simply *refused* assent to the impression).

Moreover, Foucault also more or less accurately states that this "will" is not "unconditional," because as we can also now see, the individual only wills in this manner on the condition that he or she accepts a certain impression, one that *could* be rejected. So the will is not unconditional but instead contingent upon the acceptance of an impression that, on closer examination, the individual might indeed prefer to reject. Therefore, Foucault also accurately states that the will is also not "absolute"—because it could plausibly be revised at some future time.

When Foucault proceeds to say that the stultus's will is not as it always was to be, this has a deeper truth than even he realizes. For if we ask why the subject assents to a non-katalêptic impression, the answer cannot be that the subject is necessarily caused to do so by his or her human nature, by an antecedent cause, or by an impression—or by the combination thereof. (The evidence, of course, is that not *all* human beings are disposed to accept these kinds of impressions.)[18] The subject must have, at some point, *acquired* a disposition to assent to certain impressions, and this disposition itself must have resulted from contingent causes (that is, the assent of the subject to certain impressions, which he or she was not *compelled* to assent to).[19] All this—the acquisition of a certain disposition and the resulting assent to certain impressions—is "accidental," in the sense that it could have been avoided.

Foucault is also correct to point out the necessary consequence of action that is determined by contingent external causes: it is always subject to vacillation, reassessment, and regret. As noted above, an impression

[18] All this rests on a basic principle of Stoic physics: like causes consistently produce like effects (*Nat. hom.* 105.18–21; Alex. *Fat.* 192.22–24: LS 55N). The principle is usually articulated as follows: "If the same circumstantial causes are present, . . . necessarily the same [things] happen and it is not possible that they happen now this way now otherwise" (*Nat. hom.* 105.18–21). This is consistent, in Bobzien's view, with a similar principle to be found in Chrysippus (1998, 372).

[19] The Stoics tell us that the further cause of the mind's movement must be sought in the *hexis* (*Dis.* 2.18), or *diathesis*, of the individual, his "disposition" (*Noct. Att.* 7.2.11, 12). Zeno's famous analogy makes this clear. Zeno compares the human mind to a cylinder pushed by an external force (*Noct. Att.* 7.2.11; Cicero, *De fato* 43).

that is accepted without necessity is inherently revisable, therefore unstable, and therefore always *can* be, and in time often *will* be, overturned. (By contrast, a katalêptic impression is *ametaptôton hupo logou,* "irreversible by reason" [Stob. *Ecl.* 11m23].) The revision of an impression can happen at any time: it can happen immediately, before one has even embarked on a course of action, producing vacillation; it can happen in the midst of executing action, producing a change of mind; or it can happen after an action has been carried out, producing regret. The Stoics seem to regard the revision of misleading impressions as an inevitability: if one accepts an impression without sufficient warrant, one cannot help but begin to question one's decision and the impression on which it is based. Furthermore, it is only a matter of time before the object from which an impression arises presents itself to one in a different light.[20] The Stoics are also keen to stress that if one has assented falsely to an impression, one's commitment to that impression will inevitably falter under the strain of competing and incompatible goods or the threat of impending evils, especially where they produce strong impressions of their own.[21] And even if all this is avoidable, regret is not. This is succinctly summed up in Stobeaus as follows: "Nor do they assume that a man with good sense changes his mind (*oude metanoiein*), for changing one's mind belongs to false assent, on the grounds of erring through haste. Nor does he change his mind in any way, nor alter his opinion, nor is he confused. For all these things are marks of those who waver in their beliefs (*tôn tois dogmasi metapiptontôn*), which is alien to the person with good sense" (Stob. *Ecl.* 11m5, 1999, 97). Thus, stultitia is caused by false assent, so that the elimination of stultitia requires the removal of false assent as its necessary condition.

In sum, the Stoics specify a set of causal conditions under which stultitia occurs. The Stoic telos, and the aim toward which the practice of Stoic philosophy is directed, can accurately be described as the attempt to avoid the conditions that underlie and give rise to stultitia—defined now as vacillation, hesitation, and regret, stemming from impulses determined by contingent causes (that is, a "will" that is unstable because its very existence is conditional upon the presence of contingent causes). To this extent, then, Foucault's characterization of the Stoic telos appears to be based in fact.

There is a certain irony that should be pointed out here, because the foregoing demonstrates that Foucault's account, which is often considered to be incompatible both with Stoicism's emphasis on nature and with the principles of Stoic physics, is actually directly supported by Stoic physics.

[20] Even the judgment that the death of a loved one is an evil is expected to be revised with time. *Tusc.* 3.58–59, 66–67.

[21] Seneca speaks of this when he says, "From one side the sight of what is right beckons, from the other unease about what is bad pulls him back. And so he who is setting out to do something honorably should not think that any of the obstacles is bad, even if he thinks it is dispreferred, but he should be willing and eager to do it" (*Ep.* 66.17, 2007, 20).

Notwithstanding several attempts to bring Foucault's interpretation to prominence (Sellars 2018; Bénatouïl 2003, 2011), to many, including Foucault's most sympathetic readers, the most forgiving thing that could be said is, as Timothy O'Leary writes, that in Foucault's lectures and books "there is little recognition of either reason or nature as constituting the ends of Stoic ethics" (2002, 80). Although scholars have shown, with some success, that Foucault correctly and insightfully describes different *methods* employed by Stoics to attain the telos, the general consensus remains that Foucault treats these ethical methods to the exclusion of, and in isolation from, physics, and without physics he cannot possibly provide an accurate account of the Stoic telos.[22] As the foregoing analysis will have shown, however, the account Foucault gives of the telos not only seems to be consistent with standard interpretations of the telos, as action in accord with katalêptic impression (Epictetus, *Dis.* 1.6.12; LS 63E); his claim that the telos is achieved with the removal of stultitia can be directly deduced from the principles of Stoic physics. Indeed, Stoic physics would itself proscribe the elimination of stultitia and its causes as the necessary, if not sufficient, condition for acting in accord with nature. Finally, insofar as, according to the principles of Stoic physics *themselves*, the avoidance of stultitia can only be accomplished under a specific set of causal conditions, it is accurate to describe the Stoic telos either (a) in terms of the elimination of stultitia or (b) in terms of the causal conditions that are necessary for its removal. Either account provides an accurate description of that which constitutes the telos.

Further, if Foucault's interpretation is considered in this light, then so far from presenting a distorted picture of ethical life at the *expense* of physical considerations, it actually reveals something about the relationship *between* ethics and physics.[23] Indeed, Foucault's interpretation can be read in terms of a tradition of commentary, that argues that different formulations of the telos present it from different perspectives: some from the perspective of an ethical framework, others from the perspective of a physical one, and the physical framework typically points to the hidden physical causes that underlie the ethical phenomenon (Rist 1977; Inwood 2009). Specifically, Foucault's account reveals that, in ethical and pedagogical discourse, the Stoics' are at liberty to describe their end in

[22] At the same time, most scholars find little else in Foucault, either to remark upon or to refute, besides what he says about the self. Most, like Brad Inwood, concentrate on attempting to show that Foucault fails in what they consider his self-proclaimed end, that is, he "fails to establish that the Senecan self is interestingly novel" (Inwood 2005, 333; cf. 322–52). For a review of the critiques made of Foucault by scholars of Stoicism, see Pradeau 2002, 131–54.

[23] The charge that Foucault addresses ethics in isolation from physics is in part attributable to his focus on pedagogy, and his observation that Stoic pedagogues focus primarily on instilling consistency of will in their students. Here he finds little evidence that teachers attempt to impart the knowledge of "truths, facts, principles," including the principles of physics (2005, 134).

terms of the avoidance of stultitia, while also taking it for granted that this end can only be attained under certain causal conditions, which can be fully specified only in terms available to Stoic physics. The important point is that, in characterizing the end, the Stoic can accurately describe the end *without making direct or explicit reference to physics, or its principles*, although this characterization of the end will still be "grounded" in physics.

Objections: Is Consistency of Will the Highest End?

Let me now respond to an objection that may plausibly be raised against Foucault's characterization of the Stoic telos, namely, that while there is undeniably some truth to it, it is reductive. In fact, it might be argued, the Stoics' concern is with something much larger and more expansive than the mere elimination of stultitia—such as nature or reason—and to describe the telos in these terms therefore tends to reduce the telos to that to which it cannot be reduced. The question is whether, given that the Stoics were concerned with the cure of stultitia, we should therefore generalize to the conclusion that the Stoic *has no higher end than to remove stultitia*.

In effect, the question Foucault forces us to ask is: Did the Stoics make the elimination of stultitia and the attainment of constantia, or "consistency of will," their end—their *highest* end? Or is there an even higher end?

Now, it is agreed, by modern interpreters and Stoics alike, that the telos is constituted by a rational disposition. The difficulty is that this rational disposition is itself characterized in terms of consistency, and a vague form of consistency at that.[24] This consistency is then usually interpreted in a certain way: it is usually taken to be a kind of consistency that comes with the possession of what we would today call *dispositional* beliefs—beliefs, that is, held over long stretches of time, propositional in form and universal in scope—ones both consistent with the way the world really is and logically consistent with one another.[25] Henceforward, I refer to this kind of consistency as "consistency in belief."

Hence our question might be re-posed in the following form: Given that the telos is constituted by some form of consistency, is it consistency of *belief* or consistency of *will*? Here, I shall not attempt to definitively resolve the issue but attempt to show that (a) the latter is perhaps more accurately characterized as the Stoics' primary concern and (b) to the extent that the

[24] For example, as the disposition of the soul "in harmony with itself" (*sumphonôn autêi;* Stob. *Ecl.* 5b1).

[25] An interesting case is that of Brennan, who concedes that the sage's soul must have a certain internal consistency to achieve the telos. He downplays the importance of this consistency, however, in part because he interprets it exclusively in terms of logical consistency (2005, 141).

Stoics are concerned with the former, they think of it as subsumed under, or reducible to, the latter.[26]

The fact that the Stoics are primarily concerned with what I have called "consistency of will" seems to be supported by their definition of virtue. If the Stoics say virtue is their highest end, they also say "virtue is a state of mind that makes for harmony in the whole of life" (*ousêi psuchêi pepoiêmenêi pros tên homologian pantos tou biou; Diog.* 7.89). Vice, meanwhile, is a "condition or state of being inconsistent and out of agreement with oneself over one's whole life" (*habitus aut adfectio in tota vita inconstans et a se ipsa dissentiens*; *Tusc*. 4.29, 2002, 49).[27] Here, the mere mention of life is enough to suggest that the Stoics are interested in a kind of inconsistency that occurs when a person, over the course of her life, makes decisions that are inconsistent with the decisions she has made and will make. She therefore pursues divergent courses of action. Foucault perhaps describes it best when he says these courses of action are "divergent" without necessarily being logically contradictory: now I want to fight the enemy, now I want to run and hide (2005, 133). Therefore, there is an argument to be made that, insofar as the Stoics are concerned with inconsistency of belief, they are less concerned per se with the logical inconsistency of inter-entailing dispositional beliefs than with inconsistency arising from the displacement of one belief by another, perhaps temporary, belief, and the inconsistent behavior to which this gives rise.

The question then becomes: What is the relationship between consistency of belief, meaning the logical consistency of *stable* inter-entailing beliefs, and the consistency of *temporary* beliefs that can be more clearly correlated with consistency of will?

Perhaps, we might think, the Stoics regarded inconsistency of will as little more than the most outwardly visible sign of a deeper problem: one lying in the failure to acquire and apply a set of logically consistent dispositional beliefs. A critic of Foucault's might say, for example: To be sure, the Stoics mention consistency of will, but *not* because they think of it as their highest aim in life. They think of it as attending upon the attainment of their true end in life—an aim they think is constituted by logical consistency. In a similar manner, one might also plausibly conclude that the Stoics

[26] In fact, this emphasis on logical consistency seems largely to be an imposition on Stoic texts. When knowledge is described, it is variously defined as: (1) "an apprehension which is sure and irreversible by reason" (*katalêpsin aphalê kai ametaptôton hupo logou*); (2) "a composite of such kinds of knowledge of particulars" (*sustêma ek epistêmôn toioutôn oion hê tôn kata meros*); (3) "a composite of expert types of knowledge" (*sustêma epistêmôn technkôn*); and (4) "a condition which is receptive of impressions and irreversible by reason" (*hexin phantasiôn dektikên ametaptôn hupo logou*). Stob. *Ecl.* 5121.

[27] Another, similar definition of virtue identifies it as a disposition of the soul "in harmony with itself concerning one's whole life" (*sumphonôn autêi peri holon ton bion;* Stob. *Ecl.* 5b1, 1999, 13; cf. Cicero, *De finibus bonorum at malorum* 5.66).

subsume consistency of will under the broader heading of consistency of belief, treating the former as a species of the latter.

There are, however, several reasons this interpretation is not as plausible as it might first appear. The first reason becomes apparent when we ask ourselves the following: Can the inconsistency in question be said to "exist" in beliefs because of the fact that, in the form in which they are stockpiled—namely, in the form of propositional statements—they are logically inconsistent with one another and reality? Or do they become inconsistent in application? There is reason to doubt that they are already mutually inconsistent in the form in which they exist in the mind prior to application because the most acute forms of vice, *nosêmata*, or "sicknesses," while they are referred to as opinions "deeply attached and rooted," do not seem to be propositional beliefs as we would think of them today (*Tusc.* 4.26). They are *diatheseis*, or "dispositions," to assent to at certain times, and thus to form certain judgments at those times about particular things (Stob. *Ecl.* 10e20, cf. 5k41; *Diog.* 7.98; *Tusc.* 4.29). Therefore, to the extent that vice can be identified with a disposition arising *from* and constituted *by* false and inconsistent beliefs, it seems to be considered such because it is, more accurately, a disposition resulting in false and contradictory beliefs about particular things at particular places and times. Perhaps, then, it is artificial to distinguish a disposition to hold and apply inconsistent beliefs from a disposition to *form* inconsistent beliefs. Further, if we examine the way virtue is defined, we find that vice is removed and virtue attained, not through acquiring propositional truths per se, but more precisely *katalêpseis*, or "apprehensions"—whose propositional content need not be expressed until the moment a person forms a judgment about a particular object or event.[28] It would seem therefore that—since katalêpseis are not, as such, mutually contradictory—*before* such judgments are formed there is no inconsistency or consistency proper to speak of.[29] Inconsistency, when it arises, can be spoken of only when a person makes a judgment in conflict with others she has made or will make. Hence the reason Stobaeus reports that the virtuous person possesses knowledge derived from impressions,

[28] It will be clear that virtue depends on having katalêpseis, rather than beliefs in propositional form, if we recall that virtue is constituted by knowledge, which is in turn constituted by katalêpseis. Moreover, these katalêpseis are of particular, individual things, so that a person with a katalêpsis of an object x can recognize similar objects and name them, saying: "This is an x." Other than in this sense, however, knowledge should not be identified with true propositional statements (Stob. *Ecl.* 5l21).

[29] This seems to be demonstrated by Epictetus's claim that one *prolêpsis* "does not conflict with another." Epictetus is thinking primarily of the conflicts that arise between people when he stresses that the prolêpsis of one person, with regard to goodness, justice, or bravery, does not conflict with that of another person, and that conflicts arise in "the application of *prolêpseis* to individual substances," when, for example, one person judges someone "brave" in accord with their *prolêpsis* and another person does not. However, this strongly suggests that a conflict within the individual would also arise similarly: a person judges a man brave at one moment or not the next (*Dis.* 1.22.1–4).

which is not overturned or cancelled by subsequent judgments (*ametaptôn hupo logou*; Stob. *Ecl.* 5121).[30] It would be reasonable to suppose, therefore, that the Stoic seeks a knowledge that does not simply *result in* but rather actually *consists in* the ability to make judgments that are, in some way or another, consistent with each other across time. This is a knowledge, in other words, that consists in the ability to form consistent impulses. The Stoics explicitly state, after all, that it is a defining characteristic of the ignorant man that his impulses are *akatastatous kai ptoiôideis*, "unsettled and flighty" (Stob. *Ecl.* 5b13).

In this way, one might justifiably be forgiven for concluding that, for the Stoics, all moral and intellectual faults can be more easily subsumed under the broader heading of stultitia than the narrower heading of logical consistency.

Finally, supposing Foucault's critics are right, and the Stoic seeks consistency of belief as that which constitutes his highest end, even granting the supposition, this consistency of *belief* would arguably be inseparable from consistency of *will*. For consistency of will must attend consistency of belief as sunshine attends the sun, not just accidentally but necessarily, in which case it is arguably inseparable from the end—even constitutive of it. Indeed, even granting the premise of these critics' argument, it is still possible to argue, in response, that it is misleading to describe the end in terms of consistency of belief since, presumably, consistency of belief would have no value unless it manifested itself in consistency of will. Why not then admit that consistency of will is the *real* end, rather than a mere byproduct? In short, we should not too quickly dismiss Foucault's suggestion that the Stoics may have identified their aim with consistency of will as much as, if not more than, consistency of belief.

As we have seen, it is this kind of inconsistency, inconsistency of *will*, that Foucault focuses on, resisting the temptation to reduce it to inconsistency of belief in the usual sense. He is even fairly explicit about this. He does not find much evidence, he says, that the Stoic seeks to amass a storehouse of true and consistent beliefs, as if this were an end in itself—nor much evidence that the Stoic is *simply* after "knowledge to replace his ignorance" (2005, 129). Foucault's often misunderstood approach to the Stoics might therefore be called "non-reductive": Foucault identifies a problem that he thinks Stoics are concerned to address. The particularity of his approach, however, is that he refuses to reduce this problem to another, "more fundamental" problem with which many scholars say the Stoics are

[30] Stobaeus reports this in writing that knowledge, with which virtue is identified, is "a condition which is receptive of impressions and irreversible by reason" (*hexin phantasiôn dektikên ametaptôn hupo logou*). The word *ametaptôn* stresses that, from external objects, impressions are formed such that their contents are not altered with time or canceled by subsequent judgments. The word also clearly intends to recall the vicious man "easily changing his mind and in the grip of regret over each thing" (*eumetaptôs ôn kai par' ekasta metameleiai sunechomenos;* Stob. *Ecl.* 11i16, 1999, 79).

more concerned. Hence his conception of the Stoic telos, although unconventional, might actually be considered less reductive than more conventional ones.

Conclusions

My objective here has been to show that Foucault's conception of the Stoic telos is plausible and not incompatible with more traditional interpretations of the telos. Although unconventional, there is not an obvious reason for rejecting it.

By way of conclusion, I would now like to show how Foucault finds his analysis confirmed by Stoic texts. One particularly illustrative example is to be found in Foucault's interpretation of a passage in Epictetus. In the passage, Epictetus must reprimand a father for abandoning the bedside of his sick daughter, apparently overcome by the sight of her frail condition. Epictetus, Foucault says, is able to show the father that his behavior arises from a natural impulse in human nature normally leading humans to show concern for kith and kin—a social impulse—but one that, in this case, has been corrupted or misdirected so as to become "an in some sense irregular concern" (*le souci en quelque sorte irrégulier*; Foucault 2005, 198, trans. mod.; cf. 2001, 191).

But *how* does Epictetus show the father that he should mend his ways? Here, the larger point Foucault is making is obfuscated if we focus too narrowly on the failure Foucault attributes to the father, which he has several ways of describing: the father doesn't examine his impressions, he doesn't attend to himself or to the bonds between himself and others. As Foucault knows, all these failures boil down to one decisive failure: the failure of the father to accept or reject the right impressions.[31] But this is not Foucault's main point. It is to emphasize that *if* the father had acted otherwise, *then* this result could have been avoided. In this way, Foucault says, Epictetus shows the father that he acts counter to human nature at the same time as he shows him, or *by* showing him, that it is not necessary for him to act this way.[32] As Foucault puts it, "If the father really [had] take[n] care of himself properly . . . he would not be upset by his daughter's illness in the first place" (Foucault 2005, 198, trans. mod.; cf. 2001, 191).

First, according to Foucault, Epictetus's strategy is to emphasize that the love of the family is natural, in a prescriptive and a descriptive sense: "One must love one's family because one does love one's family" (2005, 197,

[31] That Foucault is aware of this can be seen from his stress on the fact that the father has not "examined the representations which came to mind" (2005, 197).

[32] The relationship between the two things Epictetus shows, as highlighted by Foucault, is obscured in the English translation of *The Hermeneutics of the Subject*, which by using the conjunction "and" suggests that Epictetus shows two things, one not necessarily related to the other. In fact, the French, which uses only a comma, makes clear that the first thing he shows is equivalent to the second (Foucault 2005, 198; cf. 2001, 191).

trans. mod.; cf. 2001, 190). Love of family does not, however, lead one to abandon family members in their hour of need; on the contrary, it usually makes it reasonable for one to "follow the principles governing the bonds between individuals within a family" (197). *So the father's behavior is far from necessary.*

Second, and to illustrate the former claim, Epictetus points out to the father that his behavior cannot be necessary or natural because, if it were, the girl's mother and servants would have abandoned her too: "And, Epictetus says, imagine if your daughter was abandoned by all those who, like you, really love her—she would now be dead. Neither her mother nor the servants would have remained" (Foucault 2005, 197). Indeed, if this behavior were natural and necessary, every daughter in such a situation would be dead. Third, Epictetus drives home his point, which Foucault encapsulates in a string of conditionals: "*If* you had examined the representations which came to mind concerning your daughter's illness, *if* you had paid close attention . . . *then* you would not have allowed yourself to be disturbed by passion" (198).

In effect, Epictetus shows the father that his actions were not necessary, given his human nature and given the circumstances, but contingent, since not all humans will act as he did in similar circumstances, and because, in fact, none of the other family members acted that way under the circumstances. Second, Epictetus infers that the responsible variable accounting for this outcome must lie with the father, reinforcing this by pointing out that had *he* acted differently, the result would have been different. Thus, in Foucault's view, Epictetus shows the father that his actions, since they cannot be traced to human nature or be fully accounted for by circumstances outside his control, must be traced to a contingent variable *within* his control, for which he must take responsibility.

Further, we can see that Foucault reads this passage as consistent with his previous claim that it is the Stoic's end to correct stulititia. According to Foucault's account Epictetus indeed points out to the father that he is a stultus. He shows him that his will, in this particular case, is "determined by this or that," and thus it is not, in Foucault's words, an "absolute will" that wills always as it does (2005, 132). Epictetus then shows the father that this makes him vulnerable to bouts of vacillation, reversals of course, and regret. Not only did he set out to be a good father and then act in a manner that was completely inconsistent with his original aim, he now feels pangs of regret for his folly.

That said, it is unsurprising that Foucault eventually connects the problem of stulititia to subjectivity, with these by now famous lines from *The Hermeneutics of the Subject*:

> "Right from the start, at the moment of his birth, even in the lap of his mother, as Seneca says, the individual has never had the relationship to nature of rational will that defines the morally sound action and the morally valid subject. . . .

The individual should strive for a status as subject that he has never known at any moment in his life. He has to replace the non-subject with the status of subject defined by the fullness of the self's relationship to the self" (2005, 129).

Earlier, I said that, for Foucault, the Stoic's aim is to become a "subject" (127). Foucault means the Stoic's goal is to become a "subject" in the superlative, or the truest, sense of the term, much as we would say that an adolescent's goal is to become not just a "man" or "woman" but a "*real* man" or a "*real* woman." Foucault does not always spell out in exactly what sense acting on contingent causes undermines the individual's attempts to become a subject in the true sense. Like the Stoics, however, he assumes that to be a subject requires an individual to be, to some degree, a rational, autonomous, free agent, especially one who acts from an unchanging set of motivations or principles. Foucault, therefore, does not think it is reading too much into Stoic texts to assume that a person who acts on contingent causes is not *rational* because she is not acting on a reason that all rational agents would accept (that is, an impression all would assent to). She is not *autonomous* because her action is primarily accounted for, not by internal standards and measures or truth and goodness (that is, the criteria by which she determines whether an impression is to be accepted), but, in the absence of such standards, by passing impressions or thoughts that are suggested to her by external people and events. She is not *free*, *not* because she is affected by external causes, but because she is affected by external causes more than is strictly necessary (that is, "in excess of what is natural" [Galen, *De placitis Hippocratis et Platonis* 4.3.2–5: LS 64K]). We can add that she is also not a subject in the sense of capable of acting from an unchanging set of motivations. Nor can she honestly say that she always would act in the same way under similar circumstances—and always *will*. The proof is that when, as often happens, the triggering impression is reexamined and then rejected, her behavior changes, revealing that she was never really acting in a way that was rooted in deep-seated motivations or resistant to change; in fact, her behavior is revealed to have been fickle from the start and subject to change.

Perhaps, Foucault says, the Stoic has "never known at any moment in his life" what it is like to be a *truly* rational, autonomous, free, and independent agent, but, in order to approach this ideal, the Stoic must try as hard as possible to will, quoting Seneca, "freely, absolutely, and always" (2005, 133; *Ep.* 52.1, quoted in n. 4 above). Foucault seems to mean by this that the Stoic must will (i) *freely*, in the sense that the will must not be excessively determined by external causes; (ii) *absolutely*, in the sense that it must not be conditioned upon the acceptance of certain arbitrary impressions and must be absolutely grounded in and necessitated by a certain situation or set of facts; and (iii) *always*, in the sense that one must be able to "stick with" one's decision. To this end, the Stoic must regularly examine his or her own thoughts, impulses, and behavior; study their causes;

and ensure that none has been unduly determined by factors that could undermine his or her claim to be a subject.[33] In doing so the Stoic establishes a special "relationship" of self-mastery with himself or herself, and it is this special "relationship" that makes the practicing Stoic a "subject" in the truest sense of the word.

Appendix

List of Abbreviated Works

Acad.	Cicero, *Academica*
Alex. *Fat.*	Alexander of Aphrodisias, *On Fate*
Diog.	Diogenes Laertius, *Lives of Eminent Philosophers*
Dis.	Epictetus, *Discourses*
Ep.	Seneca, *Epistulae*
LS	Long and Sedley, *The Hellenistic Philosophers*
Math.	Sextus Empiricus, *Adversus mathematicos*
Nat. hom.	Nemesius, *On Human Nature*
Noct. Att.	Aulus Gellius, *Noctes Atticae*
Stob. *Ecl.*	Stobaeus, *Eclogues*
SVF	Von Arnim, *Stoicorum veterum fragmenta* (2002)
Tusc.	Cicero, *Tusculanae disputationes*

References

Arius Didymus. 1999 (cited as Stob. *Ecl.*). *Epitome of Stoic Ethics: Text and Translation*. Translated and edited by Arthur Pomeroy. Atlanta: Society of Biblical Literature.

Bénatouïl, Thomas. 2003. "Deux usages du stoïcisme: Deleuze, Foucault." In *Foucault et la philosophie antique*, edited by Frédéric Gros and Carlos Lévy, 17–49. Paris: Kimé.

________. 2011. "À la recherché d'une ars theoertica et politica." In *Michel Foucault gli antichi e i moderni*, edited by Lorenzo Bernini, 101–27. Pisa: Edizioni ETS.

Bobzien, Susanne. 1998. *Determinism and Freedom in Stoic Philosophy*. Oxford: Clarendon Press.

Brennan, Tad. 2005. *The Stoic Life: Emotions, Duties, and Fate*. Oxford: Oxford University Press.

[33] Foucault sometimes characterizes this attempt to maintain self-mastery in terms of an attitude of constant vigilance (1986, 41; cf. 1997b, 232; see further Sellars 2018, 16). On the subject of freedom, see especially Foucault 1997a.

Cicero. 2002. *Cicero on the Emotions: Tusculan Disputations 3 and 4*. Translated by Margaret Graver. Chicago: University of Chicago Press.

________. 1927. *Tusculan Disputations*. Translated by J. E. King. Cambridge, Mass.: Harvard University Press.

________. 1938. *De divinatione, De fato, Timaeus*. Edited by Otto Plasberg. Stuttgart: Teubner.

Foucault, Michel. 1986. *The Care of the Self*, vol. 3 of *The History of Sexuality*. Translated by Robert Hurley. New York: Random House.

Foucault, Michel. 1997a. "The Concern for the Self as Practice of Freedom." In *Ethics: Subjectivity and Truth*, edited by Paul Rabinow, 281–302. New York: New Press.

________. 1997b. "Technologies of the Self." In *Ethics: Subjectivity and Truth*, edited by Paul Rabinow, 223–52. New York: New Press.

________. 2001. *L'Hermeneutique du sujet: Cours au Collège de France, 1981–1982*. Edited by Frédéric Gros. Paris: Hautes Études/Gallimard/Le Seuil.

________. 2005. *The Hermeneutics of the Subject: Lectures at the Collège de France, 1981–1982*. Translated by Graham Burchell. London: Palgrave Macmillan.

Hierocles. 2009. *Hierocles the Stoic: "Elements of Ethics," Fragments and Excerpts*. Translated by David Konstan. Edited by Ilaria Ramelli. Northumberland: Sanderson Books.

Inwood, Brad. 2005. "Seneca and Self-Assertion." In *Reading Seneca, Stoic Philosophy at Rome*, 322–52. Oxford: Clarendon Press.

________. 2009. "Why Physics?" In *God and Cosmos in Stoicism*, edited by Richard Salles, 201–23. Oxford: Oxford University Press.

Long, Anthony. 1967. "Carneades and the Stoic Telos." *Phronesis* 12, no. 1:59–90.

Long, Anthony, and David Sedley, eds. and trans. 1987. *The Hellenistic Philosophers*. 2 vols. Cambridge: Cambridge University Press.

Nemesius. 2008. *On the Nature of Man*. Translated with notes by R. W. Sharples and P. J. van der Eijk. Liverpool: Liverpool University Press.

O'Leary, Timothy. 2002. *Foucault: The Art of Ethics*. New York: Continuum.

Pradeau, Jean-François. 2002. "Le sujet ancient d'une ethique modern." In *Le courage de la vérité*, edited by Frédéric Gros, 131–54. Paris: Presses universitaires de France.

Rist, J. M. 1977. "Zeno and Stoic Consistency." *Phronesis* 22, no. 2:161–74.

Salles, Ricardo. 2005. *The Stoics on Determinism and Compatibilism*. Aldershot: Ashgate.

Sellars, John. 2018. "Roman Stoic Mindfulness." In *Ethics and Self-Cultivation: Historical and Contemporary Perspectives*, edited by Matthew Dennis and Sander Werkhoven, 15–29. New York: Routledge.

Sharples, R. W. 1983. *Alexander of Aphrodisias. On Fate. Text, Translation and Commentary*. London: Duckworth.

_______. 1975. "Aristotelian and Stoic Conceptions of Necessity in the *De fato* of Alexander of Aphrodisias." *Phronesis* 20:247–74.

Seneca. 1917–1925. *Epistles*. Translated by Richard Gummere. 3 vols. Cambridge, Mass.: Harvard University Press.

_______. 1928–1935. *Moral Essays*. Translated by John Baysore. 3 vols. Cambridge, Mass.: Harvard University Press.

_______. 2007. *Selected Philosophical Letters*. Translated by Brad Inwood. Oxford: Clarendon Press.

Sextus Empiricus. 2005. *Against the Logicians*. Translated by Richard Bett. Cambridge: Cambridge University Press.

Stoicorum veterum fragmenta. 2002 (cited as SVF). Edited by Hans F. A. von Arnim. 4 vols. Milan: Bompiani. Reprint of Leipzig: Teubner, 1903. (Reprinted without the apparatus criticus as *Stoici antichi: Tutti i frammenti raccolti da Hans von Arnim*, edited by Giovanni Reale and translated by Roberto Radici.)

PART 2

MORAL PHILOSOPHY

CHAPTER 11

PHILOSOPHY AS A WAY OF LIFE TODAY

HISTORY, CRITICISM, AND APOLOGY

MARTA FAUSTINO

> The only critique of a philosophy that is possible and that proves something, namely trying to see whether one can live in accordance with it, has never been taught at universities: all that has ever been taught is a critique of words by means of other words.
>
> —Friedrich Nietzsche, *Untimely Meditations* (1997b, 187)

Introduction

Over the past few decades, Pierre Hadot's work on ancient philosophy—most notably *Exercices spirituels et philosophie antique* (published in English as *Philosophy as a Way of Life*) and *Qu'est-ce que la philosophie antique?* (*What Is Ancient Philosophy?*)—has become an inevitable reference not only for ancient studies but also in the context of an ongoing metaphilosophical discussion on the relevance and viability of reactivating philosophy as a way of life today. Indeed, the major and most fruitful contribution of his studies to contemporary philosophical debate seems to lie not so much in his reinterpretation of the birth of Western philosophical thought but in the line of continuity that, despite its multiple ruptures and interruptions, Hadot ascribes to Western philosophy as a whole. According to his interpretation, the practical and existential imperative that characterized and motivated ancient philosophy did not entirely disappear with the dawn of antiquity, even if the Middle Ages and the consequent

Philosophy as a Way of Life: Historical, Contemporary, and Pedagogical Perspectives.
Edited by James M. Ambury, Tushar Irani, and Kathleen Wallace.

Published 2021 by John Wiley & Sons Ltd.

development of universities provoked considerable changes to the way philosophy was conceived and practiced, which could only be progressively overcome from the sixteenth century onward, either *outside* or *against* the university itself: "Throughout the history of Western philosophy, we note a certain permanence and survival of the ancient notion. From the Middle Ages to today, some philosophers have remained faithful to the vital, existential dimension of ancient philosophy. At times, they have been active in the very heart of the university, but more often they were reacting against it. Sometimes they acted alone, but generally they did so from bases which were foreign to the university, such as certain religious or secular communities" (Hadot 2002, 261).

Hadot cites a great number of examples of this "genuinely creative philosophical activity" (1995, 270), ranging from Montaigne, Descartes, and Kant to Schopenhauer, Kierkegaard, and Nietzsche, all of whom, "in one way or another, were influenced by the model of ancient philosophy, and conceived of philosophy not only as a concrete, practical activity but also as a transformation of our way of inhabiting and perceiving the world" (2002, 270). This outlined continuity, as well as the intrinsic features and characteristics of the model it illustrates, has inspired recent scholarship to argue for the reactivation of philosophy as a way of life, as a means of countering and overcoming the way in which philosophy is currently practiced in the academic world. As John Sellars puts it, the true relevance of philosophy as a way of life consists in the fact that "this is not only how philosophy was once conceived long ago, but also a live metaphilosophical option that has been taken up by philosophers throughout the history of philosophy and can still be taken up today" (2017, 41).

Despite its extremely original and influential character, however, Hadot's account of philosophy as a way of life in modern and contemporary philosophy is neither complete nor uncontroversial. On the one hand, and because his main focus is undoubtedly ancient philosophy, Hadot makes little effort to prove or demonstrate his claims about the proximity of modern and contemporary philosophers to the ancient model of philosophy as a way of life. With rare exceptions, he considers it sufficient to point to the existential and practical orientation of some of these philosophers, sometimes complementing this point with indications of the presence of topics and elements in their philosophies that were clearly borrowed from ancient philosophy. On the other hand, and perhaps not by chance, Hadot's account has not been immune to criticism, and doubts have been raised about the accuracy of applying the ancient model of philosophy as a way of life to modern and contemporary philosophers, which obviously also calls into question the possibility of reactivating it today.

One of the most expressive and thorough criticisms of Hadot's approach can be found in John Cooper's *Pursuits of Wisdom*, which argues that this tradition only "lasted unbroken from Plato through to the eclipse of ancient pagan philosophizing and its ultimate replacement as a way of life in the Greek and Roman world by the Christian religion" (2012, 7). Given the complex and substantive development that philosophical ideas, concepts, and frameworks have undergone ever since that period, "modern philosophy and contemporary philosophy lack the ancient conception of philosophy as a way of life," because several important "large-scale, interconnected assumptions of the ancients have not been part of the accepted intellectual landscape for philosophical inquiry at any time since the Renaissance (nor, for that matter, in medieval philosophy)" (15). Accordingly, Cooper concludes that

> even if moral philosophy nowadays might be approached and presented as offering guidance for life, one cannot think of philosophy as a whole as having even that function. Most of philosophy today is truly an exclusively theoretical discourse, with no direct connections to the conduct of one's life. What then is someone to do who comes to academic, seriously argumentative philosophy with the idea that it is a uniquely vital subject, one that, if one succeeds in it, will alter one's life directly for the better? There seems to be no viable alternative except to study ancient philosophy—or rather, the ancient philosophies, in the plural—in the spirit in which they were written, that is, with a view to one's own self-improvement. (16)

Curiously enough, the very dissatisfaction and disappointment that philosophy students might face when embarking on their studies is an argument used by one of Hadot's most enthusiastic followers to encourage philosophers, researchers, and students to embrace philosophy as a way of life. After sharing his own experience of deep disillusionment with the boring, unappealing, disengaged, excessively technical and theoretical curricula of several university philosophy departments (both continentally and analytically oriented) and the illuminating impact that the discovery of Hadot's work had on him, Michael Chase suggests that philosophy as a way of life should be attentively considered a third way of doing philosophy that is distinct from both analytic and continental traditions (2013, 280)—and, in fact, more valuable and fruitful than the alternatives, as it guarantees a process of genuine self-transformation (266). According to Chase, this is the most valuable account of philosophy there can be, the only one that can make sense and appeal to a person who is genuinely engaged with philosophy, and also the only one that preserves philosophy's original and authentic role and task.

Clearly, Chase is not simply urging us to read the ancient philosophers to whom Cooper refers, nor is he obviously recommending a recuperation of the ancient philosophical framework and concepts. Rather, he is stressing an idea that is similar to the one expressed by Sellars above: philosophy as a way of life is a metaphilosophical option—a certain distinctive *way* of doing philosophy—that, regardless of the intrinsic peculiarities, conceptual divergences, and different philosophical landscapes of each of its representatives, has characterized a good part of the history of philosophy and, most important, might still be reactivated today (see Chase 2013, 282–83). In what follows, I would like to support the conviction shared by Sellars and Chase and, against Cooper's objections, argue for the possibility and pertinence of philosophy as a way of life in the contemporary philosophical framework and landscape. I start by outlining Cooper's main points of criticism of philosophy as a way of life in the contemporary context (section 2) and show that they do not affect the core features of the model as implied in the work of Hadot and as systematized more recently by Chase and Sellars (section 3). In the fourth section, I illustrate the clear expression of the model in the work of contemporary authors who are supposedly excluded from it in Cooper's account, through analyzing the particular case of Nietzsche. I conclude (section 5) by outlining some of the considerations that, in the wake of Chase, Sellars, and others, might persuade us to embrace philosophy as a way of life as a guiding thread, both in our work and in our lives.

Cooper's Criticism of Philosophy as a Way of Life in the Post-Antiquity Era

When one starts reading Cooper's *Pursuits of Wisdom*—to a great extent written in the wake of and as a reaction to Hadot's work—one quickly realizes that for Cooper philosophy as a way of life is *not* a model referring to a particular way of conceiving and practicing philosophy, characteristic of Greek ancient philosophy and eventually recovered by subsequent philosophers. Rather, for Cooper philosophy as a way of life is simply a trend or feature of a very limited number of philosophies in antiquity that, in a quite unique and peculiar way, indeed offered ways of life. In the preface to his work, he clearly states his opposition to Hadot's account: "I explained my dissatisfaction with Hadot's conception of philosophy, and marked out my own new path toward conceiving, not ancient philosophy itself as a way of life (as if ancient philosophy were a unique and special genre of philosophizing), but specific ancient philosophies—in fact the six to which this book is devoted—as *ways* of life" (2012, x).

Cooper dedicates his book to a thorough analysis of the six ways of life he identifies in ancient philosophy—those promoted by Socrates, Aristotle, Stoicism, Epicureanism, Skepticism, and Platonism—struggling to emphasize both how strong and interesting these philosophies are in strictly philosophical terms and how plausible and compelling their proposals as guides to life can be. Even though he explicitly expresses the wish that "these theories might open up illuminating and clarifying perspectives that both enrich our contemporary philosophical thought, and open the prospect of new self-understandings that might allow us to embrace philosophy as a way of life," he immediately adds: "in the ancient manner—to some extent, at any rate—even in our very changed modern circumstances" (2012, x–xi). On Cooper's view, these very changed modern circumstances—especially the completely different philosophical landscape of our era, which might even make it difficult to understand and accept this philosophical tradition—completely prevent philosophy from being proposed and practiced as a way of life in modern and current times, which is why, if one wants to catch a glimpse of what philosophy as a way of life is or have a hint about how to guide one's life, there is no alternative but to turn one's attention to ancient times (16).

Cooper presents three major arguments in support of his thesis that philosophy is not and cannot be conceived as a way of life in the post-antiquity era, each of which relates to fundamental philosophical assumptions that grounded the possibility of a philosophical way of life in antiquity and that medieval, modern, and contemporary philosophy lack and even reject. First, in modern and contemporary philosophies, reason no longer appears as the motivating force for action in any human life, as it did for the ancients, for whom the human power of inquiring into and recognizing truth as such, and shaping one's whole life and action accordingly, was the very basis of ethical analysis and construction (Cooper 2012, 11–12). Second, but directly connected to the previous point, precisely because reasoning was thought to have an inherent power to move individuals to action in antiquity, philosophy, as the pursuit of wisdom and truth, was held to be the only art or technique whereby reason was made perfect and truth achieved, thereby providing the form in which one should live—that is, one's *way of life* (12–13). The last assumption that ancient philosophers shared and that modern and contemporary philosophers apparently reject is the connection between truth and the good life, that is, the belief that by incorporating the truth conveyed by philosophy (and thus necessarily acting according to it), one will be safe from ever acting wrongly, thus consistently and thoroughly ensuring a good, peaceful, and happy life. Even though one can find several models of the good life in antiquity—derived from different versions of what different philosophies held to be true—all of the schools believed that their philosophical views were based on and expressed the truth, this being precisely why they were able to lead human beings to live good, complete, and happy lives (13–14).

According to Cooper, the deep interconnection between reason and action, philosophy and knowledge, truth and the good life, together with the truly unified character of ancient philosophies, was the very core of ethics and philosophical practice in antiquity. It was also what allowed philosophy to express itself as a way of life, something that seems to have become impossible after the autonomization of ethics and especially the reformulation and complexification of the theories of human action and motivation in post-Renaissance philosophy:

> The classical philosophers of the modern tradition, and also contemporary philosophy, have developed theories of human motivation that greatly complicate any connection there might be between one's philosophical views on life and

> how it is best led, or on what is right and wrong to do, and one's actual way of living and one's actions. The result is that even if moral philosophy in modern and contemporary terms could be taken to present itself as a guide to a good life and to right action, by working out theories about these matters and presenting them as true, and therefore to be followed, there remains a psychological gap to be bridged. . . . Philosophy alone—reasoned understanding of practical truths—does not suffice, in the modern and contemporary philosophical climate, as it did in the ancient one. (Cooper 2012, 15)

It is difficult to contest Cooper's extremely clear and objective account both of the framework in which philosophy as a way of life first took shape and of the important differences that separate post-Renaissance philosophy from ancient philosophy. It indeed seems undeniable that, with very few exceptions—Cooper mentions Spinoza, for example (2012, 16 n. 23)—modern and contemporary philosophers subscribe neither to the optimistic belief in the power of reason to motivate human action nor to the view of philosophy as the sole authority in what concerns human life, nor even, consequently, to the belief in an intrinsic connection between knowledge or truth and the good life or happiness. Having been seriously and repeatedly put in question since modernity, the connection between these fundamental concepts of ancient philosophy—reason, truth, wisdom, happiness, the good life—no longer even appears, without further qualification at least, in contemporary philosophical discourse.

The question is thus whether these assumptions are really fundamental to any possible conception of philosophy as a way of life, as Cooper implies, or whether it is possible to conceive of a framework in which, these assumptions being absent, philosophy as a way of life could still come to the fore as an approach that is distinctive of other ways of understanding and practicing philosophy, as Hadot and his followers seem to have in mind. Cooper is certainly right to point out that philosophy can only be a way of life if it is conceived as having some privilege over other possible techniques or arts of living, as possessing in itself a steering or motivational power for human action and as being in some way connected to the transformation and eventual improvement of one's self and life. Yet perhaps those conditions do not need to be met in the peculiar and strict way they were conceived of in antiquity, in which case we would have different versions of the ways in which philosophy can have an impact on one's character and give form to one's life—that is, express itself as a way of life. This question is particularly important if, following the recent trend in scholarly research, one is to argue for the reactivation of philosophy as a way of life in the contemporary landscape and milieu.

Hadot's Account of Philosophy as a Way of Life

If we now turn our attention to the clear and condensed account of philosophy as a way of life that Hadot offers in the essay that shares its name with his most famous book in the English-speaking world, *Philosophy as a Way of Life*, we notice that the framework in which he presents philosophy as a way of life is indeed less strict and rigid than the one that Cooper uses to contest Hadot's extension of the model to modern and contemporary philosophers. This does not mean that Hadot disagrees with the basic characteristics that Cooper ascribes to ancient philosophy; indeed, Hadot's description of philosophy as a way of life in antiquity fits relatively well with Cooper's account. Apart from the pivotal importance Hadot places on spiritual exercises in ancient philosophy, which implies a different understanding of the way philosophy provided motivation for action and self-transformation, he stresses with similar eloquence the deep interconnection between truth or wisdom and the good life, on the one hand, and the way in which philosophy as incorporated wisdom provided the form according to which one should shape one's life, on the other.[1] "Philosophy thus took on the form of an exercise of the thought, will, and the totality of one's being, the goal of which was to achieve a state practically inaccessible to mankind: wisdom. Philosophy was a method of spiritual progress which demanded a radical conversion and transformation of the individual's way of being. Thus, philosophy was a way of life, both in its exercise and effort to achieve wisdom, and in its goal, wisdom itself. For real wisdom does not merely cause us to know: it makes us 'be' in a different way" (Hadot 1995, 265).

When one looks deeper into Hadot's description of philosophy as a way of life and into recent developments of it in contemporary scholarship, however, one realizes that the distinguishing marks of this metaphilosophical model are, in Hadot's understanding and when compared to Cooper's, much more formal, general, and independent of any specific conceptual framework. Being undoubtedly present in their original ancient form, these distinguishing marks are recognizable in several authors after antiquity, even if the philosophical landscape has considerably changed since then and the particular models differ in each particular philosophical approach. These basic distinguishing marks of philosophy as a way of life can be summarized in terms of three deeply interconnected features.

First, the "philosophy as a way of life" model clearly privileges practice over theory: philosophy is conceived not primarily as a theory or body of knowledge but as a practice, a way of being and existing in the world. This need not imply that one conforms one's *whole* life to a particular philosophical theory—as occurred in antiquity and as Cooper stresses in particular—but simply that theory must necessarily have a transformative

[1] The importance ascribed by Hadot to spiritual exercises in ancient philosophy is one of Cooper's strongest points of criticism against Hadot's account of this tradition of thought in antiquity: according to Cooper, it misleadingly blurs the distinction between the strictly philosophical and the religious way of life (2012, 17–23). Discussing this criticism is beyond the scope of this essay, however.

impact on one's way of perceiving the world and living in it. Inspired by the Stoics, Hadot distinguishes between philosophy and mere philosophical discourse, which, apart from its practical application, is considered mere rhetoric or sophistry.[2] Being a philosopher means *living* philosophically, which is why "philosophical theories are in the service of the philosophical life" (Hadot 1995, 267) and of little value if they do not in some way change one's way of perceiving the world and oneself and, consequently, affect the life and character of those who practice it. The corollary of this point, as Sellars correctly notes, is that there must be a clear connection and consistency between someone's stated philosophical ideas and their behavior, such that actions are ultimately more significant than words (2017, 41).

A second deeply interconnected feature of philosophy as a way of life is its performative character, that is, its ability to have the abovementioned transformative effect on the lives and characters of individuals. According to Sellars, transformation of one's way of life is the ultimate motivation of philosophy understood as a way of life (2017, 41). This has consequences both at the level of content and at the level of style, as Michael Chase has convincingly shown, by sharply contrasting philosophy as a way of life with contemporary models, whether continentally or analytically oriented. More concretely, unlike analytic philosophy, philosophy as a way of life, despite being rigorous, is not scientifically pretentious, does not use mathematical language and signs, and most important does not avoid what Chase calls "the Big Questions" and the issues that concern everybody inside and outside the academy alike. Even though it is not necessarily dogmatic—as most schools in antiquity were—it does offer reflection and guidance on how to live and conduct one's life with a view to self-transformation. Contrary to many continental approaches, it is not hermetic, sarcastic, ironic, or relativistic but rather is expressed in clear, jargon-free language. Accordingly, contrary to the way philosophy is studied in universities today, philosophy approached as a way of life guarantees "not just an accumulation of knowledge or a display of cleverness, but a process of genuine transformation," based on a change in one's way of looking at the world, the consequence of which is "to *be* in a new and different way" (Chase 2013, 266).

Finally, the model of philosophy as a way of life implies, in Hadot's understanding, that the process of self-transformation that lies at its core is determined by a guiding ideal of human perfection, completeness, or flourishing. Hadot refers mainly to the Hellenistic tradition, in the context

[2] This must not be understood as a devaluation of discourse or theory: there is "no discourse which deserves to be called philosophical if it is separated from the philosophical life, and there is no philosophical life unless it is directly linked to philosophical discourse" (Hadot 2002, 174). Even though philosophy as an "art of living" was not *simply* a theoretical discipline, theory was the basis on which the philosophical way of life was grounded, such that philosophy was, "at the same time and indissolubly, a discourse *and* a way of life" (4).

of which philosophy as an art of living was meant to cure human suffering and bring peace of mind, which is why it was first and foremost conceived and presented as a form of therapy (1995, 265–66).[3] This fits well with Cooper's claim that in antiquity there was a deep connection between philosophy and the good life, such that those who pursued philosophy could not fail to attain happiness. As Sellars perspicaciously noted, however, this need not necessarily be so, and the "good life" or even the beneficial effects of philosophy must not be assumed to be a necessary result of philosophy as a way of life. In fact, other philosophical ideals might be at stake—ideals that do not necessarily lead to an increased sense of happiness or well-being, even if they are still related to the idea of human flourishing and/or improvement. What is fundamental, in Sellars's view, is that there is a strong connection between theory and life, such that theory necessarily has an impact on the actions, behavior, and way of life of the individual (and ultimately also of an entire society), but in principle it is not possible to determine whether this impact will be positive or negative, healthy or noxious (2017, 41). As Sellars later claims, "It may turn out that philosophy is no consolation at all" (48).

Given this sum of core characteristics of philosophy as a way of life, it is not surprising that both Hadot and his followers contrast it not with specific conceptual frameworks across the history of philosophy but with other ways of conceiving and practicing philosophy that separate it from its deep practical, existential, and transformative dimension and turn it into a mere theoretical, abstract, and logical discipline, as seems to have become the rule in most contemporary universities and even in the academic and nonacademic understanding of the term.[4] The critique by Hadot of the practice of philosophy in modern universities is consistent and harsh throughout his work, which indicates his intention of presenting philosophy as a way of life not only as a characterization of ancient philosophy but also as a powerful tool for the criticism and transfiguration of contemporary academic institutions.

According to Hadot, a general trait common to all universities is that they are made up of professors who train other professors, or experts who train other experts—that is, "professionals training professionals" (1995, 270). The tight bond that originally tied philosophy to life has disappeared, and what is at stake today is no longer the education of individuals so that

[3] On the conception of philosophy as therapy in Hellenistic philosophy, see Nussbaum 1994. On the general notion of philosophy as an art of living in antiquity, see Sellars 2009.

[4] See Hadot 1995, 107. See also Nehamas 1998, 1: "'Philosophy is a theoretical discipline.' Like many general statements, this one too conceals a perfect tense in its apparently timeless 'is.' The truth is that philosophy *has become* a theoretical discipline over time and as a result of many complex historical developments. The 'fact' that its 'nature' is theoretical is nothing but the historically given reality that philosophy has mainly been practiced as a theoretical discipline for as long as the knowledge and memory of most philosophers extend."

they may live good, complete, flourishing lives but simply the creation of professional philosophers who are able to train other professional philosophers. In short, with the development of universities, philosophy has become progressively enclosed within the academy and reduced to philosophical discourse, a "technical jargon reserved for specialists" (272), conveyed in scholarly books and lecture courses with little to no impact on everyday life and no relation to the lives of those who practice it, such that a proper philosophical life is in current circumstances nowhere to be found. As Hadot complains, "In modern university philosophy, philosophy is obviously no longer a way of life or form of life—unless it be the form of life of a professor of philosophy" (271). While philosophy seems to have lost the capacity to legitimate itself outside the university, more normative and existentially practical conceptions of philosophy tend to be devalued as philosophically irrelevant within the academy, or even criticized for seeming to imply a certain immodesty and/or a pretense of moral superiority (see Miller 1998, 872; Nehamas 1998, 4).

The Reinvention of Philosophy as a Way of Life: The Case of Nietzsche

These pessimistic comments on the way in which philosophy is currently practiced in universities and academic institutions is balanced by Hadot's acknowledgment of a few modern and contemporary thinkers who have made successful attempts to recover and reinvent the ancient model of philosophy as a way of life, most of them, not coincidentally, *outside* or *against* the university (1995, 270–71). In sharp contrast to Cooper's account, Hadot names Descartes, Spinoza, Malebranche, and Leibniz (in modern philosophy) and Schopenhauer, Kierkegaard, Nietzsche, and Wittgenstein (in contemporary philosophy) as successful revivals of the strongly practical, existential, and life-transforming potential of ancient philosophy (1995, 270–71; 2002, 270).[5] In what follows, I would like to support the account Hadot provides by adding textual evidence to his claims and showing, against Cooper, that against the background of Hadot's broader characterization of philosophy as a way of life it is indeed possible to recognize the model in contemporary philosophy and to call for its reactivation today. For the sake of economy, I focus exclusively on Nietzsche, whom I take to be a particularly illustrative example of how the previously outlined distinguishing marks of the model can be at work in post-Renaissance philosophy and be adapted to different cultural, philosophical, and conceptual landscapes and milieus.

[5] See Foucault's corroboration of this thesis in Foucault 2001, 251. On the similarity between Hadot's and Foucault's accounts of the matter, see Flynn 2005. For a thorough approach to contemporary versions of philosophy as a way of life, see Nehamas 1998 and Chase, Clark, and McGhee 2013.

A first characteristic of philosophy as a way of life that Nietzsche undoubtedly expresses is his contempt for university philosophy and his awareness of the risks involved in it. Hadot explicitly refers to the case of Schopenhauer, who considers university philosophy "mere fencing in front of a mirror," its goal being simply "to give students opinions which are to the liking of the minister who hands out the Chairs," therefore making "a joke of philosophy" (Schopenhauer, qtd. Hadot 1995, 271). Nietzsche goes even further, complementing the same criticism of academic philosophy with an explicit apology, by way of contrast, for the ancient conception and practice of philosophy. In fact, it is difficult to find a better definition of philosophy as a way of life than that which we find in *Schopenhauer as Educator*, where, praising the "philosophical life" of antiquity, Nietzsche expresses his contempt for philosophies capable of producing only "university professors and professors' philosophy" (1997b, 137, translation modified). In explicit opposition to the current "university philosophy," Nietzsche offers the following conception of philosophy: "I profit from a philosopher only insofar as he can be an example. . . . But this example must be supplied by his outward life and not merely in his books—in the way, that is, in which the philosophers of Greece taught, through their bearing, what they wore and ate, and their morals, rather than by what they said, let alone by what they wrote" (136–37).

In this passage, Nietzsche clearly subscribes to the first feature of Hadot's description of philosophy as a way of life outlined above, that is, the clear privileging of practice over theory and the idea that there ought to be some expression of one's stated opinions, thesis, and worldview in one's actual behavior, actions, and way of being. In his unfinished and posthumously published essay *Philosophy in the Tragic Age of the Greeks* Nietzsche further laments how nowadays no one ventures "to fulfill philosophy's law with his own person, no one may live philosophically with that simple loyalty which compelled an ancient, no matter where he was or what he was doing, to deport himself as a Stoic if he once had pledged faith to the Stoa" (1998, 37). In addition, Nietzsche disapprovingly observes the extent to which contemporary philosophy has not only ceased to be a way of life but has become completely dominated and policed by governments, churches, academies, custom, fashion, and "human cowardice, all of which limit it to a fake erudition" (37–38, translation modified).

Thus, just like the ancient philosophers to which Hadot and his followers refer, Nietzsche too conceived of *real* philosophy as inseparable from life and as being of little value if it does not preserve its freedom from institutions and have a transformative effect, both on the one who practices it and on those to whom it may and should serve as an example. As he states in a posthumously published note from 1873, "So long as philosophers do not gain the courage to seek a totally transformed way of life and exhibit it by their own example, they are of no consequence" (1990, 107, translation modified). And in another fragment from the same year, he claims: "The philosopher's product is his *life* (first of all, before his *works*). That is his work of art" (2009, 182).[6] Against the criticism to which Nietzsche (like some ancient philosophers, especially the Hellenists) was sometimes subjected—that of promoting an excessively individualistic or even solipsistic ethics—he adds, in the posthumous fragment previously quoted, that a work of art belongs in the first place to the artist but soon after to the whole of humanity (182). The fundamental trait of Nietzsche's way of conceiving philosophy is thus to ensure that the philosopher, through his example, has an impact on other philosophers and on those who are not philosophers, that is to say, that his practice of philosophy has performative practical, ethical, and normative effects, first on himself or herself but ultimately on the whole culture (182).

This brings us to the second feature of philosophy as a way of life that is clearly illustrated in Nietzsche's work, namely, its performativity. Indeed, rather than merely saying or teaching something, Nietzsche's texts actually *do* something to the reader. Incorporating what in *The Gay Science* Nietzsche terms "subtler laws of style" (2001, 245), they immediately affect, touch, concern, disturb, intrigue, provoke, and make one angry, or else attract, seduce, entice, stimulate, inspire, and obsess the reader, leaving no one indifferent. On a deeper level, however, all of these effects, which are clearly intentional, seem to be meant to awaken the reader and to promote in him or her the abovementioned process of self-transformation toward what, in the wake of Hadot and ancient philosophy, can be called the philosophical life. Nietzsche states that his texts are designed to "open the ears of those whose ears are related to ours" (245) and to convey to them his own innermost philosophical experiences, "changes of skin," and modulations of thought, for ultimately, as one reads in the preface to the second edition of *The Gay Science*, "this art of transfiguration just *is* philosophy" (6).

Especially noteworthy in this regard is, as Hadot himself notes, the presence of elements in Nietzsche's work that in important ways resemble the ancient "spiritual exercises" (see, e.g., Hadot 1995, 108; 2008, 155), that is, themes that are conceived not as mere "theoretical constructs" but as part of "a method for training people to live and to look at the world in a new way" (1995, 107).[7] The most expressive examples are perhaps the thought of the eternal return of the same and the idea of *amor fati*, which are indeed best understood if one approaches them not as theories about the

[6] It is interesting that we find precisely the same analogy in Foucault (2000, 261). That both Nietzsche's and Foucault's philosophies are, in the wake of the ancient philosophers, "invitations to radically transform our way of life" (Hadot 1995, 272) is a claim that finds strong support in both authors' works (see, e.g., Nietzsche 2001, 163–64; 1997a, 255; Foucault 2000, 259, 262, 272). On Nietzsche's and Foucault's ideals of self-cultivation and the influence of ancient philosophy on them, see especially Ansell-Pearson (2018) and Ure (2007; 2018).

[7] On Nietzsche and the tradition of spiritual exercises, see Hutter 2006. See also Ure 2018 for an interpretation of the thought of eternal recurrence as a spiritual exercise.

world but as tools for progressive self-transformation and self-cultivation on the basis of a modified perception of the world. Of the eternal return, for example, Nietzsche himself writes: "If this thought gained power over you, as you are it would transform and possibly crush you" (2001, 194). And the ideal of amor fati, which he frequently embodies as an example—"*Amor fati*: that is my innermost nature" (2005, 280)—is often presented as a normative device for training oneself to adopt a cosmic, universal, affirmative perspective on the Whole (see, e.g., Nietzsche 2001, 157; 2005, 99; Hadot 2008, 155, 256–67). The fact that he presents amor fati and other ideals of his philosophy from the first-person perspective clearly reveals that he intends to have a transformative impact on his readers not primarily through the transmission of a certain theoretical content but first and foremost through his own life and experience. Indeed, this intent justifies not only the personal character of his writings but also many other stylistic traits of his philosophy, such as the aphoristic form of his texts and their ironic, sarcastic, and provocative style, his frequent interpellations directed at the reader, and the abundance of autobiographical texts, especially in the last phase of his thought, including the prefaces of 1886 and, of course, *Ecce Homo*.

Finally, there is no doubt that Nietzsche aimed at a process of self-transformation on the part of his readers, on the basis of a certain ideal of human flourishing or perfection that he intended to promote as an effect of the incorporation of his thought. This remains true even if this end result was not necessarily related to "the good life" or the "happiness" espoused by ancient philosophers and was meant not only for individuals but ultimately for Western culture as a whole. What lies at the core of Nietzsche's philosophical project is the famous transvaluation of all values, which should have as a consequence a large-scale liberation from Christian herdlike values and the promotion of individuality, uniqueness, and singularity. In the early work *Schopenhauer as Educator,* for example, one reads the following: "The man who does not wish to belong to the mass needs only to cease taking himself easily; let him follow his conscience, which calls to him: 'Be your self! All you are now doing, thinking, desiring, is not you yourself!'" (Nietzsche 1997b, 127). This theme is repeated in different formulations throughout Nietzsche's work until it reaches a form that would become one of the central mottos of his philosophy: "Become who you are" (see, e.g., 2001, 152, 189).

Even though Nietzsche connects his philosophical goal with a certain idea of human flourishing and health (e.g., 2001, 116–17), in the context of his philosophy, the universalist "good life" of the ancients is substituted with a free, strong, new, incomparable, unique, individual, singular existence (see Nehamas 1998, 10)—one that, after centuries of submission to a life-denying morality, now strives for what Keith Ansell-Pearson calls "spiritual joyfulness" or "the joy in existing" (2018, 9). Insofar as this involves a process of genuine self-transformation, based on a liberation and singularization of individual existence that is to a large extent meant to be the product of Nietzsche's philosophical breeding, or education, it seems fair to include Nietzsche in the "philosophy as a way of life" model described by Hadot. Indeed, as with the ancient philosophers, it seems undeniable that the incorporation of Nietzsche's philosophy causes us not simply to know but to *be* in a different way.

Conclusion: Philosophy as a Way of Life Today

It is clear that in many senses Nietzsche's philosophy—and, in general, all modern and contemporary philosophy—cannot be compared in an absolute way with ancient philosophy. Cooper is certainly right to point out the abyssal differences that separate ancient philosophy from all later developments and transfigurations of it. It is true that philosophy never fully recovered its prominent role and authority as an art of living or guide to life and that it has mainly become an abstract and theoretical discipline. And yet, Hadot is also extremely perspicuous in noting that some fundamental aspects of the ancient conception of philosophy have never fully disappeared (1995, 271) and that modern and contemporary philosophers who were particularly influenced by Greco-Roman philosophy have tried to reinvent it in completely different philosophical, cultural, and social milieus.

I have tried to show how the model that Hadot and his followers describe as philosophy as a way of life can be clearly identified in Nietzsche, but a similar attempt could certainly be made with equal success concerning other modern and contemporary philosophers, most notably Montaigne, Spinoza, Schopenhauer, Kierkegaard, and Foucault. What unites them with ancient philosophers, as we have seen, is (i) the valorization of practice (actions, behavior) over theory (theses, books) and the consistency between the two, (ii) the performative character of their writings and their aim to promote self-transformation, and finally, (iii) a concern to provide some kind of guidance for one's life on the basis of an ideal of human flourishing or perfection. The extent to which they mirror basic traits of ancient philosophy on the one hand and run against its current practice in universities on the other justifies their inclusion in the "philosophy as a way of life" model, which is used by Hadot and his followers not only to describe a certain way of doing philosophy but, more important, also as an alternative to the model that increasingly characterizes academic philosophical practice. My aim in this essay is not to demonstrate that Cooper was wrong in his criticism of Hadot but simply to show that they indeed have different understandings of what philosophy as a way of life is and that the broader and less rigid approach taken by the latter, certainly being valid, is also more useful in metaphilosophical terms, especially in the face of current social, cultural, and academic challenges concerning the conception and practice of philosophy.

By way of conclusion, I would like to underscore certain considerations that, in the wake of Hadot, Chase, and Sellars (among others), might persuade us to reconsider our academic practice and to take the reactivation of philosophy as a way of life seriously (see Faustino 2020). First, it is a fact that, due to its increasing institutionalization, scientification, and professionalization, philosophy—like the humanities in general—is facing an unprecedented crisis and now seriously runs the risk of losing its autonomy, its particularity among the disciplines, and even its purpose. In this context, philosophy as a way of life offers a meaningful alternative to the current institutionalized practice of philosophy—an alternative that, by returning to "the Big Questions" (Chase 2013, 283) that once characterized it, might simultaneously restore philosophy's singularity and combat the increasing dissatisfaction expressed by university philosophy students, teachers, and researchers.

Second, it is interesting to note that at the same time that the philosophical community is becoming increasingly dissatisfied with the kind of philosophy practiced in universities and the demands and restrictions to which it is subjected in this context, outside the academy there also seems to be a growing interest in philosophy understood as an art of living or a guide to life—an interest to which the market has responded with a proliferation of New Age initiatives and self-help books of doubtful quality, often grounded in philosophy but completely decontextualized and deprived of their original systems, thus insulting both their philosophical roots and the intelligence of the public that consumes them. For authors like Chase, this is proof that the disappearance of philosophy as a way of life risks leaving an insurmountable gap both within and outside the academy, ultimately leading to philosophy's "proper field" being taken over by "hucksters and mass marketers, facile esotericists, and obscurantists" (2013, 283).

Finally, from a social, cultural, and political point of view, there seems to be a growing demand for the type of reflection that is at stake in this model of philosophical practice. Indeed, our era poses unprecedented challenges that call for a type of philosophical reflection that seems to be impossible in the framework of current philosophical approaches, which is necessarily limited and narrow in scope. The excessive technicization of life, the global environmental crisis, post- and transhumanism, and the refugee crisis, to name just a few modern-day concerns, are contemporary problems and challenges that arguably call for the "view from Above," that is, "the grandiose perspective of universal nature and of humanity" (Hadot 1995, 284) that was typical of ancient philosophies and that derived the good human life precisely from knowledge of the natural world and the place of the human being in it. A true reactivation of the model of philosophy as a way of life today would thus necessarily require a whole new field of reflection and experimentation, which would adapt it and reinvent it according to current material conditions and challenges. Efforts in this direction have already been undertaken, and, as interest in this tradition of thought increases, we can only expect and hope that philosophy might reemerge, even within the university, as the most efficient art for enabling individuals to live and share the world in the most flourishing, respectful, and fulfilling of ways.

Acknowledgments

This work is funded by national funds through the FCT—Fundação para a Ciência e a Tecnologia, I.P., under the Norma Transitória—DL 57/2016/CP1453/CT0042. I wish to thank Michael Ure, Keith Ansell-Pearson, and all the researchers involved in the project *Reinventing Philosophy as a Way of Life* for a fruitful exchange of ideas on the topic of this essay. A special thank-you goes to Gianfranco Ferraro and Hélder Telo for discussion and criticism of previous versions of the essay. I am also grateful to the anonymous peer reviewers of the essay for their pertinent comments and suggestions on how to improve my argument.

References

Ansell-Pearson, Keith. 2018. *Nietzsche's Search for Philosophy: On the Middle Writings*. London: Bloomsbury.

Chase, Michael. 2013. "Observations on Pierre Hadot's Conception of Philosophy as a Way of Life." In *Philosophy as a Way of Life, Ancients and Moderns: Essays in Honor of Pierre Hadot*, edited by Michael Chase, Stephen Clark, and Michael McGhee, 262–86. Chichester: Blackwell.

Chase, Michael, Stephen Clark, and Michael McGhee, eds. 2013. *Philosophy as a Way of Life, Ancients and Moderns: Essays in Honor of Pierre Hadot*. Chichester: Blackwell.

Cooper, John. 2012. *Pursuits of Wisdom: Six Ways of Life in Ancient Philosophy from Socrates to Plotinus*. Princeton: Princeton University Press.

Faustino, Marta. 2020. "'Philosophy as a Way of Life' as a Practice of Dissidence and Experimentation." In *Philosophy as Experimentation, Dissidence and Heterogeneity*, edited by J. M. Justo. Newcastle upon Tyne: Cambridge Scholars.

Flynn, Thomas. 2005. "Philosophy as a Way of Life: Foucault and Hadot." *Philosophy and Social Criticism* 31:609–22.

Foucault, Michel. 2000. "On the Genealogy of Ethics: An Overview of Work in Progress." In *Essential Works of Foucault, 1954–1984, Volume 1: Ethics*, edited by P. Rabinow, 253–80. London: Penguin Books.

________. 2001. *The Hermeneutics of the Subject: Lectures at the Collège de France, 1981–1982*. Edited by Frédéric Gros, translated by Graham Burchell. New York: Palgrave.

Hadot, Pierre. 1995. *Philosophy as a Way of Life*. Edited by Arnold Davidson, translated by Michael Chase. Malden, Mass.: Blackwell.

———. 2002. *What Is Ancient Philosophy?* Translated by Michael Chase. Cambridge, Mass.: Belknap Press of Harvard University Press.

———. 2008. *N'oublie pas de vivre: Goethe et la tradition des exercices spirituels*. Paris: Albin Michel.

Hutter, Horst. 2006. *Shaping the Future. Nietzsche's New Regime of the Souls and Its Ascetic Practices*. Oxford: Lexington Books.

Miller, James. 1998. "The Prophet and the Dandy: Philosophy as a Way of Life in Nietzsche and Foucault." *Social Research* 65, no. 4:871–96.

Nehamas, Alexander. 1998. *The Art of Living: Socratic Reflections from Plato to Foucault*. Berkeley: University of California Press.

Nietzsche, Friedrich. 1990. *Philosophy and Truth: Selections from Nietzsche's Notebooks of the Early 1870's*. Edited by Daniel Breazeale, translated by Daniel Breazeale. London: Humanities Press International.

———. 1997a. *Daybreak*. Edited by Maudemarie Clark and Brian Leiter, translated by R. J. Hollingdale. Cambridge: Cambridge University Press.

———. 1997b. *Untimely Meditations*. Edited by Daniel Breazeale, translated by R. J. Hollingdale. Cambridge: Cambridge University Press.

———. 1998. *Philosophy in the Tragic Age of the Greeks*. Translated by Marianne Cowan. Washington: Regnery.

———. 2001. *The Gay Science*. Edited by Bernard Williams, translated by Josefine Nauckhoff. Cambridge: Cambridge University Press.

———. 2005. The Anti-Christ, Ecce Homo, Twilight of the Idols *and Other Writings*. Edited by Aaron Ridley and Judith Norman, translated by Judith Norman. Cambridge: Cambridge University Press.

———. 2009. *Writings from the Early Notebooks*. Edited by Raymond Geuss and Alexander Nehamas, translated by Ladislaus Löb. Cambridge: Cambridge University Press.

Nussbaum, Martha. 1994. *The Therapy of Desire: Theory and Practice in Hellenistic Ethics*. Princeton: Princeton University Press.

Sellars, John. 2009. *The Art of Living: The Stoics on the Nature and Function of Philosophy*. London: Bloomsbury.

———. 2017. "What Is Philosophy as a Way of Life?" *Parrhesia* 28:40–56.

Ure, Michael. 2007. "Senecan Moods: Foucault and Nietzsche on the Art of the Self." *Foucault Studies* 4:19–52.

———. 2018. "Nietzsche's Ethics of Self-Cultivation and Eternity." In *Ethics and Self-Cultivation: Historical and Contemporary Perspectives*, edited by Matthew Dennis and Sander Werkhoven, 84–103. New York: Routledge.

CHAPTER 12

SETTING LIMITS TO PRACTICAL REFLECTION

AGAINST PHILOSOPHY AS A WAY OF LIFE

VITOR SOMMAVILLA

1. Philosophy as a Way of Life: Socratic Style

Human beings are typically agents. We act for reasons, frequently out of a conscious apprehension of such reasons. As rational beings, we also have a capacity to reflect on the considerations we take to be reasons, to scrutinize them.[1] In very crude form, the philosophical way of life, as proposed by Plato's Socrates, means submitting all our alleged reasons and beliefs to the test of philosophical examination. The bet is that a life conducted along these lines has a better shot at making us wiser and more capable of achieving the good.[2]

[1] Following Scanlon 1998 it has become commonplace to explain reasons as considerations that count in favor (of some action or belief). As Velleman (2009, 121–22 n. 8) correctly notes, simply saying that a consideration counts in favor of something does not explain much. We want to know *why* it counts in favor of whatever it counts in favor of. In other words, we want to know how it *warrants* or *justifies* that action or belief. Therefore, a reason is best understood as a consideration that justifies (122). The reflective scrutiny that I refer to in this paragraph is a pursuit for such justification.

[2] Discussion about philosophy as a way of life among ancient philosophers was pioneered by Pierre Hadot. For the ancients, according to him, a life dedicated to the pursuit of wisdom meant a life that brought peace of mind, inner freedom, and (for the Stoics and Epicureans) cosmic consciousness (1995, 265–66). Hadot's emphasis on spiritual progress has been criticized by John Cooper (2012). I do not wish to engage with this polemic. I register, though, that my presentation in the text follows more closely Cooper's reading.

Philosophy as a Way of Life: Historical, Contemporary, and Pedagogical Perspectives.
Edited by James M. Ambury, Tushar Irani, and Kathleen Wallace.

Published 2021 by John Wiley & Sons Ltd.

Socrates famously claimed that "the unexamined life is not worth living" (*Apology* 38a 5–6).[3] The passage is most likely best understood not as claiming that an unexamined life is worse than being dead but that one *should not* live an unexamined life.[4] His self-examination and examination of his interlocutors (so-called cross-examination) is deeply connected to the inquiry by Socrates into ethical matters, to his efforts to lead a good, virtuous life. For one thing, self-examination can help extirpate the mistaken conceptions and assumptions one inherits from culture and unreflective education.[5] Under the supposition of an objective conception of the good life, thorough, philosophical self-scrutiny can also help put one on the right track, on the track of wisdom.

Socratic wisdom is attained when one has fully grasped the truth about all human values and their systematic relations. Virtue is the condition of the soul of someone possessing wisdom. The wise and virtuous person always does what is best, for her actions always spring from her knowledge of the good (Cooper 2012, 43ff.). Therefore, constantly seeking wisdom is apparently fully justified within the Socratic model. For it disabuses us of false preconceptions and puts us on the way to a happy life.

Socrates was convinced that achieving this kind of wisdom was beyond the capacity of any real human being. Although wisdom was for him the best life in principle, in practice the best life was philosophy, the love of wisdom, or its constant pursuit. Committing to philosophy as a way of life was committing to following reason wherever it may lead.[6] As Cooper puts it, pursuing wisdom requires "constant philosophical discussion about matters of human value, and . . . constant self-examination of one's own views on the fullest range possible of those questions" (2012, 57).

An immediate thing to notice about this model is how demanding it is. It has at least three noteworthy features. (1) It requires that the agent fully examine her values and beliefs about several things; presumably all her views about what she has reason to do. (2) It requires that she know all there is to know about matters of value and reasons for action, at least when it comes to moral decision making. (3) And it presupposes that these kinds of (self-)examination and knowledge are the best guides to the happy life. Because achieving (2) is admittedly almost impossible, the follower of the model risks becoming obsessed with (1), in the expectation of reaping the benefits promised by (3). No wonder that the Socratic model was met with a great deal of suspicion and skepticism from the beginning.

Perhaps Socrates' model is to be taken precisely as a model, that is, as an ideal, which we should not expect real human beings to fully achieve. The

[3] I follow Cooper's translation (Plato 1997).

[4] Richard Kraut proposes to translate the passage as "no human being should live an unexamined life" (2007, 231). I follow his interpretation in the next phrases in the text.

[5] Kraut makes this point referring to many of the so-called Socratic dialogues (2007, 238).

[6] Cf. *Apology* 29 c–d for Socrates' persistent commitment to philosophical inquiry.

ideal model could, then, be seen either as a provider of ultimate practical reasons for actual human beings—for the model would not be plagued by the imprecisions of actual cases—or as a point of reference, to be approximated as much as our human nature allows.[7]

Independently of how difficult it is to adopt the Socratic way of life, however, what I wish to investigate in this essay is whether we have reasons to strive for such a life in the first place. In other words, I investigate whether we are justified in questioning our reasons in a self-examining process looking for firm foundations. I respond to these questions in the negative, and the better part of the essay is dedicated to arguing for the claim that there are more or less precise limits to how much practical reflection is warranted in each situation of action.[8] Just like talking or walking, deliberating is an action and, as such, demands a warrant before one justifiably engages in it. Very often one does not have reason to (further) deliberate—or so I will argue.

2. Antirealist Constructivism

In this section, I outline the metaethical view with which I am working in this essay. I will not be able to argue for its comparative merits here.[9] It is nevertheless important to have a clear starting point.

The view is called metaethical constructivism. Perhaps the best general definition of it is given by Sharon Street: "According to **thoroughgoing** or **metaethical constructivist views**, the truth of a normative claim consists in that claim's being entailed from within the practical point of view, where the practical point of view is given a *formal* characterization" (2010, 369)

When an agent makes a normative judgment, say, claims that X is a reason for him to do something, constructivism offers a model to evaluate whether the agent is correct in his claim. He occupies what Street calls the practical point of view when he makes normative judgments, takes some consideration to be a reason, or, more generally, values some things over others. His practical point of view is in a sense composed by his set of values, based on which he makes his particular normative judgments. Makes or should make: in fact, a normative judgment will be justified as long as it

[7] Idealized models have diverse problems of their own. Just to mention one: it seems that agents would have to have reasons to comply with the choices of their idealized counterparts.

[8] Practical reflection, otherwise called practical reasoning or deliberation, is reflection about what to do. Socratic self-examination and cross-examination are of course concerned with the knowledge of truth in general and for that reason do not limit themselves to reflection about reasons for action. In this regard, my discussion in this essay has a more limited range. Notice, however, that interrogating our beliefs is arguably also something we do, whose justification can just as well be cast into doubt by the exercise of our practical reasoning capacities. If that is true, my discussion here has implications that apply to the breadth of Socrates' wide-ranging concerns. But this is a matter I wish to remain neutral about.

[9] I defend it from critics in Sommavilla unpublished.

is entailed from that practical point of view, from his set of values. The practical point of view is given a formal characterization because it is not meant to have any substantive assumptions. It is the standpoint of the agent as such, regardless of which particular values a particular agent holds.[10] The notion of entailment is not defined with complete precision but is meant to include instrumental rationality, logical entailment, and conceptual necessity.

The view is internalist in at least two senses. It is a kind of motivation internalism, in that the notion of valuing or taking something to be a reason is expected to (at least partially) motivate the agent. So, for example, if an agent fails to be motivated by what he acknowledges to be a necessary means to his valued end, he either does not really count as taking it as a reason or is instrumentally irrational (Street 2008, 230). It is also a kind of judgment internalism, where it is to be determined whether a consideration is a proper reason by seeing things from the point of view of the agent. What is considered externally to be a reason for that agent does not qualify as a reason for him if it does not gain that status as a reason from within his point of view.

Moreover, on the constructivist view, justification is coherentist. A particular normative judgment will be justified if it coheres with the total set of values possessed by the judgment's utterer. No individual has a perfectly coherent set of values, so it becomes a matter of gradation how coherent the set is. Also, a particular judgment can have more or fewer connections to the other judgments, values, and beliefs in the set. More connections means more justification. Finally, particularly for the case of values and normative judgments, the more deeply attached the agent is to the value or judgment—which may or may not supervene on the level of connectedness of the value or judgment with the rest of the set—the more the judgment or value is justified. Deeply held values are closer to the core of the agent, they are more defining of his identity, and, therefore, he has less prima facie reason to abandon them.

What is the agent's total set of values and beliefs? Which ones cohere with one another? Which dispositions to believe and value does the agent possess that might be inconsistent with the normative judgment he just made? More generally, what is entailed from his practical point of view—his total set of values—in conjunction with the nonnormative facts of a given situation so that he can know what he ought to do? Answering all of these questions seems to require that the agent engage in self-examination and practical reflection, casting doubt on what might have appeared to him as a reason for action. The reflective, philosophical way of life slowly suggests itself. In fact, Christine Korsgaard, a leading,

[10]In Sommavilla unpublished, I take issue with Street's formal characterization of constructivism, but that does not have to concern us here.

Kantian constructivist, has expressed herself clearly about the high value she places on reflection in the following terms:

> Kantian positions in general set a high value on reflection and are idealizing positions in the sense that moral concepts, as Kant defines them, are derived from the ideal of a fully reflective person. The fully reflective person is a corollary of Kant's idea of the unconditioned. We seek the unconditioned by imagining a person who reasons all the way back, who never gives up until there is a completely undeniable, satisfying, unconditional answer to the question. Obviously human beings often stop reflecting very far short of that. And reflection itself is not the solution to that problem. So in that sense reflection is not the complete guide although it is the only place where we can find guidance. Something else has to get us to reflect. (2003, 60)

There are important parallels and contrasts to be drawn between the constructivist model outlined in this section and the Socratic model discussed above. The major contrast derives from the fact that Socrates presupposed a realist conception of the good and construed philosophy as the reasoned attempt to direct oneself to the independent good. Contrary to that, constructivism sees all value originating from human agency and the practical point of view. In terms of similarities, although contemporary constructivism is more explicit about it, both models highlight the importance of coherence for justification of values and beliefs. Socrates recommends knowing the whole system of values and their systematic relations and interconnections.[11] Constructivism explicitly endorses coherentism. Finally, and more important, both models seem to require a kind of reflective scrutiny on the part of the agent, before he is justified in taking some consideration as a reason for action. In other words, both models seem to posit regular practical reasoning as the only way to live according to one's reasons. This last feature is in all likelihood true about Socratic philosophy. What I attempt to demonstrate in the remainder of this essay is that it is not necessarily true of metaethical constructivism. This is a good conclusion for constructivism, for, as I also argue, the fully examined life is not a justified life policy.

4. Limiting Practical Reflection

There is a convincing case to be made against considering reflection or deliberation necessary for autonomous rational action. In fact, in many

[11] Suspending my judgment on its plausibility as a scholarly interpretation, it is worth mentioning Gregory Vlastos's classic reading of the Socratic method of refutation. Vlastos ascribes the following principled belief to Socrates: "Whoever has a false moral belief will always have at the same time true beliefs entailing the negation of that false belief" (1994, 25). From this assumption, it is possible to extract the thought that a person with fully consistent beliefs will, by necessity, have only true beliefs. Hence the importance of verifying one's consistency, according to this interpretation.

cases we seem to have no reason to engage in deliberation, cases in which we do what is rational to do "in the flow," out of habit, or in a kind of "fluent agency" (cf. Kornblith 2010; Railton 2009; Arpaly and Schroeder 2012). I do not wish to discuss the literature on these cases here. If proven correct, they provide arguments to the effect that often we should not deliberate *at all*. That is a good result for me. But I wish to grant to the defender of Socratic full-examination that we are considering only cases of conscious, deliberate, rational decision making. Limiting the discussion to cases of conscious deliberation, what I wish to confront the Socratic philosopher with is the idea that there are limits to what we should consider and to what we should challenge. In general, I claim we should not adopt a Socratic stance toward our values and beliefs.

In the case of reflective decision making, the agent is consciously taking some consideration (or set of considerations) to be a reason to do something. What warrants or justifies her taking that consideration to be a reason? Perhaps there are substantive facts, natural or nonnatural, about what counts as a reason for action. But as a metaethical constructivist, I want to assume away normative realism. The need to come up with a non-question-begging explanation for *why* a certain consideration counts as a reason for action has been convincingly put forth by J. David Velleman (2000b).

Velleman's considered view is that the ultimate criterion of justification for an action is whether the action makes sense for the agent to perform.[12] Now, Velleman is careful to say that the agent does not have to justify her actions by consciously apprehending their intelligibility. Intelligibility counts as a higher-order condition of success, while the agent justifiably attends to the specific aims she has while deciding whether or not to perform a certain action. As a constitutive aim of all full-blown action, however, intelligibility is watching over the particular aims and actions the agent decides for. An aim contrary to the higher-level aim of doing what makes sense to the agent is an unjustified aim.

Velleman believes that only a constitutive aim of action can offer ultimate justification for action and proposes intelligibility as just such an aim. For reasons I cannot explore here, I believe this kind of justification can be offered by the total set of the agent's values, coherently conceived.[13] Assuming this view, there seem to be two ways of conceiving of the

[12] I say "considered view" because Velleman changed his mind about this. In Velleman 2000b, where the problem is laid out, he takes autonomy to provide the ultimate justification. After criticism from Philip Clark, he changed his view and promoted intelligibility as the ultimate criterion (cf. Velleman 2000a, 30 n. 37).

[13] See Sommavilla unpublished. In my view, claims about the ultimate source of justification for action and claims about the nature of the agent converge on a single answer: the agent just is her total set of (coherent) values. This is a modified version of Gary Watson's view in Watson 1975. Velleman briefly considers this kind of coherentist response, in association with Street's work, and seems to find it valid but with some reservations. See Velleman 2009, 126–27 n. 12.

justification of a given action or judgment. On the more ambitious version, the agent (or some external assessor) has to evaluate whether her action or judgment coheres with her set of values before she acts or judges justifiably. This is the kind of Socratic, unduly demanding requirement I am concerned with criticizing in this essay. On a more modest interpretation, analogous to Velleman's view, coherence with one's set of values is only a higher-order aim, capable of delegitimizing a particular action or judgment, but one that need not be consciously entertained by the agent for rational, full-blown action and decision making.

The problem is how the agent can find out whether her judgment or action coheres with her set of values if she does not engage in self-examination, if she does not investigate her values, the sources of justification for her claims, and so on. My answer is that she does not know whether such coherence exists, and further, that she should not try to know as well. In the next few paragraphs, I build a perhaps surprising case for the claim that the agent is often justified in settling on the practical reason her initial reasoning presents her with. In those cases (a large majority, in my view), there is a non-negligible possibility of a mismatch between the practical reason she entertains as the conclusion of her practical reasoning, on the one hand, and the practical reason she *would have* were she strictly to follow what is entailed by her total set of values in conjunction with the non-normative facts of the situation, on the other. Since I am claiming that frequently the agent does *not* have a reason to seek total justification via a thorough questioning of her entertained reasons, I am also claiming that she is probably sometimes justified in *not* acting in accordance with what is entailed by her set of values.[14] In short, sometimes she has reason to not quite be herself.[15]

One thing we learn from commentators on nondeliberate acting for reasons is their correct construal of deliberation itself as a kind of action (cf. Arpaly and Schroeder 2012, 210; Railton 2009, 102). Being a kind of rational, consciously conducted action, deliberation is subject to criticism and in need of justification. The same is true of deliberation about deliberation, that is, practical reflection about the outcomes of a first instance of practical reflection. As stated at the beginning of this section, we are already limiting our discussion to cases of reflected decision making.

[14] Why "probably sometimes"? Because whether the mismatch occurs is an empirical matter.

[15] That is, the agent is justified in doing or judging something that fits less perfectly with her set of values than a different action or judgment. See footnote 13 above for a hint at the idea that the identity of the agent just is her set of coherent values. Notice as well that the justificatory regress can be stopped at two points. First, as I mentioned above in the text, *if* one actually goes on with subsequent challenges to one's reasons, creating the regress, I claim that it can be stopped once we reach the coherent set of values defining who the agent is. Second, I claim that there is often *no reason* to engage in the regress in the first place. I am primarily concerned with the second claim in this essay. The first claim is merely stated, not defended.

This means the agent is already engaged in the activity of deliberating about what to do. Having reasoned her way through the relevant mental states and external facts, she has settled on a practical conclusion establishing what she has reason to do. She now has the possibility of either doing what she concluded she has reason to do or engaging in second-order deliberation: she may question her conclusion and deliberate about whether to accept it. She may, for instance, ask what justifies the considerations she took to justify her initial conclusion. Is she justified in engaging in this second-order kind of deliberation? The answer, in most cases, is no.

Consider the following story. An agent deliberates and settles on a reason to act. Call the agent A. Call the act of deliberating D. Call the reason she settles on DR (for defeasible reason). And call the action that her reason favors performing X.

We are now faced with the question whether what she takes to be a reason (DR) is *sufficient* reason, in the sense that it settles *for the agent* the matter as to what she ought to do. If she were to engage in further deliberation (call it D*; for example, looking for the entailments of her values and beliefs, looking for her dispositions to value and believe, questioning directly the justification of the reason she had settled on [DR], and so forth), it is possible, though not certain, that what she would then conclude to be her considered reason for action (call it CR) will be different from DR.

Engaging in D* is exactly the kind of thing the Socratic model would recommend. But from the way the example was set, she has no reason whatsoever to engage in D*. Being an action just like any other, D* demands justification, and the agent can offer none for it. In contrast, there is a perfectly reasonable explanation for why she should perform a competing act, namely, action X. For she has reflectively come to the conclusion that she has reason (DR) for action X. Confronted with the possibility of action D*, she may do it or not. Confronted with the possibility of action X, she may do it or not. What differentiates these two courses of action is that she has a reason for one (X) and not for the other (D*). What we may conclude from this case is that what stops the potential regress of justification is that the agent has no reason to start it.

5. Extending Practical Reflection

If the argument above is sound, an agent is only going to be justified in deliberating about the outcomes of his initial deliberation if presented with a reason to do so. This might be rare, but it does happen. Sometimes we are justified in extending our practical reasoning. I want to explore two kinds of situation in which these extensions are reasonably called for. I do not claim to cover all possible cases but do consider these two kinds to be paradigmatic cases.

The first kind of case I want to consider is that of a challenge from someone else. Suppose you have to decide what to do in a particular situation.

You consider what to do reflectively, thinking about the facts of the situation and your mental states at hand (your values, beliefs, desires, and intentions that surface in your consciousness as you deliberate). Upon reflection, you settle on a course of action, taking yourself to have reason R to do it. From what we have just discussed, it should follow that you are not justified in questioning further your alleged reason for action by, for instance, checking its consistency with dispositions to believe and value that you have but did not consider at first. Suppose now someone notices you taking R to be your reason for action and presents a challenge, maybe demanding more justification from you, maybe outright claiming you are wrong about what you should do. In many such cases of a challenge, you will be justified in engaging in further deliberation.

Why is the challenge from others a reason to deliberate further? Someone may doubt that we should give any credit to challenges raised by others. In fact, unless I previously adopt the principle of paying attention to challenges raised by others (maybe only a few others), it is not obvious why I should be bothered. More precisely, why should the course of action I settled for lose in justification when presented with an external challenge, at least if I want to remain within the confines of a broadly internalist picture? It has been suggested that the very notion of a reason is a product for social consumption (Mercier and Sperber 2011), so perhaps the kind of social justification at the base of responding to challenges by others just is what reasons are meant to do. That is possible, but there is another way of explaining the role of challenges in pressing us in the direction of further deliberation, an explanation that fits squarely within the internalist framework.

Challenges are often de facto initiators of (further) deliberation. That is, they bring to mind images or ideas related to the topic and relevant to our conclusion regarding what to do. We may, of course, discard them as unwelcome intruders. But, provided we were participating in a conversation in good faith, trying to understand what we were being told, the challenge will have already made its way into our mind. We are already considering it and we may reject it as we may reject just about any other consideration we might be entertaining, regardless of how it managed to pop into our minds. And if the best reflective decision is reached by striking some kind of reasoned balance between the beliefs, desires, intentions, and values under consideration, the introduction of a new consideration may well destabilize the previous equilibrium and force a new one. In other words, a challenge de facto succeeds in broadening the scope of mental states and/or external facts under consideration by the agent and accordingly leads to further deliberation and potentially different conclusions. To disregard the challenge you would need a reason. Absent a reason, you should stick to what you have, which now also includes the challenge. Therefore, challenges do sometimes justifiably lead to greater reflection.

Another kind of situation in which it is reasonable to engage in further deliberation involves cases of dilemmas or conflicts. Sometimes reasoning through the mental states and external facts currently available to the agent does not yield a clear answer as to what the agent has most reason to do. It can be that the impasse is unavoidable; there just is no fact of the matter making action A better than action B, as seen from his perspective. But it is natural to suppose that further inquiry, either into the nonnormative facts about the case or into one's set of values, beliefs, and dispositions, will on many occasions alter the balance in favor of one or another course of action. It is difficult to specify exactly how much more inquiry is called for. One reasonable policy is (1) not to investigate so much that the inquiry impacts one's ability to implement one's (other) practical interests or (2) to stop investigating once the balance has favored one of the competing courses of action. At this point, the agent will not have reason to investigate further, for the same reasons as the ones discussed in the previous section.[16]

A related set of cases involves big, transformative decisions, such as changing one's career, getting married, or having a child. These are cases in which it seems fitting to step back and reflect on what kind of person one is or wants to become.[17] It is misleading, however, to count these as cases of further deliberation in the sense that I am considering here. These are certainly important decisions, which demand a great deal of reflection, but they do not require the kind of *further* reflection advocated by the Socratic model. It is one thing to consider what kind of person I am or want to be and how opting for such transformative experiences helps or does not help advance my ambitions. It is another thing to engage in critical reflection about the foundation of my commitments. The Socratic injunction is to fully examine the purported reasons I have to believe and act, because it is expected that only reasons endorsed after going through this critical scrutiny are really reasons for action and belief. The act of thinking about having or not having a child does not present a challenge to the justification of my values. It asks me to entertain a scenario and see whether my values support a move in this direction or not.

6. Problems with Full Analysis

What we have discussed so far shows that all-out reflection is not necessary for leading a life responsive to one's practical reasons. Deliberation about

[16] At the moment when it becomes clear that further investigation is not helping any of the competing courses of action and risks doing damage to one's capacity to do other things, the situation turns into that of an arbitrary decision. Both courses of action being permitted, there is no clear reason to favor one over the other.

[17] I cannot do justice to the complexity of this theme here. For a recent and influential discussion, see Paul 2014.

one's practical reasons is an action just like any other, an action one may or may not be justified in engaging in, depending on certain features of the context of action. The reasons against full reflection that I have given so far have been reasons to stick to a condition falling short of full reflective self-analysis. What I wish to do in this final section is discuss what might happen if one *does* go for full reflection. What do we get from engaging in such a pursuit?

An initial worry related to the project of full self-examination has to do with its feasibility. Given that we are human beings, with limited mental storage capacities, we should not go about acquiring every piece of knowledge about ourselves we are capable of and we should not go about drawing all the true inferences from our beliefs and intentions we are capable of. The consequence of this would be unjustified mind cluttering, which would inevitably stand in the way of our practical interests.[18]

A second worry relates to the coherentist model of justification underlying metaethical constructivism. In coherentism, a judgment is justified roughly to the extent that it fits into a web of mutually justifying beliefs. For any given (normative) judgment, we may assess its justification according to a (coherent) set of beliefs. Although our previous considerations recommended against it, nothing prevents an assessor from moving along a challenging regress. But coherentism has no problem with this. The coherentist will be able to stop the regress at some given higher level, at the moment in which the belonging of the assessed normative judgment in the web of beliefs of reference is proven or disproven.

As we saw above, there is often no reason to move along this justificatory chain. But now, assuming we engage in it, coherentism has a principled and traditional answer to stopping the regress. The answer only works, however, if we are assessing one judgment or belief at a time (or a subset of judgments or beliefs). But the kind of examination associated with the philosophical way of life on the Socratic model easily turns into a general challenge to one's value system. Submitting all one's values or beliefs to scrutiny with the expectation of establishing a firmer set afterward has an enormously disruptive potential. This is so because while it is possible to offer another judgment as a justification for a first judgment, there is nothing, from the point of view of coherentism about values, that one can offer as a justification for one's whole set of values. If challenged in tandem, one's values—in fact, one's identity—reveal their arbitrariness. Of course, if one adopts a detached or theoretical stance in relation to one's mental states, there might be no problem with revealing the arbitrary, genealogical

[18] See Gilbert Harman's Clutter Avoidance principle (1986, 12). Harman groups the avoidance of mind-cluttering inferences together with the idea that we need a reason to be justified in challenging a current belief (which I discussed in the previous two sections) under the label "Principle of Conservatism" (116).

processes that caused one to possess them.[19] But from the engaged, first-personal perspective of the agent looking for a justification for her normative judgments, the sense that they are arbitrary and the lack of justification that one can provide upon their being challenged as a whole may well have negative consequences for one's capacity to move on with one's practical, valuing life.[20]

Valerie Tiberius's Reflective Wisdom Account faces a similar problem. As Tiberius says: "[There] is a kind of philosophical reflection that seeks an ultimate foundation for our value commitments and the reasons we take ourselves to have for them, where we do not take for granted the value of anything. The Reflective Wisdom Account might seem vulnerable to this kind of reflection, because it does not supply an inherently normative foundation for the authority or legitimate force of the reasons we have to change our habits of thought or act on our values" (2008, 182). The way Tiberius handles the problem closely resembles my preferred solution, with one important difference:

> The meta-ethics suggested by the Reflective Wisdom Account locates the source of normativity for its prescriptive claims in the stable network of commitments of a reflective agent who has a concern to live a life she can endorse. When we engage in reflection on our commitments, some of them must be taken for granted in order to reflect critically on others (though, of course, not necessarily the same ones all the time). In particular, the underlying commitment to living a life that meets our reflective standards is always taken for granted and cannot itself be justified. On this picture, then, our reasons for pursuing the things we value and for living up to our standards ultimately derive from our concern to live well and from other particular commitments we have. (183)

The main difference between our views is that Tiberius places the value of living a life that meets one's reflective standards above all other values and assesses the other values according to that higher value. I see no reason to posit such hierarchy, so that in my view the content of what has to be taken for granted by the agent may vary from case to case.

Someone might object that knowledge has intrinsic value and that (self-) knowledge is worth pursuing for its own sake. On this view, acquiring information about one's own values and their entailments is a worthwhile enterprise, which may not be the best thing to do at all times but certainly counts as justified conduct from time to time. In reply to this line of

[19] In referring to theoretical versus practically engaged stances, I am adopting Richard Moran's terminology (2001). From the theoretical stance, nothing "really matters." But that is not what matters, or better, that is not how things matter (they matter from the engaged point of view). I borrow the talk about what "really matters" from Street 2017.

[20] This difficulty with moving on with one's life is probably part of what Nietzsche had in mind with his motto "Truth is terrible." See Leiter 2018 for discussion. Bernard Williams's reflections on the difficulties and problems associated with uncovering the contingent history of our outlooks are also relevant here. See Williams 2006.

reasoning, we must first notice that it is not the value of knowledge per se that is at stake here but rather whether we should or shouldn't engage in the pursuit of self-knowledge or self-examination. As an activity, the pursuit of self-knowledge ought to be assessed in contrast to other activities. What the previous sections have shown is that this pursuit is often detrimental to the agent's overall practical interests, by unjustifiably deviating her from what she has most reason to do. This conclusion could have been different if we presupposed some kind of good life, conceived in realist terms, whose fulfillment was inextricably connected to self-examination. This is probably true of Socrates' philosophy, but it goes against the metaethical constructivism I have been assuming all along. Furthermore, as noted in the previous paragraph, within the coherentist approach characteristic of constructivism, a full self-examination has the potential to shake the grounds of the agent's values, without having anything to offer in substitution. This means that, depending on how it is undertaken—if not piecemeal—a project of full self-analysis is likely to lead to nihilism or suffering.[21]

A final and related worry is the following. Perhaps restricting self-examination prevents an agent from obtaining (moral) understanding, and perhaps understanding why one ought to do something is rationally required of an agent or a moral obligation. In recent work, Alison Hills (2009, 2016) has argued for the importance of (moral) understanding.[22] In her view, moral understanding differs from mere knowledge that "q is the thing to do" and from knowledge why "q is the thing to do." Moral understanding requires the agent to be able to draw on her own the conclusion that q from the true reason p, by treating p to be the reason for q.[23] As Hills puts it: "Moral understanding involves a grasp of the relation between a moral proposition and the reasons why it is true" (2009, 101).[24]

According to Hills, there are four reasons why moral understanding is valuable: (1) it is a reliable method for finding out what to do (often one does not have access to a knowledgeable and trustworthy expert); (2) it enables the agent to justify her choices to interlocutors (by showing how her actions are grounded in her reasons); (3) it is a mark of good character

[21] A point I do not explore in this text is the possibility that seeking self-knowledge actually alters the content of one's mental states, so that the "self" to be known becomes different upon reflection. This point is acutely explored by Moran (2001, 59 and chap. 5). Tiberius (2008, 116) accepts this point from Moran.

[22] I thank an anonymous referee for directing my attention to Hills's work.

[23] In knowing why q you also know that p is the reason for q, but you may not be able to draw the conclusion that q from p, hence you may not understand why q. For example, you may know that the reason for q is p from the testimony of someone knowledgeable and trustworthy.

[24] See Paulina Sliwa (2017) for a contrasting, reductionist view about moral understanding, according to which moral understanding is the ability to know right from wrong. I wish to remain neutral in this dispute, since I believe both views are compatible with what I claim in this essay.

(the virtuous is "an authority into what is right" (2009 111); and (4) it is a mark of good action (acting well, as opposed to merely doing the right thing, requires acting in a way that is directly caused by the agent's recognition of her reasons to act in such a way) (2009, 106–19).

Assuming that understanding is thus valuable, it is important to see whether the restricted kind of reflective life I have been advocating for will somehow prevent the agent from obtaining (moral) understanding. Fortunately, understanding does not require full examination of the kind I have challenged in this essay. In my view, the reasons why a given practical proposition is true are often not the outcome of full examination. They are rather more modest and context dependent, as I explained above. Therefore, falling short of full reflection does not undermine (moral) understanding.

The important thing to note is that my primary concern in this essay has to do with *which* considerations to count as candidate reasons for action, whereas Hills is concerned with the nature of our *relation* to our reasons. She mounts a plausible case for the importance not only of taking some consideration to justify or to be a reason for some course of action, but also of grasping the relation between the belief that this is the right course of action, on the one hand, and the reasons why this is the right course of action, on the other. This kind of understanding is independent of how many considerations the agent is taking into account as candidate reasons, which has been my main object of concern.[25] As I argued for above, the reasons on which you should base your decision making typically do not require that you engage in full self-analysis. It is the relation between *these* reasons and the propositions or courses of action they are reasons for that you should understand, if Hills is right about understanding.

In sum, in the absence of a realist conception of the good life attached to self-knowledge, frequent conflict with one's practical interests and the potential disruption of one's system of values are the two main reasons why living a life in the pursuit of Socratic self-knowledge is in all likelihood a bad idea. Coupled with the unlikelihood that one will have reasons to progress from actual cases of deliberation to a situation of Socratic reflection, these two reasons make the philosophical way of life a good candidate for misery.

References

Arpaly, Nomy, and Timothy Schroeder. 2012. "Deliberation and Acting for Reasons." *Philosophical Review* 121, no. 2:209–39.

Cooper, John. 2012. *Pursuits of Wisdom: Six Ways of Life in Ancient Philosophy from Socrates to Plotinus.* Princeton: Princeton University Press.

[25] Though Hills correctly notes that it is impossible to understand a moral proposition in complete isolation from all other considerations (2009, 101–2).

Hadot, Pierre. 1995. *Philosophy as a Way of Life*. Edited with an Introduction by Arnold I. Davidson, translated by Michael Chase. Oxford: Blackwell.

Harman, Gilbert. 1986. *Change in View: Principles of Reasoning*. Cambridge, Mass.: MIT Press.

Hills, Alison. 2009. "Moral Testimony and Moral Epistemology." *Ethics* 120, no. 1:94–127.

________. 2016. "Understanding Why." *Noûs* 50, no. 4:661–88.

Kornblith, Hilary. 2010. "What Reflective Endorsement Cannot Do." *Philosophy and Phenomenological Research* 80, no. 1:1–19.

Korsgaard, Christine M. 2003. "Christine M. Korsgaard: Internalism and the Sources of Normativity (Interview with C. Korsgaard)." In *Constructions of Practical Reason*, edited by Herlinde Pauer-Studer, 50–69. Stanford: Stanford University Press.

Kraut, Richard. 2007. "The Examined Life." In *A Companion to Socrates*, edited by Sara Ahbel-Rappe and Rachana Kamtekar, 228–42. Oxford: Blackwell.

Leiter, Brian. 2018. "The Truth Is Terrible." *Journal of Nietzsche Studies* 49, no. 2:151–73.

Mercier, Hugo, and Dan Sperber. 2011. "Why Do Humans Reason? Arguments for an Argumentative Theory." *Behavioral and Brain Sciences* 34, no. 2:94–111.

Moran, Richard. 2001. *Authority and Estrangement: An Essay on Self-Knowledge*. Princeton: Princeton University Press.

Paul, L. A. 2014. *Transformative Experience*. Oxford: Oxford University Press.

Plato. 1997. *The Complete Works of Plato*. Edited by John M. Cooper and D. S. Hutchinson. Indianapolis: Hackett.

Railton, Peter. 2009. "Practical Competence and Fluent Agency." In *Reasons for Action*, edited by David Sobel and Steven Wall, 81–115. New York: Cambridge University Press.

Scanlon, Thomas M. 1998. *What We Owe to Each Other*. Cambridge, Mass. Belknap Press of Harvard University Press.

Sliwa, Paulina. 2017. "Moral Understanding as Knowing Right from Wrong." *Ethics* 127, no. 3:521–52.

Sommavilla, Vitor. Unpublished. "Metaethical Constructivism and Value Constitutivism." Unpublished manuscript.

Street, Sharon. 2008. "Constructivism About Reasons." In *Oxford Studies in Metaethics 3*, edited by Russ Shafer-Landau, 207–45. Oxford: Oxford University Press.

________. 2010. "What Is Constructivism in Ethics and Metaethics?" *Philosophy Compass* 5, no. 5:363–84.

________. 2017. "Nothing 'Really' Matters, but That's Not What Matters." In *Does Anything Really Matter? Essays on Parfit on Objectivity*, edited by Peter Singer, 121–48. Oxford: Oxford University Press.

Tiberius, Valerie. 2008. *The Reflective Life: Living Wisely with Our Limits*. Oxford: Oxford University Press.

Velleman, J. David. 2000a. "Introduction." In *The Possibility of Practical Reason*, 1–31. Oxford: Oxford University Press.

________. 2000b. "The Possibility of Practical Reason." In *The Possibility of Practical Reason*, 170–99. Oxford: Oxford University Press.

________. 2009. *How We Get Along*. Cambridge: Cambridge University Press.

Vlastos, Gregory. 1994. "The Socratic Elenchus: Method Is All." In *Socratic Studies*, edited byMyles Burnyeat, 1–37. Cambridge: Cambridge University Press.

Watson, Gary. 1975. "Free Agency." *Journal of Philosophy* 72 (April):205–20.

Williams, Bernard. 2006. "Philosophy as a Humanistic Discipline." In *Philosophy as a Humanistic Discipline*, 180–99. Princeton: Princeton University Press.

CHAPTER 13

WHAT IT TAKES TO LIVE PHILOSOPHICALLY

OR, HOW TO PROGRESS IN THE ART OF LIVING

CALEB M. COHOE AND STEPHEN R. GRIMM

1. Introduction: What Is a Way of Life?

What does it take to practice a way of life in general, and a philosophical way of life in particular? Is it as simple as regularly engaging in characteristically philosophical activities?[1]

We show in this essay that there are good reasons to think that living philosophically must be an achievement—something one can try to do yet fail to pull off. When a philosophical way of life is treated as an achievement, however, it is usually presented as a superlative achievement that only the wisest and best can hope to fulfill. We argue for a more moderate view: those who are making progress in their actions and understanding are already living philosophically, even if both their grasp of truth and their actions are imperfect.

You might think that living a way of life is relatively easy. We speak of the American way of life or the Chinese way of life, suggesting that living a specific way of life might only require being formed around a certain set of values (often those generally accepted in your social environment) and then using these to orient your life. Perhaps my way of life is just a description of the overall pattern of my life and the activities and practices it includes. If this is true, though, living a way of life would not really be an

[1] Hadot 1995 and Cooper 2012 give contrasting accounts, as we discuss. Popular books around this subject include Puett and Gross-Loh 2017 and Wright 2017; contemporary Stoic approaches are collected at www.modernstoicism.com.

Philosophy as a Way of Life: Historical, Contemporary, and Pedagogical Perspectives.
Edited by James M. Ambury, Tushar Irani, and Kathleen Wallace.

Published 2021 by John Wiley & Sons Ltd.

accomplishment. Just as Molière's Monsieur Jourdain was delighted to discover that he had already been speaking prose all his life (*Le bourgeois gentilhomme*, 1670), so we might be delighted to find that we have been living a way of life all along. In both cases, however, these supposed accomplishments turn out to be not as impressive as the language describing them might suggest.

There are several reasons to think that living a way of life is not that straightforward. To begin with, many characteristic ways of life, whether cultural or based in a philosophical school, are quite demanding. This comes out most clearly in cultures with well-defined and strictly enforced rankings of goods. The Spartan dictum "With your shield or on it" encapsulates the relative value of honor in comparison to injury or death, a value ordering that the warrior is enjoined to live out. Growing up in Sparta does not automatically guarantee that one will not flee battle, even if it makes it a less attractive option than it would be for someone from a less honor-focused culture. There is some sense in which everyone has a way of life, insofar as our actions and patterns of behavior (both individually and socially) embody certain value judgments. But these may be incoherent or in tension. For example, consider the mixed messages in American culture on whether Thanksgiving and Christmas are really about family and giving, as many discussions of the "real meaning" of these celebrations suggest, or about getting presents and enjoying oneself, as advertisements and some evidence from actual practice suggest.

This leads to a larger issue: many of us have conflicts between the life we want to be living and the life we are currently living. Most of those advocating for living a way of life present it as a normative goal, not simply a description of existing patterns that we may or may not value or might even regret. There is also the question of consistency. Many of us recognize tensions between our beliefs and our actions. For example, we do not always treat others as we think we ought. We also sometimes recognize tensions within our values: we can be drawn to sacrifice so that our children will have more opportunities while also recognizing a pull to act primarily for the benefit of our wider society and not just for the good of those close to us. Achieving a consistent way of life requires resolving these tensions. The goal is a harmony between our view of the world and the way we are actually living in the world.

2. Complete Achievement Conceptions of the Philosophical Way of Life

What, then, does it take to strive for and attain a philosophical way of life? Some hold that this is a supreme achievement, available only to the great and the wise. Friedrich Nietzsche, for example, insists in *Unfashionable Observations*: "The philosopher's product is his *life* (first, before his *works*). It is his work of art [*Kunstwerk*]" (1967ff. III.4, 29 [205]; 1995, 184). On this view, you show yourself to be a philosopher from the entirety of your actions, not just from a few lectures or discussions. Your whole life should embody your excellence. "I attach importance to a philosopher only to the extent that he is capable of setting an example . . . it must be presented in the way the philosophers of Greece taught, through facial expressions, demeanor, clothing, food, and custom more than through what they said, let alone what they wrote" (1967ff. III.1, 346; 1995, 183–84). Philosophers emerge here as exemplars who consistently and impressively display their mastery of life, not only in their discourse but in their entire way of being. For Nietzsche, most academic philosophers are not even close to attaining such a way of life: "As long as philosophers do not muster the courage to advocate a lifestyle [*Lebensordnung*] structured in an entirely different way and demonstrate it by their own example, they will come to nothing" (1967ff. III.4, 31 [10]; 1995, 311). A philosophical way of life is something that only the impressive few can achieve.

We see a similar idea in Michel Foucault, who also stressed the importance of making your life into a work of art. "What strikes me is the fact that, in our society, art has become something which is related only to objects and not to individuals or to life. . . . Why should the lamp or the house be an art object but not our life?" ("On the Genealogy of Ethics," 1997, 261). Fashioning your life into art requires sustained application and skill. Just as not all lamps or houses are works of art, in the societal sense of high art that Foucault is using, so not all lives are works of art. It would take impressive exercises of philosophical, aesthetic, and artistic abilities to achieve this.

This idea of the philosophical way of life as a distinguishing achievement, separating the sage from the masses (and the imitating pupils), also has ancient precedent. John Sellars notes that, in the late ancient context, it was "standard practice to preface the study of any philosophical text with a biographical account of its author" (2003, 29; cf. Mansfield 1994, 30, 97–98, 108–10). On Sellars's reading, the biography of the authors would contain telling anecdotes illustrating "the sort of transformation of attitude that might follow from a thorough understanding of [the author's] philosophy" (29). For example, Porphyry, the pupil of Plotinus and his literary executor, tells us of how Plotinus refused to sit for a sculptor. Plotinus did not want to make an image of an image or suggest that such a work would be worth looking at, showing how his philosophy had transformed his view of his own body (Porphyry 2017, sec. 1).

The various philosophical schools held the view that their leaders had lived great lives as well as thought great thoughts. Biography played a key role in ancient introductions to and summaries of the philosophical schools, as we see in Diogenes Laertius (2018). He prepares us to consider the philosophies of the various schools by first establishing the credentials of their founders, based on stories about their lives and practices. This insistence that the deeds of one's life should demonstrate one's philosophy and its transformational impact sets a high bar for living a philosophical life. It may seem that only the sort of saintly exemplars who have the credentials to start their own schools of philosophy count as living philosophically.

There is another way in which living a philosophical way of life might turn out to be extremely demanding. This comes from the thought that only the wise count as living a philosophical way of life. On this view, living philosophically requires successfully understanding things for yourself, so that every action you take displays your excellent comprehension of the cosmos and your place within it. John Cooper argues for a set of stringent requirements on the philosophical way of life based around the importance of comprehensive understanding. In his *Pursuits of Wisdom*, he maintains that a philosophical way of life consists only in activities of rational understanding and actions taken on the basis of that understanding. He insists that "philosophy itself, both in antiquity and, in fact, in its whole history, is an exercise of reason" (2012b, 40–41). He claims that "increased rational understanding" is the only way to live a more philosophical life (41), and on his view practices and therapeutic exercises have no real role to play in the philosophical life. (We discuss the role we think they should play in Cohoe and Grimm unpublished.) Further, anyone who lacks a full rational understanding of the world and our place in it is not leading a philosophical way of life. You need personally to have achieved a comprehensive rational grasp of the cosmos, one that perfectly informs your life.

3. The Appeal of a Moderate Approach

Cooper is right to think that some philosophers—notably the Stoics, late Platonists, and Aristotle—have very demanding conceptions of what it means to live philosophically. Nevertheless, we believe there are strong reasons, both historical and philosophical, not to endorse a strongly restrictive conception of a philosophical way of life. The philosophical way of life should include progressors whose lives are not yet artistic masterpieces. It should be open to those who have not yet achieved comprehensive understanding.

Cooper's view makes a philosophical way of life inaccessible to all but the most educated elites, who have the leisure necessary to cultivate such a comprehensive understanding of reality. Although elitism really is present in a number of ancient philosophers, we think this exclusivist approach is not an apt model for living a philosophical way of life in the contemporary world. While Cooper maintains that the life of reason is open to all, his narrow and demanding conception of what it requires involves a combination of intellectual, moral, and psychological attributes that is exceedingly difficult for most humans to acquire. Even if it is open to all in principle, its requirements—including a long course of study and extensive leisure—make it actually accessible to only a few.

We object to Cooper's model not only because of its narrowness but also because there are good reasons to include imperfect practitioners within the way of life. A philosophical way of life need not be perfectly achieved or completely successful, just as someone can be living a musician's way of life while occasionally missing beats or playing wrong notes. We should allow people to count as living a philosophical way of life even if their lives are not yet artistic masterpieces and they are lacking in great deeds or sayings. While it is important to connect life and action to one's vision of the world (as we discuss below), requiring a perfect embodiment of one's philosophy is too high a bar for living philosophically. We also should not build into the notion of philosophy as a way of life the idea that it must consist in perfect rational activity, even if this is the substantive position that some philosophical schools ultimately take.

In fact, the views of the schools of ancient philosophy suggest an approach more moderate than Cooper's. Even those with the highest standards for a rational life, such as Aristotle, the Stoics, and late Platonists like Plotinus, recognize the idea of making progress. They acknowledge that one can start to live a philosophical way of life even if one has not fully achieved the virtue of practical wisdom. Many discussions of philosophy as a way of life, including Cooper's, focus on the ideal cases, on what the rational life of the sage or wise person would be like. But Aristotle recognized that true virtue would be rare, while the Stoics famously questioned whether, in fact, there are any sages (*Nicomachean Ethics* X 9, 1179b10–1178a6; for the Stoics on sages see Arius Didymus, *Epitome of Stoic Ethics* 2.7.5–12; Cicero, *Tusculan Disputations* 3.10–21; Sextus Empiricus, *Adversus mathematicos* 11 ["Against the Ethicists"].181) This pushed them to allow for sorts of advancement that do not require complete rational understanding. They recognized a number of ways that we can begin to live a philosophical life, even while falling short of the ideal.

The Stoics, for example, although stringent on what true virtue and philosophy requires—a complete understanding of the cosmos—explicitly made room for improvement. Thus Epictetus asks in his *Discourses*:

> So where is progress [*prokopē*] to be found? If any of you turns away from external things to concentrate his efforts on his own power of choice, to cultivate it and perfect it, so as to bring it into harmony with nature[,] . . . if, when he gets up in the morning, he holds in mind what he has learned and keeps true to it, if he bathes as a trustworthy person, and eats as a self-respecting person, putting his guiding principles into action in relation to anything that he has to deal with, just as a runner does in the practice of running, or a voice trainer in the training of voices—this, then, is the person who is truly making progress. (2014, I 4.18 and 20–21, 12)

Epictetus thinks there will be both internal and external evidence for whether his pupils are subjecting their choices to Stoic standards. The Stoic principles of progressors should be evident in the way they live their lives: as they eat, drink, and socialize. Nevertheless, this leaves room for failure and inconsistent application. The question is whether progressors are trying and whether they keep referring their actions back to their principles, as the runner and singer in training do. For Epictetus, progress should be evident, but it takes time and may be imperfect.

4. What It Means to Take Philosophy as an Art of Living

To better understand what it takes to live a philosophical way of life, we can look to the way that ancient thinkers thought of *phronēsis*, practical wisdom or the excellence that allows one to live well, as a sort of *technē*, an art or craft. This idea of practical wisdom as a general art of living is prominent in Socrates' questioning of his fellow Athenians and is later picked up by the Platonist, Aristotelian, and Stoic conceptions of the good life (see Sellars 2003, chaps. 2–3). Epictetus, for instance, famously frames it as an art whose matter is our own lives: "Philosophy does not promise to secure anything external for the human being, otherwise it would be admitting something that lies beyond its proper subject matter [*hulēs*]. For just as wood is the material [*hulē*] of the carpenter, bronze that of the statue maker, so each individual's own life [*ho bios autou ekastou*] is the material [*hulē*] of the art of living [*tēs peri bion technēs*]" (*Discourses*, I 15.2, trans. Sellars 2003, 56). We can use this analogy to help understand the difference between merely living and practicing an art of living.

Human lives characteristically involve elements such as eating, wearing clothes, and engaging in social relations. But not all of us are practicing an art of eating, an art of fashion, or the social graces. What differentiates those with the art from the rest of us is the way their performance of these activities manifests the principles they have internalized in a consistent, well-thought-out, and beautiful way. Most human lives involve talking to others, but this does not mean that most of us possess the art of conversation. Actually practicing the art requires much more than simply performing some tokens of the general action type; it involves being able to bring the best out of our friends and acquaintances through our questions and replies.

Similarly, while we all enact certain patterns of behavior that reflect certain values, really living a way of life is an achievement. On the technē model, craftspeople possess an understanding of the relevant domain that allows them consistently to act in accordance with their understanding of the craft. Their works always manifest that understanding in the ways open to them given the circumstances. The expert shoemaker makes the best footwear—for the whole range of human feet and from the whole range of suitable materials—because the shoemaker's technē reveals how best to manifest that art in the full variety of circumstances. Those who lack the art or are novices lack the relevant understanding. We can produce pretty good chocolate chip cookies in favorable circumstances, but when we lack the technē of baking, our productive ability is modally fragile. When we don't have the exact ingredients, when we are baking at high altitude, when we are baking in really dry conditions, and so on, we do not understand how best to adjust the recipe and so we often produce a very disappointing batch.

To develop the notion of showing one's skill whatever the circumstance, Epictetus compares Socrates to the skilled ballplayer.

> [No experienced ballplayer] is concerned about whether the ball is good or bad, but solely about how to throw and catch it. It is there accordingly that the player's agility, and skill, and speed, and good judgment are demonstrated . . . an expert will catch it whenever I make a throw. . . . Now Socrates certainly knew how to play ball . . . and there in court, what ball was in play? Life, imprisonment, exile, a draught of poison, the loss of his wife, and having to leave his children behind as orphans. That was what was involved, that was what he was playing with, but play he did nonetheless and threw the ball with dexterity. That is how we too should act, with the close attention of the cleverest of ball players, while showing the same indifference to what we are playing with, as being no more than a ball. (2014, II 5.15–20, 79–80)

For Epictetus, athletes show their skill in difficult circumstances. It is the consistency of their actions and their excellent judgment that distinguish a great basketball player from someone who can dunk impressively but passes poorly and fails to use his or her athletic potential well. Likewise with philosophy. Socrates is a strong candidate for possessing the art of living precisely because his life and choices consistently reflect his value commitments across a wide range of circumstances. They show what it looks like to value virtue over externals even in the face of dishonor, ridicule, and death. Socrates displays this on the battlefield, in the marketplace, and in front of a jury. By contrast, many of us either fail to properly apply our beliefs to our lives or cannot figure out how to apply the art we are trying to practice. Just as, when stressed, the person seeking moderation may wolf food down or, when placed in a foreign setting, struggle to eat gracefully, so we, under pressure, do not have an understanding of how to live well that manifests itself in demanding situations.

Does this mean, though, that living the philosophical way of life requires being a paragon of virtue and wisdom? Do our struggles to be consistent and live out our values show that we lack any real art of living? In fact, the notion of an art allows room for degrees of progress in attaining the art. By being able to consistently and accurately follow a recipe, you might be further down the road to the art of baking than your children, even if you have not yet attained the art itself. As Epictetus suggested in discussing progress, the aspiring singer will take lessons, practice repertoire, work on technique, and listen to great singers. All these are signs of progress. In many cases, we can also trace stages on one's development toward a goal. Consider those pursuing fitness through (in part) achieving mastery of the push-up. A push-up has a certain definite form and clear conditions for success, based on the combination of muscles the movement is meant to engage and the use of bodily force that it unlocks, as well as many failures of form (sometimes dangerous) that the person performing it must avoid. Initially, most people will need to be corrected along multiple dimensions. Even when they lift themselves up, their positioning, the muscles that are used, the way force is generated, and so forth will be off on many attempts. More advanced beginners will be able to do a push-up with fairly good form. They will be engaging the right groups of muscles and getting close enough to the correct form, but they may have small errors or deficiencies. They may fail to extend all the way up or they may not be evenly lifting their chest and legs. They may also struggle with consistency. Intermediates become more consistent and deviate less from correct form. They will have good form during most push-ups but may struggle to keep that form after other taxing movements or at the end of a long series. These people are often doing push-ups well, but they do not fully have the craft, because they do not consistently move as well as their body allows. Now, who is practicing the art? It is reasonable to think that we should count advanced beginners and intermediate athletes as well as the truly expert. Similarly, it is reasonable to think that people equivalent to advanced beginners and intermediates are practicing the philosophical life.

There is, however, a complication with the analogy between philosophy and art. Aristotle notes a key difference between arts and virtuous actions: "The things that come to be by the arts have their goodness in themselves" (*Nichomachean Ethics* II 4, 1105b27–28, our translation), whereas in the case of excellence or of acting well, it matters not just *what* is done but also *how* it is done. This is relevant for living philosophically as well as living virtuously. The intention with which we do things and the manner in which we do them make a great difference for whether an action embodies a philosophical way of life. This gives flexibility in both directions. A progressor might have good intentions but be only moderately successful at putting them into practice. Alternatively, some people might be doing the actions required by a certain way of life, but if their intentions and the way in which they perform the actions are contrary to those called for by that philosophical way of life, they will not count as practicing it. Epicureans and Platonists may both eat moderately and eschew luxurious foods, but if Epicureans do so in order to maximize pleasure and avoid pain, then they are not living a Platonist way of life, even if some of their eating practices resemble those that the Platonists would recommend for separating yourself from your bodily desires.

A theoretical understanding of a philosophical way of life is also not sufficient to count as a progressing practitioner. In this sense, we agree with Epictetus (and, to an extent, with Nietzsche and Foucault). Many academics are quite competent teachers of what the Epicureans or Stoics thought without that affecting their choices and lives in any ultimately significant way. Such academics do not count as progressors in the Stoic or Epicurean life. While they may have relatively high levels of understanding, they lack commitment. They are not trying to develop and exercise the art of being Stoic or Epicurean. They show no interest in supporting practices and are not making an effort to become more Stoic or Epicurean. While having some relevant knowledge, they do not base their actions on these philosophies.

Once we take philosophy as an art of living, we see that it involves much more than the pure use of reason advocated by Cooper. Again, an analogy to the arts that promote health is helpful. Understanding health is important to achieving it, but there is much more to achieving it than that. Part of aiming at health is just to avoid certain unhealthy practices (such as not eating too much of certain foods) and committing to healthy practices (such as making it a priority to eat fruits and vegetables, committing to regular exercise). We also need certain mental habits to support this. For example, when we are apprehensive about exercising, we can think about how we'll feel afterward or think of what an exemplar of healthy living would do. These strategies can help us realize our goals. Thus both external commitments to certain actions (eating some foods and not eating others) and internal reflection on how and why our practices are improving our health and life play an important role. They play this role and help us become healthier even when our understanding of exercise science and nutrition science is quite incomplete.

Similarly, a philosophical way of life will involve some degree of reflection and understanding along with various practices, external and internal. On the more external side, we curb ourselves from performing certain actions that we take to either lack value, have negative value, or distract us from achieving things of positive value. For example, we may decide to use social media for no more than fifteen minutes a day. We might commit to doing certain actions that we take to be valuable, even when we find doing them challenging. There are a wide variety of demanding things various worldviews recommend: eating moderately, consistently showing compassion to others, sharing your resources for the greater good, committing to daily prayer, meditation, or study of sacred writings, and so on.

On the internal side, a philosophical way of life involves reflecting on the attitudes we have when acting and the intentions with which we act to improve how we are acting. For example, there is a significant difference between lovingly reaching out to a friend and doing so only in a pro forma way. As we noted, intentions matter more in the case of promoting the good life than they do in the case of promoting health. Even when it comes to improving intentions, however, self-reflection and psychological awareness often help more than a better grasp of ethical theory. We also internally reflect on our goals and motivations so as to act more effectively. Thinking about how we will feel after helping a friend can help guide and motivate us. Thinking about moral exemplars can also increase our desire to be like them and value what they value. (This may be fairly global or may instead be focused on certain values; see Zagzebski 2017.)

The analogy to health also brings out the possibility of learning from others and relying on their understanding. We can become healthy through making good use of the expertise of fitness coaches and nutritionists, even if we lack their understanding. Similarly, it is plausible that the role of defending and articulating a philosophical way of life can be partly offloaded to other members of one's community. We should be responsive to reasons, but we do not have to figure out and defend every aspect of a view of the cosmos ourselves. Those living philosophically will be intellectually humble, owning their limitations, just as Socrates did (Whitcomb et al. 2017). Other community members play vital roles in helping us discern the correct actions in our circumstances, motivating us to carry them out, and correcting and refining our mistakes.

This communal dimension is missing from the picture Cooper gives of ancient philosophy. His language suggests that ancient philosophy operated via atomistic individuals deciding which schools to endorse on the basis of abstract arguments, which neglects the social aspects of philosophical formation. In fact, one of the most striking things about philosophers who led their own schools, such as Plotinus and Epictetus, is the close relationships and back-and-forth exchanges they had with their pupils. Even if the perfect sage would have a full understanding of reality and would avoid relying on the opinions and admiration of others, the vast majority of us are progressors. Since we do not have a complete wisdom to judge things by, we can and should make use of the understanding of others, as Socrates himself tried to do (cf. the *Symposium*'s appeal to the wisdom of Diotima). Often the best way to do this is to enter into a community that seems to share your view of the good life. Through participating in such communities we can improve our vision and understanding and also come closer to practicing such a way of life (Zagzebski 2012, chaps. 7–9). Most of us need to continue to use a variety of exercises, intellectual and practical, to constantly correct and reorient our views. Doing this, however, is already to begin the philosophical way of life.

5. Conditions for a Philosophical Way of Life

5.1. Condition 1

What, then, are the key factors for living philosophically? We think there are three conditions practitioners should meet. They are: commit to a worldview, structure your life around it, and engage in truth-directed practices. These conditions are jointly necessary, but progressors can meet these conditions as well as sages can. On our view, you need not perfectly satisfy each condition to be living philosophically. Instead, you need to pass the threshold that marks you as committed to and progressing in the philosophical way of life you have chosen. The philosophical way of life involves developing and exercising intellectual and character virtues, but it does not require the perfect use of pure reason.

Our first condition is that progressors need to be committed to the truth and value of a worldview's claims. Truth-claim making is included to imply that philosophical ways of life need to be making truth-evaluable claims. For example, it may be therapeutic for you to think of your thoughts as putting positive energy out into the universe, but if someone presses you on what this means and you say it is merely a figure of speech, then you are not seriously affirming it.

A philosophical way of life includes views about humanity and our place in the cosmos: it should not just make a few claims about a very limited sphere of life; hence the idea of a worldview. We are not requiring that all those living a philosophical life be able to fully articulate and defend all aspects of these views. Nevertheless, to orient their lives and actions they need a basic sense of what a given worldview claims in order to live it out. Even if they are not scholars, Platonists need to know why they should value the soul and its activities over the body, and Epicureans need to know why they should seek pleasure and why they should not fear death. To live philosophically, you need to have thought about your life as a whole and to have consciously adopted views on your place in reality (Midgley 2018, 73). Your life needs to involve seriously contemplating the cosmos, even if your practical circumstances limit how often and how systematically you can do this (McPherson 2020, chap. 5). We are not, however, requiring that your worldview be articulated purely on the basis of reason. We will turn to our case for rejecting such a requirement after we have set out our three conditions for living philosophically.

Prescribing value is included to get at the idea that the worldview behind the way of life has to be both action guiding and comprehensive. So just accepting the truth claims of standard contemporary Western sciences and having this inform your actions (say, in getting medical treatment or forming beliefs about the age of the earth) is not enough to count as living a philosophical way of life on its own, because that does not require thinking that the sciences prescribe values in a way that structures and guides your whole life. You could think that science (or science plus reason) does, in fact, give a value ordering that should govern your whole life, but this would be a further controversial commitment requiring an account of how to get metaphysics from science, and value claims from this metaphysics. Prescribing value also excludes a lifestyle in which you think there are some reasons for you to adopt certain practices given your particular circumstances but you do not think your choice has broader normative implications or is universalizable (for example, you have arguments for why yoga or live-action role-playing are worthwhile for you).

The notion of commitment is closely related to intention and picks up on Aristotle's insistence that how you perform an action is crucial to its excellence. Your commitment is measured by your resolution to think and act in the way called for by a worldview and the concrete actions you take in response to this resolution. In the case of fitness, this involves such things as taking classes and doing exercises. For a philosophical way of life, it involves such activities as reading and reflecting on key texts, approaching significant choices in a way that is informed by your chosen philosophical school, examining how your actions could better reflect your values, and undertaking whichever supporting exercises your school supports (for example, meditation, examination of desires, dialogue with other community members, and so forth). Commitment does not require success. You can be committed to your program of exercise even if you are struggling to achieve the correct form on your push-ups. You are not committed, however, if you claim to want to improve but take no steps to do so. Similarly, as long as you continue to engage with a philosophy and keep attempting to act in the spirit of this philosophy, you count as committed.

This, then, is *condition 1: Practitioners of a philosophical way of life are committed to a truth-claim-making, value-prescribing worldview.*

5.2. Condition 2

The next condition is about the application of the first condition to one's life. As we have seen, some real level of achievement needs to be reached for one to be living philosophically. There needs to be a transition from unreflectively going along with certain values, perhaps even contradictory ones, to actively living on the basis of a global value scheme. Thus our *condition 2: Practitioners of a philosophical way of life have their practices and life structured by the worldview to which they are committed.*

How successful does your life structuring have to be to satisfy condition 2? On our view, your life does not have to be perfectly ordered. Instead, we should look at whether you have made progress in using your worldview to structure your life and practices. This involves examining the direction in which someone's practices are developing. In the case of fitness, an athletic person with a history of personal fitness may be more adept at push-ups than someone who is taking up exercise after previously being sedentary. If, however, the athletic person has abandoned the pursuit of fitness and is no longer trying to exercise his or her muscles or improve, we may judge the beginner to be closer to living a fit way of life, even though the former athlete is still the one with the better current form concerning push-ups. The direction and attitude of the person involved matter, especially at the initiation of a way of life.

For instance, in the philosophical case, those who are improving their eating choices and seeking to bring them in line with the value judgments of their philosophical schools qualify as practitioners more than someone who happens to follow the recommended sort of diet, but for quite different reasons. Committed utilitarians who are slowly and painfully, but determinedly, cutting out meat from their diets in order to reduce pain to sentient beings are practicing a philosophical way of life more than those who were raised vegetarian but are uncommitted to such practices and are adding meat back into their diets. This can be the case even if the progressing utilitarians currently eat more meat than the lapsing vegetarians.

We are not claiming, however, that those who are stuck at a given level of maximum attainment are no longer living a way of life. As long as they are committed to doing everything they can to maintain and improve their practice, they meet the directionality condition. Those who are struggling to increase their maximum number of push-ups while doing all that they can with their conditioning and diet are clearly committed to fitness, even if they are not currently improving.

There does, however, have to be real progress. Going to one or two classes sincerely while still having horrible form is not yet enough. Actual movement toward fitness must have taken place. Perfect push-ups are not required, and modifications to the exercises may be appropriate, but if your exercises are not yet engaging the right muscle groups, they are not far enough along. Similarly, philosophical progressors must have made some advance in understanding and living out their school's thought before they can count as practicing it.

How far do you need to have gone? On our view, the threshold is significantly lower than the maximum possible attainment. Where this threshold lies is influenced by the worldview in question. So Buddhism, Stoicism, Taoism, and so forth typically have developed views on what it takes to count as practicing Buddhism, Stoicism, Taoism. They may distinguish true believers from the merely nominal adherents whose lives are not significantly formed by the philosophical school. At the same time, these schools allow for progressors to count as living the school's life even if they are not yet good or excellent practitioners. You can be living out a way of life even when your application has many failures and defects. Just as advanced beginners and intermediates are doing push-ups despite deficiencies in their craft, so various progressors are already living a philosophical life despite their struggles. Instead of thinking of living a way of life as all or nothing, we should instead take it to be a notion containing degrees. We can make comparisons between those above the threshold and see how successfully they are achieving their goal. The threshold view still allows us to distinguish intermediates from experts.

Another important part of this condition is having the right relation between the diagnosis and the treatment. If you hold a Buddhist worldview but are actively engaged in pursuing wealth and status, there probably isn't the right connection between your worldview and your practices (ceteris paribus). The structuring also needs to be relatively global and sustained. Say you place flowers on your grandmother's grave once a year, out of Confucian filial piety. Even if you do this every year, it probably isn't enough to count as practicing a Confucian way of life. This is because practicing a way of life requires implementing an overall view of the world and value. The broad scope of condition 1 sets the bar for fulfilling condition 2. If the truth claims and value prescriptions are global and sustained, then the structuring of practice they imply will be as well.

On our reading, the cafeteria consumer of spiritual and philosophical wisdom won't meet the structuring features of condition 2. Meditating for stress relief isn't living as a Buddhist, because even if the practice is based on and originates in Buddhism, it is no longer structured by Buddhism in the right way. Similarly, as discussed above, abstemious Epicureans are not living a Platonist way of life, because their goal to be careful with food and the way in which they act with care are quite different.

There are also a variety of ways in which your practices and life could end up being structured by your worldview. There are some philosophical views that end up satisfying condition 2 only in a weak sense. If your philosophical commitments indicate that there is no best life or that the best life does not distinctively involve philosophy or rational activity, this will give a perspective on your actions and choices, but one that may mostly be negative. Being a nihilist will presumably inform your life, even if it does so by suggesting there are no good lives or positive values that you can achieve. You will certainly avoid value commitments that you might otherwise make.

We can distinguish approaches whose implications are primarily formal from approaches with both material and formal implications. In the primarily formal case, your philosophy primarily informs the spirit in which or the intentions with which you act. For example, Pyrrhonian skeptics always avoid dogmatism and strong commitment, no matter the topic, and existentialists always emphasize choice and freedom, no matter the content of the choice. The specific choices and actions made can vary considerably, however. By contrast, specific, concrete practices follow from some worldviews (for example, the specific commands of daily prayers and hajj within an Islamic way of life or the practices of keeping kosher and observing the 613 commandments within a Jewish way of life). Ways of life will typically have formal requirements on the way in which you perform these specific practices: few if any philosophies or religions think that performing certain actions in a purely rote way is sufficient for properly embodying that way of life.

5.3. Condition 3

These first two conditions, then, set out requirements for practicing an art of living, as opposed to just acting on socially or culturally implicit values. Our third condition captures the specific requirements that come from a *philosophical* way of life. A philosophical life should not just be guided by truth claims that one commits to, it should also *consist in* practices that are truth directed. There are many ways of life that apply a worldview, but if what it takes to live that life successfully does not constitutively involve realizing the truth, the life itself does not count as philosophical.

This bar separates practices and lives that may have philosophical justifications but are not themselves concerned with truth. Preference-satisfaction maximizers who don't care about the content of your preferences may have philosophical arguments for their position, but living that out would not be sufficiently truth involving. While such a preference-satisfaction life would involve some instrumental reasoning, that is true of almost any lived life, whether it employs a technē or not. Filling everyone's preferences for, say, watching lots of sports does not seem to be truth directed in the relevant way. Activities of preference maximizing are not themselves necessarily truth directed; only certain deliberations about them are. By contrast, worldviews on which the good life consists in contemplating the nature and order of reality are constitutively truth directed. Thus we have *condition 3: The practices and life of practitioners of a philosophical way of life are constitutively truth directed and are responsive to reasons.*

We use "truth directed" because, as discussed, a philosophical way of life does not need to consist primarily in discursive reasoning or other exercises of our rational powers, contra Cooper. There are other ways of getting to the truth. Experiences of beauty sometimes give us insight and allow us to contemplate reality in a way that arguments on their own do not. They allow us to see the truth of things in a distinctive way. Simone Weil and Iris Murdoch both make the case that appreciative attention to beautiful and good things can help us both morally and intellectually, allowing us to see and act better (Weil 1951, "Reflections on the Right Use of School Studies with a View to the Love of God," Murdoch 1997, esp. "The Sovereignty of Good over Other Concepts"; cf. McPherson 2020, chap. 5). Plotinus, whom even Cooper wants to include as living a philosophical way of life, thinks that the culmination of his way of life consists in a union with the One that cannot be achieved via any intellectual activity: this activity is reality directed but is not a rational activity in the standard sense (*Enneads* V.3, 14.5–8; VI.9, 4.1–4; though, of course, for Plotinus, developing intellectual virtues and activating one's understanding is an important part of the preparatory process). Truth-directedness, as we conceive it, requires that the characteristic activities of your way of life be truth conducive, conditional on your worldview being right. If, conditional on the truth of Buddhism, Buddhist meditation would help you appreciate emptiness, then it is a truth-directed practice.

Our view allows for a wide range of practices to contribute toward achieving truth. The most central sorts of practices are those that themselves give access to truth, whether through successful use of discursive reason or through a more direct aesthetic or intellectual experience. Other practices, however, can be truth directed insofar as they prepare you to see what's true or orient you in the right direction. Practices can count as truth directed in this sense just by making you more convinced of your worldview and more committed to living it out. Even practices that do not directly change your credences can still be truth directed. For example, in the context of an Abrahamic religion, praying to God might be a truth-directed practice because if such a God exists, it is plausible that prayer is a way of connecting to God. This might hold even if, in some cases, praying does not increase one's credence or directly result in any positive experience. You might still be engaging in a truth-directed practice. Similarly, for Buddhists, engaging in meditation while also accepting the transitory character of the self could be truth directed even in cases when your meditation does not immediately succeed in affecting your view of the self. If Buddhism is right, the practice is conducive to truth even when it does not immediately get you to where you are trying to go.

Living philosophically, then, means leading a life characterized by truth-directed practices, including argument, cognitive self-reflection, and contemplative appreciation of the true and the good. There are also, however, requirements for how practitioners of a philosophical way of life go about forming their beliefs and pursuing truth. On our view, those living a philosophical way of life must be reasons responsive. Reason has an important role to play in why they hold the views they do. They are also sensitive to defeaters of their views. They do not merely hope that the practices they are following turn out to be truth conducive. They are following them because they reasonably believe them and are open to being convinced otherwise. This does not, however, mean that living philosophically requires being able to individually address any question or objection about the way of life you are following. Practitioners are allowed to consult others and to admit they are not sure about an issue. They will both develop their own intellectual virtues and be open to learning from the excellences of others. The crucial thing is to be responsive to reasons, in whichever direction they ultimately point, and not to ignore defeaters. To live philosophically you constantly need to be developing intellectual virtues that make you responsive to reasons. You need to be willing to consider objections to your view and be open to the truth.

5.4. Summation

We have seen, then, that a philosophical way of life is a value-oriented and lived-out way of life that is responsive to reasons and directed at truth. To embrace it you need to have a vision of the good and live on the basis of that vision in a way that is conducive to reaching truth. These conditions are demanding, and meeting them is a significant achievement. They are, however, still attainable. Further, religious or tradition-based ways of life can count as truth directed as long as their practices are reasons responsive and will be truth directed if the claims made by their way of life are correct. Our three conditions for living philosophically are summed up in table 1.

TABLE 1. Conditions for living philosophically

	Paradigm of philosophical way of life	Philosophically informed life	Not living philosophically	
Examples	*Sage or adept*	*Progressor (includes both inarticulate practitioners and those who are articulate but deficient in practicing)*	*Cafeteria consumer*	*Practitioner of a non-philosophical worldview*
1. Committed to a truth-claim-making, value-prescribing, coherent worldview	Yes	Yes	No	Yes
2. Practices and life structured by this worldview	Yes	Yes, but not perfectly	No, because they are not ultimately committed	Yes
3. Practices and life are constitutively truth directed	Yes	Yes, but not perfectly	Not as uncommitted consumer	No

6. Conclusion

A philosophical way of life involves reflection and the use of reason but does not require perfection or solitary achievement. Making progress in how one acts in the world and improving one's understanding and direction through being part of a community *is* living a philosophical way of life. Our view acknowledges the wide number of ways in which people can live philosophically. Even if we do not all have the leisure to fully articulate and defend a view of reality, each of us can reflect on what is beautiful and true in our experience of the world. We can also make use of the practices, techniques, and ideas shared with us by others in our communities. This allows us to benefit from their work and move together toward our shared goal of living well.

Acknowledgments

We would like to thank participants in the 2018 National Endowment for the Humanities Summer Seminar entitled *Philosophy as a Way of Life* for their thoughtful and inspiring discussions. We are particularly grateful to Alison Krile Thornton and Susan Brower-Toland for their discussions of what the conditions on a philosophical way of life should be.

References

Cohoe, Caleb M., and Stephen R. Grimm. Unpublished. "What Is Philosophy as a Way of Life? Why Philosophy as a Way of Life?" Unpublished manuscript.

Cooper, John. 2012. *Ancient Philosophies as Ways of Life*. The Tanner Lectures on Human Values. Salt Lake City: Utah University Press.

Diogenes Laertius. 2018. *Lives of the Eminent Philosophers*. Translated by Pamela Mensch, edited by James Miller. New York: Oxford University Press.

Epictetus. 2014. *Discourses, Fragments, Handbook*. Translated by Robin Hard. New York: Oxford World's Classics.

Foucault, Michel. 1997. *Ethics: Subjectivity and Truth*. Volume 1 of *Essential Works of Foucault, 1954–1984*. Edited by Paul Rabinow. New York: New Press.

Hadot, Pierre. 1995. "Philosophy as a Way of Life." In Hadot, *Philosophy as a Way of Life*, edited and introduced by Arnold I. Davidson, 264–76. Malden, Mass.: Blackwell.

Mansfield, Jaap. 1994. *Prolegomena: Questions to Be Settled Before the Study of an Author, or a Text*. Philosophia Antiqua, 61. Leiden: E. J. Brill.

McPherson, David. 2020. *Virtue and Meaning: A Neo-Aristotelian Perspective*. Cambridge: Cambridge University Press.

Midgley, Mary. 2018. *What Is Philosophy For?* London: Bloomsbury.

Murdoch, Iris. 1997. *Existentialists and Mystics: Writings on Philosophy and Literature*. Edited by Peter Conradi. New York: Penguin.

Nietzsche, Friedrich. 1967ff. *Werke: Kritische Gesamtausgabe*. Edited by Giorgio Colli and Mazzino Montinari. Berlin: W. de Gruyter.

________. 1995. *Unfashionable Observations*. Translated by Richard T. Gray. Volume 2 of *The Complete Works of Friedrich Nietzsche*. Palo Alto, Calif.: Stanford University Press.

Porphyry of Tyre. 2017. "On the Life of Plotinus and the Order of His Books by Porphyry of Tyre." In *Plotinus: The Enneads*, edited by Lloyd Gerson and translated by George Boys-Stones, John Dillon, Richard King, Andrew Smith, and James Wilberding, 17–38. Cambridge: Cambridge University Press.

Puett, Michael, and Christine Gross-Loh. 2017. *The Path: What Chinese Philosophers Can Teach Us About the Good Life*. New York: Simon and Schuster.

Sellars, John. 2003. *The Art of Living: The Stoics on the Nature and Function of Philosophy*. Farnham: Ashgate.

Weil, Simone. 1951. *Waiting on God*. Translated by Emma Craufurd. New York: Harper and Row.

Whitcomb, Dennis, Heather Battaly, Jason Baehr, and Daniel Howard-Snyder. 2017. "Intellectual Humility: Owning Our Limitations." *Philosophy and Phenomenological Research* 94, no. 3:509–39.

Wright, Robert. 2017. *Why Buddhism Is True: The Science and Philosophy of Meditation and Enlightenment*. New York: Simon and Schuster.

Zagzebski, Linda. 2012. *Epistemic Authority: A Theory of Trust, Authority, and Autonomy in Belief*. New York: Oxford University Press.

________. 2017. *Exemplarist Moral Theory*. New York: Oxford University Press.

CHAPTER 14

WHY PRACTICE PHILOSOPHY AS A WAY OF LIFE?

JAVIER HIDALGO

1. Introduction

Many ancient philosophers thought that philosophy was a way of life. They believed that philosophy should improve and transform our existence. In his influential work on ancient philosophy, Pierre Hadot (1995) observes that although ancient philosophers engaged in theoretical discourse, they also sought to integrate their doctrines into their ordinary lives.[1] Ancient philosophers engaged in spiritual exercises in order to change their attitudes and behavior. Different schools of philosophy favored different exercises. But common spiritual exercises included meditation, dialogue with others, negative and positive visualization, ascetic living, contemplating one's life from the perspective of the cosmos, subjecting negative patterns of thought to critique, and more. Philosophers sought out communities of like-minded people to assist them in self-transformation. Stoics, Epicureans, and others formed schools and communities to support one another. Philosophy as a way of life was hardly the exclusive preserve of Greek and Roman thinkers; non-Western philosophical traditions, such as Buddhism and Confucianism, were also guides to living.[2]

In contrast to ancient thinkers, few present-day academic philosophers study philosophy as a way of life. Contemporary philosophers tend to

[1] But for criticisms of Hadot's depiction of ancient philosophy, see Cooper 2013.

[2] And, of course, Buddhism and Confucianism, along with other Eastern philosophical traditions, are alive and well today.

Philosophy as a Way of Life: Historical, Contemporary, and Pedagogical Perspectives.
Edited by James M. Ambury, Tushar Irani, and Kathleen Wallace.

Published 2021 by John Wiley & Sons Ltd.

focus on puzzles and problems, such as the mind-body problem, the problem of free will, the correct analysis of conditionals, how we can acquire knowledge of moral and mathematical truths, and so on. Yet there's growing interest in philosophy as a guide to life. That's certainly true outside academia. Consider Stoicism. There's a vibrant Stoic movement replete with organizations, conferences, workshops, and best-selling books. Eastern philosophies, such as Buddhism, are ever more popular in the West. Aspects of Buddhism, such as mindfulness meditation, are pervasive. Academics too are becoming more interested in philosophy as a way of life. There are initiatives under way to make it a more mainstream component of academic philosophy.[3]

Why should we practice philosophy as a way of life? Some may find the answer to this question easy to answer. Isn't it obvious that philosophy should guide life? After all, that's why many of us became interested in philosophy in the first place. Maybe it's *so* obvious that philosophy should guide life that it's not worth discussing. But if it's that obvious, then it's hard to explain the limited interest in philosophy as a way of life among contemporary philosophers. On the other hand, some people consider philosophy as a way of life to be obsolete. Advice on how to live is best left to positive psychologists who study which interventions actually improve well-being. What's left for philosophers to do?

In this essay I explain why we have good reasons to practice philosophy as a way of life. My aim is not to defend a particular philosophy of life. Instead, I want to give a general argument in favor of practicing philosophy as a way of life. I discuss what I mean by "philosophy as a way of life" more precisely below. But, provisionally, philosophy as a way of life involves philosophical reasoning and reflection about how we should live combined with behavioral, cognitive, and social strategies to alter our behavior and attitudes so that they're in line with our philosophical commitments. I argue that many of us have a reason to pursue philosophy as a way of life in this sense.

2. A Defense of Philosophical Discourse

My argument begins with the assumption that we should live well. By this, I mean at a minimum that we should do what contributes to our own good and fulfills our obligations. I don't have much to say in defense of this assumption. I take it for granted that we should promote our own good and avoid wrongdoing. You could deny this premise. But I suspect that most readers will share it. Some philosophers reject the view that there are any reasons that are independent of our thoughts and attitudes. Yet even these philosophers can agree that we have subjective reasons to improve our lives and meet our obligations to ourselves and others (Streumer 2017).

[3] See, for instance, the "Philosophy as a Way of Life" Initiative at: https://philife.nd.edu/

I try to avoid committing myself to substantive views about prudence or the content of our obligations. Sure enough, I give examples that *assume* substantive views about what makes life go well and what's morally right. But these are only illustrations. I'm not committed to the views that these examples presuppose. My argument is compatible with different views about prudence and morality.

So, we should live well. Yet we can live badly. One way in which we can live badly is because our goals in life can be mistaken and our understanding of our obligations can be wrong. Furthermore, philosophical reasoning can help us to identify these mistakes. Here's an illustration. In the early 1970s, a young graduate student named Peter Singer decided to become a vegetarian (Singer 2009, 15–19). Singer was having lunch with a fellow graduate student named Richard Keshen. The choice was between spaghetti and salad. Keshen asked whether the spaghetti sauce had meat in it. When he discovered it did, he chose the salad. Singer asked Keshen why he didn't eat meat. Keshen told Singer that he objected to the way that humans treated animals. Intrigued by Keshen's argument, Singer was put in touch with other vegetarian graduate students and intellectuals.

Their influence and his own reflections led Singer to conclude that our treatment of animals was wrong and that it's immoral to eat meat. But he was reluctant to act on this judgment. He and his wife, Renata, were not "animal lovers." Moreover, he liked meat, and "vegetarians were very rare then, and most people thought them decidedly odd" (Singer 2009, 18). He was tempted to shrug his shoulders and ignore the conclusion of his own arguments. But eventually the Singers became vegetarians. Singer comments: "It seemed especially contradictory to take a theoretical interest in ethics and yet push its conclusions to one side when they became difficult to act upon" (18).

The point of this example is to illustrate how mistaken we can be about how well our lives are going, and whether our conduct is permissible. Singer identified a mistake in how he was living his life. But how do we identify these kinds of mistakes? How do we know if we're living badly? We need reasoning and reflection to identify our mistakes. Much of this corrective reasoning is instrumental. Perhaps you have certain goals and you're failing to effectively pursue them. Maybe you want to be happy, but your lifestyle results in unhappiness. You can use reasoning to discover this and correct your behavior. Yet we can also be mistaken in more fundamental ways. Our deeper aims can be defective, and our understanding of our obligations can be wrong. Philosophical reasoning can help us to identify and correct these mistakes. For instance, philosophical reasoning influenced Singer to condemn the treatment of animals. The philosopher Roslind Godlovitch was writing an article on animal ethics, and Singer gave Godlovitch feedback on it. Singer says: "In the process of putting her arguments in what seemed to me the strongest possible form . . . I convinced myself that the case for vegetarianism . . . was overwhelming" (2009, 17).

Philosophical reasoning can also identify mistakes in our prudential aims. Philosophical reflection can even unseat foundational assumptions about prudence. Here's another illustration. Buddhist philosophers argue that the belief in the self is the root cause of human suffering. We cling to our desires and projects because we believe that we are enduring selves. Yet our projects and pursuits are fragile. Bad luck can put an end to our projects in an instant. It's true that we can achieve happiness and pleasure on occasion. But according to a Buddhist simile, the pursuit of worldly pleasures is like licking honey from a razor blade (Perrett 2016, 37). Each of us faces the inevitable loss of everyone and everything that we love.[4] The passage of time and death will rob us of much of what we value. The realization that our lives are fragile and our egoistic pursuits are in a sense futile may cause us to feel existential anxiety and suffering.

Yet Buddhist philosophers contend that egoistic pursuits and the existential anxiety that they provoke rest on a mistake. The suffering that we experience is predicated on the belief that we are enduring selves with projects, plans, and meaningful goals that require an open future.[5] But there are no selves. Why believe that there are no selves? Some Buddhists argue that we lack introspective evidence that there is a self, and, in addition, it's unnecessary to posit a self in order to explain our experience. Others defend a brand of mereological reductionism according to which entities with composite parts, like the self, are unreal. Some philosophers, such as Derek Parfit (1986), use thought experiments to claim that our ordinary conception of the self is unjustified. I won't discuss the arguments against the enduring self here. My point is this: if these arguments are sound, they may cause us to change our attitudes and beliefs about our lives.

According to Buddhists, we should fetishize our projects and attachments less and end our grasping and clinging to life. We should live in the moment more, as dispelling the illusion of self means that we should stop clinging to our desires and projects and worrying about their fulfillment. We can suffer from existential anxiety because we worry that our lives are meaningless, but if there is no self, then there is no subject whose life can lack meaning in the first place (Siderits 2007, 77). We should also care about the suffering of others more. The badness of suffering doesn't depend on whether this suffering is mine, as it's false that suffering belongs to any self.[6] So, suffering ought to be reduced wherever it occurs. More generally, the case against the self should arguably transform our relationship with our own projects and the lives of others.

[4] I borrow this poignant formulation of the Buddha's First Noble Truth from Sharon Street (2016).

[5] This interpretation of Buddhist philosophy draws heavily on Siderits 2016.

[6] This is one interpretation of Śāntideva's famous "ownerless suffering" argument for altruism in the *Bodhisattvacaryāvatāra* (Garfield, Jenkins, and Priest 2016). But it's controversial whether Śāntideva was offering an argument for the rationality of altruism or instead a guide to meditative practice.

These examples illustrate how philosophical reasoning and reflection can lead us to change our understanding of our obligations and aims in life. But what exactly is "philosophical reasoning"? It would likely be futile to come up with a precise definition of this concept. For one thing, I doubt that there's a category of philosophical reason that would make it distinct from other kinds of reasoning. I'm also skeptical that I could come up with a definition of philosophy that could cover much of what philosophers do. So, I won't try. Instead, I'll stipulate that *one* kind of philosophical reasoning is reasoning and reflection on what our aims in life should be and the content of our moral obligations. And by this I don't mean something especially rarefied. As I understand it, philosophical reasoning is continuous with ordinary reasoning about our obligations and life goals, although it tends to be more systematic and abstract.[7] I make no other claims about where the boundaries of philosophy lie or what distinguishes it from other kinds of reasoning.

One of my major claims so far is that philosophy can cause us to change our views about what we should seek in life and what's right and wrong. But that's not enough for my argument to work. Remember that my aim is not to show that philosophy can change our beliefs. My aim is to show that we have reason to use philosophical reasoning to guide our lives. For that claim to be true, philosophy needs to be reliable. Suppose that philosophy changes our minds, but always in the wrong direction. Instead of getting us closer to the truth about morality and prudence, philosophy leads us further away. If that were the case, then philosophy would be unreliable. And it would be a bad thing if we changed our lives on the basis of an unreliable method. Suppose that my doctor is unreliable. If I took her advice, this would make my health worse. Obviously, I should avoid listening to my doctor. Similarly, if philosophy delivers up bad advice about how I should live my life, then I should ignore it.

The question of whether philosophy is reliable or not is itself a philosophical question. Some philosophers deny that philosophy can help us reach the truth, while others argue that philosophy is reliable after all (Brennan 2010). I'm unable to resolve this disagreement here. But my argument relies on fairly modest premises about the reliability of philosophy. My view is that philosophy can alter our credences in a reliable way. By "credences," I mean how likely you think a belief is to be true. We can be more or less confident that something is true. For instance, I'm only weakly confident that the current president of the United States will win reelection. There's a reasonable chance that another candidate will win. We can also understand our philosophical beliefs in terms of credences.

[7] Toby Svoboda writes that rational, philosophical reflection on the good life "will include argumentation, appeals to coherence, reasoned objections to competing views, and other devices familiar to philosophers—it presumably will not include dogmatic appeals to divine revelation, historical authorities, or prevailing social norms" (2016, 41–42). I agree.

Philosophical reasoning can move our credences. Philosophy can lead us to rationally conclude that certain philosophical views are more likely to be true, even if philosophical reasoning is often insufficiently powerful to make us confident that we've arrived at the truth. In this sense, philosophical reasoning can be weakly reliable.

Before Singer encountered the arguments for vegetarianism, he likely attached a high credence to the belief that eating meat is morally acceptable. For the sake of illustration, let's imagine that he would have said that it's more likely than not that eating meat is morally acceptable before hearing the case for vegetarianism. But after listening to and evaluating the arguments against eating meat, he revised his credences. At some point, he concluded that vegetarianism was indeed more likely justified. It's hard to deny that philosophical arguments can rationally move our credences in this fashion. At first glance, good philosophical arguments can shift our views about which positions are more probable or less probable.

Let's consider my example of the Buddhist view on the self. Before reading Buddhist philosophers and fellow travelers, I had a high credence in the "further fact" view, the view that we are enduring selves and that our identities are irreducible to psychological connectedness and continuity. After hearing and considering arguments against this view and in favor of a reductionist conception of the self, I adjusted my credences. I now place a higher credence in the reductionist view after hearing these arguments. Maybe I'm still not fully convinced. But I now believe that the reductionist view is more probable than I once thought. My claim is that it's rational to adjust one's credences about the plausibility of a philosophical position in light of strong philosophical arguments.

If it's possible for philosophical reasoning and reflection to move our credences in a rational way, then philosophy can be reliable in a sense. I see no reason why philosophical reflection would only be reliable about the topics that I've discussed. So, it stands to reason that philosophical reasoning can potentially be reliable in other cases too. It's true that philosophical arguments rarely command agreement. The philosophical community notoriously fails to reach consensus on which philosophical views are correct. Nonetheless, this observation is compatible with my argument. Philosophical arguments can lead us to rationally adjust our credences even though philosophers will continue to disagree about which views are best justified overall. But arguments that prompt rational belief revision can help guide our lives despite the fact that they fall short of generating consensus. For instance, when Singer adjusted his credences about the truth of vegetarianism, doing so led him to stop eating meat. The fact that other philosophers disagreed with him seems irrelevant.

To be clear, it would be absurd to claim that philosophical reasoning is reliable per se. Philosophical arguments can easily point us away from the truth as well. Philosophical reasoning is more likely to be reliable if the reasoner has other epistemic virtues, such as humility, fair-mindedness, and intellectual curiosity. But that holds true for all reasoning. Scientific reasoning can go astray if the reasoner in question lacks epistemic virtues. There are also no guarantees. Even a scrupulous and fair reasoner can reach the wrong conclusion. Nonetheless, it's plausible that philosophical reasoning can be weakly reliable under the right conditions.

3. From Philosophical Discourse to Philosophy as a Way of Life

3.1 The Problem of Philosophy's Inefficacy

So, philosophical reasoning can help us better understand how we should live. But understanding is insufficient. We must be able to use this understanding to inform our lives.

Recall that when Singer first came to believe that vegetarianism was morally required, he was reluctant to stop eating meat. To support his reluctance, he gave an analogy between vegetarianism and poverty relief. He reasoned that he was also required to spend more money on helping the global poor. Yet he didn't do this. He asked: "If we can live in the knowledge that we are not doing what we ought to be doing with starvation in India, why can't we live with the knowledge that we are not doing the right thing about eating animals?" (2009, 17). Singer's wife, Renata, was not impressed with this argument. She insisted that, in addition to becoming vegetarians, they also give more to famine relief. Singer relented.

But let's suppose that Singer had failed to reform his behavior. That would have been a mistake. That is, he would have been making a mistake if philosophical reasoning revealed a better way to live and he nonetheless failed to adjust his behavior in light of this knowledge. Here's a plausible principle that could explain these judgments. If you should live well, you have a justified belief that you are living badly in some respect, and you have a justified belief that some other way of living is better, then you have a strong reason to change the way that you live to conform to the way of life that's better. This principle implies that Singer had reason to change his life.

Yet most of us refrain from changing our lives on the basis of philosophical reasoning. We reason ourselves to some conclusion about how to live and yet we refrain from adjusting our behavior and attitudes in light of this conclusion. One source of evidence for these claims comes from the behaviors and beliefs of ethicists. In a series of provocative studies, Eric Schwitzgebel and Joshua Rust (2014; 2016) have examined the moral behavior of moral philosophers through both self-reports and direct behavioral measures. They've found that the behavior of professional ethicists is not significantly different from the behavior of other philosophers or academics. Sure enough, the *beliefs* of professional ethicists are different from those of other academics. But those views fail to translate into action.

According to Schwitzgebel and Rust's survey, most ethicists agreed that eating mammals is morally problematic (2014, 306–7). Sixty percent of surveyed ethicists said that "regularly eating the meat of mammals, such as beef or pork," is morally bad (ethicists were much more likely than other groups to view this behavior as bad). Ethicists were also more likely than other philosophers and college professors to say that they are vegetarians. Despite their disapproval of eating meat, ethicists reported eating meat at about the same rate as other groups did. Nearly nine out of ten ethicists also said that it is a good thing to give 10 percent of your income to charity, which is a higher rate than nonethicists said. Nonetheless, ethicists did not give significantly more of their incomes to charity than did nonphilosophers (314).

Other researchers have replicated Schwitzgebel and Rust's findings. Philipp Schönegger and Johannes Wagner (2019) surveyed ethicists in German-speaking countries. They found that ethicists did have moral beliefs different from those of nonphilosophers: they were both more stringent on some measures (charitable giving) and less stringent on others (keeping in touch with your mother). But, once again, ethicists did not report having more moral behavior than nonethicists in general.[8]

We should interpret these findings with caution. Surveys can be unreliable, especially when researchers are asking about conduct that could cast the respondents in an unflattering light. Perhaps some of the surveyed groups are more likely to misreport their behavior or beliefs. For this reason, we're unable to rule out the possibility that ethicists do in fact behave differently from other academics. Schwitzgebel and Rust do, however, provide observable measures of ethical behavior. For instance, in Schwitzgebel and Rust 2014 they examine how often ethicists vote from publicly available data, whether ethicists are more likely to respond to charitable incentives to complete their surveys, pay conference registration fees, and other such measures. Once again, they find that the behavior of ethicists does not differ from that of other groups.

The evidence from surveys of ethicists is consistent with the hypothesis that engagement with philosophy can change beliefs. Professional ethicists have beliefs different from those of other philosophers and nonphilosophers. Perhaps we can explain this via selection. People who already are disposed to favor vegetarianism and charitable giving may disproportionately decide to become ethicists. But it also seems plausible that philosophical reflection and reasoning is partially causally responsible for the difference between ethicists and other groups.

Yet the scope of philosophy's impact appears to be limited. If philosophical reasoning significantly influenced behavior, we would expect philosophical reasoning and reflection to change the ethical behavior of the

[8]Schönegger and Wagner do find that professional ethicists are more likely to be vegetarians. Schwitzgebel suggests, however, that some of the respondents in Schönegger and Wagner's study are giving inaccurate self-reports and that different statistical techniques may eliminate the difference between ethicists and non-ethicists. See Schwitzgebel 2019.

people who engage in this reasoning. But their behavior doesn't differ from the behavior of the control groups. This is evidence that philosophical reasoning has few effects on behavior on average. Research on the gap between the beliefs and the actions of philosophers fits into a broader empirical literature on the "value-action" gap (see, e.g., Flynn, Bellaby, and Ricci 2009). According to this literature, we often express value judgments and attitudes that are at odds with our behavior. People say that they value environmentally friendly products, but they end up buying whatever product is cheapest or most convenient. Recent research on the value-action gap suggests that people have trouble translating abstract values into specific behaviors. Similarly, while philosophical reasoning might change abstract values and beliefs, the gap between values and behavior remains about as wide as ever.

Other strands of evidence support the claim that moral reasoning fails to influence behavior or attitudes. A small empirical literature examines the impact that ethics classes have on the moral attitudes, judgments, and behavior of students. This literature generally finds that ethics instruction has, at best, modest effects on outcomes (Schwitzgebel 2013). One study examined the impact of an ethics course in the philosophy department on perceptions of fairness (Konow 2017). This research concludes that ethics instruction had no impacts on students' judgments of fairness. Only a handful of studies have examined whether ethics instruction changed the behavior of students outside a laboratory. These studies generally find no effect. To illustrate, several studies consider whether business ethics instruction affects rates of cheating, and these studies find that there are minimal differences between the control and the treatment groups on average (Konow 2017, 191–93).

Why does abstract moral reasoning seem to have little impact on attitudes or behavior? I explore this question in more detail in the following subsection, but one possibility is rationalization. Perhaps people who engage in philosophical reasoning end up justifying their prior beliefs and conduct. People adopt whatever ethical and philosophical views that ratify their past behavior and judgments. While the rationalization view likely explains the limited impact of philosophical reasoning in part, it's hard to square with the discrepancy between ethicists' judgments and behavior. Many ethicists agree that they should give more to charity and become vegetarians, but they don't do these things. Another possibility is what Schwitzgebel and Rust call the "inert discovery view" (2014, 295–96). On this view, philosophical reasoning and reflection does lead to the discovery of moral truths, and yet this doesn't cause a corresponding change in behavior. The inert discovery view is consistent with my background assumptions. I've argued that abstract moral and philosophical reasoning can be reliable at least in the weak sense that it can cause us to rationally revise our credences. So, it's possible that people who engage in more moral reasoning have better justified ethical views than other groups. Yet, for whatever reason, this moral reasoning falls short of causing behavioral changes.

3.2 Philosophy as a Way of Life as a Potential Solution

Suppose that you agree that philosophy's inefficacy is sometimes a problem. How can we mitigate this problem? Let's return to the question of why philosophical reasoning fails to cause attitudinal or behavioral change. Consider a simple model of how people could change their lives. Imagine that you engage in reasoning and you arrive at the conclusion that you ought to X, and you respond to this judgment by doing X. More concretely, suppose that I conclude on the basis of moral reasoning that I ought to become a vegetarian and give more to effective charities and, as a result, I change my life so that I become a vegetarian and give more to charity. On a purely rationalist model of personal change, a reasoned judgment that I ought to do X would be sufficient to cause me to X.

A simple rationalist model of personal change, however, faces four key problems:

(i) *The problem of knowledge*. I may lack knowledge about how to change my life in light of my judgments. An illustration: maybe I don't know how to cook vegetarian meals or might not know where best to donate my money. Even if I believe in the abstract that I should become a vegetarian, I lack the knowledge to concretely apply this conclusion to my day-to-day life.

(ii) *The problem of motivation*. The simple rationalist model overlooks the problem of motivation. I might lack the motivation to make my behavior consistent with my judgments. After reading Singer's famous arguments for charitable giving, some of my students agree that they should give much more to charity. Yet few do. Why? Although they agree on a theoretical level that they should give to effective charities, my students still lack the motivation to give away their money. Their reasoned judgments fail to motivate them.

(iii) *The problem of context*. The simple rationalist model ignores the importance of context. It seems undeniable that our behavior is influenced by the situation we find ourselves in. Cues in our environment trigger judgments and behaviors. Social cues are especially important. If other people are behaving in a certain way, most of us are strongly inclined to go along with the crowd. Few of us enjoy being the odd one out.

(iv) *The problem of habits*. Much of our decision making and behavior is automatic and the product of habit rather than explicit reasoning. So, to change our behavior in an enduring way, we need to cultivate new habits. Here's a common problem: you should exercise more, but you consistently don't. Why? One reason is probably that you haven't

> cultivated the habit of exercising. Thus, you need to motivate yourself to exercise in any given case, which is difficult to do. If you acquire the habit of exercising, the decision to exercise would become more seamless and automatic.

These four reasons are interrelated. You could lack the motivation to change your behavior because you lack the right kind of social cues and incentives in your environment to motivate this behavior. Moreover, these four factors help explain why abstract reasoning fails to translate into action. While we may believe on the basis of abstract reasoning that we ought to behave differently, factors (i) to (iv) prevent us from consistently acting on this belief. So, to align our behavior and attitudes with our philosophical commitments, we need a solution that addresses (i) to (iv).

Here's a motivated hypothesis: philosophy as a way of life is a potential solution to philosophy's inefficacy because it addresses problems (i) to (iv). Let me start by clarifying what I mean by "philosophy as a way of life." As I use the phrase, philosophy as a way of life includes philosophical reflection on how to live combined with strategies for living in accordance with our convictions about the good life. To flesh this idea out, I'll draw heavily on the pioneering work of Hadot (1995; 2004). Hadot argues that ancient philosophers realized that reason and philosophical discourse have limits. To be a true philosopher in antiquity, you needed to do more than engage in philosophical reasoning. You also had to live philosophically. A true philosopher integrated philosophy into his life. Epictetus illustrated this insight as follows: "A carpenter does not come up to you and say 'listen to me discourse about the art of carpentry' but he makes a contract for a house and he builds it. . . . Do the same thing for yourself" (qtd. Hadot 1995, 267).

How did ancient philosophers integrate philosophy into their lives? Hadot identifies several strategies, but he emphasizes "spiritual exercises." Spiritual exercises are practices that seek to make us into the kind of being that our chosen philosophy endorses (Hadot 2004, 6; May 2017, 171). Ancient philosophers advocated such spiritual exercises as meditation, dietary regimens, physical exercise, gratitude exercises, and other strategies. Spiritual practices are intended to be repeated routines rather than one-off actions or realizations. According to many ancient philosophers, we should frequently engage in spiritual exercises in order to gradually modify our dispositions and mental habits in the desired direction.

Here's an illustration. Many Stoics believed that, to achieve tranquillity and virtue, we should focus only on what we can control and rid ourselves of the desire to change things that exist outside our control, such as the inevitable misfortunes of life. Events outside our control are indifferent to us, and we must train ourselves to respond to these events with equanimity. To internalize this lesson, Stoics practiced negative visualization, which requires practitioners to vividly imagine painful or tragic outcomes (the Romans referred to this technique as *premeditatio malorum*, the premeditation of evils). Seneca advises us to "remind our spirits all the time that they love things that will leave—no, better, things that are already leaving" (2015, 47). Along similar lines, Epictetus tells that when kissing your child you should imagine that she will die tomorrow (2014, 207). Stoics believed that negative visualization was a useful tool for preparing us for events outside our control and for instilling gratitude for the good that we possess. Negative visualization was just one in a repertoire of Stoic spiritual exercises. Other Stoic exercises included regular practice in subjecting our reactions and impressions to rational critique, mediation on the cosmos, and reflecting on the impermanence of all things.

Eastern philosophical traditions pioneered their own distinctive spiritual exercises. The most famous is the practice of mindfulness meditation in the Buddhist tradition. The Buddha recommends meditation and breathing exercises in order to cultivate insight into the nature of reality and liberate ourselves from clinging. One aspect of the Buddha's teaching seems to be that concentration through meditation can lead us to see that all possible candidates for the self are impermanent and thus unable to serve as the basis for a self.[9] In this way, meditation can help us to confirm that the self is an illusion. Furthermore, meditation and breathing exercises can cultivate habits that counter emotions that reinforce the sense of "I"—that is, the sense that we have selves. Loving-kindness meditation is one meditative practice that aims to counter emotions, such as greed, that prioritize and reify our self-interest. Loving-kindness meditation involves extending compassion toward ourselves, our associates, our enemies, and a progressively larger circle of beings. Through this practice, we can reinforce habits that calm and overcome egocentric emotions. This is one step on the path to internalizing the truth of nonself.

Spiritual exercises can help us to apply philosophy to our lives. Recall that one of the factors that explain why abstract values fail to translate into action is the problem of habits. Habits are cognitive and behavioral dispositions that tend to rely more on unconscious and automatic decision making. Habits are sticky. Once you cultivate a set of habits, it's hard to change the structure of your life. Spiritual exercises aim to change habits. These exercises cultivate new cognitive and affective dispositions to replace old habits. Stoic practices seek to reform our habits of fixating on and worrying about events that are outside our control. Buddhist serenity meditation undermines our habits of clinging to our thoughts and desires, soothing the turmoil in our minds. Loving-kindness meditation weakens our tendency to react with feelings of hatred, anger, and other egocentric emotions, instead promoting compassion and empathy for all other beings. By restructuring our habits, spiritual exercises change how we act and think

[9] Hence the Buddha says: "Develop meditation on the perception of impermanence; for when you [do so] the conceit 'I am' will be abandoned" (Nanamoli and Bodhi 1995, 424).

about the world. They may also address the problem of motivation. For example, one goal of loving-kindness meditation is to help motivate you to act with compassion toward all suffering beings.

But do spiritual exercises work? It's not enough to seek to change our habits and motivations. We must provide evidence that spiritual exercises do have this effect. This is not the place to provide a comprehensive review of the evidence. There's now a large literature in psychology, however, that supports the claim that certain spiritual practices can change our attitudes, dispositions, and behavior. Stoic spiritual exercises bear close affinities with modern cognitive behavioral therapy. Similar to Stoic advice, cognitive behavioral therapy directs people to challenge mental distortions and disrupt negative patterns of thought. Cognitive behavioral therapy is one of the most well-supported strategies for treating depression, anxiety, and other mental health problems (Hofmann et al. 2012). This therapy appears to have real behavioral consequences as well—for instance, cognitive behavioral therapy reduces violence and crime among treated populations (Heller et al. 2016; Blattman, Jamison, and Sheridan 2017). Psychologists have also begun studying mindfulness meditation in recent decades. While researchers continue to debate the effects of mindfulness meditation, there is evidence that this practice can change our cognitive and behavioral dispositions (Goleman and Davidson 2017).

Another component of philosophy as a way of life that Hadot identifies is communal engagement. He remarks that ancient philosophy "was always a philosophy practiced in a group" (2004, 274). This may help explain the proliferation of philosophical schools and communities in ancient Greece, from Plato's academy to the garden of Epicurus. Ancient philosophers joined philosophical schools in order to create a community of research and mutual assistance. Extended networks of spiritual advisers, disciples, and supporters were also important. A community of like-minded adherents supported philosophy as a way of life in several ways. For one thing, this community could communicate the philosophical teachings and principles of their school.

The members of this community could also provide spiritual guidance and advice. For example, the Stoic Junius Rusticus was the spiritual adviser to the emperor Marcus Aurelius. According to one account, "[Marcus] received most instruction from Junius Rusticus, whom he ever revered and whose disciple he became, a man esteemed in both private and public life, and exceedingly well acquainted with the Stoic system" (Magie 1921, 139). More generally, a community can preserve a tradition of thought on how to incorporate philosophical teachings into your life. A tradition in this sense may serve as a repository of experience and wisdom that transcends the knowledge of any individual (Scheffler 2012). Remember that one problem philosophy as a way of life faces is the problem of knowledge. You can accept philosophical principles in the abstract and lack the right kind of knowledge to apply them to your life. A community of fellow travelers can transmit a tradition of thought on how to live in accordance with philosophical teachings on a day-to-day basis.

Communal engagement also addresses the other problems we face when applying philosophy to life, such as the problem of motivation and context. Humans are an intensely social species. As a result, our motivations are often social. We tend to act as others around us do and are motivated to behave in certain ways because people around us encourage this behavior. We desire esteem from others and need to belong. People harm others in order to conform to their group, and they also help others for the same reason (Nook et al. 2016).

So, a philosophical community can harness social motivations to change behavior and attitudes. Suppose that you want to adopt a new way of life. The fact that the other members of your community are trying to live this way can provide a powerful motivation for you to change as well. In addition, community helps solve the problem of context, the problem that much of our behavior is a response to cues in the environment instead of abstract, principled reasoning. Consider the importance of communal rituals. Communal rituals can serve as cues to engage in some activity that you may otherwise not engage in. When the members of a congregation pass around the collection plate at the same time every week, this serves as a cue to engage in charitable giving—something that you may neglect to do otherwise.

Consider a contemporary illustration of the power of community. Effective altruism is a social movement that aims to effectively make others better off through rigorous evidence and reasoning. In several respects, effective altruism is an example of philosophy as a way of life. Philosophical reasoning is an important part of effective altruism. Many of the people who helped found the movement, such as Peter Singer, Toby Ord, and Will MacAskill, are philosophers. Most effective altruists endorse consequentialist philosophical views, and they're famous for arguing that we should give a substantial amount of our incomes to highly effective charities. Yet effective altruists acknowledge that there's a gap between moral reasoning and behavior. It's one thing to claim that we should make substantial sacrifices in order to improve the world, and another to make these sacrifices.

This is in part why effective altruists form communities. They have created social clubs and chapters throughout the world. These chapters host events and discussion groups. They're a way for effective altruists to support each other in their giving and projects. In addition, effective-altruist podcasts, conferences, and discussion forums dispense moral advice and guidance on how to live according to effective-altruist principles. Effective altruists also create commitment devices to encourage effective giving. For instance, Giving What We Can is an effective-altruist organization. The goal of Giving What We Can is to create a supportive community for effective altruists and to leverage a commitment device and social pressure to encourage people to follow effective-altruist principles. To join, you must publicly pledge to give 10 percent of your lifetime income to highly effective charities. By taking the pledge, members become part of a community of like-minded people, and they also promote their reputation and status, which encourages people to stick to the pledge (Giving What We Can 2019). In these ways, effective altruists use social motivations to encourage moral improvement.

Let me now bring the different strands of my argument together. My argument in this essay amounts to a defense of philosophy as a way of life. How? Philosophical reasoning is crucial because we're fallible. Our understanding of our obligations and aims in life can be mistaken. When used appropriately, philosophical reasoning can improve our understanding of how we should live. Yet we have trouble living according to abstract moral and philosophical principles. The evidence that I've surveyed suggests that there's a gulf between abstract reasoning and the philosophical life. This inconsistency can be a mistake. If philosophical reasoning is at least weakly reliable, then it can identify ways in which we can improve our lives in these cases. A failure to act on philosophical conclusions is sometimes a lost opportunity to live a better life.

Philosophy as a way of life can help bridge the gap. Drawing on the work of Hadot, I've discussed two strategies in particular: spiritual exercises and communal engagement. These strategies mitigate the factors that plausibly explain the gap between our philosophical commitments and our dispositions and behaviors. Spiritual exercises modify our habits and motivations, and communal engagement can address the problem of knowledge, motivation, and contexts. If these practices aid us in living well or, at least, living more in accordance with justified beliefs about the good life, then we have reason to engage in them. There are likely other strategies besides these two that can assist us in living more coherent and perhaps better lives. I don't pretend that my account is comprehensive. My point is merely to establish that there are compelling reasons to pursue philosophy as a way life.

4. Scope, Religion, the Value of Philosophy, and Other Clarifications

In this section, I clarify my argument and respond to some objections.

One question about my argument involves its scope. I've sometimes implied that my argument has universalist pretentions. My argument began with the assumption that we should live a good life. I then argued that if this assumption is true, there's good reason for us to practice philosophy as a way of life. But who exactly should practice philosophy as a way of life? Does my argument imply that *everyone* should practice philosophy as a way of life?

To answer this question, we should first note that philosophy as a way of life is not an all-or-nothing concept. Philosophy as a way of life is instead a spectrum of behaviors and activities. Recall that philosophy as a way of life consists in philosophical reasoning and reflection on how you should live, along with strategies for changing your attitudes, dispositions, and behaviors to conform to your philosophical commitments, particularly spiritual exercises and communal engagement. Most people partake in these activities to some extent. While the majority of humanity will never take a philosophy class, most people wonder whether their lives have meaning and value, and whether they're living well. Most reflect on their goals in life and whether they're behaving morally, occasionally adjusting their attitudes and behavior in light of these reflections.

So, philosophy as a way of life is not necessarily a rarefied or elite activity. People often participate in it to some degree. And if that's true, then it doesn't sound so strange to claim that most people have good reason to pursue philosophy as a way of life. It seems like a good thing for people to reflect on and reason about their ends in life and try to make their behavior consistent with these ends. On a related note, consider religious ways of life. Religions incorporate the components of philosophy as a way of life that I've defended. Religions encourage spiritual exercises, such as prayer and meditation, and create communities to support norms of behavior. These practices aim to effect change among their adherents. Does a religious life therefore count as philosophy as a way of life? It can. If a religious life involves rational and philosophical reflection on the good life along with spiritual exercises and communal engagement, then it counts as philosophy as a way of life in the sense that I've defined it. Some religious ways of life rely on dogmatic appeals to divine revelation and authority. To the extent that this is true, I'd resist classifying these as philosophy as a way of life. But other religious conceptions of the good life would match the description of philosophy as a way of life that I've given.[10]

Yet I feel that this concessive response to the concern about scope is somewhat inadequate. Most of the examples that I've used throughout this essay are not cases of people who occasionally reflect on whether their lives are good and change their behavior in light of these reflections. Instead, my examples are often of people, such as professional philosophers, who engage in systematic philosophical reasoning about ethics and the good life. Some of the cases that I've discussed include people who also make it a major focus of their lives to live in accordance with their philosophical conclusions. For ease of reference, I'll refer to a way of life that involves (i) regular and systematic philosophical reasoning and reflection on the good life and (ii) a sustained focus on integrating philosophical principles into one's life through spiritual exercises, communal engagement, and other strategies as *robust philosophy as a way of life*. Should people generally pursue robust philosophy as a way of life?

[10] Hadot (1995) points out that some Christians in the ancient world conceived of Christianity as a philosophical way of life. See also Löhr 2010.

No. It seems false that everyone has an all-things-considered reason to pursue philosophy as a way of life in this more robust sense. A variety of mundane factors can defeat the reason to pursue this way of life. The most important one is opportunity costs. Engaging with philosophy takes time and effort. Most of us need philosophical training to assist us first. So, to engage in philosophical reasoning in a serious way, you need to forgo other options. And this trade-off isn't worth it for everyone. Suppose you could either spend more time reading philosophy papers or spend more time with your friends and family. Many people should take the latter option because that would make their lives better. This point generalizes to: once we consider opportunity costs, it's false that most people should practice philosophy as a way of life in a robust way.

My point is that there's probably no general answer to the question "Should people practice robust philosophy as a way of life?" The answer depends on a complex set of factors that vary across individuals. Some people lack the time, resources, and inclination to engage in philosophical activity. Others lack the epistemic virtues that make philosophical reasoning and reflection more likely to be reliable and useful. Some people have more valuable things to do. My argument aims to show that we have a *reason*—potentially a strong one—to engage in philosophy as a way of life. It doesn't aim to show that this reason is decisive in any particular case.

Yet this concessive response may still be too strong for some critics. I'm claiming that the life of someone who refrains from practicing philosophy as a way of life is in some respect deficient. For example, imagine that a person, Samantha, follows a traditional way of life inherited from her community. She rarely or never reflects on whether these traditions are good ones, considers alternative ways of life, or engages in philosophical argumentation. But let's imagine that her life is a rich and happy one, filled with friends, family, and community. Can I really claim that this person's life is missing something valuable that philosophy could deliver?

I think so. The factor that makes Samantha's life worse in one respect is fallibility and risk. Samantha may be living badly in some way and not know it, and philosophical activity and practices could help correct her way of life. A happy and rich life isn't always good in all respects. Samantha may unknowingly be making serious moral mistakes in the course of living her life, where careful philosophical reasoning and reflection would uncover this mistake. Again, this possibility fails to imply that she has an all-things-considered reason to pursue philosophy as a way of life. Perhaps the opportunity costs of pursuing philosophy as a way of life are too great. Maybe pursuing this would require Samantha to sacrifice projects that she's right to value. Nonetheless, that's compatible with the claim that she has a reason, albeit a defeasible one, to practice philosophy as a way of life.[11]

[11] There's a complex question about how to weigh the benefits and costs of philosophical activity against other options. For an insightful discussion, see MacAskill 2014, chap. 7.

Finally, let me consider another concern about the scope of my argument. How does philosophy as a way of life relate to the rest of philosophical activity? Epicurus wrote: "Vain is the word of a philosopher which does not heal any suffering of man. For just as there is no profit in medicine if it does not expel the diseases of the body, so there is no profit in philosophy either, if it does not expel the suffering of the mind" (qtd. Irvine 2008, 4). Like some other Hellenistic philosophers, Epicurus rejected the view that philosophy is a merely academic subject. The point of philosophical reasoning was to achieve the good life. On Epicurus's view, philosophical activities that are unrelated to this aim should be discouraged. Does my account imply a similar conclusion?

No. My claim is that we should live well, and this means that we have some reason to pursue philosophy as a way of life. Yet I don't claim that the philosophy related to questions about the good life is the only kind of philosophy that's worthwhile. Perhaps we have good reason to learn the truth about philosophical questions because this knowledge is valuable in itself irrespective of any practical benefits that it offers. It's plausible that learning more about the nature of, say, consciousness, causation, or universals is worthwhile regardless of whether it makes my life better or not. A defense of philosophy as a way of life is compatible with pluralism about the aims of philosophy.

5. Conclusion

I've tried in this essay to defend philosophy as a way of life. Let me conclude by saying something about why this defense could be valuable. Some readers will think that philosophy as a way of life sounds like amateur self-help advice. These readers may conclude that this subject is best left to positive psychologists who study well-being from a scientific perspective. Others will likely find my argument in this essay to be banal. They'll take it as obvious that philosophy should guide life. I want to briefly respond to these concerns.

Philosophy as a way of life should integrate insights from psychology. We must understand how spiritual exercises and other techniques actually impact the people who use them, and how to translate abstract principles into real changes in our lives. We can't understand these issues merely by reflecting on them. Instead, we need rigorous empirical evidence to test whether our strategies achieve the aims that we seek. But questions about the good life have an irreducible normative component. The question "How should I live my life?" is not reducible to the question of how I can increase the amount of positive affect or perception of meaning in my life. Sometimes it's wrong to take certain actions to increase your happiness, sometimes your own happiness is the incorrect thing for you to value, and sometimes there's a gap between what you think is meaningful and what is actually meaningful. Insofar as that's true, it's false that positive psychology gives us a complete answer to the question of how we should live. It's always possible that my goals are mistaken or that my way of responding to others and the world is wrong. Psychology is incapable of identifying more fundamental mistakes about what we ought to value and the content of our obligations. For that reason, philosophical reasoning and reflection are necessary.

At the same time, few philosophers seriously study how to incorporate philosophical teachings into our lives. This is a crucial omission because the available evidence indicates that the impact of philosophy is quite limited. Studying philosophy appears to have few effects on our attitudes and dispositions on average. While philosophy should guide life, it doesn't seem to. I've argued in favor of one motivated hypothesis, inspired by the work of Pierre Hadot, about how to make philosophy more relevant to life. But this hypothesis requires further investigation and support. The more fundamental point is that we must better understand how to integrate philosophy into our lives.

References

Blattman, Christopher, Julian C. Jamison, and Margaret Sheridan. 2017. "Reducing Crime and Violence: Experimental Evidence from Cognitive Behavioral Therapy in Liberia." *American Economic Review* 107, no. 4:1165–1206.

Brennan, Jason. 2010. "Scepticism About Philosophy." *Ratio* 23, no. 1:1–16.

Cooper, John M. 2013. *Pursuits of Wisdom: Six Ways of Life in Ancient Philosophy from Socrates to Plotinus*. Princeton: Princeton University Press.

Epictetus. 2014. *Discourses, Fragments, Handbook*. Translated by Robin Hard. New York: Oxford University Press.

Flynn, Rob, Paul Bellaby, and Miriam Ricci. 2009. "The 'Value-Action Gap' in Public Attitudes Towards Sustainable Energy: The Case of Hydrogen Energy." *Sociological Review* 57, 2 suppl.:159–80.

Garfield, Jay, Stephen Jenkins, and Graham Priest. 2016. "The Śāntideva Passage: Bodhisattvacaryāvatāra VIII. 90–103." In *Moonpaths: Ethics and Emptiness*, edited by The Cowherds, 55–76. New York: Oxford University Press.

Giving What We Can. 2019. "The Giving What We Can Pledge." 2019. https://www.givingwhatwecan.org/pledge/

Goleman, Daniel, and Richard J. Davidson. 2017. *Altered Traits: Science Reveals How Meditation Changes Your Mind, Brain, and Body*. New York: Avery.

Hadot, Pierre. 1995. *Philosophy as a Way of Life: Spiritual Exercises from Socrates to Foucault*. Edited by Arnold Davidson, translated by Michael Chase. Malden, Mass.: Wiley-Blackwell.

_______. 2004. *What Is Ancient Philosophy?* Translated by Michael Chase. Cambridge, Mass.: Harvard University Press.

Heller, Sara B., Anuj K. Shah, Jonathan Guryan, Jens Ludwig, Sendhil Mullainathan, and Harold A. Pollack. 2016. "Thinking, Fast and Slow? Some Field Experiments to Reduce Crime and Dropout in Chicago." *Quarterly Journal of Economics* 132, no. 1:1–54.

Hofmann, Stefan G., Anu Asnaani, Imke J. J. Vonk, Alice T. Sawyer, and Angela Fang. 2012. "The Efficacy of Cognitive Behavioral Therapy: A Review of Meta-Analyses." *Cognitive Therapy and Research* 36, no. 5:427–40.

Irvine, William B. 2008. *A Guide to the Good Life: The Ancient Art of Stoic Joy*. New York: Oxford University Press.

Konow, James. 2017. "Does Studying Ethics Affect Moral Views? An Application to Economic Justice." *Journal of Economic Methodology* 24, no. 2:190–203.

Löhr, Winrich. 2010. "Christianity as Philosophy: Problems and Perspectives of an Ancient Intellectual Project." *Vigiliae Christianae* 64, no. 2:160–88.

MacAskill, William. 2014. "Normative Uncertainty." Ph.D. thesis. University of Oxford.

Magie, David, trans. 1921. *Historia Augusta*. Volume 1. Cambridge, Mass.: Harvard University Press.

May, Todd. 2017. *A Fragile Life: Accepting Our Vulnerability*. Chicago: University of Chicago Press.

Nanamoli, Bhikkhu, and Bhikkhu Bodhi, trans. 1995. *The Middle Length Discourses of the Buddha: A Translation of the Majjhima Nikaya*. Sommerville, Mass.: Wisdom Publications.

Nook, Erik C., Desmond C. Ong, Sylvia A. Morelli, Jason P. Mitchell, and Jamil Zaki. 2016. "Prosocial Conformity: Prosocial Norms Generalize Across Behavior and Empathy." *Personality and Social Psychology Bulletin* 42, no. 8:1045–62.

Parfit, Derek. 1986. *Reasons and Persons*. Oxford: Oxford University Press.

Perrett, Roy W. 2016. *An Introduction to Indian Philosophy*. Cambridge: Cambridge University Press.

Scheffler, Samuel. 2012. "The Normativity of Tradition." In *Equality and Tradition*, 287–311. New York: Oxford University Press.

Schönegger, Philipp, and Johannes Wagner. 2019. "The Moral Behavior of Ethics Professors: A Replication-Extension in German-Speaking Countries." *Philosophical Psychology* 32, no. 4:532–59.

Schwitzgebel, Eric. 2013. "Do Ethics Classes Influence Student Behavior?" https://faculty.ucr.edu/~eschwitz/SchwitzAbs/EthicsClasses.htm

_______. 2019. "Most U.S. and German Ethicists Condemn Meat-Eating (or German Philosophers Think Meat Is the Wurst)." *The Splintered Mind* (blog). March 22. http://schwitzsplinters.blogspot.com/2019/03/most-us-and-german-ethicists-condemn.html

Schwitzgebel, Eric, and Joshua Rust. 2014. "The Moral Behavior of Ethics Professors: Relationships Among Self-Reported Behavior, Expressed Normative Attitude, and Directly Observed Behavior." *Philosophical Psychology* 27, no. 3:293–327.

________. 2016. "The Behavior of Ethicists." In *A Companion to Experimental Philosophy*, edited by Justin Sytsma and Wesley Buckwalter, 225–33. Malden, Mass: Wiley-Blackwell.

Seneca. 2015. *Seneca: Selected Dialogues and Consolations*. Translated by Peter J. Anderson. Indianapolis: Hackett.

Siderits, Mark. 2007. *Buddhism as Philosophy*. Indianapolis: Hackett.

________. 2016. *Personal Identity and Buddhist Philosophy*. 2nd edition. Burlington, Vt.: Routledge.

Singer, Peter. 2009. "An Intellectual Autobiography." In *Peter Singer Under Fire*, edited by Jeffrey Schaler, 1–74. Peru, Ill.: Open Court.

Street, Sharon. 2016. "I-Constructivism in Ethics and the Problem of Attachment and Loss." *Aristotelian Society* suppl. 90, no. 1:161–89.

Streumer, Bart. 2017. *Unbelievable Errors: An Error Theory About All Normative Judgements*. New York: Oxford University Press.

Svoboda, Toby. 2016. "Environmental Philosophy as a Way of Life." *Ethics and the Environment* 21, no. 1:39–60.

PART 3

PEDAGOGY

CHAPTER 15

ON THE BENEFITS OF PHILOSOPHY AS A WAY OF LIFE IN A GENERAL INTRODUCTORY COURSE

JAKE WRIGHT

1. Introduction

Philosophy as a way of life, or PWOL, is, in many important respects, quite different from what Stephen Grimm (2019) has called "standard operating procedure" philosophy, or SOPP. For example, SOPP often views the discipline as a series of discrete, though often interconnected, problems and subproblems. We see this frequently in our research specialties, where one may focus intently on the particulars of causal explanation, material composition, the nature of warrant, and so forth, in an effort to arrive at the fact of the matter within these comparatively narrow domains. By contrast, PWOL often focuses on broader themes of the good life and how one ought to live in pursuit of one's own good life. This distinction between consideration of discrete problems and a broad investigation into one's conception of the good life is becoming increasingly clear as a number of instructors move toward PWOL-focused philosophy courses. At the conclusion of such courses, students are often expected to articulate their own vision of the good life and how they can live in accordance with that view. Whereas SOPP-based courses begin and end with consideration of discrete questions, PWOL-based courses use such problems as instrumental tools to motivate personal growth.

As a result of the differences between these two approaches, if one were to reframe one's SOPP-based course to function as a PWOL-based course the resulting course would look and operate quite differently. This is especially true at the introductory level, where general introductory and survey

Philosophy as a Way of Life: Historical, Contemporary, and Pedagogical Perspectives.
Edited by James M. Ambury, Tushar Irani, and Kathleen Wallace.

Published 2021 by John Wiley & Sons Ltd.

courses seem especially amenable to SOPPorific smorgasbords, with a bit of epistemology here, some philosophy of religion there, and often little effort to connect the units together. Put somewhat differently, the switch from SOPP to PWOL is not a small lift from an instructional point of view. Further, while there has been increasing discussion regarding *how* to teach a PWOL-based course, little, if any, scholarship has been developed on the benefits of such a course. Thus, an explicit articulation of these benefits, as well as consideration of potential challenges associated with such courses, seems warranted.

This essay presents such a discussion, focusing especially on general introductory courses. I argue that, compared to SOPP-based general introductions, PWOL-based introductions have at least four benefits. PWOL courses are better positioned to (1) incorporate high-impact pedagogical practices, (2) draw on extant literature on first-year transitions from high school to college, (3) allow students to more explicitly think like a philosopher—that is, engage in successful philosophical practice—and (4) give novice students a holistic understanding of philosophy's importance both generally and to their own lives.

My discussion proceeds as follows. First, I begin with a discussion of general introduction to philosophy courses and their aims in section 2. Section 3 briefly sketches what a PWOL-based general introduction might look like. I next discuss the aforementioned benefits of a PWOL-based general introduction in section 4, followed by consideration of concerns in section 5. Finally, I present concluding remarks in section 6.

2. General Introduction to Philosophy and Its Goals

Perhaps there is no more challenging philosophy course to teach than a general introduction. This is for two reasons. First, the course's potential scope is essentially limitless. Second, the course's introductory nature requires us to assume no formal background or philosophical ability among enrolled students. In addition to these challenges, general introductory courses often represent the only formal exposure to academic philosophy that most enrollees will experience; the majority of students in the class will not go on to take another philosophy course. Given these facts, it is worthwhile to begin by reflecting on the aims of our general introductory courses. This section considers implications raised by the scope of general introductory courses, the assumed abilities of students enrolled in such courses, and how we ought to approach the idea of successful general introductory courses.

2.1. The Scope of the General Introductory Course

Often, a course's scope is neatly circumscribed by the course title, the course description, or both. For example, students will have a clear idea of what to expect from courses with titles like "Contemporary Moral Issues," "History and Philosophy of Science," "Intermediate Logic," and "Modern Philosophy from Descartes to Kant." By contrast, "Introduction to Philosophy" establishes no subdisciplinary boundaries that the course may not transgress. One could conceivably include *any* philosophical topic, provided the topic is presented at a level appropriate for introductory students. As a result, general introductory courses can vary wildly not only from institution to institution but also from instructor to instructor and occasionally from semester to semester.

One side-effect of this scope—where the number of potential topics is dramatically constrained not by content but by factors like the length of the class, instructor comfort, or perceived importance—is that instructors are regularly forced to make editorial judgments vis-à-vis course material. Professor Smith may include a unit on feminist philosophy that Professor Jones omits in favor of Confucian philosophy. Dr. Brown may include neither, instead incorporating a unit on ethics. In each case, Smith, Jones, and Brown presumably have worthwhile and defensible reasons for these decisions. Perhaps Smith and Jones omit a unit on ethics on the grounds that an introductory ethics course is regularly offered. Perhaps they chose feminist philosophy over Confucian philosophy (or vice versa) out of a relative comfort or discomfort with such subfields, or chose to include them out of a commitment to including underrepresented philosophies. Perhaps Brown included a unit on ethics out of a belief in the importance of ethics and in recognition of the relatively low odds that enrolled students will subsequently enroll in an ethics course.

In each of the above cases, the sort of curricular judgments made by Smith, Jones, and Brown with regard to their respective classes is neither unusual nor controversial. As philosophy instructors, we might individually disagree with their respective decisions, but it seems difficult to argue that their respective courses could not constitute a successful general introduction to the discipline per se.

If one must start with *all of philosophy* and edit one's course down accordingly, one will need to consider how the course is structured. In the case of general introductory courses, a common framework is to structure the course in terms of discrete units based on particular philosophical problems or questions. For example, one might have a unit on epistemology followed by a unit on God's existence, followed by the problem of free will. Because most philosophers are engaged in SOPP in their professional lives, these units are typically presented accordingly as discrete, often unconnected units seeking to answer a particular philosophical question. A unit on God's existence, for example, becomes more narrowly focused on whether there is good evidence for the Abrahamic God's existence, which, in practice, is more narrowly focused on whether students ought to accept or reject a subset of arguments in favor of or in opposition to that of God's existence. Once the unit is completed, it is not uncommon for the instructor and the course to move on, never to speak of the unit again or, at best, vaguely wave at some ideas from a previous unit while moving on to the next problem.

The end result in such SOPP-based courses is that a general introduction to the discipline is often presented as a sampler platter of various discrete philosophical issues that do not form a coherent whole. As I argue later, this "sampler platter" structure limits the ability of students to see not only how their respective views in one area influence their views elsewhere but also how these discrete problems directly impact their lives. It is not difficult for us, as professional philosophers, to understand how one's commitment to physicalism rules out certain options with respect to the concept of a nonphysical God or immaterial soul, but such connections do not seem especially clear to our introductory students.

2.2. *Student Skills and Background Knowledge*

The second key challenge, faced by introductory courses of all types, is the fact that introductory students are novices with no assumed disciplinary knowledge or skills. Their status as novices impacts how the course is taught because such students neither understand the current state of any debate nor possess the ability to successfully engage in the debate. Thus, much of any general introduction must be dedicated to skills development via basic argumentative analysis (Cashmore 2015), paper-writing strategies (Burkard 2017; Cashmore 2015; Turner 2013), metacognitive development (Stokes 2012), and so on, while presenting manageable chunks of limited debate so that students are not overwhelmed. It would be inappropriate, for example, to begin one's semester with the latest issue of *Synthese* and ask students for their thoughts.

In addition to the significant time that must be devoted to skills development, the status of students as novices significantly impacts the degree to which they are capable of truly engaging in what one might call objectively meaningful philosophical investigation. By this, I don't mean to suggest that students' efforts are meaningless; I think that student progress at the introductory level is both vital and meaningful. Instead, I mean something like this: It is unlikely that introductory students will be able to settle, once and for all, whether, say, explanations can be distinctively mathematical. In other words, while students leave with a greater understanding of particular issues than they did when they began the course, they will not extend the boundaries of disciplinary knowledge. One simply cannot go from zero to expert in a matter of weeks, and our introductory courses recognize this by the way in which they are structured. This is, in part, why starting with the latest issue of *Synthese* is inappropriate. Not only do students lack the skills necessary to engage with the articles in that issue, they also lack an appropriate knowledge of philosophical debates themselves to be able to successfully engage at an expert level.

The end result of this novice status is that what we can reasonably expect from students in a general introductory course will rarely constitute good philosophy. Students will make basic mistakes, fail to anticipate important objections, and present well-worn arguments as somehow novel. They will be unable to engage successfully with particularly technical or cutting-edge arguments. They will, however, be in a position to make meaningful personal or subjective progress, in terms both of their individual understanding of various philosophical positions and their view of these positions.

2.3. The Successful General Introductory Philosophy Course

The concerns raised in the preceding subsections naturally prompt the question of what a successful general introduction course *does*. Clearly, success cannot hinge on successfully introducing all of philosophy. Neither does it seem that a successful general introduction requires coverage of certain core material or views. If this were the case, we would expect some formal set of APA guidelines outlining such standards and expectations. For example, in chemistry, the American Chemical Society has engaged in a nearly ten-year project to identify content that arises at varying stages of a chemistry curriculum (Holme et al. 2018; Holme, Luxford, and Murphy 2015; Marek et al. 2018; Raker, Holme, and Murphy 2013), mapping "Anchoring Concepts and Enduring Understandings [that] are consistent across the undergraduate curriculum" (Raker, Holme, and Murphy 2013, 1115). Though this chemistry project is not intended to provide a set-in-stone collection of topics that *must* be covered, even such a rigorous, systematic project to outline common areas of core coverage from course to course has not been undertaken in philosophy.

It seems more plausible, therefore, that the successful general introduction develops particular skills and dispositions. Whether one thinks of these as specific, enumerated outcomes like the list of learning objectives found at the beginning of many syllabi or the development of more abstract goals like "the ability to think philosophically," or a combination of both, the sorts of things we say we want students to actually leave our class with are not content related. Put differently, *what is* engaged with in a successful general introduction is far less vital than *how* it is engaged with.

One way of seeing this is to imagine what you would think if you were to meet, ten years after teaching them, some students who enrolled in your class but did not go on to study philosophy as a major or minor. Would you be more disappointed if they were unable to craft Gettier cases or present a coherent version of Jackson's knowledge argument, or would you be more disappointed if they clearly did not take time to think critically or consider important questions? While I can only speak for myself, I imagine that I am not alone in preferring dispositional success over content-retention-based success.

3. Introduction to Philosophy as a Way of Life

At this point, it may be helpful to say a bit about how a general introduction course can be reframed as a PWOL-based course. I have little novel to say in this section, mostly in deference to excellent PWOL courses that already exist both at the introductory level—for example, the University of Notre Dame's "God and the Good Life" ("God and the Good Life" 2019), Suffolk University's "Meaning of Life" (Cheraksova 2014), and the University of California at Santa Cruz's "Introduction to Philosophy as a Way of Life" (Donley, Haug, and Rule 2018)—and at more advanced levels—for example, Wesleyan University's "Philosophy as a Way of Life" (Angle 2011) and Yale-NUS College's "Philosophy as a Way of Life" (Walker 2018).

For such courses, a more-or-less standard framework has emerged in which students examine a series of explicitly interconnected topics framed around questions of value, the good life, and how one ought to live. "God and the Good Life" (2019), for example, asks students to consider four basic questions: How should I decide what to believe? What are my moral obligations? Should I follow a religion? And, what will it take for my life to be meaningful? Throughout PWOL-based courses, students are frequently asked to engage in traditional philosophical skill development (for example, close reading and argument reconstruction) while also engaging in explicit reflection on how the course's questions and topics relate to their efforts to live well. At the conclusion of the course, students are commonly assigned a final assessment that asks them to synthesize what they have learned into a coherent, personalized vision of the good life. In short, they are asked to present and defend an account of flourishing, as well as say how they plan to live in accordance with the values that lead to such flourishing.

At this point, PWOL-based introductory courses may sound like SOPP-based courses, but with a bit of self-reflection and more explicit links between various sections of the course. All one need do, if this is the case, is take one's SOPP-based intro and gussy it up with a bit of reflection and brief notes on why one's stance on *p* might affect one's view of *q*. As Grimm (2019) noted at the inaugural "Philosophy as a Way of Life" conference at the University of Notre Dame, one could plausibly make a case for *any* topic's impact on one's conception of the good life. Indeed, one could argue passionately and persuasively, as Grimm did, that our ability to engage in such examination is, by itself, a powerful force that drives human flourishing.

While this may be true, what distinguishes PWOL-based general introductions is the courses' ability to adequately capture these connections at a level that introductory students are able to make between the course, the good life, and their own lives, even with the expert guidance of professional philosophers. Thus, the sorts of questions included in a PWOL-based general introduction will likely obviously tie into how one conceptualizes the good life—perhaps, in the view of instructors, painfully so.

4. The Benefits of "Introduction to Philosophy as a Way of Life"

My primary goal in this discussion is to articulate the benefits of a PWOL-based general introduction, relative to a SOPP-based introduction. As I argue below, these benefits are both philosophical and pedagogical. Philosophically speaking, PWOL-based general introductions give students a vital chance to not only think like philosophers but also *live* like them. By so doing, PWOL-based introductions represent a particularly powerful defense of philosophy's value to such students via the course's overt focus on philosophy's implications for their own flourishing. Pedagogically, PWOL-based courses present unique opportunities for students to think like a disciplinarian and for instructors to incorporate high-impact practices while drawing on pedagogical principles that have been shown to be especially useful for first-year students and students in transition.[1]

4.1. Philosophy as a Way of Life and the Defense of Philosophy's Intrinsic Value

One of the greatest challenges we face when teaching philosophy at the introductory level to novice students, most of whom will not pursue formal philosophical study beyond the current course and are simply present out of a desire to check some box on a list of degree requirements, is to explain philosophy's value both broadly and within students' own lives.

As a professional philosopher, I'm always shocked when nonphilosophers remark to me that their minds don't work in a philosophical way. For example, at my home institution, first-year students are given a choice of continuing with a second semester of philosophy or a second semester of sociology. Because my campus is quite small, I often have the chance to discuss students' choices informally with them. By far, the most common response I get from students who showed great skill as novice philosophers is that they enjoyed the class but they are opting for sociology over philosophy because their mind "just doesn't work that way." Similarly, when other adults find out I am a philosophy professor, they frequently remark that they took a philosophy course in college, but it wasn't for them. Again, their mind "just didn't work that way."

[1] I discuss such practices later in this section (4.2.1. High-impact practices), but as a brief description, *high-impact practices* like capstone projects and collaborative learning are teaching and learning practices that have been widely shown to increase learning for students from a variety of backgrounds (Kuh 2008).

What shocks me about such responses is that philosophical thinking, writ large, is neither different from nor harder than any other thinking. As a colleague of mine describes the practice of philosophy to his students, it is, in essence, the act of thinking in slow motion. Such responses are especially distressing when given by my former students; I know their minds work that way because I've experienced their minds working that way firsthand!

One possible cause of this disconnect is the nature of philosophical debate itself at the introductory level. Another possible cause is the highly specialized, problematized nature of SOPP. A third possibility is the lack of a clear connection between the practice of philosophy and one's own life. PWOL-based introductory courses address each of these concerns.

4.1.1. The nature of the debate at the introductory level. The presupposition that novice students have no background in formal philosophical practice has important implications for how one is able to teach any introductory course. One of the most important implications is that students are not equipped to engage deeply with any philosophical debate in the sense that they lack the skills, background knowledge, and time to get up to speed on the contemporary state of the debate for any philosophical problem over the course of a semester. Thus, in a particular sense, the goal of introductory courses from a content perspective is not to bring students to this point but rather to familiarize them with the broad outlines of a particular debate (Wright 2019). One curious effect of this is that students are unlikely to make definitive objective progress with respect to any philosophical problem. They are, however, in a position to make personal progress in their understanding of various questions and how they relate to their lives.

PWOL-based courses are especially well suited for student progress in this area precisely because PWOL is intrinsically focused on student personal progress. If students are asked to philosophically defend how they should live and have started the course with no formal background in the practice of philosophy, successfully completing the course seems to require that students use the course not as an opportunity to become content masters or expert philosophers but as an opportunity to develop a clearer sense of what they value and how they should live in accordance with those values. Put differently, success in a PWOL-based general introduction is predicated on personal progress. They know that they can think like a philosopher because they have done so in response to vital questions related to their own lives.

4.1.2. The problematized nature of SOPP and the connection between philosophy and one's own life. Regarding concerns about SOPP's specialized, problematized nature and the lack of connection between SOPP-based topics and the good life, recall Grimm's earlier point that essentially any philosophical problem can be refocused on questions of flourishing and the good life. While this is certainly the case, such connections are not immediately obvious to novice philosophy students (and occasionally practiced professionals). For example, how would a philosophical novice relate the question of distinctively mathematical explanations to their conception of the good life? I might do so by noting that explanations in general have important implications for what we can know and how we can predict—and if necessary, intervene in—events. These abilities then rule in or rule out certain beliefs and actions as appropriate, which in turn rule some goals in or out. If explanations cannot be distinctively mathematical, a certain set of beliefs and dispositions is therefore ruled out. But introductory students do not see this, nor do I think they could be made to see this without a herculean effort on the part of the instructor. Without such effort, many discrete philosophical problems are little more than so much esoterica. The drawback of SOPP-based introductory courses is that such an effort to connect material with students' lives either is not made or falls flat.

By contrast, PWOL makes the connection between course materials and students' lives explicit by examining material that cannot help but inform the views students have of their own lives. By focusing the course on questions like "Should I practice a religion?" and "Is my death bad for me?" philosophical questions are explicitly framed not only as a search for truth but also as an interrogation of how one's justified beliefs impact one's own life.

In my experience, students find topics interesting to the extent that they are able to relate to them. In end-of-semester surveys, my students regularly rate questions about life's meaning and God's existence as the most interesting and enjoyable units. One advantage of PWOL-based general introductions is that the connection between philosophy and one's everyday life is made explicit. If the course centers on what the individual student ought to value and how the individual student ought to live his or her life using philosophy as the lens through which such investigation takes place, the value of philosophy cannot help but be clear to students.

Such an explicit connection between philosophical practice and students' own lives is more than a motivating pedagogical tool. It is a powerful defense of the value of philosophy per se. My institution is not the only university to require a philosophy course while offering neither a major nor a minor. Even at institutions that grant such degrees, the overwhelming majority of introductory students will not go on to obtain a philosophy degree. Indeed, most will not go on to take a second philosophy course. If one is studying to be a chemist or a consultant, it can be difficult to see why philosophy requirements exist. But by focusing the class on using philosophy to help students sort out important questions in their own lives, often in a way that other disciplines simply cannot, students are able to experience the value of philosophy directly.

4.2. The Pedagogical Benefits of Introduction to Philosophy as a Way of Life

In addition to the purely philosophical benefits of PWOL-based general introductions, there are also a number of pedagogical benefits. Most notably, PWOL-based general introductions are more naturally able to incorporate high-impact pedagogical practices, implement skill-building strategies found to be especially effective for first-year students, and allow students to think like a disciplinarian (that is, think and practice like a philosopher).

In most cases, as I discuss below, it is not the case that PWOL-based courses are uniquely suited to achieve these benefits. Rather, such courses are more likely or better positioned to achieve these benefits, relative to SOPP-based introductions. Put differently, it is certainly the case that innovative assignments are often content neutral, but that doesn't mean that certain pedagogical choices, like teaching a PWOL-based general introduction, can't be more or less amenable to such assignments.

4.2.1. High-impact practices. High-impact practices are teaching and learning practices that have been widely shown to increase learning for students from a variety of backgrounds (Kuh 2008). While these practices are often discussed at the curricular level (for example, in learning communities that encourage students to discuss so-called big questions in the context of their wider course load), there is no reason in principle why their primary goals cannot be realized at the course level. Though philosophy courses are generally able to integrate high-impact practices, PWOL-based general introductions are especially well suited to do so.

For example, the aforementioned learning communities that encourage discussion of big questions can naturally be integrated into PWOL-based introductions. In such communities, students work closely as a group to explore questions whose importance extends beyond the classroom. It is hard to think of such a question with more obvious import than what one should value and how one should live. Further, it's clear that the consideration of such questions benefits from regular discussion, rather than relying solely on solitary meditation. Thus, a natural pedagogical strategy for a PWOL-based course would be to regularly encourage students to work in groups when thinking through these bigger questions.

Similarly, a course that asks students to articulate a view of the good life can also promote diversity by exposing students to a variety of conceptions of the good life as defended by their fellow students. One advantage of teaching a philosophical debate within a philosophy class is the ability to expose students to views and arguments that they might not share or might even fundamentally oppose (Besong 2016). Framing this exploration in the context of students themselves being asked to articulate their view of a fundamental question for which there exists a wide variety of defensible answers enhances this goal by requiring students to engage not only with views that are different from their own but also with individuals who hold such views.

Both the creation of learning communities and strategies amenable to the promotion of diversity speak to the course's ability to incorporate collaborative work into the course. As Kuh (2008) notes, there is a great deal of benefit in students listening seriously to their fellow students, especially when those students' experiences are different from their own, and such collaboration has been a hallmark of publicly available PWOL-based courses. Indeed, the recent "Philosophy as a Way of Life" conference was a veritable cornucopia of such assignments, with presentations and discussions of debates ("God and the Good Life" 2019), games (Cheraksova 2014), and opportunities to create visual representations of students' views on a particular topic (Christy 2019).

Further, at a minimum, structuring the course so that the final unit is a synthesis of previous units seems to naturally lend itself to collaboration, even if such collaboration does not take place within the bounds of a formal assessment. Asking students to finish the course by constructing their own meaning would make little sense if that construction was largely facilitated via the instructor's lecture. On the other hand, asking students to work through these issues together and respond to each other's ideas seems like a much more natural fit for such a unit. Such collaborative work could easily be extended to reflective assignments scattered throughout the middle section of the course, with students discussing and responding to one other's takeaways, questions, and insights.

4.2.2. Situated skill development. If the mark of a successful general introductory course is skill based and dispositional, it is useful to consider how best to develop the sorts of skills that we want to develop, like critical thinking, argument construction and analysis, and philosophical writing. Research on this issue exists across the scholarship of teaching and learning, but literature from the perspective of first-year academic seminar courses, often explicitly aimed solely at skill development, is especially useful because the students in such courses are so likely to be first-year students.

This research demonstrates that skill development is most effective when it is practiced rather than presented (Zerr and Bjerke 2016) and is contextualized in student construction of meaning on a topic of interest to them (Brent 2005; Kenny et al. 1998), a finding noted throughout teaching and learning scholarship (Abrantes, Seabra, and Lages 2007; Bergin and Reilly 2005; Pintrich and De Groot 1990; Yuretich et al. 2001). As Doug Brent notes, "The road to academic literacy involves pedagogies of integration, extended process, and grounding in genuine inquiry" (2005, 258).

In other words, it is not enough to ask students to simply learn how, for example, to take notes, nor is it enough to simply give students an exercise in which they are asked to take notes using whatever method has been demonstrated. For maximum effectiveness, students must be put in a position where their notetaking skills are a necessary component of their own knowledge construction for a question of interest to them. Thus, developing philosophical skills and dispositions should ideally take place within a context of interest to students where student success at applying these skills has a direct bearing on their own knowledge construction. It is again difficult to think of a topic of more interest to students than how they ought to live their own lives, so it is again difficult to think of a philosophical topic that would be better positioned to develop these skills in novice students.

4.2.3. The ability to think like a disciplinarian. One of the most frustrating aspects of teaching philosophy, especially at the introductory level, is that it can often be unclear whether students are genuinely engaging in successful—though nascent—disciplinary practice or whether they are merely engaging in what Meyer and Land (2005) call mimicry, simply regurgitating what students believe the instructors want to hear. Such mimicry is common in a variety of disciplines and has been explicitly noted in philosophy (Besong 2016; Momeyer 1995). While disciplinary practice represents genuine understanding of critical disciplinary threshold concepts (Meyer and Land 2005), mimicry is not indicative of any genuine philosophical learning beyond a student's potential ability to suss out what the instructor is looking for. Put in terms of Bloom's taxonomy, students who think like a disciplinarian are creating, while students engaged in mimicry are often at best evaluating or analyzing. At the introductory level especially, however, the distinction between these two can be difficult to distinguish because students' lack of disciplinary content knowledge can make it difficult for even more gifted students to extend their analysis beyond the sorts of basic moves contained in literature they have read for class.

For example, suppose introductory students are assigned an essay on abortion, having read and discussed standard introductory-level sources like Judith Jarvis Thomson's "A Defense of Abortion," Don Marquis's "Why Abortion Is Immoral," and Michael Tooley's "Abortion and Infanticide." Given the lack of knowledge among students with respect to the current state of the debate and their lack of disciplinary background knowledge, the student who genuinely engages in thoughtful philosophical practice and the student who mimics such practice can be difficult to distinguish. Both will likely stick close to the assigned readings and class discussion, make the same sorts of moves, and advance roughly the same arguments. Yet it is only thoughtful practice that allows for genuine understanding, both of the material itself and of how to engage with the material philosophically.

This ability to think like a disciplinarian has several pedagogical benefits, including motivating students to create their own knowledge and make novel distinctions (Langer 1993), to distinguish between the stability of their own internal views and the stability of consensus surrounding the underlying phenomenon (Langer 2000), and to creatively and spontaneously apply information they have learned (Langer et al. 1989). By contrast, more traditional pedagogical strategies (for example, strategies common to SOPP-based courses) can inhibit student learning of critical threshold concepts (Land et al. 2005). In short, thinking like a disciplinarian makes students better able to understand disciplinary threshold concepts—in this case, the sorts of skills we seek to develop in our students.

PWOL-based general introductions are better able to position students to think like disciplinarians. The sorts of questions PWOL-based courses ask often diverge significantly from mere repetition or rearrangement of content knowledge by asking students to synthesize course material and apply it to their own lives. For example, some PWOL-based courses ask students to reflect not only on their view of the good life but also on what in their own lives is preventing them from achieving the good life. In other PWOL-based courses students are asked to live like a member of a particular philosophical school for a week and critically reflect on the experience. Such requirements make it easier for instructors to distinguish between genuine cases of successful practice and mimicry. This distinction encourages genuine philosophical engagement in two ways.

First, if students recognize that successful completion of the course cannot be accomplished (or can be accomplished less well or less reliably) via mimicry, they will be disincentivized to engage in such mimicry and instead be motivated to engage in genuine disciplinary practice, even if their underlying motivation is to earn the grade they think is necessary and move on.

Second, by providing assignments that are better able to distinguish between genuine engagement and mere mimicry, instructors can craft assessment tools like rubrics that more clearly delineate for students what the difference between engagement and mimicry looks like in a successful assignment. In other words, instructors are better positioned to help students see in advance what sorts of submissions will lead to genuine engagement and therefore a better grade.

5. Concerns About "Introduction to Philosophy as a Way of Life"

Though I have argued there are a number of philosophical and pedagogical benefits to a PWOL-based general introductory course, there are also concerns in need of consideration, especially if many of the pedagogical benefits discussed above are not exclusive to PWOL-based courses. It may be worthwhile to design a SOPP-based course, even if the pedagogical benefits are less fully realized or require greater effort to realize if the drawbacks of PWOL-based courses are significant enough.

In this section, I address two potential concerns with PWOL-based general introductions: the concern that PWOL-based courses are ultimately ethics courses and the need for traditional philosophical training within a philosophy class.

5.1. "Philosophy as a Way of Life" Is Ultimately an Ethics Course, Not a General Introduction

As described above, one may reasonably conclude that a course focused on concepts of the good life and how to live in accordance with one's values may be an appropriate introductory course, but it is more clearly "Introduction to Ethics" than "Introduction to Philosophy." There are, I think, two responses to such an objection.

In the first case, let us grant the objection. At a certain level, it is difficult to see what rides on its truth. "Introduction to Ethics" is a common introductory philosophy course at nearly every institution and is often as or nearly as popular when compared to general introductory courses. If a particular instructor feels that the course structure outlined here would be better suited for an ethics course, then such a course could be straightforwardly designed and largely retain the benefits discussed above.

My view, however, is that the proposed course structure will function better as a general introduction because the sorts of questions one must answer to articulate a vision of the good life extend beyond ethics. Thus, relying on an "Introduction to Ethics" course, rather than an "Introduction to Philosophy" course, as the lens through which students interrogate questions of meaning and value in their own lives will likely leave some important feature out simply on the grounds that consideration of that feature does not constitute ethics.

For example, suppose one wishes to consider whether the good life is one led in strict obedience to God's commands. Such a view is often considered within introductory ethics courses—at least as a normative ethical theory—and the pros and cons of such a view are discussed. What is typically left behind in ethical discussions of divine-command theory, however, is whether we have good reason to suppose that God exists. This is typically because such a question is metaphysical, rather than ethical, in nature; it is assumed out of necessity that students at least have a view on the matter and ideally have a defensible argument in favor of that view. But because the course is an introductory one, such an assumption is largely inappropriate even if necessary. Introductory courses, by their nature, presuppose no formal background in a particular discipline, which means that, absent some good reason to believe to the contrary—for example, an intro-course prerequisite where the instructor knows that philosophy of religion has been discussed—we ought not assume that students have thought systematically about such topics.

This inability to assume that students have considered arguments for and against, in this case, God's existence, can have profound effects on students' views of the good life and how it ought to be lived. After all, if there is no God, one probably ought not to live according to God's commands. Yet an ethics course is not really in a position to engage in a sustained interrogation of arguments for and against God's existence in the way that a general introduction can. "Introduction to Philosophy as a Way of Life" may ultimately lean more heavily in an ethical direction than many other general introductory courses, but its ability to step back and investigate other areas of philosophy offers a richer tapestry from which to pull than a dedicated ethics course.

5.2. The Need for Traditional Philosophy in a General Introduction

A second concern one might raise is that by focusing on PWOL rather than SOPP, a general introductory course will, at some level, stop being about philosophical goals like the search for truth and instead devolve into relativistic navel-gazing that hardly constitutes philosophy. If we are to offer a general introduction to philosophy, it must involve philosophy as it is traditionally construed.

Setting aside the view that introductory courses are not fruitful avenues for the investigation of the sorts of truths philosophers seek (Wright 2019), such concerns are understandable, especially if one is unfamiliar with PWOL and its aims within the classroom. They represent, however, either a misunderstanding about how to successfully engage in PWOL or a legitimate—but reasonable—disagreement about the relative focus of SOPP- and PWOL-based course content.

In the case of how to engage in PWOL, it may be helpful to think about what is meant by philosophy as a way of life. As Grimm (2019) has characterized the project, the focus of PWOL is twofold. First, one might ask what it is to have a *way of life*, which is a genuinely philosophical question worthy of consideration in a PWOL-based course. Second, one might ask what it means to have a *philosophical* way of life. There are genuine disagreements about this, for example between Pierre Hadot's view of PWOL as a series of philosophically oriented exercises (Hadot 1995) and John Cooper's view of a life based on a commitment to reason (Cooper 2012), but what is inescapable from any such view is that successful practice of philosophy is a prerequisite for engaging in PWOL. Thus, one cannot successfully practice PWOL either in the classroom or in one's own life without the ability to engage in SOPP-based philosophy at some level because living a philosophical life requires the ability to engage in conceptual analysis, argument evaluation, and so on. Thus, any minimally satisfactory PWOL-based introduction will engage in SOPP at some level; to do otherwise would remove the philosophy from philosophy as a way of life.

If one accepts the view that SOPP will necessarily be incorporated at some level into a PWOL-based introduction, the concern voiced above comes down to the *degree* to which SOPP is incorporated, rather than a concern about its total exclusion. To such concerns, I return to the idea of editorial judgment expressed when outlining PWOL-based general introductions earlier in this essay. Reasonable philosophers can disagree on how much SOPP is enough (or too much) based on their individual goals, the abilities of their students, and so forth, and it seems that, other things being equal, we ought to have no complaint with such assessments in our colleagues' own courses. But the reverse is also true; if a colleague views a PWOL-based general introduction as less desirable in its treatment of SOPP, that does not seem to be a convincing indication that such a course is insufficient, irresponsible, or unphilosophical.

6. Conclusion

Philosophy is a rich discipline that can critically inform our views of ourselves, the world around us, and how we ought to live. Unfortunately, few students get the opportunity to see this because the only course most students enroll in is a problematized general introduction that has little to say about questions of meaning and value. Framing one's introductory course via the lens of PWOL is an opportunity to refocus the course in a way that brings such questions front and center. Doing so has a number of benefits, both philosophical and pedagogical. Most notably in my view, a PWOL-based general introduction represents a forceful defense of the power of philosophy to contribute to leading a good life by providing the opportunity to engage in investigations vital to students' own lives. This is in addition to pedagogical benefits like the enhanced ability to engage in high-impact practices, situate skill development so that students are more likely to succeed, and engage in meaningful disciplinary practice.

Throughout the inaugural "Philosophy as a Way of Life" conference, speakers frequently employed metaphors distinguishing between tourists, travelers, and natives. Two key distinctions that separated the groups were the time one spent engaged in a particular place or culture and one's willingness to step off the well-trodden path to seek one's own experiences. Tourists, for example, often stay with the guide or visit only well-known locations over brief visits, while travelers linger longer and seek out their own adventures. With enough time and exposure, such travelers may even become natives or something like natives.

Traditional SOPP-based introductions function much more analogously to tour guides, shepherding students from an exhibit on epistemology here to the philosophy-of-mind wing of the museum there. PWOL-based courses, on the other hand, invite students to become philosophical travelers, immersing themselves in philosophical practice even as it leads them off the beaten path of more traditional introductory offerings. They may never become natives like us—indeed, they are unlikely to engage in such disciplinary travel again during their education—but like travelers whose life is forever changed by their backpacking or study abroad or extended stay, a course focused on philosophy as a way of life can give students an experience whose contours positively influence their lives and how they live them. In my view, at least, it is hard to see how a general introduction could be more successful.

Acknowledgments

I am indebted to the many participants at the inaugural "Philosophy as a Way of Life" workshop for their presentations, discussion, and insights; the helpful suggestions of two anonymous referees; Xavier Prat-Resina for his discussion of chemical education standards; and my students for their good humor as I have integrated these practices into my own teaching.

References

Abrantes, José Luís, Cláudia Seabra, and Luís Filipe Lages. 2007. "Pedagogical Affect, Student Interest, and Learning Performance." *Journal of Business Research* 60, no. 9:960–64.

Angle, Stephen. 2011. "PHIL 221: Philosophy as a Way of Life (Syllabus)." Wesleyan University. https://wesfiles.wesleyan.edu/courses/syllabi/1119-sangle-013195-321.pdf.

Bergin, Susan, and Ronan Reilly. 2005. "The Influence of Motivation and Comfort-Level on Learning to Program." In *Proceedings of the 17th Annual Psychology of Programming Interest Group*, edited by Pablo Romero, Judith Good, Edgar Acosta Chapero, and Sallyann Bryant, 293–304. Brighton, U.K.: Psychology of Programming Interest Group.

Besong, Brian. 2016. "Teaching the Debate." *Teaching Philosophy* 39, no. 4:401–12. https://doi.org/10.5840/teachphil2016112256.

Brent, Doug. 2005. "Reinventing WAC (Again): The First-Year Seminar and Academic Literacy." *College Composition and Communication* 57, no. 2:253.

Burkard, Anne. 2017. "Everyone Just Has Their Own Opinion: Assessing Strategies for Reacting to Students' Skepticism About Philosophy." *Teaching Philosophy* 40, no. 3:297–322. https://doi.org/10.5840/teachphil2017101773.

Cashmore, Sarah. 2015. "Changing Values in Teaching and Learning Philosophy: A Comparison of Historic and Current Education Approaches." *Teaching Philosophy* 38, no. 2:297–322. https://doi.org/10.5840/teachphil201532634.

Cheraksova, Evgenia. 2014. "Philosophy 235: Meaning of Life (Syllabus)." Suffolk University. http://meaningoflife.cherkasova.org/wp-content/uploads/2014/05/Meaning-of-Life_Web-Syllabus_2014.pdf.

Christy, Justin. 2019. "Peer-Led Dialogue and Philosophy as a Way of Life." Paper presented at the inaugural Mellon "Philosophy as a Way of Life" Workshop, University of Notre Dame, June 17.

Cooper, John M. 2012. *Pursuits of Wisdom: Six Ways of Life in Ancient Philosophy from Socrates to Plotinus*. Princeton: Princeton University Press.

Donley, David, Steven Haug, and Thomas Rule. 2018. "Introduction to Philosophy as a Way of Life (Syllabus)." University of California at Santa Cruz. https://summer.ucsc.edu/courses/course-syllabi/2018/2018-phil-11-donley.pdf.

"God and the Good Life." 2019. University of Notre Dame. https://godandgoodlife.nd.edu/.

Grimm, Stephen. 2019. "What Is Philosophy as a Way of Life? Why Philosophy as a Way of Life?" Paper presented at the inaugural Mellon "Philosophy as a Way of Life" Workshop, University of Notre Dame, June 17.

Hadot, Pierre. 1995. *Philosophy as a Way of Life: Spiritual Exercises from Socrates to Foucault*. Edited and with an introduction by Arnold I. Davidson. Oxford: Oxford University Press.

Holme, Thomas, Cynthia Luxford, and Kristen Murphy. 2015. "Updating the General Chemistry Anchoring Concepts Content Map." *Journal of Chemical Education* 92, no. 6:1115–16. https://doi.org/10.1021/ed500712k.

Holme, Thomas, Jessica Reed, Jeffrey Raker, and Kristen Murphy. 2018. "The ACS Exams Institute Undergraduate Chemistry Anchoring Concepts Content Map IV: Physical Chemistry." *Journal of Chemical Education* 95, no. 2:238–41. https://doi.org/10.1021/acs.jchemed.7b00531.

Kenny, Shirley Strum, Bruce Alberts, Wayne Booth, Milton Glaser, Charles Glassick, Stanley Ikenberry, Kathleen Hall Jameson, et al. 1998. *Reinventing Undergraduate Education: A Blueprint for America's Research Universities*. Stony Brook, N.Y.: Boyer Commission on Educating Undergraduates in the Research University.

Kuh, George. 2008. *High-Impact Educational Practices: What They Are, Who Has Access to Them, and Why They Matter*. Washington, D.C.: AAC&U.

Land, Ray, Glynis Cousin, Jan Meyer, and Peter Davies. 2005. "Threshold Concepts and Troublesome Knowledge (3): Implications for Course Design and Evaluation." In *Improving Student Learning Diversity and Inclusivity*, edited by Chris Rust, 53–64. Oxford: Oxford Centre for Staff and Learning Development.

Langer, Ellen. 1993. "A Mindful Education." *Educational Psychology* 281, no. 1:43–50. https://doi.org/10.1207/s15326985ep2801_4.

———. 2000. "Mindful Learning." *Current Directions in Psychological Science* 9, no. 6:220–23.

Langer, Ellen, Michael Hatem, Jennifer Joss, and Marilyn Howell. 1989. "Conditional Teaching and Mindful Learning." *Creativity Research Journal* 2, no. 3:129–50. https://doi.org/10.1080/10400418909534311.

Marek, Keith, Jeffery Raker, Thomas Holme, and Kristen Murphy. 2018. "The ACS Exams Institute Undergraduate Chemistry Anchoring Concepts Content Map III: Inorganic Chemistry." *Journal of Chemical Education* 95, no. 2:233–37. https://doi.org/10.1021/acs.jchemed.7b00498.

Meyer, Jan, and Ray Land. 2005. "Threshold Concepts and Troublesome Knowledge (2): Epistemological Considerations and a Framework for Teaching and Learning." *Higher Education* 49:373–88. https://doi.org/10.1007/s10734-004-6779-5.

Momeyer, Richard. 1995. "Teaching Ethics to Student Relativists." *Teaching Philosophy* 18, no. 4:305–11.

Pintrich, Paul R. and Elisabeth V. De Groot. 1990. "Motivational and Self-Regulated Learning Components of Classroom Academic Performance." *Journal of Educational Psychology* 82, no. 1:33.

Raker, Jeffrey, Thomas Holme, and Kristen Murphy. 2013. "The ACS Exams Institute Undergraduate Chemistry Anchoring Concepts Content Map II: Organic Chemistry." *Journal of Chemical Education* 90, no. 11:1443–45. https://doi.org/10.1021/ed400175w.

Stokes, Patrick. 2012. "Philosophy Has Consequences! Developing Metacognition and Active Learning in the Ethics Classroom." *Teaching Philosophy* 35, no. 2:143–69.

Turner, Dale. 2013. "How to Teach: Critical Thinking." *Teaching Philosophy* 36, no. 4:399–416. https://doi.org/10.5840/teachphil20131015.

Walker, Matthew. 2018. "Philosophy as a Way of Life (Syllabus)." Yale-NUS College. file:///Users/jake/Downloads/Philosophy_as_a_Way_of_Life_Yale-NUS_Col.pdf.

Wright, Jake. 2019. "The Truth, but Not Yet: Avoiding Naïve Skepticism via Explicit Communication of Metadisciplinary Aims." *Teaching in Higher Education* 24, no. 3:361–77. https://doi.org/10.1080/13562517.2018.1544552.

Yuretich, Richard F., Samia A. Khan, R. Mark Leckie, and John J. Clement. 2001. "Active-Learning Methods to Improve Student Performance and Scientific Interest in a Large Introductory Oceanography Course." *Journal of Geoscience Education* 49, no. 2:111–19. https://doi.org/10.5408/1089-9995-49.2.111.

Zerr, Ryan J., and Elizabeth Bjerke. 2016. "Using Multiple Sources of Data to Gauge Outcome Differences Between Academic-Themed and Transition-Themed First-Year Seminars." *Journal of College Student Retention: Research, Theory and Practice* 18, no. 1:68–82. https://doi.org/10.1177/1521025115579673.

CHAPTER 16

PHILOSOPHY AS EMPIRICAL EXPLORATION OF LIVING

AN APPROACH TO COURSES IN PHILOSOPHY AS A WAY OF LIFE

STEVEN HORST

When Pierre Hadot wrote his landmark book *Philosophy as a Way of Life* (Hadot 1995), he would probably have been surprised if anyone had suggested that there would eventually be a movement of philosophers developing college courses exploring philosophical ways of life, some of them integrating what he called "spiritual exercises." Indeed, organizers of recent summer institutes exploring such courses were themselves surprised by the number of applicants, some of them people who were already teaching such courses and others who were intrigued by the idea and wanted to learn more about how to begin teaching them.[1] I have been teaching such courses for several years now, and courses involving immersive exercises for much longer. In this essay, I wish to share my experience in teaching such courses and offer some ideas about how to use a series of immersive exercises to help tie together the units in a course.

First, a bit of background. In the late 1990s, I began to teach a course called "Moral Psychology: Care of the Soul." This was not a course focused narrowly on the psychology of moral cognition but one focused on "moral psychology" in the older sense of the intersection of theories of the good life, theories of the soul/mind/self/psyche, and practices of therapy and self-cultivation. That particular class was a bit different from what

[1] Wesleyan University hosted an NEH Summer Institute entitled "Reviving Philosophy as a Way of Life" in 2018. http://nehwayoflife.com. In 2019, the University of Notre Dame hosted the first of a three-year program of summer institutes funded by the Mellon Foundation. https://philife.nd.edu.

Philosophy as a Way of Life: Historical, Contemporary, and Pedagogical Perspectives.
Edited by James M. Ambury, Tushar Irani, and Kathleen Wallace.

Published 2021 by John Wiley & Sons Ltd.

I would now think of as a philosophy as a way of life (PWOL) class, in that a good half of it consisted in readings from more contemporary authors from fields other than philosophy: theoretical psychologists, psychotherapists, spiritual practitioners, and cognitive ethologists. But it was around that time that my colleague Brian Fay drew my attention to Pierre Hadot's *Philosophy as a Way of Life*, which had recently appeared in English, as he saw that it had a great deal in common with what I was exploring. (I should perhaps note that, although Hadot's books have provided much inspiration for my classes, they have proven very difficult to use successfully as assigned readings in introductory-level courses. The central lecture of *Philosophy as a Way of Life*, in particular, is written for fellow scholars familiar with the traditions with which Hadot is dealing and does not make for a good point of entry for students.) I recently began to teach a PWOL course based principally on the classical Western and Eastern philosophical schools. This was something that another colleague, Stephen Angle, had begun a few years before, and a third colleague, Tushar Irani, was exploring in his courses in classical Western philosophy. I have now taught the course four times, all as first-year seminars that combine reading and discussion of texts with what Hadot called "spiritual exercises." Some of these exercises are taken from the well-known Live Like a Stoic Week.[2] Others were devised to explore other classical schools by Professor Irani, and still others are of my own devising.[3]

PWOL courses are quite different from most of the courses I have taught, and certainly different from any that I took as a student. Designing them involves some of the same issues we face in designing most of our classes, such as the trade-offs between depth and breadth. But they involve different sorts of issues as well, particularly issues of how to give students some sort of experience in trying to live philosophically, whether by trying to emulate (for a brief period) some of the experiences one might have found in the ancient schools or by finding new ways to explore philosophical ideas in daily practice. Initially, both my moral psychology class and my PWOL class may have ended up being something of a motley: anything between a single class session to two weeks on each of a number of different philosophical traditions, exploring their ideas and trying out some practices, with a bit of intellectual comparison of the theories. At first, I thought of this as introducing students to a number of separate ideas and activities that they could "try on," in the hopes that they would find some that would help them to lead richer and more reflective lives. I have, however, continually sought ways to try to tie the units of the course together

[2] https://modernstoicism.com.

[3] Some of the resources for these can be found at Notre Dame's Philosophy as a Way of Life site: https://philife.nd.edu/resources/. A downloadable PDF of the 2018 syllabus with exercises can be found at https://philife.nd.edu/assets/322484/fullsize/horst_wesleyan_pwol_course_f2018_with_exercises.pdf.

into something more unified, even though the course necessarily presents a number of very different and often incompatible ways of life. This essay presents some of what has emerged from that, in the form of an open-ended set of exercises that build upon one another and can be adapted to fit with many different readings.[4]

Before I describe these exercises, however, a few brief words about my own orientation toward the idea of philosophy as a way of life and to teaching PWOL courses.

Brief Orienting Reflections

The most important foundational texts in the revival of PWOL are Pierre Hadot's *Philosophy as a Way of Life* (1995) and *What Is Ancient Philosophy?* (2004) and John Cooper's *Pursuits of Wisdom* (2013). My basic perspective on PWOL is closer to Hadot's than to Cooper's. I take Hadot's central claim to be that each of the ancient Western philosophical schools had its own distinctive way of life. That is, Hadot's claim was not that there is a single, well-defined thing called "philosophy" that has a unique "way of life" associated with it. Rather, there are a variety of schools we call "philosophical," each with its own way of life. (Indeed, as many of the schools had their own internal conversations, disagreements, and developments, there might be more than one possible way of life associated with broad categories like "Platonism" and "Stoicism.") Cooper's view, by contrast, seems to be more that what we call "philosophy" is characterized by something quite specific—seeking a life guided entirely by Reason—and that whatever the differences among the classical schools, what made them count as *philosophical* was a particular shared view of how a life might be guided by Reason: in particular, that Reason provides motivation to action that can be definitive in determining how we act. Hadot's emphasis on exercises, in Cooper's view, was misplaced: at most, they played a role in only a few of the schools of late antiquity (Stoicism, Neoplatonism) and were tangential to what made those traditions philosophical. While Cooper is no doubt correct that an emphasis on Reason, as a central and perhaps determinative motivating force, is a distinctive feature shared by the Western schools, I side more with Hadot on the question of whether spiritual exercises also played an important role in most or all of them. Cooper may be correct that formal exercises (of a sort that might be compared with the Ignatian exercises) played central roles in only a few schools of late antiquity. But it is difficult not to read things like Plato's prescriptions for *musike* and *gymnastike* as recommending particular forms of practice (*Republic* 376e–379b). And we find similar elements in other Western

[4] In the 2019 version of the class, I began with a week of these exercises. The content of these should be sufficiently clear from this essay, but instructors wishing to obtain copies of the exercises as used in class may contact the author.

schools as well: for example, the Epicureans practiced a distinctive communal form of living, and the Pythagoreans seem to have practiced a variety of religious rituals and followed a specific diet in addition to cultivating Reason through mathematics and natural philosophy.

I am also inclined to go beyond explicit statements by Hadot (though I think this is compatible with his view) to include non-Western traditions like Confucianism, Daoism, some forms of Buddhism, and some Vedic traditions as "philosophical," even if they lack the distinctive emphasis on Reason found in the Greco-Roman philosophers. Most of these clearly have distinctive practices aimed at the cultivation of the person, some of which could quite plausibly be counted as spiritual exercises even in a narrow sense. (For example, some of the Confucian Rites and the variety of Buddhist mindfulness techniques.) As this is a statement of a *perspective* rather than a *thesis*, I shall not argue for it, except to say that viewing the field in this broad way allows important commonalities to stand out that might otherwise be overlooked and also allows for a multicultural curriculum. I shall, however, stress one implication: that the focus thus becomes on philoso*phies* as *ways* of life rather than a single thing called "philosophy" that has a single way of life qua philosophy. This, however, does not mean that the different traditions have nothing in common: in particular, they are all *reflective* ways of life in which there is an important interaction between theoretical reflection and practice, and this is an important part of what makes them count as *philosophical*.

To this I shall add three somewhat theoretical claims, though given the scope of this short essay I shall not attempt to argue them in a scholarly way. First, I regard each of the philosophical schools as a kind of *empirical* or *experimental tradition* in which people were attempting to live well, and often doing so in a community of living dialogue and pedagogy. This indeed involved the formulation and propagation of theoretical ideas, not only about the nature of the good life, but also (in varying degrees and mixtures) about moral psychology, epistemology, metaphysics, political philosophy, logic, and natural philosophy. But it also involved practices of cultivation. And the theory and practice stood in an important reciprocal relationship. On the one hand, theory was grounded in self-examination and observation of individuals and communities; and both theory and particular practices were tested through reflection upon attempts to live out the theory through the practices. Conversely, practice was guided by theory, and in some cases by a dialectic between different theoretical positions, both within and between philosophical schools. Think, for example, of Aristotle's disagreement with Plato on how to cultivate the moral virtues (*Nichomachean Ethics* 1.13–2), or disagreements within Neoconfucianism about the importance of their practice of "quiet sitting" (see Mabuchi 2016). There were clearly *debates* about the merits of particular cultivating practices, but it also seems almost certain that these were informed by experiments with different practices and reflection upon their outcomes.

Second, those who considered making a "profession" of philosophy often tried out several different schools and their ways of life, and the schools competed for adherents.[5] Aspiring philosophers were indeed attentive to the *arguments* of the different schools, but the biographies and *apologias* of the founders and major proponents of the schools also played important roles in the process of "conversion" (*metanoia*), and I cannot help but think that many who were attracted to philosophy made a decision between schools by trying out their various ways of life and seeing what was most beneficial in their own aspirations to life-transforming philosophical cultivation.

Third, in some cases, this led to a kind of syncretism that combined elements drawn from more than one school. Much of this may be difficult to document—who knows how many people led lives woven from strands of different philosophical schools? But we also see it in the ways that dialogue both within and between schools led to changes within particular schools or the formation of new schools. In the West, Socrates inspired not only Plato but also the Cynics and Skeptics, and Stoicism grew out of these. Neoplatonism combined elements of Platonism, Aristotelianism, and Stoicism. In medieval China, many neo-Confucians incorporated ideas and practices that had originated with Daoists and Buddhists. (And, conversely, Chinese Buddhism became something quite different from Indian Buddhism.) In some ways, I regard it as quite natural for students in a PWOL course to undergo a similar process of discernment by exploring several philosophical schools and perhaps adopting something from each of them, though of course on a much shorter timescale.

Issues in Designing a PWOL Course

This process of exploring and drawing from several schools presents interesting issues for how to teach a course in PWOL. If my perspective is apt, pursuing a philosophical way of life is not something that a person could do within the scope of a college course—it is more of a lifelong journey. Moreover, taking a modern college course is something quite different from going to live in an Epicurean garden, a Buddhist monastery, or Plato's Academy: one is not subscribing to the teachings of a single school or committing to its lifestyle, and indeed a modern university would quite rightly be suspicious of a course that even hinted at such an undertaking, much less an instructor who sought converts to his or her teachings or personal devotees as a kind of guru. The furthest one might go in this direction would be, say, for a professor of Buddhism who was also a Buddhist teacher to offer instruction in mindfulness practices or a

[5] The word "profession" meant something quite different in ancient philosophy from what it means today. It did not mean pursuing philosophy for pay in an academic setting but meant something like an explicit adoption of a philosophical way of life.

practicum in following the Eightfold Path for the semester, or for a Jesuit to offer a unit or a course in the Ignatian exercises. (And doing even this much would require a great deal of sensitivity to things like the personal religious commitments of individual students, with explicit forewarnings to potential students.) At the other end of the spectrum, we might find more traditional courses that taught *about* the theories of the good life presented by one or more schools and described their practices without asking students to try them out. In the middle—and I think that this middle ground is what most faculty interested in PWOL classes are exploring—are courses that present the theories and practices of several schools, with an attempt to provide students with some ways of trying out some of them for themselves—say, by offering immersive spiritual exercises as a part of the course. This has been my own approach, and indeed the only approach available to me, as I do not consider myself a sage or philosophical master in any one school.

As with any course, there is a trade-off here between depth and breadth. One could easily develop a *very* full course that integrated theory and practice that was confined to, say, just the major classical Western or Chinese schools, and even such a course would really do little more than scratch the surface. While I worry about the extreme of a course that could be caricatured as "If it's Tuesday, it must be Aristotle," I think that a bit of eclecticism is actually quite in the spirit of what the person in late antiquity who was considering making a profession for philosophy might have experienced, listening to teachers of the different schools and perhaps trying several out. And if I am correct about the syncretism and the empirical nature of philosophical exploration, such an eclectic course can, I think, capture the spirit of PWOL if it succeeds in engaging the student in reflective self-examination and a dialogue between theory and practice by studying and trying out several alternative philosophical paths. While I do not wish to encourage the "cafeteria" view of "self-improvement" that fuels popular self-help movements, I do think that getting students to think about living philosophically requires more than educating them about the *views* and *practices* of the schools purely as book learning; it involves getting them to engage reflectively with their own lives in a fashion that allows them to make the most of what has already been explored by several traditions, and to determine for themselves what rings true and what proves to be edifying. Just as Socrates never accomplished more than to inspire others to start out upon philosophical journeys of their own, our best hope is to do so as well, but with the addition of orienting them to certain guideposts that have withstood the tests of time.

Finding a Unifying Strand

In order to make an exploration of multiple philosophical traditions into something more than a hodgepodge of views, however, it is useful to have a uniting strand. There are doubtless many ways to do this. I wish to present one approach, which has emerged out of several years of teaching PWOL courses, and before that, courses in moral psychology.

The uniting strand of this approach is the notion of what we *want* or *desire*. Our wants, desires, and appetites are of course an important topic in most classical philosophies, and the various schools take different views on such matters as the *nature* of desires, *which* desires are to be cultivated and which to be resisted, and the best *techniques* for addressing them. It is also an easy point of entry for the beginning student. Philosophical theories may be difficult, abstruse, even alien to the novice student. But the question "What do I want?" is something anyone can relate to, even if it turns out to lead into reflections that might cause the student to conclude that it is not such a simple question after all. (And that, in itself, is an important kind of philosophical maturation. Realizing that we do not really understand the things we have always taken for granted is at the core of philosophy in the Socratic lineage.)

Over the years, I have developed a set of exercises involving reflections upon desire, which can be deployed in different ways depending upon the topics, traditions, and readings selected for a course. They introduce a student to things like reflection, self-examination, and mindfulness. They also provide practical ways of looking at what might otherwise seem like purely theoretical claims in texts. And they provide a point of entry for the empirical project of testing one's own experience (clarified successively in several types of self-examination) against philosophical theories, and vice versa.

The Foundational Activity: Compiling an Inventory of Desires

The foundational exercise is quite simple in outline. I ask students to take a period of time (perhaps half an hour to an hour) and make a list of things they want or desire. It is important that they understand from the outset that this list—at least in its initial form—is for their eyes only, as otherwise they might censor their list. Doing this initial exercise, even by itself without others that build upon it, can be an important philosophical initiation in more than one respect. Taking an inner inventory of their desires invites students to be reflective in ways they may never before have been—perhaps not yet *critically* reflective but engaged in self-examination. But there is also more than this. For students used to studying to the test, it can be quite a novel experience to be asked to do an exercise that no one, including the teacher, will ever see. This is something that most have them have never before experienced—and, I daresay, something that most readers of this essay have never assigned. And it can in itself be quite a powerful experience. Indeed, if we are trying to get students to live philosophically, there may be no accomplishment more crucial than breaking them out of the mind-set of doing things for external validation or figuring out how to play the system to get a good grade.

Taking an inventory of one's own desires can also lead to the beginnings of practices of *mindfulness*. Sometimes I have done the first exercise in class, which necessarily makes it a very short exercise. Sometimes I have had students do it as a homework assignment, which allows more time. But, both in my own experience in doing it for myself and in what I have seen from my students, it is something that takes on a life of its own. Once we begin to be attentive to our desires in an explicit exercise, we are likely to begin noting more of them as they occur and eventually to end up with a much richer inventory of desires than we might have come up with the first time we thought about it. Here is how it went for me. Personally, I started out with high-minded goals and aspirations. I thought of things like this: *I want world peace. I want to do good for others. I want to be a successful and respected scholar whose work makes a difference in the lives of others.* Then I realized there were a motley of other respectable things I want. *I want to be a good cellist and give others pleasure in my playing. I want to be healthy, perhaps even athletic. I would like to see Prague, the Grand Canyon, and the Alhambra before I die.* Then I realized there were many little things I wanted at the moment—*I really want a cup of coffee, I really like fatty food.* Then perhaps some things I was ambivalent about: *I'd like to have a mansion on the sea, be famous,* and so on. And eventually things were tugging at my mind that I indeed wanted but suppressed as taboo. (I shall not disclose the details of these, and of course your students should not disclose theirs to you. You might also do well to make contact with resources in behavioral health and spiritual counsel should some students come up with something they find they need to talk about. There is the outside chance that you may have a budding Hannibal Lecter in your class. More likely, you will have someone with gender or sexuality issues, or problems with rage, depression, or despair, that he or she finds distressing to think or talk about. Unless you are a trained psychotherapist or spiritual director, you should not take these on but should be sensitive to their signs and know your local resources for referral. Reflective philosophical exercises can bring serious psychological issues to the surface that most philosophy professors are not trained to deal with, and it is wise to know in advance whom to turn to should they arise.)

I think it is a good idea to give instructions for this exercise that involve keeping a journal or at least a piece of paper that can be added to over the following days or weeks. I sometimes invite a few students to present a bowdlerized list (without the bits they do not wish to disclose) to the group, and the comparisons of these often lead students to realize that there are whole classes of "desires" that they had not thought about. (Some may have thought only of fleeting desires and not life goals, and others the reverse. Some may have only listed desires for themselves and not for others, or vice versa. And some may find items on other students' lists that they realize they share as well, though they had not initially thought of them.) And whether or not this is the case, once you have started thinking about your desires, you may well become more attentively mindful to your inner life and realize, a few days later, that there are all these other things that could be added to the list. I believe that this is a very easy and gentle *introduction to a practice of mindfulness*, in which students become more reflectively attentive to the things they desire, which can pave the ground for further, deeper, and more intentional mindfulness practices, should you include them.

Next Steps: Mapping Desires and Empirical Engagement with Texts and Theories

How does one introduce such an exercise? Often, I have done so in conjunction with a text, and as part of a longer sequence of exercises. For example, both Plato and Aristotle talk about how we do some things for their own sake and other things for the sake of something else. You can do the first exercise without signaling how it will later be connected to texts, or you can do it in conjunction with a text like Plato's discussion of means and ends in book 2 of *Republic* or Aristotle's in *Nicomachean Ethics* 1.1, or indeed in looking at the Sophists' view of the good life as getting what you desire, either in conjunction with a Sophist text or a longer reading of Plato's *Gorgias*, which has the additional merit of vividly contrasting the philosophical way of life with that of Sophists and rhetoricians.

A follow-up exercise I use is to ask students to take items from their list and make them into a diagram of the relations between their desires: whether some are means to the others as ends. For example, a student might list "get good grades," "get into medical school," and "become a doctor," which clearly stand in a means-ends relationship. I ask students to connect means to ends with arrows, producing a kind of map or diagram of their motivations. A third step would be to consider passages where the philosophers claim that there is some one thing *all* our actions aim at—"the Good" (Plato, *Gorgias* 468a) or *eudaimonia* (Aristotle, *Nichomachean Ethics* 1.7)—and ask students, first, to see whether this corresponds to how their diagram already shapes up and, second, whether their diagram might reasonably be put into greater order by adding this.

In these second and third steps, we have begun a dialectic between experience and theory. On the one hand, do means-ends analysis and the idea of a final end help make better sense of what one has discovered in oneself through a naive listing of desires? On the other hand, does what one finds in one's own experience confirm or perhaps challenge such analyses? Are there things that we pursue for their own sake that are not pursued for the sake of happiness or that even we ourselves might not indeed consider good?

These are questions that ought to be pursued in any philosophical course examining such texts: for example, are the authors' claims *correct?* In a more traditional course, this question might be pursued chiefly by examining the authors' *arguments*. We analyze and evaluate arguments in my PWOL classes as well. But questions about the nature of our desires, the relations between them, and the effective means of transforming them are not questions that can be settled by a priori argumentation, as they are at least in part empirical questions about human psychology. A PWOL approach invites students to explore these in the one case about which they have direct evidence and the ability to test claims through experience and experiment—their own—and then discuss their findings together. Even if a course is not specifically devoted to PWOL—if it is, say, a course on classical Western philosophy—this seems like a useful and salutary addition to the reading and analysis of texts and arguments.

An Entry Point to Further Exercises

Such preparatory exercises also provide the basis for a number of further sorts of exercises. I have never used all of them in a single course—they are more like a stockpile of activities to be drawn upon. Some of these are practical and pedestrian. I might, for example, ask my students to reflect on one or more of the following topics:

1. Is it really possible to attain *all* of the desires you have listed, or are some in conflict with one another? As a friend put it to her daughters, "You can do *anything* you want, but you can't do *everything* you want." For example, perhaps you could become a surgeon *or* a concert pianist, but probably not both. Perhaps you can be famous and widely celebrated or you can choose to lead a quiet and secluded life, but probably not both, because they involve incompatible ways of living. How would you go about resolving the practical conflicts?
2. Are there some goals on your list that would require you to do other things you are not now doing in order to accomplish them? If so, what other desires, habits, skills, and practices might you need to cultivate in order to realize them? (If, for example, you wish to become a doctor, you will have to study and succeed at some very particular things, and this may in turn require greater habits of self-discipline.)
3. Are there things on the list that you cannot realistically expect to attain—perhaps because you do not really have the aptitude for them or perhaps because they depend on factors that are outside your control? If so, what should you do about these?

Such questions might quite reasonably be incorporated, say, into a unit on the Sophists, who view the good life in terms of getting what you desire.

A second set of exercises would involve trying to apply the interpretive lenses of different philosophical schools to one's list. For example, in a unit on Confucianism, students might be prompted to ask themselves, *Which items on the list are what Confucians describe as desires for "profit" or "the pleasures of the eyes and ears"? What attitude would Confucians recommend that we take toward such desires? Are any of them manifestations of Mencius's four sprouts?* (Mencius 2001, 2a6). *Does your list confirm or refute Xunzi's claim that "human nature is bad?"* (Xunzi 2001). In a unit on Socratic/early Platonic thought, *Can all of your desires reasonably be interpreted as beliefs that the things desired are good?* (Or, conversely, are there some that you find you *desire* even though you also believe them to be *bad*?) Here we are engaging the student in an empirical project of testing a theory against experience and experience against theory.

A third type of exercise involves deeper exploration of moral psychology. This might be done in connection with a text or as an open exploration. I have already described one such reflection: whether the Socratic or early Platonic view that desires are beliefs about what is good (*Gorgias* 468) is psychologically realistic. This might involve, not only an analysis of the desires themselves, but also exercises in trying to alter desires by changing beliefs and seeing if doing so is effective in changing desires. If you wish to stress moral psychology heavily, you might go on to introduce modern ideas like cognitive behavioral therapy (CBT), which proceeds on the assumption that changing beliefs can alter desires. (And even if you do not bring it up, you may well find that some of your students are intimately familiar with CBT, as they have been involved in that form of therapy.) I have also often contrasted this intellectualist psychology of the *Gorgias* with Plato's later tripartite psychology, which adds nonrational types of motivation from the appetites and *thumos* (*Republic* bks. 4, 9), and with Aristotle's discussion of the differences between intellectual and moral virtues (*Nichomachean Ethics* 1.13).

Aristotle's account of moral virtues, of course, is itself a wonderful topic for exploring moral psychology. From the perspective of PWOL, one of the most useful things to do here is to have exercises that attempt to test the view that moral virtue can be cultivated by way of continence through habituation (*Nichomachean Ethics* bks. 2, 7). Reflection on desires may well have put students in a position where they recognize that there is something they need to cultivate—say, courage or temperance—even if only because they realize they will also need these things in order to attain the things they already desire. A straightforward exercise is to pick one of these, formulate a practicum of things to do to try to "fake it 'til you make it," and see if it bears fruit. Even if the period allotted for the exercise is unrealistically short for this to be effective, students will have been introduced to a *strategy* they can apply over a longer span of time for themselves well after the course is over.

One could also do something similar with Plato. In my view, there is a striking difference between the moral psychology put forward by Socrates in the *Gorgias* and the richer tripartite theory of the *Republic*, which introduces nonrational sources of motivation (the appetites and thumos). I have sometimes paired a reading of the myth of the many-headed Beast in book 9 of the *Republic* (588b–89b) with an exercise in which I ask students to draw a picture of their own souls (or motivational structures) as a beast with many heads corresponding to their different appetites, drives, or sources of motivation, labeling these and tying them to their more particular desires. (That is, there might be more than one relevant *level* of analysis: one type of *drive* might be the source of many distinct *desires*.) For some students, exploring such a topic artistically rather than verbally opens up new insights for them, even if they are not talented artists. I then ask them to reflect upon Plato's claim that Reason can domesticate these (with the help of thumos) by knowing and working with their natures—not trying to cut off the heads like Heracles cutting off the heads of the Hydra, but like animal trainers or gardeners working with their knowledge of the natural tendencies of the plants or animals (*Republic* 589b). I ask the students to think about such questions as these: *If you were to regard your own soul in this manner, what would the implications be? What are the "beasts within" that need to be tamed? What are their natures, and how can you use your understanding of these in an attempt to gentle them? Can you find a way to love, care for, and nurture them rather than either giving in to them or regarding them with repugnance and shame?* The text also offers opportunities for comparison with other theories: for example, how does Plato's view of the appetites differ from Xunzi's (2001) characterization of them as "bad," and what different types of "therapy" do the different theories seem to recommend?

Plato's tripartite psychology also provides one of many good entry points to invite deeper analysis of the things we started out labeling as "desires." If you agree with the classical philosophers that Reason itself can motivate but also allow that there are other, nonrational sources of motivation, it turns out that things we initially called "desires" are of several different psychological kinds. Aristotle's claim that the virtues motivate in a way different from Reason, and require a different type of cultivation, introduces the same kind of issue, and we could similarly pose the question of whether Mencius's "sprouts" are sorts of psychological faculties different from whatever produces the motivation for profit or the pleasures of the eyes and ears. There is ample material here to lead students to be more reflective about their own moral psychology by examining the implications of different theories and testing them against their own experience. If one wishes to bring in materials from outside the classical traditions, an additional useful topic to include might be Hume's claim that reason and belief cannot themselves provide any motivation at all—that this comes *solely* through the emotions, including moral emotions. This is a fundamental challenge to the classical Western schools, particularly as described by Cooper, and knowing about it helps students to understand how radical those schools' view of Reason really was. Similarly, in my moral psychology class, I have used John Riker's *Ethics and the Discovery of the Unconscious* (Riker 1997), which presents challenges to

Western intellectualist ethics arising from philosophical and psychological theories of the unconscious developed by such figures as Nietzsche and Freud. I think it is also useful to give students pointers to the ways these questions are still being debated, not only in philosophy, but also between different schools of therapeutic psychology, even if these are not part of the course syllabus. (This is something I emphasize more in a class on moral psychology but might supply suggestions for additional reading in a PWOL class.)

It would also be possible, however, to begin such an examination without direct connection to a classical text. Indeed, the more perceptive students may realize, in looking over their list of "desires," that they are not all of the same type. Some might be something like ultimate life goals, others core values, fleeting momentary wants, or even troubling compulsions. A few students might even suggest in discussion that we really need a more nuanced set of terminology rather than lumping all of these under the single heading of desire. The most analytically minded students may be able to come up with their own vocabulary that reflects what they see as the major divisions into psychological categories, but this is also a topic that makes for excellent classroom discussion if students are asked to work together to sort through the different types of "desire" and produce a classification of different sources of motivation. In a seminar-sized class, this could be done as a whole-class exercise; in a larger class, it could initially be done in small groups, followed by a comparison of the categories different groups have come up with and further plenary discussion. This, in effect, invites students to do what philosophers like Plato, Mencius, and Aristotle were doing in formulating their theories: beginning with experience and ordinary language, and moving beyond them to try to craft a more psychologically realistic theory.

Grading, Assessment, and Feedback

What I have tried to describe here is not exactly a concrete plan for a course. It is more like a set of related exercises that might be regarded as a deck of cards that can be played differently, depending on which philosophical traditions you wish to explore in a particular class. This will, I hope, provide readers with a set of ideas and activities that can be worked into courses of their own design. I should add that these are not the *only* types of exercises I use in my course. For example, I generally have students do a full week of "Live Like a Stoic" exercises, write their own apologia, and try basic mindfulness techniques involving quiet sitting, breath control, or repetition of a word or phrase. And the course syllabus was originally organized not around the desire exercises but by philosophical schools, with exercises assigned throughout the semester in conjunction with particular texts. In the 2018 version of the course, there were units on Confucianism, Daoism, the Sophists, Socrates, the Cynics, Plato, Aristotle, the Stoics, existentialism, Buddhism, and Christianity, and the desire exercises were assigned in conjunction with book 1 of the *Nichomachean Ethics*. In 2019, I began the course with a full week of the desire exercises before having the students read any texts, and several subsequent exercises invited students to bring particular philosophical treatments of desire they were reading about to bear in interpreting their own lists and desire maps. Students reported that this worked very well, as it got them reflecting on themselves before being introduced to any philosophical interpretations that might influence their reflections, and they had a variety of interesting observations at the end of the course about how the desires they had initially listed had changed, or how they now regarded them in a different light. I believe this was a successful experiment, and I plan to keep this format in future versions of the course.

But how does one give a *grade* in a course where much of the work consists in reflective exercises? My own brief answer is that I do *not* grade the students. My university allows professors to offer courses pass/fail, and this has been my practice for PWOL. I realize that this is not something that is possible at every institution, but I think it is an option worth considering if it is available. I initially decided against letter grades specifically because so much of the course is oriented toward self-reflection. On the one hand, there are some types of reflection that are really not possible to grade. A student's list of desires simply is what it is. If I see students' lists at all, I might regard what I see on one more positively than what I see on another, but that does not make one more academically respectable than another, and I am not in the business of evaluating students' character. On the other hand, doing such an assignment for a grade would make it into a different kind of assignment, in which the students are guided by whatever they may assume the standards of evaluation to be, rather than one in which they are trying to be transparent to themselves. Indeed, as I said earlier, I do not even collect the initial exercise in unedited form, and at most ask for volunteers to share expurgated versions of their lists.

I have also come to see another and more fundamental reason that *not* grading PWOL courses has value. Many students think of school work as something that they do entirely for external validation and approach an assignment or a course thinking "What do I have to do to get an A?" This, however, is entirely the *wrong* attitude with which to approach PWOL. Trying to live philosophically in order to get an A is not trying to live philosophically at all. And I have found that some students actually find the reorientation toward their work that can ensue from this—thinking of an assigned activity as something to be done because one actually finds it rewarding in its own right—to be the most important thing they get out of the course. Last year, for example, one of the comments in the course evaluations went something like this: "The most important thing I got out of this course was when I realized I had an assignment that would not be turned in or graded. I could have blown it off, but I did it anyway, just for its own sake, and got a lot out of it, and this totally transformed my orientation towards learning." This in itself was at least as much of a step toward living philosophically as anything the student might remember from the *content* of the course.

This does not mean that assignments involving or based upon exercises cannot receive some form of evaluation and feedback. Even with something like the exercise in which students trace the means-ends relationships between their desires it is possible to assess how thoroughly and perceptively they have identified such relationships. This could be assessed and assigned a grade, but personally I find the more important type of feedback to come in the form of suggesting further questions they might wish to explore. For example, I might say: "You have listed 'being a doctor' as a goal that does not have a further goal beyond it. Is being a doctor really something you seek only for its own sake, or is there also some further goal you have not considered, like status, financial security, a sense of fulfillment, or making a difference in the lives of others?" Or, if the map tends to focus on just one sort of desire—becoming a particular kind of person, achieving particular things, receiving external goods, or perhaps only desires for abstract things like world peace—I might prompt the student to think about whether there are also things he or she desires in some of the other categories. This helps students to understand that thinking about a question is not really finished when they turn in a paper or have it returned—in philosophy (and in many other subjects as well), when you do something well, it tends to open up further questions to pursue, and the more philosophical you have become, the more you will wish to pursue them. I could, of course, assess how much work a student has put into such an assignment and how well he or she has seen connections, but I prefer to tread carefully here. There can be psychological reasons, having nothing to do with academic skills or diligence, that students might experience difficulty examining their own experiences or be unwilling to express them, and I am not in a position to know whether the fact that a student did not go further might be the result of healthy psychological defense mechanisms that it would be dangerous to try to push past outside a psychotherapeutic relationship. On a short assignment like this one, I tend to comment on one thing they did well and suggest one thing to work on more or think through further.

Of course, even in an exercise-intensive course, it is also quite appropriate to assign more traditional papers as well. I often assign such familiar topics as comparing (early) Plato and Aristotle on the question of whether virtue consists entirely of knowledge, or Mencius and Xunzi on human nature. Such essays can be evaluated as they would be in any other class, though they may end up being deeper and more vigorously engaged if students have first done exercises that provide direct evidence on the questions addressed in the essay. If a PWOL course is to be graded, the bulk of the assessment leading to the grade can come from much more traditional assignments and whatever standards an instructor uses to assess classroom participation, and the exercises can be given "completion points." (That is, you get the points simply for doing the exercise without it being graded for quality.)

Conclusion

The recent initiatives in teaching PWOL classes are, to my mind, an exciting development in philosophy, and I think that Hadot would have been pleased to see his work bearing this kind of fruit. I have been surprised, in my discussions with other professors interested in such courses, at just how varied their approaches to them can be. What I have offered here is only one model, and perhaps one that makes about as much use of immersive exercises as is prudent or practical within a college curriculum. The *kinds* of exercises I have described, however, can also be used more selectively in more traditional kinds of courses. And I have found that crafting and teaching such courses is also an empirical undertaking: we try things out, see what works, and try to improve upon a course each time around, and we learn as well from the experiences of our colleagues.

References

Cooper, John. 2013. *Pursuits of Wisdom: Six Ways of Life in Ancient Philosophy from Socrates to Plotinus*. Princeton: Princeton University Press.

Hadot, Pierre. 1995. *Philosophy as a Way of Life*. Translated with an introduction by Arnold Davidson. Malden, Mass.: Wiley-Blackwell.

________. 2004. *What Is Ancient Philosophy?* Translated by Michael Chase. Cambridge, Mass.: Belknap Press of Harvard University Press.

Mabuchi, Masaya. 2016. "'Quiet Sitting' in Neo-Confucianism." In *Asian Traditions of Meditation*, edited by Halvor Eifring, 207–26. Honolulu: University of Hawai'i Press.

Mencius. 2001. "*Mengzi* (Mencius)." Chapter 3 of *Readings in Classical Chinese Philosophy*, Second Edition, edited by Philip J. Ivanhoe and Brian W. Van Norden, 115–60. Indianapolis: Hackett.

Xunzi. 2001. "Human Nature Is Bad." Translated by Eric L. Hutton. In *Readings in Classical Chinese Philosophy*, Second Edition, edited by Philip J. Ivanhoe and Brian W. Van Norden, 255–310. Indianapolis: Hackett.

INDEX

Philosophy as a Way of Life: Historical, Contemporary, and Pedagogical Perspectives.
Edited by James M. Ambury, Tushar Irani, and Kathleen Wallace.

Published 2021 by John Wiley & Sons Ltd.